THE FIRST POLISH AMERICANS

THE FIRST POLISH AMERICANS

Silesian Settlements in Texas

By

T. LINDSAY BAKER

TEXAS A&M UNIVERSITY PRESS
College Station

Library of Congress Cataloging in Publication Data

Baker, T. Lindsay.
The first Polish Americans.

Bibliography: p.
Includes index.
1. Polish Americans—Texas—History. 2. Texas—History.
I. Title.
F395.P7B33 976.4'004'9185 78-6373
ISBN 0-89096-725-3 (pbk.)

Manufactured in the United States of America
SECOND PRINTING, 1996

For
Krystyna,
without whose help
this work would never have been written

Contents

Acknowledgments xi

1. The Upper Silesian Origins 3

2. Founding the First Polish Colonies 21

3. Polish Life on the Frontier 39

4. The Civil War 64

5. Reconstruction 78

6. The Growth and Development of Silesian Institutions and Settlement 99

7. The Silesian Way of Life in Texas 126

8. The Twentieth Century 150

9. The Significance of the Silesians in Texas 164

Notes 173

Bibliography 231

Index 257

List of Illustrations

following page 48

Reverend Leopold Bonaventura Maria Moczygemba, about 1852
St. Stanisław Church, Płużnica, Poland
Typical rural scene in Upper Silesia
Handbill advertising passage to America
Upper Silesian peasant girl in nineteenth-century folk dress
Present-day Upper Silesian woman in folk dress
Yoke of oxen plowing
Long, narrow agricultural fields
Thatch-covered dugout cellar
Felix Mika, Sr., residence in Panna Maria
St. Mary's Church at Panna Maria
John Twohig's stone storage barn at Panna Maria
Reverend Adolf Bakanowski
Reverend Vincent Barzyński
Map of Panna Maria colony prepared by Rev. Bakanowski in 1869
Church and school at Panna Maria drawn by Rev. Bakanowski in 1869
View toward St. Joseph's School at Panna Maria today

following page 144

Reverend Felix Zwiardowski
Cibolo Creek between Panna Maria and Helena
Abandoned Protestant church at Helena
St. Hedwig, patroness of Silesia
Joseph Moczygemba
John Dugosh family making molasses, ca. 1900–1915
Philip Kowalik, cattle buyer at Kościuszko, ca. 1915
Tom Mórawietz family at Bandera, ca. 1900–1915
Hog slaughtering at Falls City, 1921

Pete Kaczmarek with his dogs at La Vernia, 1914
Members of St. Adalbert's Society
Henry Czerner and Ben Urbanczyk
Threshing wheat at the White Deer Polish colony
Waiting for cold beer, ca. 1910
Kaczmarek family on an excursion, ca. 1915–1918
An issue of *Nowiny Texaskie*
Grave of August Moczygemba at Panna Maria
Reinterment rites for Rev. Leopold Moczygemba at Panna Maria, 1974

Maps

Map 1. Upper Silesia, Kingdom of Prussia, in the 1850's, showing area of emigration *page* 4
Map 2. Silesian settlements in Texas *page* 26

Acknowledgments

HAVING prepared this study of the Silesians in Texas, I stand indebted to a large number of people who made it possible for me to compile the source materials and then to mold them into the shape of a historical narrative. I would like to acknowledge their invaluable assistance over the years, but at the same time to retain for myself responsibility for my own interpretations and for any factual errors.

Throughout my several years of research on the oldest Polish colonies in America, my wife has been my most steadfast supporter. It was through her that I gained my ability to read and speak in Polish, poorly though I do, and thus she opened for me the vast Polish-language sources on the Silesian immigration. She served as the principal translator for both manuscript and published materials that I identified but because of various pressures was unable to translate either quickly or accurately enough. Furthermore her encouragement was the most important factor in keeping me going in the rough spots. And, it must be added, we had a grand time as we struggled through the reams of material together.

For both the knowledge of research techniques and whatever literary ability I possess, I owe thanks to Dr. Seymour V. Connor, who supervised my graduate study at Texas Tech University. A constant supporter and friend, he is more responsible than any other person for my determining to become a professional historian.

Many friends and members of my family contributed to the preparation of the manuscript, but none more than my parents, who aided me both psychologically and materially. In a larger sense they are the people who shaped me into a person who could both enjoy and appreciate the study of history.

Archivists and librarians, the custodians of the materials I have used, were among the most significant people to contribute to my work. Among these individuals in America who were the most helpful were Roy Sylvan Dunn, Southwest Collection, Lubbock, Texas; Ray Janeway, Frank Temple, and Mrs. Gloria Lyerla, Texas Tech University Library; Paul Robert Scott and Dr. Larry D. Sall, Archives Division, Texas State Library; Sister Gertrude Cook, MSSA, Archives, Archdiocese of San Antonio; George Chalou, Old Military Branch, National Archives; and Dr. Chester V. Kielman, University of Texas Archives. In Europe their counterparts, among them the following, were equally helpful and considerate: Dr. Jerzy Pabisz, Archives of the City and Voivodeship of Wrocław; Dr. Ryszard Dermin, Opole Voivodeship Archives; Antoni Wróbel, Silesian-Wendish Collection, University of Wrocław; the Reverend M. I. Kiefer, CR, Congregation of the Resurrection, Rome; Dr. Z. Jagodzinski, Polish Library, London; Mrs. Helvi Wendeler, Archives, Ludwig-Missionsverein, Munich; and Dr. Annemarie Fenzel, Archives, Archdiocese of Vienna.

In Poland many historians generously assisted me in identifying and finding potential sources of data for the book. Of these the most important was Dr. Andrzej Brożek, of Katowice, who pioneered research using European sources on the Silesians in Texas. Without his previous work in finding source materials, which he has shared with me in personal conferences over the past seven years and in his publications, I would have been forced to spend many more days in library and archival research. Other scholars similarly provided me with large amounts of information on suggested historical materials, some of which I hardly imagined could exist. Among these people were Dr. Andrzej Szefer, Director, and Teresa Służałek, Adjunct, Silesian Library, Katowice; Dr. Stanisław Michałkiewicz, Department of Silesian History, University of Wrocław; Dr. Zygmunt Kubacki, Department of Foreign Languages, Technical University of Wrocław; and Dr. Witold Zatoński, Wrocław. Vice-Rector Bogusław B. Kędzia and his staff at the Technical University of Wrocław were indefatigable in helping me gain access to various collections and in securing copies of manuscript materials. I owe a special debt of thanks to all these people.

American historians were among the most generous of all people in both time and materials. The Reverend Jacek Przygoda offered many fugitive items from his private collections and a ready ear to some of my interpretations of Polish Texan history, while James P.

McGuire, of the Institute of Texan Cultures in San Antonio, opened the files of that institution to my examination and gave me constant encouragement and copies of newly found data. Robert H. Thonhoff, historian of South Texas, likewise helped me with information, particularly dealing with the majority American population of that region. Dr. Maria Starczewska provided well-balanced criticism and her views on the spatial relationships involved in the study of Polish colonization.

A battery of translators helped me through the bulk of foreign-language material. First among these was my wife, but she was followed closely by Arkadiusz Bryczkowski, Urszula Jakubowska, Jerzy Wroński, Maria Stobiecka, Laura Buck, and Helena Titiriga, all of the Technical University of Wrocław.

Catholic priests, both as pastors of local parishes and in other roles, greatly facilitated my search for material. In Texas I conducted research in the parish records preserved by the Reverend Bernard Goebel, Panna Maria; the Reverend Peter Steubben, Castroville; and the Reverend P. Flanagan, New Braunfels. The Reverend John W. Yanta, through his sincere encouragement, introductions to individuals within the Catholic hierarchy and the Polish community, and loan of historic documents, was one of the most helpful of all individuals. In Germany the Reverend Berard Schloer, OFMConv., opened all the pertinent archival collections of the Bavarian Province of the Friars Minor Conventual, while in the United States the Reverend Peter D. Fehlner, OFMConv., provided me with very large amounts of rare material from American and North Italian archives of the same order. At Rome the Reverend M. I. Kieffer, CR, spent hours directing my wife and me through the voluminous archives of the Congregation of the Resurrection. While conducting research in Poland, the two of us were graciously received for examination of parish records cited in this work that were administered by the Reverend Rudolf Krupop, Jemielnice; the Reverend Stanisław Prochacki, Toszek; the Reverend Rudolf Porada, Wiśnicze; and the Reverend Władysław Robaczynski, Sulisławice. Father Rafał Kaczmarczyk, of Płużnica, not only permitted us access to his parish records but also gave us almost a second home in Upper Silesia by allowing us to use his rectory as a base for historical research in the source villages of the Texas immigrants.

Oral informants, either Silesians or persons who know them very well, gave much of the living character to the materials used in this work. Among these informants the following were especially helpful: Ben P. Urbanczyk, Elias J. Moczygemba, Mr. and Mrs. Felix Mika, Sr., Felix Mika, Jr., Clem Kaczmarek, Mr. and Mrs. Felix V. Snoga, Panna Maria; Mrs. Mary Lyssy and Fletcher B. Kuhnel, all of Karnes City; the Reverend Henry Moczygemba, of Yorktown; Emil A. Kosub, of Saint Hedwig; Mr. and Mrs. Prosper A. Mika and Dr. Robert Malina, of Austin; the Reverend John W. Yanta, LeRoy Moczygemba, Arthur J. Moczygemba, Mrs. Valerie Grace, and the Reverend Peter Kolton, of San Antonio; Mr. and Mrs. Franciszek Karkosz, the Reverend Rafał Kaczmarczyk, and Mrs. Krystyna Popanda-Jaksik, of Płużnica; and the Reverend Jan Karkosz, of Piotrówka.

Much of the early research that provided material for this work was assisted by a Sendzimir Scholarship from the Kościuszko Foundation in 1973–1974, while the final research and writing was conducted during a Fulbright-Hayes Lectureship sponsored by the United States government at the Technical University of Wrocław, Poland, in 1975–1977.

THE FIRST POLISH AMERICANS

1

The Upper Silesian Origins

"THE desire for immigration to America has spread like an epidemic disease. . . . I have been flooded with applications for papers allowing emigrants to leave."[1] In this way in 1855 the high sheriff of an obscure county near the southeastern tip of Prussia described the beginnings of Polish peasant migration to the New World. The people he wrote about were on their way to Texas, where they founded the first Polish colonies in America. Arriving in late 1854 and early 1855, the initial parties established a core of settlements that predated any such communities in the northern United States. These Silesian peasants not only began agricultural colonies but also organized the first Polish Catholic parishes and the first Polish school in the United States.[2] The settlements remain in existence and today exhibit a surprising level of preserved nineteenth-century Slavic culture in an area dominated by American, German, and Hispanic peoples.[3]

Upper Silesia, the homeland of the mid-nineteenth-century Polish immigrants to Texas, had been separated from the Polish state for five centuries when the peasants began their migration. In the fourteenth century it had passed from Poland to Bohemia and subsequently was held by Hungarian kings and Habsburg rulers until Frederick the Great acquired the territory in 1742. Despite the long alien control of Upper Silesia, the Polish language, Polish traditions, and the Roman Catholic religion survived among its peasantry.[4]

Prussian land reform in Upper Silesia, which began with a royal decree ending serfdom in 1807, increased personal freedom for the peasants but at the same time hurt them economically. Under these reforms the peasants were released from most of their responsibilities to the lords of the manors. In exchange for this freedom, however, they had to give the lords between one-third and one-half the land they had held as feudal tenants; the peasants retained any indebted-

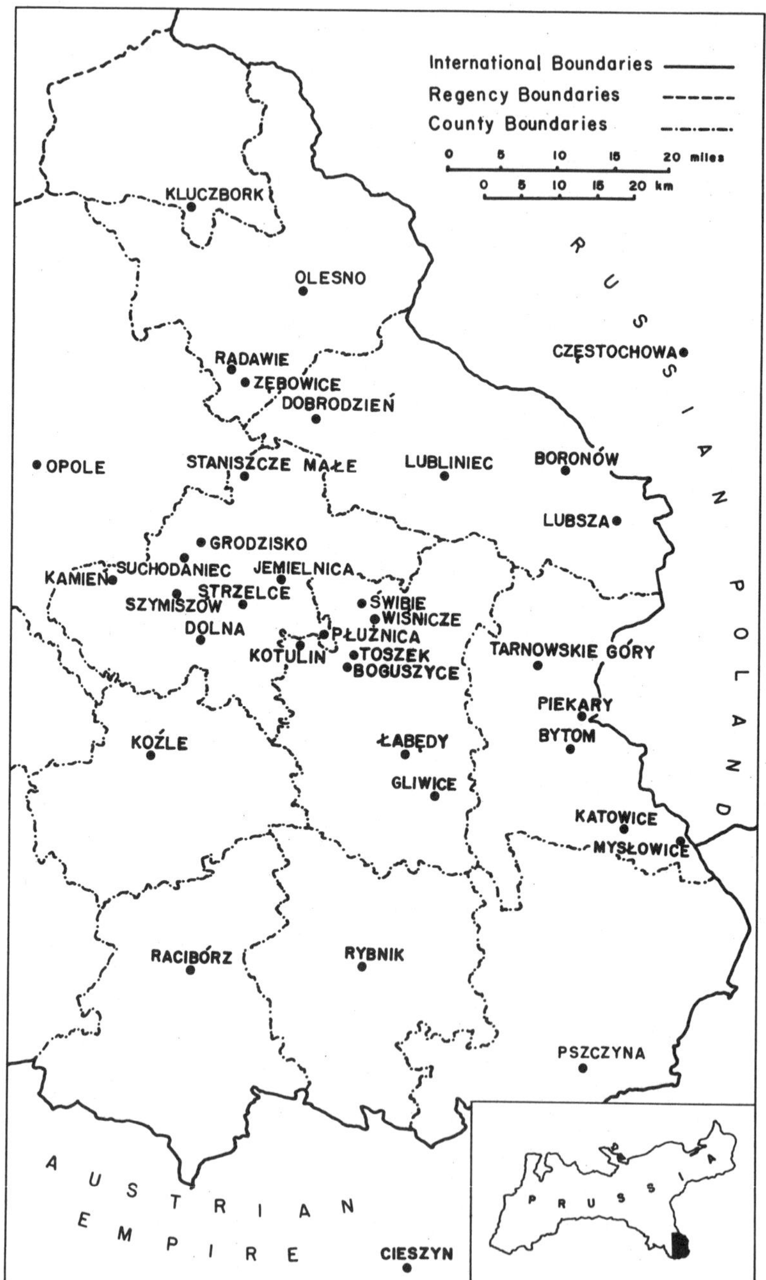

MAP 1. Upper Silesia, Kingdom of Prussia, in the 1850's, showing the area from which Poles emigrated to Texas.

ness on this land, however. In addition, when the peasants were seperated from the manors, the nobles were released from their responsibilities to them. After this time, for example, the lords no longer allowed the small farmers to graze their livestock on manorial lands. Thus, although the fundamental reforms gave the peasants some personal liberties, they frequently placed them in more difficult economic situations.[5]

In the mid-nineteenth century Upper Silesia constituted the extreme southeastern end of the Kingdom of Prussia. Administratively it composed the Regency of Opole, a political subdivision created in 1815–1816, after the agrarian reforms. Half a century later, when the Silesian peasants were departing for America, the Regency of Opole consisted of sixteen counties, five of the largest of which are known to have contributed immigrants to Texas. These counties were Opole (Oppeln), Strzelce (Gross Strehlitz), Toszek-Gliwice (Tost-Gleiwitz), Lubliniec (Lublinitz), and Olesno (Rosenberg).[6] This geographical source area of Polish immigration to Texas was divided approximately evenly between forests and open land, with most of the properties held by German nobles. The Polish peasants themselves owned small farms or worked on the manors, and they lived in small villages scattered through the countryside. The population of the five counties providing Texas immigrants was 288,390 in 1855, with an average annual increase at the time of 1.5 percent. Of this population 90 percent was Catholic, 8 percent was Protestant, and 2 percent was Jewish. All the known Polish immigrants were Roman Catholics.[7]

Upper Silesia was by no means a wealthy region. It was characterized by the poverty of the Polish lower classes contrasted with the relative wealth of the German ruling elite. A Prussian writer of the period noted that the "common people" in Strzelce County, source of some of the first Texas immigrants, lived very simply and that "the servant class goes barefooted in the summer and many houses have no floors."[8] The reputation of the region as a poor one went beyond the borders of Germany itself. The *Times* of London, for example, described it as "the Ireland of Prussia . . . an ever open sore in her body politic."[9] The economic problems of the Polish peasantry were aggravated by the fact that they were separated both socially and linguistically from the German rulers. They were, in fact, pawns in a German-dominated society.[10]

Conditions were ripe among the Polish peasantry of the Regency of Opole in the 1850's for emigration abroad, but first a stimulus was needed to initiate the movement. The basic causes for emigration, to be discussed later in some detail, were all present, but someone had to go first in order to give the others directions. A young Roman Catholic priest named Leopold Bonaventura Maria Moczygemba was the catalyst.[11]

Leopold Moczygemba was born at one o'clock on the morning of 24 October 1824 in the little village of Płużnica, situated between the county towns of Strzelce and Toszek. He spent his boyhood here and in the nearby village of Ligota Toszecka. In these villages his father, a native of Płużnica also named Leopold, supported his numerous family of ten children as an innkeeper and miller. Little is known about Leopold's mother, Ewa Krawiec, other than that she was the daughter of a farmer from the neighboring village of Boguszyce.[12] As a young man Leopold studied in the gymnasiums in Gliwice and Opole but then made the momentous personal decision to join the order of Friars Minor Conventual and become a priest.[13]

Leopold traveled to Italy, where in Osimo on 17 November 1843 he received the Franciscan habit. He remained in Italy for the next five years, studying and preparing himself to become a priest. Accepted into the order, he became affiliated with the Convent of Santa Vitoria delle Fratte in Osimo, where after a year's novitiate he made his profession on 18 November 1844. He began his studies for the priesthood at Ascoli-Piceno, continuing them in 1846 at Recanati. In that year he was transferred to Urbino and then was ordained a priest on 25 July 1847 in Pesaro at the age of twenty-two. He was sufficiently young that the procurator general of the order had to ask for a fifteen-month dispensation from age requirements for him to be ordained. Probably because of his youth, next he was transferred in 1848 to southern Germany for additional studies.[14]

As early as his departure from Italy, Father Leopold had considered going as a missionary to some distant part of the world. His desires had to wait, however, until a suitable opportunity presented itself. This chance came in early 1852, when Bishop Jean-Marie Odin, of Galveston, Texas, a Frenchman by birth, traveled to Europe seeking both priests and monetary assistance for his far-flung diocese in the wilds of North America.[15] Among his stops during the tour was the Conventual Franciscan cloister at Schönau, near Würzburg, in the same Franciscan province as the Oggersheim convent where Moczygemba was staying. When Odin and his party visited Schönau, they recruited Father Bonaventure Keller, who at the same time recommended Moczygemba, "a Polish priest," to accompany him in missionary work among the German settlers in Texas. As soon as Leopold heard of this opening to go as a missionary to America, he wrote to the commissary general of the order for Germany, the Reverend Robert Zahradniczek, asking for permission to go with Keller to Texas. After some delay, on 30 April 1852 the commissary general wrote to Moczygemba that his long-entertained plans for becoming a missionary had been approved in Rome and that he could leave for America.[16]

Moczygemba's departure for the New World was not without its complications. Just a few months before he learned that he might become a missionary in Texas, he had made a surprise trip home to Upper Silesia to visit his family and friends, his first time to see them in the eight years since he had become a Franciscan. Thus in the spring of 1851 he requested permission to travel to see his family for six to eight weeks, and by midsummer he was already in his birthplace. Not long thereafter Leopold wrote back to his superiors describing how everyone in the church at Płużnica had wept when he said his first mass after his return. At the same time he asked to have his stay prolonged for four weeks so that he could take the place of the priest in the village of Wiśnicze while the latter took a cure. He added that the additional stay would give him the opportunity to practice his native Polish.[17] Moczygemba's parents were so overjoyed at having their son back that they wrote to his superiors asking that Leopold be placed in the convent at Troppau, in Austrian Silesia, where they could see him every year. At the end of his permitted stay Moczygemba returned to Oggersheim, but his family continued its efforts to have him moved to the nearer monastery, especially in 1852, when they learned that he wanted to leave for the New World.[18] Their opposition was to no avail, however, and in July 1852 the Reverend Leopold Moczygemba, wearing the black robe of the Friars Minor Conventual, set out as a missionary to Texas with Father Bonaventure Keller and two other German Franciscans.[19]

Traveling via Le Havre to Galveston, the four friars reached their posts in Texas by September 1852. In that month Bishop Odin assigned the German Catholic parishes of New Braunfels, Fredericksburg, and Castroville to their care. In addition to these three major settlements the friars received as missions several smaller German communities, including Vandenburg, Quihi, Seco, Comal, Santa Clara, Cibolo, Llano, and Pedernales. Father Moczygemba was assigned to the parish in New Braunfels, where he served as its first resident pastor until February 1854, when he moved to the Alsatian colony at Castroville, staying there through December of that year.[20]

Living among the German immigrants in Texas, Moczygemba quickly observed their economic and social advancement in the open society of the Texas frontier.[21] He decided that his family and friends back in Upper Silesia could experience the same success if they came to the New World. Consequently he began examining various potential sites for settlement and pricing land, at the same time writing letters suggesting and even urging people in his boyhood home to come to a place he was preparing for them in Texas. Although none of these letters from before 1855 has been found, slightly later correspondence suggests that he wrote back to Upper Silesia about the freedom and opportunities found by European immigrants in Texas.[22] The tone of one of his letters written from Texas in summer 1855 suggests what the ones just a few months before must have been like: "I wrote to him to come here. . . . because he would live better here. . . . I told him only because I wish for him to come. There will be a time, and it will not be long, when Franc will want to leave for America and he will not be able. . . . John of the Uncles is very happy that his parents are coming here because they will live here in peace."[23]

Letters like this, and later correspondence written by the peasant immigrants themselves, created a sensation in Upper Silesia. The Polish farmers treated them like "religious relics" as they passed the letters from family to family, often affecting whole localities.[24] Father Leopold, in fact, addressed them to groups of people: "I greet all of you, Franc and his wife, sisters and Wrobel, also Uncles from Toszek, people from Boguszyce, Jemielnica, and Dolna, and everybody."[25] As early as summer 1855, the local Prussian bureaucracy had become aware of the influence of Moczygemba's correspondence. At that time the high sheriff of Strzelce County reported to the police administration in Opole that the tendency toward emigration from his area was being excited by letters from "the missionary, Father Moczygemba, who works in Texas and who comes from Płużnica." The official added that the priest had many relatives and friends in the Toszek vicinity and that he was trying to persuade them to emigrate to Texas "with prospects of a better life."[26]

These letters from Texas provided the stimulus for the first Polish peasant immigration to America. In late 1854 the first parties of emigrants sold their properties and left Upper Silesia. They were followed by sizable contingents of farmers in 1855 and 1856 and by smaller numbers in the subsequent few years. The correspondence from Texas, however, was by no means the reason for the emigration. It was only the spur. The actual causes lay much deeper and were based in the economic and social problems of the Upper Silesian peasantry.

Poverty presented probably the most serious difficulty for the Polish peasants of Upper Silesia in the 1850's. Among the reasons for this poverty was the change in society caused by the early-nineteenth-century agrarian reforms, which had reduced the sizes of the peasant landholdings. With the fragmented properties the peasants became less and less able to support themselves. When natural disasters struck, as they did in the period, they were among the first victims.[27]

High food prices plagued Upper Silesia in the mid-1850's. A major cause for this inflation was the Crimean War. When the war broke out in 1853, the Russian government prohibited the export of Russian grain to European markets, driving grain prices skyward in neighboring Prussia. At the same time several natural disasters hit Silesia. A potato blight caused by a fungus spread across the North European Plain and from there into Silesia. The decay of the potatoes in the fields either destroyed or heavily damaged several years' crops of this staple in the Polish peasant diet. Food supplies became so short that the Prussian government was forced to import maize from Hungary to feed the indigent.[28]

Accounts of poverty and suffering filled contemporary government reports and newspapers. The president of the Regency of Opole, for example, wrote to Berlin in May 1855 that "one can speak of a steady increase in poverty" rather than an improvement in the standard of living of the poorer classes. He continued that, although employment was available for day laborers in agriculture, road building, and railways, the salaries for such work were insufficient to pay "the high prices for food." The next year the same official reported that the greater part of the population in the Regency of Opole had lived through the winter of 1855–1856 in comparatively good condition but that "it is not unusual to encounter lean figures who lack the strength and vigor to live." He noted that the spring was the most difficult season for the peasants because by that time they had consumed their stored food, and then "the starving people reach for herbs and other unwholesome products."[29]

Across the boundary in Austrian Poland, where Polish-language publishing was much freer than in Prussian territory, the Polish press covered economic conditions in Prussian Upper Silesia in considerable detail. From Kraków, *Czas* reported in autumn 1855 that "the material conditions in Silesia have not changed at all" and that "this year the winter very easily could be the saddest ever." The author stressed the problems of inflated food prices, which he saw as created by the combination of poor harvests with curtailed grain imports, notably from the belligerents in the Crimean War. The writer of another article about the same time emphasized the significance of the potato blight, which destroyed "the only hope of the poor," while a third observer warned that "with true fear they wait in many places for the winter."[30] In the border town of Cieszyn, the local Polish newspaper, *Gwiazdka Cieszyńska*, concluded that the desire of Upper Silesian peasants to emigrate to America was founded on bad crops and "the rotting of the potatoes."[31]

In addition to the inflated food prices were high taxes, which the peasants greatly resented. Reflecting on the immigration to Texas a decade afterward, the Polish Upper Silesian newspaper *Zwiastun Górnoszląski* stated that, among the various reasons the peasants had departed for Texas, "first of all" in importance was that "they wanted to pay less taxes." Chronologically in the midst of the emigration *Gwiazdka Cieszyńska* reported that what the settlers liked best was that "they do not have to pay taxes" in the new land. Even a local Prussian official commented in his reports that one reason people were leaving his district was to escape increased levies.[32]

In response to the poverty, inflation, and high taxes some of the Upper Silesian population turned to begging as a means of sustenance. In all the region the number of beggars reached into the hundreds if not the thousands. In a typical report the Opole correspondent of the Wrocław *Schlesische Zeitung* wrote that in the summer of 1855 increasing food prices had caused beggars to proliferate on the streets of his city, despite efforts by charitable organizations to help the poor. He described how in Opole "both old and young beggars stand in the doorways asking alms from morning until night, swallowing what potatoes and bread are given to them." In the same article the correspondent coldly reported that the trade in the local grain markets was brisk and bringing substantial profits because of the high prices paid as the products passed through the hands of the merchants. In an article the next year the correspondent from Toszek-Gliwice County declared that in the preceding ten years the poverty of the Upper Silesians had become severe, "in contrast to the great wealth of some individuals." He went on to say that many people from childhood preferred to beg rather than to work, "a born proletariat that grows up without school or church." From Katowice came the demand for a special police force to act against beggars who had perpetrated several brutal robberies.[33]

Increased criminal activity, indeed, accompanied the economic difficulties. The contemporary press is filled with reports of crimes against private property. From Toszek-Gliwice County, for example, came serious complaints against a band of gypsies that in 1856 was moving back and forth across the county from village to village, begging and stealing whatever was available. Not all the new criminals engaged in petty crimes. The number of highwaymen also increased noticeably in the 1850's. The best known of these robbers was a former student of the university in Wrocław named Kahle, who finally was caught by the authorities.[34] The numbers of criminals apprehended grew so large that the prisons in the Regency of Opole could not contain all of them. To help alleviate the overcrowding, the royal government moved about four hundred inmates from the severely crowded penal institutions to the old Szymiszów Castle near Strzelce. Despite the crowded conditions in Prussian prisons, however, many prisoners felt that the living conditions there were better than in the poverty of the outside world, and they preferred to remain incarcerated and be assured of warmth and wholesome food. As one of them reportedly asked, "Where can we find better conditions than here?"[35]

Making the economic problems of the Upper Silesians more difficult were natural disasters, among which were repeated outbreaks of typhus and cholera. Such epidemics in the 1840's are comparatively well known in the history of the region and were described at the time by the noted German physician Rudolph Virchow.[36] Less well known are the continued outbreaks of cholera, at times accompanied by typhus, which claimed victims numbering in the hundreds almost every year during the first half of the 1850's. The summer and autumn of 1855 were a particularly severe time in which 1,351 lives were lost. Country people suffered especially from the feared disease. In the village of Mozurów in northern Racibórz County, just south of the area that supplied immigrants to Texas, 55 of the 480 inhabitants died of cholera.[37] Mortality was also high among urban dwellers. In the city of Wrocław, for instance, so many people died that official reports by the president of the police appeared daily in the press giving the death toll.[38] In the cities as well as in the villages the people undoubtedly scrutinized the newspaper advertisements like that of Herman Gochaczewski for his "cholera-liqueur," as they tried to decide whether the patent medicines would indeed protect them from the dread killer.[39]

A much more serious natural disaster for the peasants of Upper Silesia was the great flood of summer 1854. By mid-August of that year unusually heavy precipitation had filled rivers and streams of the area to overflowing, and between the seventeenth and the twenty-fourth of the month there was such a heavy and continuous rainfall that the water levels rose higher than at any other time in over half a century. The flooding occurred not only in the valley of the Odra, the principal river of Silesia, but throughout the region on all the smaller watercourses.

All the areas that sent peasants to Texas in the next few years were subject to the flooding. A newspaper correspondent from Lubliniec County, the easternmost district providing immigrants, wrote a few days after the downpour that, though there was no main river in the county, the small streams had destroyed or damaged many peasant cottages and that most of the road bridges and levees along watercourses were ruined. He reported that in most of the county only half of the crops had been harvested before the rains began and that the wheat and oats had not been gathered at all. A week and a half after the flood these grains were still lying in the water-soaked fields, overripe and rotting. From Strzelce County came a report at the same time that, even that far away from the rivers, "we have a small picture of the Great Flood." This correspondent also remarked that the water was still in the fields and that it was impossible to drive wagons there because the wooden wheels sank into the mud. In such situations some of the desperate Upper Silesian peasants, fearing famine in the winter, with great difficulty trudged through the wet to cut and carry armfuls of grain to the barns.

Some of the greatest damage was caused by the collapse of levees and dams. In Kluczbork, just beyond the northwestern corner of the area from which the immigrants came, the church bells began ringing the alarm at ten o'clock on the night of 19 August 1854. There had been continuous rains and storms for three days, and the inhabitants of the town had been forced to stay indoors. That very night they were complaining about the inclement weather, unaware that the rains had been even heavier upstream in Olesno and Lubliniec counties, areas that later contributed immigrants to Texas. Water had filled the ditches, streams, and lakes; on the night of the nineteenth it overtopped the dams, washing great gaps in them. By the time the alarm was rung in Kluczbork, waves of water from these higher reservoirs were pouring through the streets of the town with a frightening hissing sound. The flow took away everything in its path, removing even the solid cobblestones and leaving only mud in their places.

The most severe damage was in the valley of the River Odra. There the houses in many places were flooded up to the windows and even the roofs, forcing the unfortunate residents to seek shelter in their attics, or, if that was impossible, to be rescued in boats. In this area many of the houses were destroyed by undercutting of their foundations. Few bridges could withstand the powerful pressure of the floodwater, and most of them were either damaged or destroyed.

All communications in Upper Silesia were disrupted. A report from Gliwice, for example, stated that the waters of the normally calm Kłodnica River had overflowed their banks and flooded the road to Kraków, turning the outskirts of the town "into a river." There beside the Kraków road people were standing in water "up to their hips" and looking for help. All the major railway lines were closed and were returned to service only after the construction of temporary bypasses. The line between Gliwice and Koźle, for example, was put out of service by washed-out embankments near Łabędy. The tracks could not be repaired for three days, and hundreds of grumbling Vienna-bound travelers were stranded in provincial Racibórz.

The flood caused the greatest harm to agriculture. All the hopes for a good harvest, which would have allayed the poverty of the region, were dashed. The rye harvest everywhere and the wheat and barley harvests in some places had already begun by the time the flood started, and the results had been satisfactory, but most of the grain crops either were washed away or rotted in the muddy fields, where they could not be harvested. Even the crops that had been taken into the barns were not safe. The humidity was so high in the days after the heavy rains that the stored crops molded badly. The fate of the potato harvest was as sad as that of the grain. As a result of the downpour virtually all the potato fields were flooded, and some of them did not show even a trace of their former crops. The president of the Opole Regency reported that less than a third of the normal crop of this mainstay in the peasant diet would be harvested. Although most of the livestock was able to escape from the rising waters, many of the animals subsequently had to be slaughtered because of lack of fodder or because of ailments they had contracted from days of standing in the water. Even after the flood receded and the sun finally came out again, the farmers were plagued with problems. One of the most serious was that their fields were covered with undesirable heavy, wet silt that prevented normal cultivation of the soil.[40]

Throughout Germany charitable people launched a campaign to provide aid to the sufferers in Silesia. A main committee was organized in Berlin to coordinate the relief activities in the various German states, while newspapers bore large advertisements soliciting donations. Typical of the fund-raising efforts was the "monster concert *al fresco*" held in Berlin in September at which a total of sixteen thousand thalers was subscribed for the relief campaign. The benevolent efforts, sizable though they were, were insufficient to provide more than a token service to the thousands of destitute people in the region for whom the flood only increased the general poverty.[41]

Economic problems, while the most important cause of the emigration from Upper Silesia, were by no means the sole reason for the peasant exodus. With the economic motivation came social impulses to try for a better life elsewhere. This incentive for leaving was rooted in the basic inequalities and discrimination of the society in which the ruling German minority dominated the majority Polish peasant population.

The contemporary Polish press demonstrated a clear understanding of these additional causes of Upper Silesian emigration. *Gwiazdka Cieszyńska* wrote that the Polish population was leaving not merely because of "physical reasons, overpopulation, etc.," but for "social reasons." In Kraków, *Czas* stressed the gap between the peasants and the "well-off German landlords," with whom they were connected "by neither religion nor language."[42] A decade later the editors of the Polish Upper Silesian weekly *Zwiastun Górnoszlazki*, in an open letter addressed to the emigrants in Texas, stated that the only reason they could imagine for the people to have left their homes was that in America they had "an equality of classes and greater freedom of life than here."[43] At the same time that *Zwiastun* was writing to the Silesian colonists about their liberty in America, a local Polish priest in Texas could calm even the most severe complaints of the settlers by reminding them of the social discrimination they had suffered in their motherland:

> I thank you for your Prussian joys . . . and what freedom did you have? Didn't you have to work a great part only for the king? As soon as a boy grew up, they took him to the army, and for the defense of whom and what? Not your kingdom but the Prussian one. You lost your health and lives for what purpose? And taxes? Were they small? Did you forget how you were racked? You talked among yourselves that they took holy pictures from the walls and covers from the beds of the poor. Wherever you went, you had to have a certificate from the officer of the Diet in the village.[44]

When the Revolution of 1848 failed to alleviate the heavy discrimination against the Polish population of Upper Silesia, many of the peasants gave up hope for social reform in their homeland. Such an individual was Stanisław Kiołbassa, a farmer from the village of Świbie who with his family left for Texas in 1855. After a temporary liberalization of election laws, on 8 May 1848 he had been elected to represent the Forty-second Electoral District of Gliwice in the Prussian national parliament. Kiołbassa was a theretofore obscure man with whom only his electors were familiar. Once chosen to serve as their representative, he traveled to Berlin, and there, despite his inability to speak any language except Polish, he participated in the parliamentary activities and served on the Committee for Mines and Foundries. Because Kiołbassa could not communicate in German, another deputy introduced a motion to have him expelled from the assembly, but other members came to his support and successfully defeated the attempt. Current historians have disagreed over Kiołbassa's political philosophy, one claiming him for the leftists and another for the moderates. Whichever is correct, at least some of his constituents were dissatisfied with his performance in office. A conservative German newspaper in Olesno complained that, as long as the election laws remained so liberal, "the Kielbasas [*sic*] will always keep the field." When he returned to Upper Silesia after the close of the sessions in late 1848, the dissatisfaction of some of the natives reached him in a more concrete form. When he visited Toszek, an angry soldier from the reserves physically assaulted him, blaming Kiołbassa and his "political friends" for being called up for military service.[45]

Returning to his home in Świbie, Kiołbassa undoubtedly met the Reverend Leopold Moczygemba when he visited Upper Silesia in the summer and autumn of 1851. It was in Kiołbassa's own parish of Wiśnicze that the priest substituted for the local pastor while he went to take a cure. One can hardly imagine the young clergyman who had just returned from Bavaria and Italy not having personal meetings with the most active politician among the local parishioners.[46]

Another cause for Upper Silesian emigration abroad was the desire of many men to evade conscription of themselves or their sons into the Prussian army. Service in this rigidly disciplined military body was known throughout Europe for its severity. At the age of twenty every Prussian subject, with certain exemptions, was compelled to begin a three-year term of duty in the regular army followed by a two-year term in the active reserves. After this period the men were released into civilian life but were transferred to inactive reserves, called the Landwehr, where they remained until their fortieth year. During these fifteen years they were required to spend fifteen days annually in military exercises. Even at the age of forty they were not free of their obligations. They were then transferred to secondary inactive reserves, called the Landsturm, where they remained until they reached the age of sixty. During this time they were subject to be called out in the event of foreign invasion. To avoid this onerous duty for their offspring, many fathers sent their sons to America, keeping at home one son, who as an "only son" was exempt from duty. This subterfuge was successful for some time, but after the government authorities realized how people were evading military service through emigration of all but one son, the law was changed so that the "only son" left after the emigration of all his brothers would no longer be exempt from the normal conscription.[47]

Added to the economic and social reasons for emigration was a vast array of personal motives. To the individual peasants themselves these reasons for leaving probably figured more importantly than the actual causes. People emigrated to avoid family friction, to escape scandals, to join relatives, to see new country, because others had gone, and for scores of other such reasons. The decision to stay in Europe likewise frequently was based on personal motives. Father Moczygemba, for example, wrote back to Płużnica about his brother, saying that "he doesn't want to come because he follows his and his wife's own ideas."[48]

While the several causes discussed were the most important in both beginning and continuing the emigration from Upper Silesia to Texas, many additional factors promoted or stimulated the movement. Among these elements were the continued arrival of favorable reports from America, the activities of emigration agents, the promotion of emigration by German landlords, and the spread of exaggerated rumors.

In the beginning Father Moczygemba's letters provided the catalytic agent that started the peasant movement, but as soon as the first Polish immigrants arrived in Texas, they also began writing letters back to their families and friends in Upper Silesia. Generally praising the new country, this correspondence convinced more and more farmers that they should try their luck overseas. Among the first people outside the peasant population to recognize the importance of the letters were, as might be expected, the local government authorities. As early as February 1855 the high sheriff of Olesno County wrote to Opole that the reason for the emigration from his and adjoining counties was reports from the people who had left the area and were writing back home about their "well-being in America." Later the same year the high sheriff of Toszek-Gliwice County blamed Father Moczygemba's letters for the movement. By 1856 the entire bureaucracy was aware of the influence of the American letters, with the president of the Opole Regency writing to Berlin that "favorable news" from Texas was even further increasing the tendencies toward emigration from his province.[49]

The naïve letters of the immigrants were recognized by the more critical intellectuals as one-sided but made a tremendous impression in the countryside. When the topic of such letters came up in the 16 September 1857 meeting of the Wrocław-based Central Emigration Society for Silesia, one member of this German organization pointed out to his fellows that, while they should be careful about believing everything in the laudatory reports, the letters did have a large influence "not only on single families but also on whole localities." Similarly questioning the content of the American letters, the Silesian correspondent of *Gwiazdka Cieszyńska* wrote that, although the reports from Texas sounded good, "we cannot tell if the immigrants are doing well or whether they want to delude others in order for them to bring help from home."[50]

Perhaps more can be learned from the letters of the peasants themselves than from the comments of contemporaries about them. Four letters from Texas in 1855 were preserved by the officials of the Regency of Opole in a file of papers concerning the activities of emigration agents and therefore are available today.[51] In one of the letters a peasant wrote home as follows about the opportunities he found in Texas: "If you have money, you can keep even one thousand head of cattle, as the Americans do. You can plant cotton, which is very expensive, and I, John Moczygemba, plan to grow it."[52] The same writer in another letter attempted to persuade some of his relatives to come to America: "I talked to Joseph about it and he told me with tears in his eyes that it would be best if you came. When he came he was alone, but it was not so hard as in Silesia, because here he can breed whatever animals he wants and it costs nothing. He told me that with the help of God he could sell his wheat for one hundred dollars. . . . Now I would like to greet my Parents and my Brother and his Wife and . . . come the sooner the better."[53]

Making the way smooth for the travelers were the emigration agents, who represented shipping companies in North German ports and who arranged transportation for specific emigrants or parties of emigrants. As early as 1852 such businessmen appeared in the Regency of Opole, and within three years a number were active in the region, including several in Opole and even one in the county town of Strzelce.[54] By 1854 the number of emigration agents active in the Kingdom of Prussia had grown sufficiently large that the minister of commerce, trade, and public works found it necessary to issue directives for the protection and regulation of their activities.[55]

The work of the emigration agents generally was criticized by their contemporaries. The Polish press of the 1850's condemned the agents in Upper Silesia for deluding the country people with impossible promises. Even prospective immigrants criticized them. One peasant from the Regency of Opole, for example, complained to a government official that some of the ships had been sold as unseaworthy by their original owners and were too dangerous to be trusted for overseas travel.[56]

Not everyone, however, was so critical of the agents. The same peasant who found fault with the ships provided by some of the firms represented by local businessmen, for instance, described another agent as looking after his emigrants "as a father does for his children."[57] Another emigrant similarly characterized the man who booked his travel as caring for "every person, even for the smallest child."[58] Yet another immigrant to Texas stated that his agent exchanged all his money honestly and "went with us up to the moment we sat on the ship."[59]

The emigration agents, whether honest or unprincipled, did provide a valuable service to the emigrants by arranging their transportation. This assistance in facilitating the movement of families from the villages to the ports and from the ports to Texas, coupled with their own limited publicity, undoubtedly promoted the emigration. Their role was in making it easier.[60]

The German landlords, instead of opposing the departure of the Polish peasants, at times even encouraged it. They reasoned that they could replace the native Poles with German colonists from other parts of the country whom they considered to be more efficient workers. Commenting on the situation, *Gwiazdka Cieszyńska* noted that it was strange that the new German settlers were able to live from the same fields where the Poles could not live. Decrying the critics who accused the native peasants of "mental indolence," the writer declared that the problem was that they lacked "direction, energy, knowledge, and guidance," all of which the new German colonists had in abundance. He sadly observed that through the emigration, which the landlords furthered, "the Polish population of Silesia is disappearing every week."[61]

With the increasing misery in Upper Silesia conditions were ideal for the spread of stories about better life elsewhere. The tales about Texas were believed by the peasants in every respect, for the more difficult material circumstances had dulled their normally sharp reason. The villages of Upper Silesia, in fact, were rife with rumors about Texas, about living conditions there, and about means of emigration. One of the most frequently repeated rumors concerned "golden mountains," tales that had most likely originated in the California gold rush five years before. Other stories dealt with free land, fertile fields, and a waiting church in the New World.[62] Many of the peasants had no concept of how far they were going or what difficulties they might meet along the way. The Prussian consul in Bremen, for example, wrote to the authorities in Opole that Polish families from Upper Silesia were arriving at the port believing a rumor, told to them by the brother of a man who had successfully immigrated to Texas, that there was a Frenchman in Bremen who was offering people free passage to Galveston if they would sign contracts to work for him in Texas. According to the official, "They thought that they needed only enough money to get to the water."[63]

Even more extreme was the gossip believed by other families, who merely walked to the nearest railway stations, from which they expected "to go directly to America."[64] Although most of the rumors were false, they provided an additional stimulus for the peasants to try their luck in the New World. At the same time they set the stage for their great shocks and severe disappointments both in travel and in the expected "land of milk and honey."[65]

2

Founding the First Polish Colonies

AS we have seen, letters from Texas, combined with the difficult social and economic conditions in mid-nineteenth-century Upper Silesia, precipitated a peasant exodus that contemporary observers characterized as a "mania," a "fever," and an "epidemic." This flow of emigrants, beginning in 1854, remained strong for three years before it decreased to a trickle. As early as October 1854 a member of the Wrocław-based Central Emigration Society for Silesia noted that among the Polish population of Upper Silesia a trend had begun for emigration "in the direction of Texas." Calling the movement a "disastrous fever," *Czas* declared from Kraków that nothing could stem the flood because of the severe poverty of the areas from which the peasants were departing. When the high sheriff of Olesno County tried to convince prospective emigrants that they would not succeed in improving their situations in the New World, they replied: "Whether we rot here or there, it's all the same to us. At any rate, we want to try our luck."[1]

Unlike the stereotype of Slavic immigrants as poverty-stricken masses longing for just enough bread to live, the Silesians who were leaving for Texas were propertied people with a stake in society. It was only substantial individuals with some capital who could afford to move their families a third of the way around the world, an expensive matter even in the cheapest steerage quarters of the emigrant ships of the day.

The Texas immigrants came exclusively from the peasant class, a group generally misunderstood in America both in the nineteenth century and at the present time. They were people with small landholdings living in country villages where most land was owned by local lords. They had a stable social position between that of the gentry above and that of the landless laborers beneath. While they showed an inherited deference to the gentlemen, they also stood far above their inferiors. As important members of their rural world the peasants were property owners, taxpayers, and permanent constituents of an old social order. They were known to and known by all in the community and enjoyed positions appropriately adjusted to their means and families. For them the marriage of children, the pensioning of aged parents, and the compensation for portions of brothers' or sisters' inheritance all constituted significant questions of property of almost dynastic character.[2]

People like these, although hurt by bad harvests, epidemic diseases, and floods, could never be compared with the beggar class. They were, however, frightened by the prospect of poverty and very much disturbed by the misery and lawlessness they saw growing around them. A typical encounter between a peasant girl and a beggar illustrates that the members of the farming class were distressed by the increasing economic problems and demonstrates the kinds of events that caused many of them to try for more security and advancement in Texas. In the summer of 1854 a beggar approached a peasant cottage in the village of Lubsza, in Lubliniec County. An eighteen-year-old servantgirl met him at the door and replied to his requests for food that she was the only person in the house and that she had nothing to give him. Rejecting her refusal, the pauper forced his way inside, took a plate in the kitchen, and served himself a large portion of dumplings. When the maid protested that the food had been prepared for the owners of the house, the man, without stopping his meal, picked up an ax and threatened her life if she dared disturb him further. After finishing his dinner, the tramp set off, leaving the girl so frightened that she was unable even to leave the house to ask the neighbors for help.[3]

Contemporary European sources uniformly described the immigrants to Texas as landowning peasants, and some of them deplored the loss of such valuable members of society. As early as February 1855 the high sheriff of Olesno County, for example, described the departing emigrants as "mostly farmers, gardeners, and cottagers."[4] The president of the Regency of Opole complained to Berlin that through the migration "the country is losing its better people, as concerns both the human and the material sides of the matter."[5] The press across the boundary in Austrian Poland called the emigrants "the richest parts" of the Polish population in Upper Silesia and declared that they were "not loose people, but rich and settled ones who are looking for a new motherland overseas."[6] An Upper Silesian newspaper a few years later noted that the emigrants went to Texas not merely for land but for "larger properties."[7] The peasants who began leaving for America very obviously were people of substance.

The first group of emigrants departed from Upper Silesia in late September 1854. Coming predominantly from the villages around Toszek and Strzelce, the initial group traveled together by train to the harbor at Bremen.[8] An article in the German press at Poznań, repeated by the Polish press, recounted their journey: "On the 26th of September, 150 Poles from Upper Silesia arrived by train in Berlin and on the next day in the afternoon left by the Cologne Railway for Bremen, from where they plan to go by ship to Texas (to America). This is worth mentioning because, as is known, Slavic people are so attached to their native land that emigration among them is extraordinary."[9]

Once at the port the farmers and their families boarded the 265-ton wooden bark *Weser*, which in October set sail on a two-month voyage to the Texas coast. A handful of Silesians, for reasons unknown, failed to board the *Weser* and followed the main party several days later on the brig *Antoinette*.[10]

After crossing the Atlantic and the Gulf of Mexico, the *Weser*, with its combined cargo of merchandise and immigrants, slowly sailed into Galveston Harbor on 3 December 1854. It docked at the long wooden Merchant's Wharf, where Pier 15 now stands, and discharged its passengers, while the customs agent noted that another load of immigrants "from Germany" had arrived.[11] They entered the strange city, filled with white, brown, and black people who spoke languages unknown to the Polish farmers. One can only imagine what they must have thought about their exotic new surroundings. They undoubtedly were happy to find German residents with whom some of them could converse. Father Leopold Moczygemba, who had drawn them to America, was not on hand to meet them. He was absent probably because he recently had assumed new duties as the superior of the Franciscan Minor Conventual missions in Texas.[12]

The Silesians secured transportation by boat from Galveston to the port of Indianola, farther down the Texas coast. From this second harbor they turned inland toward San Antonio, some of them walking and others riding in hired Mexican oxcarts.[13] Most accounts of the first Polish immigration stress the exposure and illness of the new settlers as they traveled overland toward San Antonio. This may be an assumption on the part of later writers, for none of the preserved peasant correspondence of the period says anything negative about that part of the journey. On the contrary, one of the Silesians wrote back to his family that "there is no winter here." Nevertheless, the travelers undoubtedly were subject to the elements during the tiresome trek, and it probably was not a pleasant one, particularly since the man who had invited them to Texas had not yet appeared. After the colonists, who at this time numbered 159, arrived in San Antonio on 21 December, however, Father Leopold hastened from Castroville to greet them and guide some of them to a place he had selected for their settlement.[14]

Moczygemba, in fact, had been busy preparing for the new arrivals. As early as 1853 he had started planning the settlement of Poles near New Braunfels, where he had bought a parcel of land at a previously platted townsite named Cracow. For some reason he abandoned his plans for the Cracow settlement and chose two new locations on opposite sides of San Antonio. One of these was an unnamed open plateau above two river valleys in Karnes County, about sixty miles southeast of the city, and the other was the already established American town of Bandera, about forty-five miles northwest. There had been no previous settlement at the former site, which he planned to be the major community. Before the arrival of the immigrants the priest had ridden on horseback through the area with its owner, an Irish immigrant named John Twohig, and had made an agreement with him about the proposed settlement of Poles on the land. Although the details are unclear, the general agreement was that Twohig would hold the land for the Poles exclusively until they were able to buy it from him. It is not recorded whether the two men discussed the prices to be paid.[15]

After Father Leopold met the immigrant band in San Antonio, he led most of them the remaining sixty miles southeast to the place he had chosen for their main colony. There, above the confluence of the San Antonio River with Cibolo Creek, on an open knoll on which stood a few clumps of live-oak trees, the Silesians found their new home.

Some of the settlers, still believing rumors they had heard in Silesia, were disappointed to find waiting for them neither houses nor a church but instead only tall grass, brush, and a few trees. Nevertheless, having finally completed their wearisome three-month journey, the immigrants were thankful for their safe arrival. In this mood Father Leopold, under one of the largest of the oaks at the site, offered a Christmas mass of thanksgiving, which for many of the immigrants also served as a petition to the Almighty for strength to carry on in the face of adversity. In this way the founders marked the establishment of the first Polish colony in America.[16]

The new settlement in Karnes County soon came to be known as Panna Maria, meaning Virgin Mary in Polish.[17] There are several theories about how the name was chosen. One hypothesis is that, in the very same month that the colony was founded, Pope Pius IX in Rome proclaimed the dogma of the Immaculate Conception of the Virgin Mary. According to this interpretation the Silesians and their priest, under the influence of the enunciation of the dogma, decided to build their church under the invocation of the Immaculate Conception and to name the place Virgin Mary.[18] A second theory regarding the name Panna Maria stems from its Polish origin. According to this version, "many of the settlers" had seen the beautiful Church of Saint Mary in Kraków, and they wanted to name their settlement after it.[19] Another interpretation of the story is that Father Moczygemba while on a mission at another settlement had a vision of Saint Mary's Church in Kraków surrounded by a great light and took the vision as a sign that he should name his new colony Panna Maria.[20]

While most of the Silesians from the *Weser* and the *Antoinette* chose to settle in Karnes County, sixteen families went in the opposite direction to Bandera. Situated in the scenic hill country northwest of San Antonio, it had been established in 1853 by John James, Charles DeMontel, and John H. Herndon, who had pooled their resources to build a sawmill at the new townsite. In search of settlers to occupy the place, the promoters were delighted with the opportunity to people it with new Slavic immigrants. Americans had been reluctant to locate there because of the town's constant danger of Indian attacks in its exposed position on the fringe of settlement.

American teamsters working for James and DeMontel met the immigrants in San Antonio (some sources say Castroville) and in early

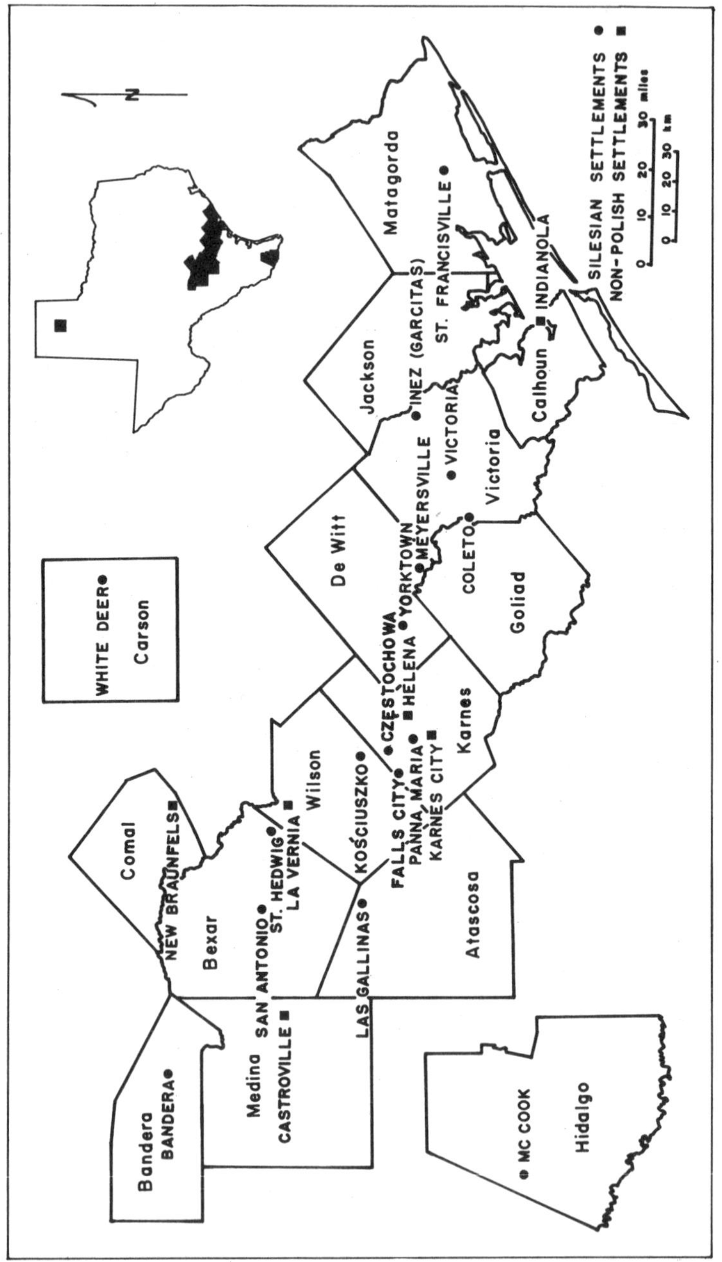

MAP 2. Silesian settlements in Texas.

February 1855 hauled them and their baggage to Bandera. The teamsters' orders were to carry the immigrants free of charge but not to permit any of them to return in the wagons. An American who witnessed their arrival recalled, "When these Polish people were dumped off here they had to stay, as they had no way to leave." The Silesians immediately went to work for the Americans, doing manual labor, working in the sawmill, and cutting cypress shingles. Soon they were able to erect log and picket houses on land they bought from the townsite promoters. The Polish population of the town during the next three years grew to about twenty families, primarily through the arrival of people who left Panna Maria because they felt that Bandera was situated in a more healthful location.[21]

Least known of the early Silesian colonies in Texas is the community that in the second half of the 1850's sprang up on the southeast side of San Antonio. Soon after the arrival of the immigrants many of the craftsmen gravitated toward the city, where they could live better from their skills. The colony was able to retain its ethnic identity in the heterogeneous population of the city, and within just over a decade its members had established their own separate Polish Catholic parish. In the interim their religious needs were met by Polish-speaking priests from the other settlements. Three years after the first Silesians entered the city, San Antonio had at least fifty Polish artisan families.[22] Because Father Moczygemba was heavily occupied with the Panna Maria colony and with his duties as superior of the Franciscan missions in Texas, the San Antonio Poles chose a fellow countryman, Erasmus Andrew Florian, as their guide and adviser. Florian was a native of Zasław, in Russian Poland. His original name was Florian Liskowacki. He was a political exile from the unsuccessful Polish Insurrection of 1830 against the Russians. After coming to America, he worked for several years in New York and Memphis before moving to San Antonio, where he became a successful businessman and banker.[23]

While the first Polish immigrants were traveling to and settling in Texas, other groups of peasants were preparing to leave Upper Silesia. During this second year of emigration the "Texas fever" spread somewhat north to villages around Olesno and Dobrodzień, where large numbers of families began preparing to seek their fortunes in the New World. The president of the Regency of Opole reported to Berlin that the movement to America was increasing, "especially in Olesno County," where it would have increased even more "if the owners of properties could find immediate buyers." During this second year of migration the role of emigration agents appears to have increased significantly. These businessmen sought personal gain from arranging travel for peasants already predisposed toward leaving and for others whom they persuaded to go.[24]

One of the most active agents involved in arranging transportation for Silesians to Texas was a forty-year-old German merchant from Opole named Julius Heinrich Schüler. More is known about his activities in Toszek in the summer of 1855 than about the work of any of his contemporaries. For this reason his endeavors present a case study in what the other entrepreneurs were doing elsewhere in Upper Silesia at the same time.

Having received his concession as an emigration agent from the royal administration only a few months before, Schüler went to Toszek in early August in his ordinary role as a merchant. There he learned that the local peasantry was interested in immigration to Texas, and he began talking with people about the possibility of traveling with the Carl Pokrantz Company of Bremen, the firm he represented. After discussing the subject with a local merchant, Alexander Czerner, who himself was interested in emigration, Schüler placed one of his posters on the door of the tavern owned by Czerner. While he was in the town, Schüler also talked about emigration with several other people, including the local baker, John Rzeppa, who also wanted to go to Texas. Six days after he had left Toszek, Schüler signed a contract with Stanisław Kiołbassa, of Świbie, the former deputy to the Prussian parliament, and made definite arrangements to transport him and his family to Texas. Immediately Kiołbassa began telling his friends and acquaintances in Toszek-Gliwice County about his plans and about Schüler's services and in this way aroused even more local interest in emigration. The news spread quickly.

Only a few days later a messenger came to Schüler in Opole, asking him to return to Toszek, where a number of people wanted to confer with him about the conditions of travel and the technicalities of the contracts. Meeting in Czerner's tavern on 12 August, a cattle market day when the town was filled with country people, the German described the journey to a large crowd of peasants and praised the prospects for life in Texas. In that one day he made contracts with seven heads of households. While he wrote some of the contracts, the daughter of John Rzeppa, the baker, prepared the others for him. Although Schüler's words to the peasants were not recorded, the way he described his work to the local authorities undoubtedly has a similar ring:

> All the emigrants have gone to the state of Texas to a parish established by the Catholic clergyman, Moczygemba, from Płużnica near Strzelce, which is under the name Panna Maria. It is located on a plateau near Castroville, where the air is healthful and the soil is fertile, leaving nothing more for the farmer to desire. . . .
>
> The emigrants . . . are transported . . . in copper-covered, three-masted vessels by experienced and friendly captains for the lowest possible prices. . . . There is nothing more for them to wish for in emigration in ships with high middle decks and other conveniences. Therefore it is quite common for emigrants to change their agents and to go with the Pokrantz firm.

During these discussions at Toszek some of the prospective emigrants, according to one of the merchant's critics, became intoxicated by drinking "red wine, liquor, and beer" and were under the influence of alcohol when they signed their contracts. The same detractor further claimed that some of the peasants who agreed to sign had not considered the idea before and that they did not even have the required five-thaler deposit and had to borrow it from merchant Czerner. Schüler defended himself by saying that the peasants in Toszek drank in moderation only to compensate the innkeeper for using his tavern as a meeting place and that "all had been warned" that the five-thaler deposit was necessary. During this second visit to the town several illiterate peasants approached Schüler wanting to sign contracts, but he asked them to wait until a later date to make their marks on the contracts in the presence of the local authorities, because it was too late in the day to ask them to serve as witnesses.

After returning to Opole, Schüler was called back to Toszek once more that month to make several additional contracts. In this way, a little at a time, he made arrangements for a number of peasant families to leave one small area, just as other agents were doing in their vicinities.[25]

Although almost all the Silesian emigrants to Texas came from the property-owning peasant class, by the second year of movement a few families with less income attempted to make their way to America. Some poorer peasants begged or borrowed money from their more affluent friends and relatives to pay for their passage, but others sold everything that they owned for just enough money to get to the ports. The Prussian consul in Bremen wrote to the officials of the Regency of Opole complaining about two such peasant families for whom he had assumed responsibility. According to the consul, in the spring of 1855 the two families had come to Bremen from Staniszcze Małe, a village about midway between Olesno and Strzelce. They had arrived without enough money to pay for their passage to Texas and had waited several weeks for more emigrants supposedly coming from their village in hopes of borrowing money from them to pay for their tickets. The two families had so little cash that the keeper of the inn where they had been staying had agreed not to charge them for their lodging. Some families like these succeeded in getting the help they needed, but others had to return home disappointed, embarrassed, and empty-handed. The practice of borrowing money from friends for emigration must not have been too uncommon, for Father Moczygemba himself warned his family, "I tell you this, don't pay for anyone else's passage with your money."[26]

Some young men were able to secure transportation as indentured servants for more wealthy peasants. Discussing the possibilities of securing the services of this type person, John Moczygemba from Panna Maria advised his family: "Now, my Dear Brother, take with you Peter Rafliczyn, because he will be very useful here and he also wants to come and you will need him for the journey. Arrange with him for a year, two, or even more, up to the time that your children will grow up, because it is difficult to keep cattle yourself. And if not this one, look for another boy, because it is worth money."[27]

The second major party of Silesians left their homeland after harvests were taken in during autumn 1855. Traveling as a large group, they also went by rail to Bremen, and from North Germany they sailed to Texas in at least three ships, the *Weser*, the *Ostend*, and the *Gessner*.[28] As they journeyed toward the sea, the press noted their movement: "On the 26th of September, during travel to Texas, there passed through Wrocław a group of Polish peasant emigrants from Upper Silesia which consisted of 700 persons. The view of these people made a sad impression on me as I saw them depopulating the land of their fathers."[29]

Setting sail in October 1855, the main contingent of immigrants landed on the Texas coast about Christmastime after a two-month voyage. While the *Gessner*, after completing a fifty-nine-day passage, docked at Galveston, the other two known vessels landed at Indianola. From the coast the new settlers made their way inland toward San Antonio, as the previous immigrants had done. This time some of the farmers had brought their own wagons from Silesia, and they reassembled them on the spot for their overland journey, while the others hired oxcarts from the Mexican teamsters. The big procession slowly moved up the distinct cart road from the coast to the interior, arriving in the Alamo city in approximately two weeks.

At San Antonio the contingent broke up. Most of the new immigrants settled in the Silesian colonies that already had been established in the city, at Panna Maria, and at Bandera, but thirteen families went to a new location on Martinez Creek, about eighteen miles east of San Antonio.[30] The colonists learned about the available land from a German named John Demner. He met some of the immigrants just after their arrival in San Antonio, told them about the desirable land, and suggested that they investigate it. The Silesians then formed a committee to examine the conditions, and its members were sufficiently impressed with the locality that they recommended passing up equally fertile land nearer San Antonio to settle at the place east of the city.

Once they arrived at the site, which later the immigrants came to call Saint Hedwig, they found that there was already a Pole living nearby. This man was John Dorstyn, who has been confused in some writings with John Demner. Said to have been an exile from the ill-fated Polish Insurrection of 1830 and to have come to Texas about 1835, Dorstyn settled in Bexar County in 1852. Prematurely aged from a hard life, he married into a respectable American family and became known locally for his honesty. During the next years the quiet expatriate served the Silesians in the neighborhood as an adviser and assisted them in their dealings with the American landowners. Over the years his ties with the new settlers became so close that one of his daughters, Faustyna, entered a convent of Silesian nuns that had been organized at Panna Maria.[31]

In 1856, the last year of mass movement to Texas, the emigration continued. Though the total number of people departing is not known precisely, the press reported that in spring of that year a total of 500 peasants had left Prussian Silesia for America, "the larger part of them . . . departing for Texas."[32] Emigration agent Julius Heinrich Schüler, of Opole, in his annual report for 1856 stated that he alone during the year had transported 239 persons, who "with few exceptions" had gone to Texas "to the colony established by the Catholic clergyman, Moczygemba."[33] Only scattered information is available about the vessels that carried the colonists during the third year of emigration. One such fragment concerns Joseph Cotulla, who at the age of twelve left Strzelce County with his widowed mother and grandmother to join his aunt and sisters, who had gone to Texas the year before. The three traveled alone with non-Poles on the bark *Von Beaulieu*, which landed in Galveston on 9 January 1857. From the port they traveled overland by oxcart to San Antonio and from there south to an outlying community to rejoin their relatives.[34]

Today, in an age of rapid, convenient transportation, it is worthwhile to reflect on what travel was like for the peasants leaving Silesia in the mid-1850's. Preserved records provide a vivid image of what the farmers and their families experienced on their way from the little villages in the Regency of Opole to the ports, from the European harbors to Galveston and Indianola, and finally from the Texas coast to their new homes on the frontier. The Silesian correspondent of *Czas* in 1856 described the departure from the villages in this way:

> Let us suppose that a Polish peasant from the center of Upper Silesia . . . decides to leave his homeland. In such a case, as quickly as possible, not bargaining too long, he sells all his property, packs his bed linens, clothes, several axes, shovels, and saws, and when the formalities in the high sheriff's office do not hold him up for too long, one can see him together with his whole family walking to the nearest railway station.[35]

At the age of eight or nine Constantina (Pyka) Adamietz, with her family left the village of Sucho Daniec in Strzelce County, joining one of the initial groups of emigrants in 1854. She recalled that her family's preparations were hasty and that they were ready long before the starting time. After they had waited for what seemed to her a long time, word finally came that they were to leave on a certain day. She was full of anticipation for the excitement of the journey, but when she "kissed loved ones goodbye," little Constantina "could not keep from crying," because at that moment she realized that "we never expected to meet again . . . unless they should come to America."[36]

An important step in preparing for departure was the sale and disposal of one's property. The contemporary press recognized the significance of this activity when it noted in spring 1855 that "many families are selling out" in order to "go to Texas." The time consumed in selling one's farm and belongings delayed some emigrants who would have left sooner if they could have found buyers quickly. The prices many peasants received for their holdings were not necessarily small. One nineteenth-century Upper Silesian account stated that they sometimes were paid as much as five to six thousand Prussian thalers, "probably enough money for them and their families to live quietly and without problems" had they elected to stay in Europe.[37]

All the Polish emigrants traveled by trains on the initial leg of their journey. Railway construction in the 1840's and 1850's had made travel comparatively fast and easy by way of Opole, Wrocław, and Berlin or Leipzig to Bremen and other ports. The first line had connected Opole with Wrocław in 1842, and the route from Opole to Myslowice, passing through Strzelce and Toszek, was completed in 1846. By the next year Opole had gained a connection south through Koźle to Racibórz. In 1855 work began on a line eastward from Opole to Tarnowskie Góry, passing through the heart of the territory from which peasants were flocking to Texas. These railroad connections meant that the prospective emigrants were only two or three days from their ports of departure. The railway companies encouraged emigrants to go by train by offering them special rates, for example, allowing them to ride third class to Bremen from either Leipzig or Berlin for only about three Prussian thalers, with children under ten years of age going for half fare and infants free. As further inducements to travel by rail, the adult emigrants received an allowance for one hundred pounds of free baggage, children received an allowance for fifty pounds, and emigrants were permitted to carry excess baggage at the rate of two pfennigs a mile per ten pounds.[38]

Most of the emigrants leaving for Texas headed for Bremen as their first stop. A few of them, however, finding that ships to Texas were not immediately available upon their arrival in Bremen, transferred to other ports like Hamburg, Szczecin, and even Rotterdam. Some may have gone to ports other than Bremen because they lost their way in unfamiliar train travel in a country where no one could understand their Polish speech. The peasants might have avoided such difficulties had they not been reluctant to accept the free advice they could have received from the German-operated Central Emigration Society for Silesia.

From the North German ports most of the Silesians sailed to Galveston and Indianola, although a few individuals landed in New York and New Orleans. Indianola quickly became the favored arrival point because of its comparative nearness to San Antonio, only two weeks away by oxcart. Father Moczygemba in 1858 recommended the port to any future immigrants.[39]

Once at the port in North Germany or in the Low Countries, if their travel had been arranged by an honest agent or if they themselves had booked travel with a reliable shipping company, the emigrants generally had good treatment. If they had not made such preparations, however, but blindly had set off for the ports, they frequently had to wait at inns for Texas-bound ships and then had to make their own arrangements for the voyage. All of this time they were waiting and spending money that they knew they would need in America.

The best available information on the transatlantic passage of the Silesians is that for travel on ships operated by the Carl Pokrantz Company of Bremen. That is the firm for which Julius Schüler was agent in Opole and that is known to have carried large numbers of Polish peasants to Texas. One emigrant who sailed with this firm wrote back to Toszek describing the conditions and treatment at the port: "We happily arrived in the Big Ship and . . . have had good food and the people have received blankets to cover themselves and everything has been provided. . . . Tonight, the 2nd of October, we will leave Bremerhaven at one o'clock."[40]

On a typical voyage the emigrants sailed for about two months, spending most of their time in the gloomy steerage quarters inside the creaking vessels. This was a dark, windowless area of a ship near the steering apparatus, which gave it its name. On eastbound transatlantic trips it was used as cargo space for carrying loads of cotton, tobacco, rice, and other staples, but for the westbound voyage from Europe it was fitted with rough wooden floors and platformlike bunks for transporting emigrants. For the people in the steerage, apart from occasional distractions like storms or illnesses of passengers, the crossings were monotonous. One immigrant recollected that on the ship "every day was just alike," adding that during the evenings "a stillness of death settled about us." According to a handbill distributed by the Pokrantz firm, "At night it is lighted between decks with lanterns." Sleeping quarters inside the vessels were crowded at best. Every voyager had his assigned place, normally two persons to a stiff wooden bunk. For the beds each passenger was allowed to bring a mattress, a pillow, and a woolen blanket. All of these were sold at the port, a mattress stuffed with sea grass for one and a half thalers, stuffed with straw for half a thaler, and blankets for one and a third thalers apiece.

The unfortunate among the travelers suffered from seasickness and other illnesses. On the voyage of the *Weser* in October–December 1854, three of the passengers succumbed to their maladies and were buried at sea. Constantina Adamietz recalled that the corpses were wrapped in canvas, weighted, and dropped overboard. As a little girl, she remembered, she could not help but wonder if "the fish would eat the bodies."

The shipping company boasted that the passengers on its vessels received meals "in abundance" and that each ship carried enough supplies for a voyage of up to thirteen weeks. Among the foods prepared for group eating were salted pork, salted beef, rice, potatoes, butter, barley, peas, beans, sauerkraut, and dried plums. Each day was broken in the morning and in the evening by rations of coffee or tea, ship biscuit, and drinking water. Although there was no "individual eating," the emigrants were permitted to bring along a reasonable amount of food for themselves to supplement the meals that were provided. The ship's cook prepared the communal meals, but all the passengers were expected to take turns assisting in its preparation.

The fare for adult passage from Bremen to Galveston in 1855 was between thirty-five and forty-five gold thalers. Children under the age of ten received a five-thaler discount, and infants under the age of one traveled free. The price of passage varied with the number of voyagers on each ship. With the payment of the passage each traveler received the right to twenty cubic feet of baggage and to space for one trunk measuring three by three by two and a quarter feet. This baggage was stored in the hold of the ship for the duration of the voyage. In addition to this allotment passengers could bring on board a limited amount of hand baggage in the form of small crates. In these the immigrants carried articles that they would need during the voyage, valuables that would not be safe in the hold of the ship, and their own food. The smoking of tobacco and the lighting of fires, as well as the carrying of matches and gunpowder, were specifically prohibited, and during the voyage the passengers were required to deposit all firearms with the captain of the vessel.[41]

Letters of advice that the immigrants of 1854 wrote back to Upper Silesia provide valuable insight from their perspective into what the movement of a family across the Atlantic was like. One Pole counseled members of his family to leave all their legal affairs in proper order so as to avoid difficulties with the local court, while in the next breath he admonished them to find a good agent to arrange their travel and to "pay attention not to be cheated once more."[42] Much of the advice concerned financial matters. Telling what money to take, John Moczygemba recommended that "the best is gold, and thalers are good, but heavy." He added, "Don't take many bank notes, and if you have them, take only new ones."[43] Thomas Moczygemba and John Dziuk also advised the Poles to "take as much gold as you can . . . because you can make a profit from it," but they reminded the future emigrants that they must carry enough German money to pay for their railway tickets.[44] Father Moczygemba spoke directly when he urged his family, "Hide your money well." Betraying suspicions about their possible traveling companions, the priest also warned his relatives to "take care on the ship; the less company that you have the better."[45] Plaintively wondering about who would join the colonists in faraway America, a peasant farmer in Texas asked his correspondent to "write who will come."[46]

One Silesian recalled the arrival of his emigrant ship on the coast of Texas: "At last we reached Galveston Bay, and there was much hurrying and scurrying about when the ship dropped anchor. Everybody began collecting their scant belongings, mothers calling their children, and the men giving directions for all to keep together."[47]

From the coast they turned inland, most of the peasants going either on foot or in hired Mexican oxcarts. These vehicles, necessary for moving heavy and bulky possessions, must have made an impression on the immigrants, as they did on almost all people who saw them for the first time. They were durable affairs, made almost entirely of wood, that rolled on pairs of large, solid wooden wheels mounted on squeaking wooden axles. The contents were protected from the elements by rawhide sheets. Such a cart when drawn by two yokes of oxen could move up to five thousand pounds of freight at a rate of about twelve to eighteen miles a day. For use by immigrants—for the Mexican drivers already were familiar with German settlers—the contents could be packed so that weary women and children could ride together with enough supplies for a family for its first nine months in the new land. Even more novel to the immigrants than the unusual carts were the Mexican teamsters themselves, whose "swarthy complexions, broad sombreros and striped blankets . . . as they flourished their long whips wielded with both hands" left deep marks on the memories of newcomers.[48]

It was generally as described here that hundreds of Polish peasants emigrated from Silesia to Texas in the three years from 1854 to 1856. After that time, however, the movement declined to merely a few individuals annually and then ceased entirely with the outbreak of the American Civil War. A number of factors contributed to this comparatively rapid close of migration. The most significant of these were improved economic conditions in the source area. Beginning in 1856, Silesian harvests improved, and the end of the Crimean War in that year reopened the flow of Russian grain to German markets. Both of these factors combined to lower food prices and thus relieve the suffering of the poor. At the same time the expansion of industrial development in Upper Silesia, particularly in the coal basin, gave an outlet to the rural population that before had migrated to Texas. The widely used expression for Upper Silesia as the "Prussian California" not only boasted of the prosperity of the region but also may have served as an antiemigration slogan. Most of the out-migration that continued appears to have shifted in the direction of Austrian Galicia. Factors in America also influenced the decline in immigration. The most important of these was the great Texas drought of 1856–1857, which created such a desperate situation in the areas of Polish settlement that the colonists dared not encourage their countrymen to join them. Other negative American elements may have included the Panic of 1857 and the rise of Know-Nothing sentiment opposed to immigration.[49]

With virtually all the Upper Silesian immigrants settled in Texas by early 1857, the subsequent five years served as a trial not only of their ability to adapt to the new social and physical environments but also of their capacity to stay together as a cohesive social group. The peasants had left a stable rural society in Europe, experiencing the trauma of leaving behind all that they had known, and they had been transported to a completely alien land where the foods, the climate, and the people were utterly foreign to them, where they could not even make themselves understood to the natives. The next years would be their initial trial. Would they survive? And if so, what would they be like?

3

Polish Life on the Frontier

THE vast areas where the Silesians settled in Texas were far different from their compact European homeland. Leaving a densely populated country with towns and villages scattered through a countryside of green cultivated farmland and regulated forests, they moved to a thinly populated frontier area with comparatively sparse vegetation. From villages they migrated to a land where, as one peasant wrote, "one cottage lies from the other ten miles or even more." They were both frightened and encouraged by the great expanse of new land in which they found themselves living.[1]

Thomas Ruckman, an American living in Karnes County when the Silesians arrived there, described the site of the Panna Maria colony, on the high ground above the confluence of the San Antonio River with Cibolo Creek: "In this region . . . there had not been a sign of a settlement or habitation. The fires had been running over the rolling ground between the two streams, & kept it burned off, so that it was clean prairie except patches of Musquete [*sic*] in the low places & clumps of live oaks on the ridges. We could ride anywhere & see long distance[s]."[2]

The initial view of Bandera was more pleasing to the Silesians, but the first impression was deceptive. A Polish priest writing from San Antonio described the locality in this way: "There it is quiet and calm, between the mountains as in Italy. The water is clear and there are many springs. The air is more healthful than anywhere here."[3] The same clergyman, however, also wrote that Bandera was "the most dangerous" of all the settlements because of its constant exposure to raids by warlike Indians, which kept the Polish farmers in their houses at night "from fear of attacks."[4]

In appearance the site of the colony on Martinez Creek in eastern Bexar County was more similar to that of Panna Maria, although it lacked the more picturesque elevated location of the earlier settlement. One of the original settlers described the site as "steppe with thick-spreading oaks growing on it." It was these trees that drew the Silesians to the location; the immigrants crossed several miles of open country before reaching the place where they found the oaks, which they wanted for both fuel and building material.[5] Father Moczygemba described the vicinity pessimistically in 1858, commenting that, although the Martinez location possessed fertile soil, it had no perennial streams, and, in his words, "because of the lack of water there are no good prospects for the future."[6] He was unable to foresee that the proximity of the settlement to San Antonio and its agricultural markets would ensure the prosperity of the community for the next century and a quarter, making it one of the most wealthy of the Silesian colonies.[7]

When the immigrants began arriving in 1854, they discovered that no preparations had been made at the sites of settlement. The lack of food and shelter naturally caused them both discomfort and inconvenience. They were forced to camp under the trees during the difficult first weeks while they built temporary shelters, sowed their first crops, began learning how to prepare the strange new foods, and met for the first time the curious-looking natives who seemed constantly to be mounted on horseback.[8] One of the Silesians recalled these initial weeks in this way:

> What we suffered here when we started! We didn't have any houses, nothing but fields. And for shelter, only brush and trees. . . . There was tall grass everywhere, so that if anyone took a few steps, he was lost to sight. Every step of the way you'd meet rattlesnakes. . . . And the crying and complaining of the women and children only made the suffering worse. . . . How golden seemed our Silesia as we looked back in those days![9]

Especially frightening to the colonists were the large numbers of rattlesnakes that infested the areas where they settled. Almost without exception the settlers carried hoes or sticks as they walked about to protect themselves from the poisonous vipers, which reportedly caused the deaths of several settlers. One anecdote has come down to the present time about a snake disrupting a dinner Father Moczygemba held for a group of newly arrived Polish farmers. The priest had planned a meal to reassure the somewhat apprehensive immigrants about their new homes. Just as he was serving the soup, a rattlesnake tumbled down to the table from one of the rafters above and stampeded the alarmed guests from the hut.[10]

Records indicate that the first employment of the Silesians at Martinez and Panna Maria was in their own agricultural pursuits, whereas at Bandera and San Antonio it was for salaries from the Americans. All the known letters from Panna Maria in 1855 contain information about peasants clearing and working their land, but none of them mention working for the natives. One peasant wrote from Panna Maria, "We did not sow much because we had only three oxen and only one plow."[11] In another letter he reported, "There is no prepared land, but everybody must get it ready for himself," because, he went on to explain, "the land is covered with trees and brush and no one has ever plowed it before." He further informed his brother, who was planning to immigrate, that he already had secured and fenced land for him and that "we both have much. I think that 100 [acres] is more than enough for the two of us."[12] One of the founders of the agricultural colony in Bexar County recollected that in the first years most of the settlers there grew corn and vegetables for their own consumption and "for the most part raised cattle."[13]

At Bandera and San Antonio, on the other hand, most of the immigrants immediately went to work for the people who were already living there. In Bandera, for example, John Dlugos, a carpenter by trade, found his first employment in building a combined house and store for a merchant named August Klappenbach. When a gristmill was built on the Medina River in the town, a group of Polish women dug the millrace. The surprisingly large excavated channel was three-quarters of a mile long, ten feet wide, and as much as four to five feet deep. Probably the most common initial employment for the Bandera Poles was cutting cypress roofing shingles to be sold in San Antonio. The Bandera colonists viewed the employment for others as interim occupations to be followed until they had earned enough money to set up their own farmsteads. Most of the Silesians in San Antonio were either artisans or craftsmen, and they automatically began working either for the Americans or independently, and as the years passed they remained at their trades.[14]

Many of the accounts of the first Polish colonies in America stress the poverty of the immigrants upon their arrival in Texas.[15] This view seems to have been produced by later historians who assumed that the immigrants were poor. During the initial period of settlement in Texas, a time of favorable weather conditions,[16] the colonists in fact lived well and were optimistic about their prospects for the future. The writers of letters back to Silesia stated that they had to work hard in Texas but that their lives were better than in the motherland. For this reason they encouraged their families and friends to join them on the frontier. As one peasant wrote home to Płużnica: ". . . now I greet you, my dear Uncle Leopold, and your Wife and daughter. . . . I want eagerly for you to come this year."[17] If conditions were so bad in the Polish settlements during the first months, as later historians have written, this farmer certainly would not have been eager for his family to join him in the suffering.

There are two reasonable explanations for the stories of poverty during the initial settlement. One of these is that the Silesians did not know where to buy the things that they wanted, a problem aggravated by their isolation on the edge of the frontier. One peasant expressed his frustration: "We had money, but there was nothing to buy with it."[18] Another wrote home, "Don't wonder that we ask for so many things, because here there are no people and that's why no things."[19] A second explanation for the tales of poverty is that the Poles clearly were dissatisfied with some American counterparts of things to which they had been accustomed in Europe: "If you, Brother, come yourself, bring a wagon for me, the same as I had, . . . bring a harrow for you, and for me too, because they are available here, but only made from wood, and these are bad. And bring thread, because it is here too, but is very weak and made of cotton. . . . Dear Brother Tom, bring two plow blades and one strong winch, the same kind as I used to have."[20]

Probably the Silesians' most urgent need upon their arrival was shelter. During the first months in Texas the immigrants lived under the trees while each family built its own hut. Most of these were dugouts or picket houses, although some log huts were erected during the first weeks both in Bandera and in Martinez. Most commonly the huts were covered with thatch roofs made from prairie grass.[21] One of the early settlers recalled that some of the people "lived in burrows, covered with brush and stalks," while others put up shelters of "stakes and brush, using strands of grass to make the roofs."[22] Upon visiting one of the settlements in 1855, an American found the people there "huddled together on little patches of land living in their pole cabins & sod houses."[23] About the same time a peasant wrote home to Silesia, "Here one can get a house very easily," because, he explained, "everybody builds his house himself."[24] The exceptions were the Silesians at San Antonio, who were able to rent houses. There, however, they found that they had to pay as much as five to six dollars a month for poor Mexican *jacales* (huts).[25]

After a few months more sophisticated housing began appearing at the colonies. At least as early as 1858, John Gawlik, who had been trained as a stonemason, built his sturdy stone cottage, which still stands in Panna Maria. He was followed in erecting masonry homes by settlers including Albert Kasprzyk, John Rzeppa, and Philip Przybysz. Not all the houses were stone, however; log houses also were popular in the settlements where trees were available for building material. Thus a decade after the settlements were founded, a Polish priest described some of the cottages in Karnes County as "made of wood, similarly to Lithuanian houses."[26]

In Texas the Silesians built their homes on their own land, frequently somewhat removed from the towns. This physical distance from the other residents of the communities made an impression both on the peasants and on later Polish visitors. Describing the location of his house at Panna Maria, for example, one peasant wrote home, "There are no villages. . . . We live quite a distance from the church. It is farther than you live from the manor."[27] A decade later a Polish priest stationed at Martinez wrote to Rome that in his parish "the houses of the Poles are situated in the brush, far from the church, and all I can see are clouds and trees."[28] The pastor at Panna Maria at the same time described the homes of his parishioners as "hidden in the woods" outside the village.[29]

When they started building their houses in the new land, the Polish peasants used techniques handed down for centuries in the old country and built homes in the same way that they would have in Poland. Consequently today there is a remarkable similarity between the cottages at Panna Maria and surrounding communities and those in rural Upper Silesia. Among their common characteristics are building materials, arrangement of rooms, steep pitched roofs (designed in Europe to allow snow to slide off), rear roofs that come very near to the ground, meat smoking rooms within the houses, and the location of ventilation openings for upper-floor rooms. Although none today are preserved in Texas, thatch roofs constituted another parallel element of folk architecture in Texas and Poland. This roofing material continued to be used by Silesians in Texas up to the turn of the century and still can be seen in rural Upper Silesia.[30]

The warmer climate in Texas caused some modifications in the style of folk architecture followed by the peasant immigrants. They quickly came to prize the coolness of the prevailing southerly winds during the hot months of the year. They often built their houses with entrances facing the south and with windows at the rear to provide cross ventilation. To benefit from the cool breezes to the utmost, they soon added porches to the cooler windward sides of their cottages, as the German immigrants in the state had learned from the Americans over a decade before. The covered gallery quickly became the standard appendage to Silesian homes in Texas. Under its cool shade the family members carried on almost all their activities, from dressing animal hides to sleeping. The porch, in addition, became the common place to keep things like saddles, fishing tackle, guns, flowering plants, and comfortable chairs. Both day and night for nine months of the year it was the most desirable place in the house.[31]

The dress of the Silesians set them apart from the general population during their first years in America. The best description of the folk dress of the immigrants comes from Lyman Brightman Russell, an American living in Helena, the county seat of Karnes County, at the time the Polish farmers were arriving and settling in the area.[32] Later in life he recalled the Silesians wearing

> the costumes of the old country, many of the women having what at that time were regarded as very short skirts, showing their limbs two or three inches above the ankles. Some had on wooden shoes, and almost without exception they had broad-brimmed, low-crowned black felt hats, nothing like the hats then worn in Texas. They also wore blue jackets of heavy woolen cloth, falling just below the waist, and gathered into folds at the back with a band of the same material.[33]

The short skirts of the Polish girls and women evidently created some excitement among the males of the native population, because, only six months after the first Silesians arrived, Father Leopold advised his family: "Don't take any country dresses for Hanka, because she will not need them here. Our country dresses are the reason that the native people make fun of us and they cause sin."[34] Even as recently as the beginning of this century, people in Texas were surprised by the comparatively short skirts worn by women just immigrating from Silesia.

It is difficult to believe that Polish peasants went clomping about the Texas prairies in wooden shoes. Yet such footgear, known as *drewniaki*, was daily wear for nineteenth-century peasants in Silesia. The old-style *drewniaki* were hand-carved from solid blocks of wood and resembled Dutch wooden shoes with squared heels. More recent wooden shoes, worn in both Upper Silesia and in Texas, were clogs modified from the original design. They consisted of thick carved wooden soles to which heavy leather tops were attached. Both styles of wooden shoes were worn by the Texas colonists as recently as the turn of the century and in Upper Silesia until after World War II.[35]

Living on the sparsely settled frontier, the immigrants felt very isolated. Having come from a densely populated region, they were impressed by but ill at ease in the vast, empty spaces. One peasant revealed his sense of the remoteness in Texas when he wrote to his friends and family in Poland about the northern United States being "as far away as we are from you."[36]

Feeling this alone, the European farmers had a real fear of attacks by warlike Indians. Their fear was well founded. In the summer of 1855, Indians raided into the country both north and south of the colony in Karnes County. During these incursions (near the place where peasants would settle on Martinez Creek only five months later) a war party killed the twelve-year-old son of a local preacher and came very near catching and slaying his companion, who "narrowly escaped by the fleetness of his horse." About the same time Lipan Apaches raided into Goliad and Atascosa counties, stealing livestock and murdering those who resisted them.[37]

Indian attacks posed the most serious problem for the Silesians living at Bandera, where they had been brought by the town developers to bolster the population against such forays. Fear of attack became a part of everyday life for the settlers, who from the outset were subject to incursions. The attacks were so severe in the summer and autumn of 1855 that some of the residents considered abandoning the town. Then the raids declined for a while, but they continued in varying intensity for the next twenty years.[38]

In a typical incident Albert Haiduk, an immigrant from Strzelce,[39] was attacked just outside his cottage at Bandera. Hearing noises in his corn patch one night, he went out expecting to find cattle breaking into the field. Instead he vaguely saw the figures of three Indians coming through the darkness toward him. Concealing himself behind a tree, he successfully hid from the first two warriors, but the third discovered him and shot an arrow into his side. The Pole was able to make his way back to his house, where his frightened wife cut out the arrow with a small knife. Fearing to light a lamp or candle, thinking that the raiders might see it and return, she conducted her crude surgery in the dark. Haiduk fortunately had turned aside as the warrior shot, so the arrow did not penetrate too deeply, and he survived his encounter with the Indians.[40]

Not all the Silesians were so lucky.

The most celebrated Polish victim of the Indians was Theodore Kindla, a twenty-five-year-old shepherd who was attacked and cruelly killed in the summer of 1862. The young man was herding sheep for an American in the Sabinal Canyon, southwest of Bandera. One evening he left his camp to look for another water hole. After going only a short distance, he was surprised by a party of Indians. An unarmed Mexican herder who was with him successfully sought cover and observed in horror the event that followed. The warriors first roped Kindla and then proceeded to lance him and shoot several arrows into his body. While he lay on the ground still alive, the attackers scalped him and finally peeled the skin from the soles of his feet. After the marauders left, Kindla, although terribly wounded, got up and began staggering toward his camp, but after going about two hundred yards he fell and died. When the danger had passed, the Mexican herder left his hiding place to aid the Silesian but found him dead. He ran to spread the alarm, returning for the body late the next day with a party of settlers. They found the remains already so badly decomposed that their only choice was to bury him where he had fallen.[41]

The Silesians were by no means the only victims of the Indian attacks. Two Bandera Poles had the unhappy task of informing Jacob Huffman, a German from Castroville, of the death of his brother. Huffman had been hauling corn to army troops at Camp Verde and was returning to Castroville by way of Bandera with a load of timber for DeMontel's sawmill. When he was five miles outside Bandera, his wagon stalled on a steep grade, where the two Silesians happened to meet him. There they gave him the sad news that Indians had just killed his brother. Then they helped him up the hill with his heavy load and tried to console him in his loss.[42]

The new Polish immigrants had more than Indians to fear. They were also attacked by thieves and robbers in the areas where they lived, a danger that added another hazard to travel between the settlements. In April 1855, in an incident that, though it did not involve a Pole, was typical of the period, a German immigrant was murdered on Calaveras Creek about twenty miles southeast of San Antonio. The spot was on the general route taken by the Silesians on their trips between Karnes County and the city. A few days earlier the German had been visiting on a ranch in the vicinity. He had left in the company of a Mexican, who ostensibly was showing him the way. A few days later the disfigured body of the immigrant was found with cuts about the head and several gashes in the side. The wounds evidently had been made with a large knife, the description of which fit one in the possession of the companion. The same Mexican afterward was seen trying to exchange German gold coins for silver money at a small store near the crime, but he disappeared, never to be seen again.[43]

In spring 1855 the first Silesian colonists began planting crops. Their basic goal in the beginning was to become self-sufficient in food production and then to start raising surplus products to market among the Americans. Consequently their initial crops were foodstuffs. The Poles immediately adopted corn, the staple crop of the land, giving it their own name. One of them wrote home: "There is no grain like yours, but there is Turkish wheat [corn]. . . . A bushel of this wheat costs one dollar."[44] Another peasant wrote back to Poland that the soil in Texas was fertile and good, particularly for potatoes, melons, cucumbers, and pumpkins. He added that the grass grew unusually abundantly. Father Moczygemba, visiting Europe in 1858, reported that the land where the Silesians had settled was good for raising sugar cane, cotton, and tobacco.[45] Even though one farmer reported to his family in 1855 that he planned to grow cotton, such cultivation did not reach any large scale among the Silesians until after the Civil War.[46]

The spring the first crops were planted, the entire area of Polish settlement in Texas was subjected to a plague of grasshoppers. The local press described them as passing through the country "in divisions," eating all vegetation in their paths. Farmers saved some of the fields from the pests by what they called the "herding process." As soon as the insects were seen approaching, all hands turned out to "hurry them on their course," not giving them time to consume the crops.[47] The grasshoppers posed a recurring problem. In spring 1858, for example, an American at Helena wrote to Goliad that in Karnes County grasshoppers had destroyed "all the prospects for a crop," but he added that there had been a good rain and that the farmers were planting again in May just as if it were early spring.[48]

Another perspective on agriculture among the Silesians in the 1850's comes from the manuscript schedules of the census of agriculture that was conducted in 1860 as part of the decennial American census. During this enumeration a large variety of information was recorded about the possessions and production of farmers throughout the country. The somewhat restricted data on the Silesians, probably limited because of difficulties encountered by the enumerator in communicating with the Poles, gives an interesting view of rural life in Silesian Texas.[49] Among the Karnes County immigrants, at that time the largest concentration of agricultural Poles in the state, the average farm size was sixty-eight acres, thirty in improved land and the remainder in unimproved land. The cash value of such a farm was just over $300 and of farm implements $48. A typical farm had one or two horses, seven milk cows, four oxen, and twenty-five other cattle. Some of the farmers had a few pigs for home use, although one of them specialized in hog production and had one hundred swine. The average value of livestock per farm was $325, and of animals slaughtered, $56. According to the census, none of the Poles interviewed grew any cotton in 1860, but they raised an average of 76 bushels of corn. From his milk cows the average farmer produced sixty-four pounds of butter yearly.[50]

An important aspect of agriculture among the Polish colonists was animal husbandry. From the first weeks of settlement livestock played a significant role in their lives. Among the most important animals for them were oxen. Without these animals the immigrants never would have been able to move their heavy possessions from the coast to their settlements. After the first movement inland these beasts of burden, which could live on grass alone, not only provided transportation but also pulled agricultural implements and moved heavy

The Reverend Leopold Bonaventura Maria Moczygemba about 1852, when he first traveled to Texas. (From Joyce, *Our Polish Pioneers*.)

The cemetery, building, and churchyard of St. Stanisław Church in Płużnica, Poland, the home parish of the Reverend Leopold Moczygemba and of many of the first Silesian immigrants to Texas. (Photograph by the author, 1977.)

A typical rural scene in Strzelce County in Upper Silesia, showing the mixture of forest and agricultural land in the region. (Photograph by the author, 1972.)

Agentur bei J. H. Schüler in Oppeln

Bedingungen der Ueberfahrt

von Bremen nach den Vereinigten Staaten von Nord-Amerika,

unter denen

das Handlungshaus Carl Pokrantz & Comp. in Bremen

Passagiere annimmt und mit vorzüglich guten Schiffen befördert.

1) Die Bremischen Gesetze enthalten die zweckmäßigsten Bestimmungen über die Beschaffenheit der Schiffe, welche zu einer Reise mit Passagieren angenommen werden dürfen. Es wird deren Tüchtigkeit vor dem Antritt jeder Reise von Seiten der Behörde untersucht. Außerdem lassen wir es uns angelegen sein, nur solche Schiffe zu wählen, welche ein geräumiges, hohes Zwischendeck haben und von einem menschenfreundlichen Capitain befehligt werden.

2) Die Ausrüstung übernehmen wir selbst, oder überwachen solche auf's Sorgfältigste, so daß wir für die gute Beschaffenheit der Lebensmittel einstehen, zur Vermeidung von Klagen und zur Beruhigung der Passagiere.

3) Die Passagiere erhalten während der Überfahrt freie und reichliche Beköstigung, so wie solche am Bord der Seeschiffe üblich ist, bestehend in gesalzenem Ochsen- und Schweinefleisch, Erbsen, Bohnen, Mehlspeise, Grütze, Reis, Kartoffeln, Sauerkraut, Pflaumen, Butter rc., alles hinreichend und gut; ferner Morgens und Abends Caffee oder Thee, Schiffsbrot, Trinkwasser u. s. w. In Krankheitsfällen werden dem Kranken dienliche Speisen gereicht, so wie die erforderliche Medizin, wozu eine vollständig ausreichende Kiste mit Arzeneien mitgenommen wird. Damit auch bei einer langen Reise kein Mangel auf dem Schiffe entstehe, werden die benannten Lebensmittel, so wie das zur Bereitung derselben erforderliche Brennmaterial in einer überflüssigen Quantität, nämlich für eine Reise von 13 Wochen berechnet, für jeden Passagier, gleichviel ob groß oder klein, angeschafft, unter Andern circa 68½ ℔ Brod, 26 ℔ Fleisch, 13 ℔ Speck, 5½ ℔ Butter rc. per Kopf. Hierüber muß der Obrigkeitlichen Behörde vor Expedition des Schiffs Nachweisung ertheilt werden. — Aus diesem Grunde und um Unordnungen vorzubeugen, findet eine Selbstbeköstigung der Passagiere nicht statt, obwohl es Jedem erlaubt ist, einige Lebensmittel für sich besonders mitzunehmen. — Bei Bereitung der Speisen für die Passagiere haben von denselben immer einige Männer und Frauen dem Schiffskoch hülfreiche Hand zu leisten.

4) Die Schlafstellen (Cojen) im Zwischendeck werden den Passagieren an Bord gehörig eingerichtet, in der Regel jede Coje für 2 Personen. Das Zwischendeck wird Nachts durch Laternen erleuchtet. Für Betten oder Strohsäcke, so wie auch für Eß-, Trink- und Waschgeschirr, Löffel, Messer und Gabeln haben die Passagiere selbst zu sorgen.

5) Das gewöhnliche Reisegepäck der Passagiere geht frachtfrei mit über und zwar für jede zählende Person 20 Cubikfuß Raum, also eine Kiste ungefähr 3 Fuß lang, 3 Fuß hoch und 2½ Fuß breit. Es kommt hierbei nur auf die Größe, nicht aber auf die Schwere der Kiste an. Sollte das Gepäck ein Bedeutendes mehr austragen, so wird dafür in der Regel nach **Baltimore** und **Newyork** circa 8 bis 10 Dollars Fracht per 100 Cubikfuß, nach **Philadelphia** und **New-Orleans** 10 bis 12 Dollars bezahlt. Jeder Passagier hat in allen Fällen auf sein Gepäck selbst zu achten, dasselbe auch mit seinem Namen zu bezeichnen.

6) Sollten Effecten von Passagieren vorausgeschickt werden, so werden wir dieselben bis zur Hierkunft der Eigner auf gutes Lager nehmen, die Kisten, Koffer rc. marken, repariren und auch die Feuer-Assecuranz besorgen, wenn uns die Versicherungs-Summe aufgegeben und der Auftrag dazu ertheilt worden ist. Auch sind wir gern bereit, Frachtgüter per Dampf- oder Segelschiff nach den Vereinigten Staaten zu spediren.

7) Das Passagegeld für die Ueberfahrt im Zwischendeck wird einschließlich guter und reichlicher Beköstigung und einschließlich des Amerikanischen Armengeldes gestellt und beträgt gewöhnlich nach **Newyork, Baltimore** oder **Philadelphia** 30—40 Thaler Gold oder 60—80 Gulden Rheinisch, nach **New-Orleans** 33-43 Thaler Gold oder 66—86 Gulden Rheinisch und nach **Galveston** in **Texas** 35—45 Thaler Gold oder 70—90 Gulden Rheinisch für jede Person über 10 Jahr alt; für jedes, bei der Einschiffung unter 10 Jahr alte Kind tritt eine Ermäßigung von 5 Thaler Gold oder 10 Gulden Rheinisch ein. Säuglinge, die bei der Einschiffung unter ein Jahr alt sind, werden ganz frei mitgenommen. Diese Vergünstigungen bei der Ueberfahrt von Kindern sind jedoch davon abhängig, daß die betreffenden Geburtsscheine bei der Einschiffung beigebracht werden, geschieht das nicht, so ist der volle Ueberfahrtspreis zu entrichten, da nach den Bremischen Gesetzen für jeden Kopf über 1 Jahr alt, ohne Unterschied des Alters, das volle Quantum Lebensmittel angeschafft werden muß. In keinem andern Hafen wird die Ausrüstung so reichlich besorgt wie hier; dagegen können aber auch die sich in Bremen Einschiffenden Passagiere sicher sein, daß sie auch bei einer ungewöhnlich langen Reise keinen Mangel leiden. — Der Ueberfahrts-Preis richtet sich nach dem jedesmaligen Verhältniß der Passagiere zu den vorhandenen Schiffen und kann zu Zeiten höher und auch niedriger wie vorbemerkt gehen, doch werden wir den Passage-Preis jederzeit möglichst billig stellen.

8) In vielen Schiffen können Passagiere gegen Zahlung von 10 Thaler Gold oder 20 Gulden per Kopf außer dem festgestellten Passagegelde, Plätze in einer bequem eingerichteten zweiten Cajüte auf Deck erhalten.

9) Das Passagegeld für die Ueberfahrt in der Cajüte des Schiffs beträgt gewöhnlich 80—90 Thaler Gold oder 160—180 Gulden für die erwachsene Person; 2 Kinder unter 10 Jahren, wenn sie zusammen 1 Bett benutzen, werden für eine volle Person gerechnet; Säuglinge unter ein Jahr alt sind ganz frei. Der Cajüts-Passagier erhält Beköstigung am Tische des Capitäns, hat sich jedoch mit Wein, so wie mit Matratze, Bett- und Handtüchern in der Regel selbst zu versorgen. — Die freie Beköstigung der Cajüts-Passagiere fängt an, sobald das Seeschiff aus dem Hafen legt. Das in Amerika zu zahlende Armengeld berichtigt der Schiffs-Rheder oder Schiffs-Befrachter für eigene Rechnung. — Die Besorgung der Passage mit den jeden Monat nach Newyork abfahrenden Amerikanischen Dampfschiffen übernehmen wir zu 190 Thaler Gold für einen Platz im Salon; zu 160 Thaler Gold für die erste Cajüte und zu 100 Thaler Gold für die zweite Cajüte oder den geringsten Platz. Alles für die erwachsene Person berechnet.

10) Die Passagiere müssen mit genügender Legitimation zur Reise versehen sein und bleiben für die Richtigkeit der Alterszeugnisse von Kindern rc. verantwortlich.

11) In Amerika werden nur gesunde, mit keinem körperlichen Gebrechen behaftete, überhaupt nur solche Personen angenommen, welche fähig sind, sich selbst zu ernähren, und haben demnach diejenigen, deren Aufnahme aus diesen Gründen bei den amerikanischen Behörden Schwierigkeiten findet, oder welche wegen Gebrechlichkeit, ansteckender Krankheit, Blödsinn oder sonstiger Hülflosigkeit schon hier von der Aufnahme in's Seeschiff ausgeschlossen werden müssen, die Folgen davon selbst zu tragen, und sind zu keinerlei Ansprüchen berechtigt; eben so wenig als diejenigen, welche die Abfahrt des Schiffes versäumen. — Personen, welche mit genannten Gebrechen behaftet, dieselben bei der Einschiffung zu verheimlichen wußten, und später in Amerika entdeckt und zurückgewiesen wurden, sind für alle Kosten verantwortlich, die aus ihrer Zurücksendung entstehen. Am strengsten sind die Einwanderungsgesetze gegenwärtig in Newyork: schwangere Frauenzimmer ohne Männer; Frauen mit Kindern, die nicht in Gesellschaft ihrer Ehemänner anlanden; Kinder unter 13 Jahren und Personen über 60 Jahre, wenn dieselben ohne Begleitung ihrer Familie reisen, werden unnachsichtlich zurückgewiesen. Es ist daher durchaus erforderlich, daß Personen, welche nach den verschärften Einwanderungsgesetzen des Staates Newyork daselbst nicht zugelassen werden können, sich nach einem andern Seehafen einschiffen. Auf Anfrage werden wir und unsere Herren Agenten denjenigen Platz bezeichnen, wo deren Anlandung ohne Schwierigkeiten statt finden kann. — Verbrecher und Sträflinge dürfen durchaus nicht aufgenommen werden.

12) Wenn sich Passagiere ihre Ueberfahrt im Zwischendeck auf eine bestimmte Zeit fest sichern wollen, so haben sie für jeden Kopf ein Handgeld von 5 Thaler Gold oder 10 Gulden Rheinisch per Kopf franco einzusenden, oder an unsere bevollmächtigten Herren Agenten zu zahlen, wogegen ihnen ein Aufnahme-Schein in doppelter Ausfertigung zugestellt wird. Das eine Exemplar bleibt im Besitz der Passagiere, während sie das andere uns gegen einen denselben zu ihrer Legitimation auf dem Schiffe dienenden, beim Antritte der Reise dem Capitain einzuhändigenden Ueberfahrtsschein abzuliefern haben. — Den Rest des vereinbarten Ueberfahrtsgeldes haben die Passagiere hier vor der Einschiffung an die Unterzeichneten baar zu zahlen, da [illegible] nur zur Empfangnahme des Handgeldes bevollmächtigt und mit Aufnahmescheinen zu diesem Zwecke von uns versehen sind. — Jeder Cajüts-Passagier hat [illegible] Thaler Gold als Handgeld zu entrichten.

13) Durch die Zahlung von Handgeld tritt die gegenseitige Verbindlichkeit nach Maaßgabe dieser Bedingungen ein, und sofern keine anderweitige Vereinbarung getroffen, halten wir uns verpflichtet, die mit Zwischendecksloos engagirten Passagiere nebst ihrem Gepäck an dem zur Abfahrt bezeichneten oder an einem der beiden nächsten Tage von hier nach dem circa 6 Meilen entfernten Seehafen in verdeckten Flußschiffen frei hinzubefördern, woselbst

One of the handbills advertising passage to America for immigrants on the vessels of the Carl Pokrantz firm in Bremen. This handbill is the one that was posted in one of the taverns in Toszek by emigration agent Julius Schüler in summer 1855. (Original document in the Archives of the City and Voivodeship of Wrocław, Wrocław, Poland.)

An Upper Silesian peasant girl in nineteenth-century folk dress. (Illustration from Kretchmer, *Deutsche Volkstrachten*.)

A present-day Upper Silesian peasant woman in folk dress. (Photograph by the author, 1976.)

A yoke of oxen plowing a field near Sucho Daniec, in Strzelce County, Upper Silesia. Oxen were the beasts of burden commonly used by the Silesian Polish farmers in Texas during the early years. (Photograph by the author, 1977.)

Long, narrow agricultural fields stretching out from the village of Płużnica, Poland. Dating back centuries, this form of land tenure was used by the Polish farmers at Panna Maria, Texas, when they laid out their first farms. (Photograph by the author, 1972.)

A thatch-covered dugout cellar in southwestern Poland. Shelters like this were first used by many Polish immigrants in Texas after their first arrival on the frontier. (Photograph by the author, 1976.)

The Felix Mika, Sr., residence in Panna Maria. This house, which originally had a wooden stable attached to one side, was erected about 1863 by August Moczygemba, one of the brothers of the Reverend Leopold Moczygemba. It still stands opposite the village church. (Photograph by the author, 1978.)

St. Mary's Church at Panna Maria, home of the oldest Polish Roman Catholic parish in America. (Photograph by the author, 1971.)

John Twohig's stone storage barn at Panna Maria, today the United States Post Office and general store of Felix V. Snoga. (Photograph by the author, 1978.)

The Reverend Adolf Bakanowski, superior of the Resurrectionist missions in Texas and pastor at Panna Maria, 1866–1870. (Original photograph in Archives, Congregation of the Resurrection, Rome, Italy.)

The Reverend Vincent Barzyński, Resurrectionist missionary and pastor at San Antonio, St. Hedwig, and Panna Maria between 1866 and 1874. (Original photograph in Archives, Congregation of the Resurrection, Rome, Italy.)

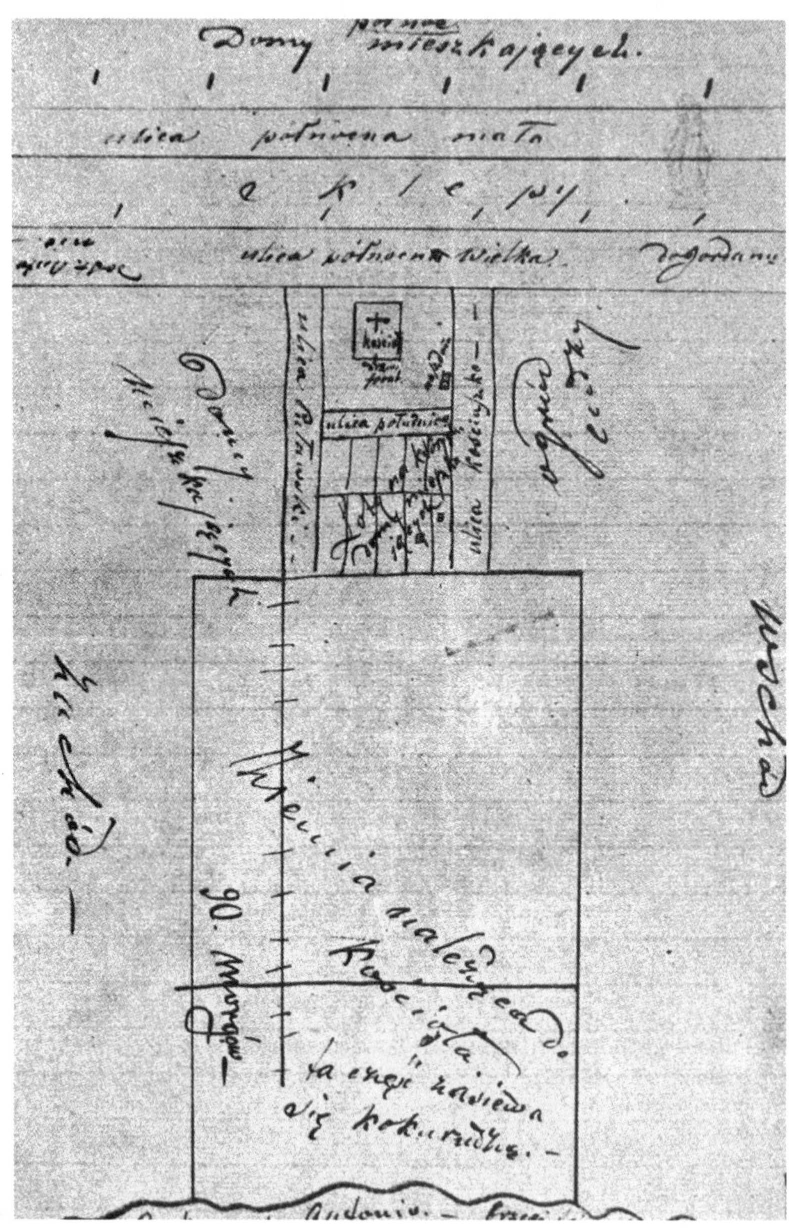

Map of the Panna Maria colony prepared by the Reverend Adolf Bakanowski in April 1869. (Archives, Congregation of the Resurrection, item no. 9368. Photograph by the author.)

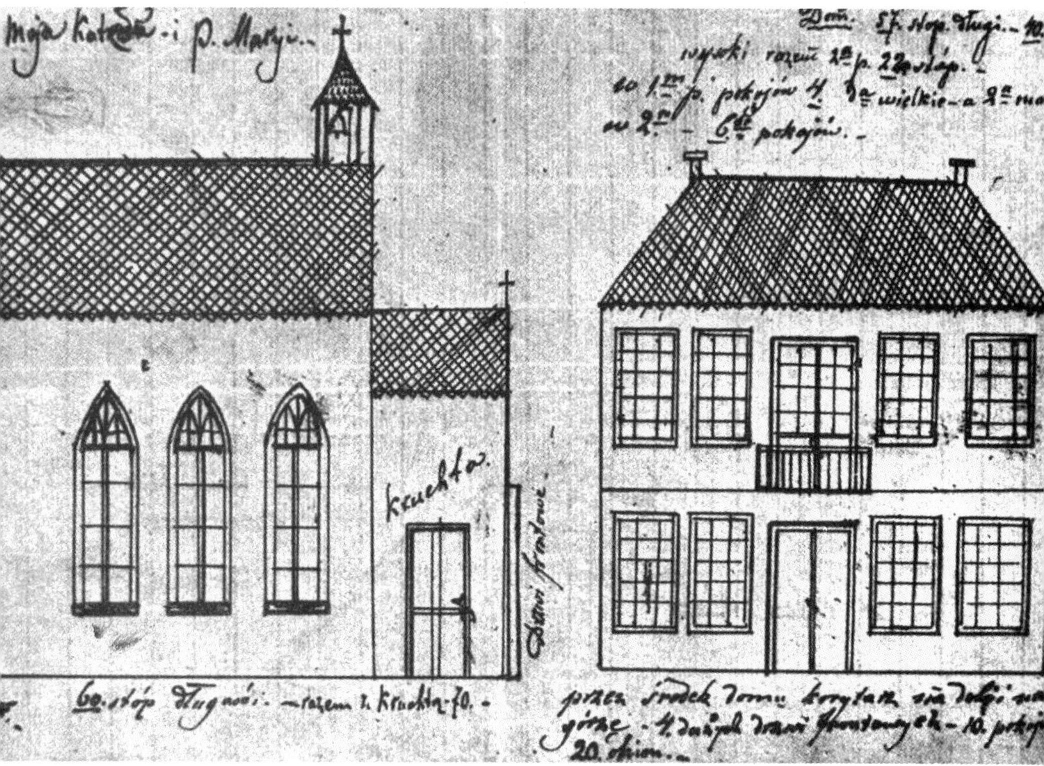

The church and school at Panna Maria as drawn by the Reverend Adolf Bakanowski in April 1869. This is the only known picture of the first Polish church in America actually prepared while the structure was standing. (Archives, Congregation of the Resurrection, item no. 9368. Photograph by the author.)

A view up the hill toward St. Joseph's School at Panna Maria as it appears today. (Photograph by the author, 1971.)

timbers. They were essential to the peasant economy, so important, in fact, that all but one of the identified Karnes County Poles in the 1860 census of agriculture owned at least one yoke. Oxen were used by the Silesians for agricultural work until the beginning of this century, when they were gradually replaced by horses and mules.[51]

Cattle raising assumed an important role among the Poles, particularly among the Martinez Creek settlers in Bexar County. It was necessary for time to pass, however, before the new immigrants would adopt the local methods of handling the animals. In spring 1855, John Moczygemba obviously was still thinking in European terms when he advised his brother to arrange for a boy to tend cattle for him. Reflecting on the colonists' early experiences in cattle raising in Bexar County, Thomas Kozub recollected that after the animals were branded they "wandered in complete freedom over the vast steppe." Before winter began, the colonists drove the stock into the woods, and then in the spring they allowed the animals to go where the grass was green. "Under such conditions we completely lost control of our property," Kozub commented. The settlers, unaccustomed to Texas methods of ranching, felt that it was strange to have to "make excursions long distances" to collect their animals. The old settler continued, "Sometimes we found our cattle with young, but other times we lost them entirely." Delighted with the mild climate and impressed by the fact that he did not have to ask permission for his cattle to feed on the unfenced prairie, one peasant wrote home favorably, "You don't need to leave anything in the fields for feeding stock because there is very much for them far and near." The purchase of a first milk cow was an important event, especially in families where there were children and infants to feed. This was the case in the John Pyka family of Bandera. One of the daughters remembered, "We bought our first milk cow at Castroville. . . . father went down there afoot and drove her home." During the early days cattle were raised primarily for milk and meat consumption within the colonies, but usually the farmers sold a few animals each winter to buyers who already had spoken for them. The non-Polish buyers, who had contacts in other parts of the state, then marketed the stock elsewhere at a profit.[52]

Oxen and cattle were not the only animals raised on the Polish farmsteads. Describing his barnyard in 1855, one farmer wrote: "I bought cows for myself two days ago. A cow costs from 15 to 20 dollars with a calf. I have six cows and five calves and two oxen and one mule for work and one mare that will foal in two weeks. A mule costs 20 dollars and a mare costs 30 dollars, so all my animals cost 198 dollars. . . . [In addition] I have . . . nine maranusses, in our language pigs, and ninety chickens."[53]

As time passed, the use of horses instead of oxen or mules for agricultural work became a status symbol among the Silesian farmers, and they and their families treated their horses almost as if they were pets. Other animals that the transplanted peasants kept on their farms were ducks, geese, goats, and, to be sure, dogs.[54]

The diet of the Silesian pioneers provides additional insight not only into their agriculture but also into their daily lives. One of the peasant farmers, an immigrant from Lubliniec County, wrote back to Silesia that the colonists were eating well in Texas. He reported that they had bread, fish, and coffee on the table every day and that the hunting was free. Because the settlements had skilled hunters, he related, the colonists frequently had wild game.[55] Among this game were deer, turkeys, wild pigs, and rabbits. One reason why wild game may have been so popular, in addition to its abundance, was that there was no refrigeration for beef carcasses when cattle were slaughtered. The meat therefore could not be kept from spoiling for more than a day or two during the warm months of the year, and so when families butchered large animals, they were forced to distribute the meat among their neighbors at very low prices to prevent it from spoiling in the heat. One possible remedy for this problem was salting the beef, but that was not always successful during the warmest months. Another method employed by the Silesians was to cut the beef into thin strips and dry them in the sun for later use in cooking. Still another way they avoided meat spoilage was by using it in smoked sausages.[56]

The colonists did not neglect their milk cows as sources for nutrition and variety in their meals. They used the milk not only for the obvious purposes of drinking and cooking but also as the principal ingredient of dairy products, including sour cream and cottage cheese, both favorites in the Polish peasant diet.[57]

Corn soon became a staple food for the Polish Texans. It was the universal crop of the natives the immigrants found in the state, and soon the newcomers developed a taste for it. One of the founders of Bandera many years later recalled that an American neighbor named

Curtis first showed her family how to cook roasting ears on the cobs and that they never had eaten anything like it in Silesia. According to several accounts a Mexican rancher named Andreas Coy gave the Poles at Panna Maria their first corn for bread and seed. One reason for the almost immediate appeal of corn to the colonists may have been that they had to travel to other somewhat distant towns, such as Seguin or San Antonio, to buy flour, for they knew of no other mills more convenient to their communities during the period of initial settlement.[58]

Fruits and vegetables were especially popular among the Silesians. Almost every house had a garden that provided the residents with a great variety of fresh foods. One of the colonists wrote that the soil was especially well suited for cucumbers, melons, pumpkins, and potatoes, while a Polish priest stated that all vegetables grew well and that during the summer months crops of cabbage, lettuce, potatoes, and watermelons were particularly bountiful and cheap. He added that peaches and figs were generally available, though not everywhere. In Texas the immigrants encountered a number of strange new foods, but sweet potatoes seemed to puzzle them the most. One of the Poles wrote home, "Potatoes are of two kinds: some like yours and others that are sweet, which are called 'patets.'" Another described the curious tuber as shaped "like our cucumbers" but with a "sweetish taste." Expressing the desire for more variety on his dinner table, one farmer asked his brother in Silesia, "When you come, take all vegetables with you, and particularly beans, enough so that you could give some to me."[59]

The settlers also utilized wild foods that they found growing around them. Among the most popular of these were the nuts produced by the wide-spreading pecan trees that grew luxuriantly along the river bottoms. One Polish writer described them as excellent, like walnuts, "only heavier and longer." When a farmer was fortunate enough to have several of these trees on his property, the pecans he and his family gathered in the autumn could bring him a handsome profit. The peasants also tried to use the native muscadine grapes, which the local Americans claimed were suitable for wines, but most of them found the fruit so sour as to be "unfit for use."[60]

With the opening of farms in Texas came the need to arrange for the land legally. Father Moczygemba already had made plans with

John Twohig for the sale of land at Panna Maria. After the immigrants arrived, however, they found that Twohig and his partner, Colonel W. J. Hardee, had set the prices at the settlement comparatively high, much higher, in fact, than in the surrounding country. The average price for unimproved land in Karnes County in 1858 was only $1.47 per acre.[61] Twohig and Hardee, however, charged the Silesians between $5.00 and $10.80 for equivalent land at the Polish colony. The average price for the 728 acres of land that the two men sold to the immigrants in transactions completed before the Civil War was $5.88 per acre. Perhaps the new arrivals were willing to pay such sums because they were accustomed to high land prices in Europe and because one of their purposes in immigrating had been to own larger farms than they had possessed at home. Commenting on the sales, an Upper Silesian newspaper related that the colonists in Texas bought "for several hundred dollars" so much land that in their motherland "it could be compared with our knights' properties." Land prices were much more reasonable at the other Polish communities, $1.00 to $2.00 an acre at Martinez and $2.00 an acre at Bandera.[62]

To provide land for the less affluent settlers at Panna Maria, Father Leopold bought a block of 238 acres at $5.00 an acre and then proceeded to parcel out all but 25 acres for the church to the colonists who could not afford Twohig's high prices. The priest made the purchase with money he had received from his order to establish a Franciscan convent in Texas. After the transaction was completed, he wrote to his superiors in Rome that the plans for a proposed convent in San Antonio had failed because his agent, "Mr. Twohig," had been unable to purchase the desired location. Then Moczygemba related that instead he had chosen a site "for the convent" elsewhere: "Your instructions were to buy land well situated. This I did by buying it in another place, . . . the new colony of Panna Maria."[63]

The exorbitant prices charged by John Twohig can best be appreciated when they are compared to land prices in the same area during the next fifty years. In 1859 the average price for land in Karnes County was $1.81.[64] After the Civil War, in the second half of the 1860's, the price of an acre of unimproved land went down to between $0.50 and $1.00.[65] In the decade beginning in the early 1870's the price of unimproved land went up again to between $1.00 and $2.00

an acre.[66] From the second half of the 1880's through the 1890's it still could be bought for as little as $2.00 an acre.[67] Even as late as 1904 unimproved land in the area was selling for $5.00 an acre, the minimum price that Twohig had required from the immigrants upon their arrival half a century earlier.[68]

One severe natural disaster beset the immigrants during their first years in America, the great Texas drought of 1856–1857, one of the worst in the history of the state. The weather problems commenced before Christmas 1855, when a series of cold, wet northers began. They followed each other until late March 1856. This unfortunate weather set back planting a number of weeks into the spring.[69] By the time the late crops were beginning to mature, the drought had begun. By late summer the local press was complaining that the weather was the driest in memory and that many of the best wells in the country were going dry.[70]

The siege of dry weather continued for over a year. According to several accounts no rain fell at Panna Maria for fourteen months. On the prairies around Seguin, about twenty miles northeast of Martinez, the earth cracked open a foot wide and thirty to forty feet deep. All vegetation seared, shriveled, and finally disappeared entirely, leaving only the bare ground. Cattle became lost and died as they ranged far and wide searching for water and grass that no longer existed.[71]

With the dryness came inflation and hard times for country people who lived by what they could raise. Corn became so scarce that it was transported from Ohio down the Mississippi River to New Orleans and thence to Texas ports. From there it went overland to inland markets, where it brought a price of two dollars a bushel. Several months earlier, before the rainless period, a bushel of the same product was selling in San Antonio for only seventy-five cents to a dollar. In Karnes County the price for corn rose as high as three dollars a bushel, almost four times the normal price. Flour was considerably more expensive, twenty-four dollars a barrel. Sweet potatoes and syrup became rare delicacies. With food prices soaring, the Silesians who had been able to save some of the money they had brought from Europe were forced to spend it on food. By the end of the drought the economic positions of the immigrants generally had leveled as a result of the spending on food. Some of the Silesians may indeed have faced serious malnutrition. An American who knew them at the time wrote that "had it not been for the abundance of wild game" the new settlers "would have starved to death."[72]

One of the immediate results of the drought was pressure on many of the Polish immigrants to seek employment with the Americans who lived around them. Men went to work on the ranches and farms, usually earning fifty cents a day plus board, while women and girls took jobs in the homes of their American neighbors as housekeepers. Some of them had to leave their farms to go to San Antonio to find work. Through such employment, coupled with what scant crops they could raise, the immigrants were able to live through the drought. Many of them, however, went so deeply into debt that it took them several years to recover financially.[73]

The great drought not only ruined the economic hopes of the Silesians but also destroyed the relationship they had with their founder, Father Moczygemba. Ever since the establishment of the settlements some of the colonists had grumbled about conditions in Texas. Having believed rumors they had heard in Silesia about a land of milk and honey in America, they were disheartened when they found instead a land filled with scrub brush, waist-high grass, and rattlesnakes.[74] The discontent remained suppressed for the first months but when the immigrants began feeling the effects of the drought, their dissatisfaction broke into open hostility against the priest who had brought them to such a desolate wilderness. According to one version some of the colonists wanted to hang Moczygemba, and according to another they wanted to drown him in what little water was left in the San Antonio River.[75]

Father Leopold, while deeply troubled by the plight of his Silesians, had more problems worrying him than those of the colonists. As the superior of his order in Texas, he was responsible for supervising the activities of the other Franciscan missionaries in the field at such places as Fredericksburg, Castroville, and New Braunfels. He wanted, in fact, to be free from the Polish colonies to pursue his official duties, and even before the first immigrants arrived he began requesting his superiors to send a Polish priest to care for them. Making his problems as superior of the missions even more difficult was the feeling of isolation that he experienced; sometimes he went for months and months without receiving replies to his frequent letters to the mother house in

Rome. Moreover, he was asked repeatedly when additional European priests whom he had promised would arrive. Most of the expected missionaries were never sent by the order, and Moczygemba was left having made empty pledges both to the people and to the bishop.[76] Expressing his depression in the face of the problems coming from all directions, the lonely missionary wrote to the minister general in Rome in 1856: "After having written several times . . . asking for missionary fathers . . . and having not received any answer to my letters, I am so desolate and oppressed that I cannot express myself. . . . On my knees I beg you to send a Polish father as soon as possible, for I cannot visit all our missions." After chronicling his previous year, when he had been very ill from hard travel and exposure to rough life, Father Leopold concluded, "My great sadness does not permit me to write more."[77]

The Polish colonists undoubtedly could not understand all the simultaneous demands that were being made on their leader. They only knew that they needed bread and that all he could offer was prayer. As a later pastor among the people wrote, "They complained and cursed this priest so strongly that he had to escape."[78] In October 1856, Moczygemba left the Silesians to go back to Castroville, where he remained until July of the next year. He stayed in Texas at least through mid-October 1857, when he is known to have visited New Braunfels, but then he left the state entirely. Probably because of his many unpleasant experiences there, Father Leopold, after conferring with his superiors in Rome in 1858, moved the Franciscan Minor Conventual missions away from Texas to the northern United States, where, with interruptions for additional trips to Europe, he resided until his death in 1891. The anger of the Silesians did not abate for several years. In 1867 missionaries among the settlers stated that they "cannot forgive him up to this day."[79] Finally, twenty years after he had brought the immigrants from Upper Silesia, Father Moczygemba was able to return to the settlements to visit with his brothers and their families.[80]

Taking the place of Father Leopold as the spiritual guide for the Silesians came the Reverend Anthony Rossadowski. He was a native of Wilno, in Russian Poland, who came to America first as an exile after serving as a chaplain in the Polish forces in the Polish Insurrection of 1830. After spending several years in the eastern states, during which time he served as an army chaplain in the Seminole War, Rossadowski returned to Europe for a time before the superiors of the Friars Minor Conventual directed him to Texas in May 1856.[81] As soon as Rossadowski arrived at Panna Maria, Father Leopold departed for Castroville, leaving him to cope with the problems created among the parishioners by the drought. Although Rossadowski was active in developing the Silesian parishes, neither Moczygemba nor the people were satisfied with him. A later pastor declared, "He was such a spitfire that he thrashed the parishioners' backs for the slightest offense." Father Leopold complained to Rome, "He acted so tyrannically that the people asked me to remedy it."[82] The next year, however, Father Leopold withdrew from Texas entirely, leaving the short-tempered Rossadowski on his own.

The same year as Moczygemba's departure, 1857, another Polish priest, the Reverend Julian Przysiecki, arrived and took charge of the Silesian parish at Bandera. Rossadowski and Przysiecki shared the priestly duties for the Polish colonies until 1860, when the former left for New York State. There Rossadowski joined Father Moczygemba and became the master of novices at a Franciscan convent in Syracuse, where he died in 1865. When Rossadowski departed Texas on the eve of the Civil War, he left Father Przysiecki the only Polish priest to care for all the Silesian communities.[83]

During the first years of Silesian settlement the population expanded beyond the initial four colonies at Panna Maria, Bandera, San Antonio, and Martinez. One reason for this growth was continued immigration, another was the belief that the site of the Panna Maria settlement was unhealthful, and a third was the desire to try life elsewhere. The largest of the new colonies were Yorktown and Meyersville, communities with intertwined histories. About 1856, Silesians began moving to these two already established towns, which are respectively twenty-five and thirty-five miles east of Panna Maria, in DeWitt County. In both places the Poles lived with Germans, and in time antagonism developed between the two ethnic groups over which language would be used in the churches. Finally the Meyersville Silesians, who were outnumbered two to one by Germans, moved their religious affiliations to Yorktown, which by the 1860's had a Polish church and later a Polish school. Yorktown, known to the Silesians as Jordan, became the center of Polish life in DeWitt County. About a decade after the Silesians began moving eastward into this area, they formed another Polish parish at the Coleto community, near Meyersville. For a time it was served by Polish priests, but after a few years its population became integrated with that around it, and Coleto lost its distinctive Polish character.[84]

Another series of Silesian communities developed between the original settlements and the Gulf of Mexico. These included the Polish colonies at Victoria, Inez, and Saint Francisville. The first two of these communities were on the general route that the immigrants took from the harbor at Indianola toward San Antonio, and they frequently are said to have been established by colonists who, either unable or unwilling to go farther, left the main contingents on the way inland. Victoria had over a dozen Silesian families in the 1860's and sufficiently strong ties to the more important colonies to send at least one of its daughters to become a nun at the Silesian convent that had been formed at Panna Maria. Inez, at the time called Garcitas by the Americans and Gazeta by the Poles, likewise had about a dozen Silesian families. Both of the communities retained their Polish consciousness to such an extent that they required the ministrations of traveling Polish-speaking priests at least into the 1870's.[85]

Saint Francisville, near the Gulf of Mexico in Matagorda County, about midway between Galveston and Indianola, had a comparatively separate existence from the other Silesian colonies. Like Victoria and Inez, it is reported to have been established by some of the first immigrants from Upper Silesia who did not wish to go farther inland. Settling in what the Americans soon called the Polish Village, a handful of the Silesians became successful farmers in the coastal area near what today is Bay City. In the late nineteenth century the inhabitants of the community built their own Polish Catholic church, but their population was never sufficient to support a resident pastor. Among the surnames of settlers in the colony were Petrucha, Gola, Sisky, Waschka, Ryman, and Bonk. Today the old wooden frame church stands empty at Saint Francisville except on All Souls' Day, when the descendants of the original immigrants gather to tend the cemetery and to celebrate a mass of remembrance for the dead.[86]

South of San Antonio, in Atascosa County, another handful of Silesians founded a colony in what was purely ranching country. This settlement, known as Las Gallinas, but called Gaina by the Poles, at one time had twenty-five families, and at least through the 1870's was visited by traveling Polish priests from the other colonies. It was the home of, among others, Joseph Cotulla and his family when they immigrated to Texas in the 1850's. Today, like many of the other small Polish communities, it has lost its Silesian identity.[87]

The great drought of 1856–1857 provided the stimulus for the establishment in Missouri of the one colony by Silesians who first came to Texas and then left the state. Escaping from the suffering of the rainless period, one party of Poles departed from the settlements and traveled overland to a site near the Missouri River in Franklin County east of Saint Louis. There they settled in the Saint Gertrude community and were instrumental in changing its name to Krakow, the name by which it is known today. The initial group was joined there by Poles from both Texas and Russian Poland, and within sixty years they had expanded their settlement to include the nearby villages of Clover Bottom and Owensville.

The area where they settled in the 1850's was woodland. After they had bought the land, cut down the trees, and burned out the stumps, they learned to their disappointment that they had chosen a place with inferior soil. They had no choice except to stay, however, and in time they became recognized for raising on the poor land crops that compared favorably with the yields of any other farmers in the area. The Poles of Franklin County first used the already existing Catholic church at Krakow, but as the German population in that vicinity increased, they shifted their religious activity to a church that they established at Clover Bottom, which now is the center of the ethnic community.[88]

Contact between the Silesians in Franklin County and those in Texas has remained remarkably strong for over a century. During the 1870's, for example, Polish newspapers published in Franklin County printed articles written in Texas, and one paper was edited by the former schoolmaster of Panna Maria, John Barzyński.[89] During the same period at least one Texas pastor traveled to the settlement in Missouri. There always have been occasional visits by family members between Missouri and Texas, and a "pilgrimage to Panna Maria" was organized by the local newspaper in 1973.[90]

Although precise statistics are not available, it is possible to estimate the Silesian Polish population of Texas in the middle of the nineteenth century. When Father Leopold Moczygemba passed through Paris on his way to Rome in 1858, he was interviewed by correspondents of two Polish newspapers. He gave them approximate population figures for the four major Silesian colonies. He told them that Panna Maria had 120 families, San Antonio 50 families, Bandera 20 families, and Martinez 25 families. Assuming that the average family had 4.66 members, as may be calculated from the data recorded for Silesians enumerated in the United States census of 1860, this meant that the major concentrations of Silesians, excluding peripheral settlements such as Meyersville and Las Gallinas, had in 1858 a total population of 1,002.[91] The population schedules of the census of 1860, which at first would appear to be ideal sources for Silesian population figures, in reality are disappointing, although they may be used for computing some statistical averages. The English-speaking enumerators frequently garbled information they obtained from the peasants, confused nationalities, and failed to record known individuals.[92]

The next somewhat reliable population statistics on the Silesians in Texas come from 1867. In that year a Polish priest conducted a census of the Silesian parishes, and he determined the following numbers: Panna Maria, 75 families; San Antonio, 43 families; Bandera, 12 families; Martinez, 34 families; Yorktown, 13 families; Coleto, 14 families; Victoria, 13 families; and Inez, 12 families. If the same estimate of family size is employed, this provides a total population for the Silesian colonies of 1,007, almost the same figure that Father Moczygemba had estimated a decade earlier.[93]

Both of these population estimates, however, may be less than the actual number of Silesians in Texas in the middle of the nineteenth century. Undoubtedly the priests enumerating their parishioners missed some of the immigrants—people who, for example, lived in non-Silesian communities or were members of non-Polish parishes. Furthermore, European sources suggest a somewhat larger number of immigrants. The contemporary estimates of emigrants from Upper Silesia to Texas indicate about 150 in 1854, 700 in 1855, and 500 in 1856, or a total of approximately 1,350 for the three years. Sources do not indicate numbers for the subsequent years, but by 1857 the emigration had subsided, and the movement had become quite small.[94]

One of the initial goals of the Silesian immigrants was the erection of Polish churches in their communities. There they could worship the Almighty in their Polish manner. This construction consumed much of the energy of the peasants during their first years in Texas and served as a unifying element during that time of difficulty. As early as spring 1855, Father Moczygemba was examining stone to be used in building the church at Panna Maria. Work proceeded with many interruptions through 14 August 1855, when the priest blessed the cornerstone, to 29 September 1856, when Moczygemba consecrated the place of worship. Even before the shell of the building was completed, the parishioners, in a visible manifestation of their faith, erected a large wooden cross in front of the entrance and in spring 1856 mounted on it a Christ figure that John Rzeppa of Toszek had brought from Upper Silesia.[95]

An unsolved mystery about the church at Panna Maria, the oldest Polish church in America, concerns the funds used for its construction. As early as March 1855, Father Moczygemba, as head of the Franciscan missions in Texas, had spent over a thousand dollars to purchase 238 acres of land at the Panna Maria colony "for the convent." In reality he distributed the land among the settlers, putting aside 25 acres for the church. Then in the next year and a half he reportedly spent approximately two thousand dollars more to erect the church. Not only did the colonists pay nothing for the construction, but the priest even paid them for their labor. A number of theories have arisen to explain how Father Moczygemba secured the money to build the sanctuary. In 1902 one of the stonemasons, John Gawlik, recollected that the funds had come from Father Leopold's Bavarian superiors. A second hypothesis is that the priest and John Twohig may have split the excess money that the landowner charged the settlers for their land.[96] A third and probably the most reasonable theory is that the funds came originally from the Ludwig-Missionsverein, a German missionary society based in Munich, which donated large sums of money for Catholic work among the Germans in the United States.[97] It is known that the organization made substantial contributions to the Friars Minor Conventual for their activities in Texas. At the time that the society was giving the money, Moczygemba was the superior of the Franciscan missions in America and was busily engaged in building the church at Panna Maria.[98]

Not long after the Silesians at Panna Maria completed their

church, the immigrant farmers on Martinez Creek and at Bandera started building their own houses of worship. The Bexar County group began erecting their log church in either 1856 or 1857 on land that Ludwig Zając donated. He allowed his fellow parishioners to use any timber on the land for building purposes. The methods used by the Poles amazed their neighbors. "When our people began the work," one of the pioneers recalled, "the Americans looked at them in wonder" as "without proper tools they managed those thick oak trees." After felling the trees, the peasants squared the timbers and transported them to the construction site with the aid of oxen. Soon the small church at the colony was completed, and the parishioners could say proudly that they had built it "with no help from anyone." The erection of a church at Bandera followed in 1858. Built under the supervision of Father Anthony Rossadowski, it also was a humble log structure similar to the one at Martinez. Both of these wooden churches remained in use until after the Civil War, when in more affluent economic circumstances the settlers were able to replace them with masonry buildings. The urban Silesians at San Antonio were unable to worship in their own building until 1866, when they moved their services from the old San Fernando church to a former bakery and warehouse in the Polish Quarter of the city.[99]

Although information about it is sketchy at best, available data indicate that a Polish school existed at Panna Maria as early as 1858. When Father Moczygemba was interviewed by the newspaper correspondents in Paris that year, he reported that in Panna Maria there was a "small school" and that during his travels in Europe he would like to "take a young Pole to be teacher" there.[100] Another nineteenth-century source stated that, before the Civil War, Peter Kiołbassa, son of the deputy to the Prussian parliament in 1848, was the "first teacher" in Panna Maria "under Father Anthony Rossadowski."[101] Yet another source said that, before the construction of a separate school at Panna Maria in the late 1860's, a portion of the stone storage barn built by John Twohig at the settlement was partitioned off to be used as a schoolroom. All these Polish educational activities predated any elsewhere in the United States, giving the Silesian immigrants in Texas the additional distinction of having had not only the first Polish colonies and churches in America but also the first Polish school.[102]

Relations between the Silesians and the Americans in Texas were mixed. During the initial months of settlement the two groups eyed each other with curiosity from some distance. As an illustration of the kinds of encounters that occurred, an American who accidentally rode into one of the settlements in 1855 later recalled: "In the month of November [1855] . . . while on that hunting trip we came upon some dug outs not far from the Cibolo, but we found people there that couldnt [*sic*] understand what we said to them. . . . They might have fallen from the moon or stars for what we knew or could find out."[103] About such chance meetings one of the immigrants remembered: "Sometimes one of the Americans would appear. We couldn't talk with them, so they just gazed at us in wonder, smiled, and . . . went away."[104]

After the beginning of the drought in 1856, some of the Americans who lived around the Poles became their benefactors. By employing the peasants on their ranches and farms and in their homes, the Americans perhaps unknowingly ensured the preservation of the new ethnic communities. Some of the Texans went out of their way to be helpful to the newcomers. Upon learning of hunger at Panna Maria, for example, a local rancher named William Butler drove a dozen fat steers into the village. Finding that Alexander Dziuk had learned enough English to converse with him, Butler announced through his interpreter that he was presenting the cattle to the villagers with the injunction to butcher them and to eat and be merry. Similarly both John Twohig and Mexican rancher Andreas Coy sent loads of corn to the settlement.[105]

Not all the relations between the Americans and the Silesians were so friendly. It is likely that the local feelings toward the new Catholic immigrants were tainted by the nativism then prevalent in the state. In San Antonio during this period there were a number of unfortunate incidents in which, for example, young American hoodlums pelted stones at pupils and teachers at the Catholic boys' school and drunken Americans tried to ride on horseback into churchyards during Catholic religious services. Some of the negative activity was directed specifically against the Poles. About the time that the third large contingent of Silesians was arriving in central Texas, the local press carried rumors of public speakers warning "the late immigrants from Poland . . . not to settle in this section."[106]

Numerous accounts chronicle episodes in which the Americans

took advantage of the strange, silent foreigners. Frequently they sold the new colonists livestock only to return later and steal it back. Other times they sold them ostensibly sound animals that turned out to be inferior or diseased. When some of the Silesians, after working for Americans for several weeks, asked for their salaries, their employers turned them out and threatened them with revolvers, warning them not to come back and ask for anything.[107]

A final question about the life of the Silesians on the Texas frontier is a subjective one. It concerns whether the immigrants were happy in the new land they had chosen. Examining this matter in the 1860's, an Upper Silesian newspaper described one family as an example of what the transplanted peasants experienced. The family, consisting of a mother, a father, and one son, left Silesia to try for a better life in Texas. They bought several hundred dollars' worth of virgin land and immediately set to work clearing it for farming. The work went slowly as they cleared acre after acre, but they were able to support themselves from the livestock they were beginning to raise. The father, who was about fifty years old, the mother, and the only son worked day and night to build a house and surround it with a fence. They found the manual labor very hard because "they were used to being well off in Upper Silesia." Wisely keeping aside a substantial portion of their money, not spending everything for land, the father slowly built up a sizable herd of cattle and horses. Through overwork, however, he died before he could realize his dream of returning to Silesia a wealthy man. After several years the son married the daughter of another peasant, and she brought to him in her dowry more land, cattle, and horses. Thus he became a success by immigrant standards and even was able to send home to Poland two hundred American dollars for his family. According to the report, however, the peasant's latest letter asked if it would be possible for him to return and settle in Silesia for five or six thousand thalers. Despite the fearsome journey across the ocean, he reportedly was ready to go back "to his motherland . . . to live, work, and die there."[108] Today one can only wonder how many of the immigrants after a few years of the rough life in Texas wanted to go back to their soft, green Silesia and how many of them wanted to stay. Undoubtedly, after the Civil War began, most of them would have preferred to have been back at home.

4
The Civil War

PERHAPS unknown to the Silesian peasants of central Texas at the time, the Civil War began for them in February 1861, when the voters of the state of Texas decided overwhelmingly in favor of seceding from the Union. The Poles had not been in the United States long enough to participate in that election. The subsequent four war years were disastrous for the immigrants, who just then were recovering financially from the severe drought of 1856–1857.[1] For the families who remained home during the war, these were times of isolation and hardship, and, for the men who went to battle, times of danger and privation. Both the families and the men lived under severe tensions that caused many of them to lose hope. As one of the Poles related, "We were looking forward to our end."[2]

The Silesian peasants in Texas appear never to have supported the Confederate cause enthusiastically. Some of them, in fact, became its active adversaries. Why did this occur? None of the Silesians were slaveholders.[3] Their opposition probably did not stem from revulsion against the institution of slavery, however, although such feelings may have played some part. One reason many Poles had left Europe for Texas had been to evade conscription into the Prussian army.[4] They did not want to fight in anyone else's wars either in the Old World or in the New. Consequently after the hostilities broke out in America, one of the worst fears among the Polish peasants was of induction into the Confederate army and subsequent separation from their families. This fear most likely prompted their opposition to, or at most lukewarm support of, the southern cause.

As early as January 1862 the press in San Antonio began carrying notices concerning the issuance of conscription laws and orders. The readers, at least some of whom included Silesian Poles who had begun using English, learned that all male inhabitants of the state between the ages of eighteen and fifty, except those exempted for occupational reasons, were liable for military service.[5] In the spring of that year further notices appeared that all affected men were to enroll themselves with the military authorities. Primarily to ensure this supply of fighting men, General Paul Octave Hébert, commander of the Department of Texas, declared martial law in the state.[6] A few months later the *San Antonio Weekly Herald*, noting lax compliance with the rulings, lamented "what a sad spectacle" would be presented when "free Southern citizens, native or adopted," had to be escorted into the ranks to defend "their own firesides."[7] After all men presumably had been registered, military surgeons began appearing in county seats to give them medical examinations before induction. These teams visited the centers of Silesian population at Yorktown and Helena in the late summer and early autumn of 1863.[8]

Though many of the Silesians already were able to communicate in English, as a group they did not fully understand all that was going on around them. They greatly feared the breakup of their families, and many of them mistakenly thought that boys as young as fourteen years were being taken. Furthermore, some of them believed that all those who did not comply would be hanged.[9] Because of such fears and uncertainties many Silesians tried to avoid all Confederate officials, conscription officers in particular. This fact is attested to by the tales still told in the Silesian households.[10] The defiance of the Poles at Martinez provides an example from a contemporary source. In spring 1862 a correspondent of the local press from eastern Bexar County reported that all men from his area except the old and invalid had departed for the army. Then he added, however, that he had forgotten to mention the inhabitants of the Silesian settlement near him. In scathing irony he declared that "not one of the *brave* compatriots of Kosciusko has gone to the wars," and he went on to speculate that the reason the Poles had remained at home was to prey on the herds that the local cattle raisers had left behind.[11]

Relations between the Silesians and their neighboring Americans on the home front did not improve as the war dragged on. This would have been very difficult with all the Americans knowing that the foreigners were evading the draft, and it became impossible when they learned that some of the Poles had in fact left the Confederate army to fight against it. This news became common knowledge in spring

1863, when the local newspaper published the names of soldiers who had changed sides to fight for the Union and included at least a dozen Silesian Poles in the list.[12] In what seems to be an unfeeling description of the violent death of a Silesian in Helena later that year, an anonymous American writer illustrates what may have been a common attitude: "In the evening . . . a Polander was killed by a horse. He was going to ride him bareback and Albert Mayfield lifted him up by the foot and gave him [al]most too much of a lift . . . [because] he slid over on the other side and got his arm entangled in the rope. The horse started off and directly he commenced kicking and killed him."[13]

With the war came also inflation and the almost inevitable shortages of a wartime economy. By the second year of the conflict both problems had become evident in central Texas. Not only were things becoming more expensive, but also they were increasingly difficult to find. The local press in September 1862 went so far as to warn of the possibility of starvation in the region before spring.[14]

The shortages and high prices were everywhere, in both city and country, and they became worse as time went on. In San Antonio in the second year of the war flour sold for $40.00 a barrel, corn meal for $2.50 a bushel, and coffee for between $7.00 and $9.00 a pound or, outside the city, for $1.00 in gold. Manufactured goods also soared in price. Calico cloth sold for $0.75 to $1.00 a yard, shoes for $8.00 to $10.00 a pair, and boots for $20.00 a pair. Some critics blamed the inflation and shortages on the lack of transportation, for most draft animals had been taken for military use, while others blamed the merchants for profiteering.[15] In rural Karnes County the problems were similar to those in the city. Certain food items, even staples like flour, were available only intermittently. Because it was a stock-raising area, beef generally remained available. The women from Panna Maria went to Helena when they had a few extra cents to buy small quantities of meat from a German butcher there. Because they lacked the money to purchase good cuts, they carried with them large squares of cloth and used them to wrap up and carry away the less expensive scraps not wanted by the Americans. A constant problem for the Silesian mothers in the countryside, especially those whose husbands and older sons were away at war, was to keep cows to provide milk for their children. Some families in the area were forced by the high prices of cloth to return to home weaving to make clothing.[16]

Added to the difficulties between the Poles and the Americans was the problem of rising lawlessness in the area south of San Antonio, where many of the Silesians lived. Particularly after the fall of Brownsville and other South Texas points to federal forces in late 1863, the region between the Rio Grande and the San Antonio River became overrun with renegades and bandits. The situation became so serious that residents of Karnes County felt it necessary to appeal to the state government for assistance. In their subsequent petition for authorization to form a volunteer company to protect themselves, they stated that the lawless men in the area were increasing in number alarmingly and were threatening to devastate the countryside.[17]

During the second half of the war the Silesians in Texas were troubled by a serious natural calamity, recurring drought. The cycle of dry weather began in 1862 and continued through 1865. Despite occasional rains most streambeds remained parched and empty. An American who in January 1863 moved to a farm on Ecleto Creek in Karnes County, an area heavily populated with Poles, recalled that he "must have been living there three months" before "it rained a drop." In spite of sporadic rains the drought persisted for months until the San Antonio River "stunk with carrion from its head to its mouth." Not only were agricultural and livestock raising interests disrupted, but the residents of the area even had trouble finding potable water.[18]

The Poles were beset not only with war-related and natural difficulties but also with religious problems. In the middle of the war they lost their only Polish priest. As early as 1857 the Reverend Julian Przysiecki had begun meeting the religious needs of the Silesians at Bandera and Martinez. How and when this enigmatic man came to Texas is uncertain. When the Reverend Anthony Rossadowski departed for New York in 1860, he left Przysiecki the only Polish priest to minister to the Silesians in the state. Riding on horseback from place to place, he cared for all the Poles from Bandera on the northwest 105 miles to Panna Maria on the southeast.[19]

This last Polish priest in Texas was killed in a riding accident near the Martinez Creek settlement on 25 November 1863. The circumstances of his death are as unclear as the mystery that surrounds his life. Some secondary writers have praised him.[20] Others closer to him in time were more critical. His successors in the same decade uniformly denounced him for frequent and public intoxication. One called him a drunkard and accused him of being unable to read the mass because he was unconscious from drink.[21] Another declared that, when he left the church, "you saw him everywhere—by the table and under it." The latter priest, however, accorded blame to the parishioners at Martinez, whom he accused of "gross and familiar relations" with the pastor.[22]

As the story can be reconstructed, Przysiecki's death occurred at a party in the Bexar County community. Seeing several men racing on horseback, the reportedly intoxicated priest called out: "Let me ride that horse. I'll show you how to ride." He mounted one of the horses, and a few moments later it passed at a gallop under a low-hanging mesquite branch, which knocked the rider to the ground and immediate death. It remained for the Reverend P. Amandus of the German Catholic congregation in San Antonio to bury Przysiecki in the parish cemetery, where the colonists erected a still-standing grave marker in his memory.[23]

The death of Father Przysiecki brought to the Silesians the period of greatest isolation during their life in Texas. There was no possibility of securing another Polish priest. The Civil War prevented any effective communication with possible Polish clergymen in the northern United States, and the Polish Insurrection of 1863 disrupted contact with Poland. During the next three years the Silesians received occasional ministrations from visiting priests, most of them French and German Benedictine fathers from San Antonio. To maintain their faith, the Poles in the rural communities frequently gathered in the churches on Sundays without priests to chant the rosary, to sing hymns, and to recite the mass in the vernacular. Because of the lack of Polish-speaking priests, the people were unable to say confessions, some of them for several years, and a number of them died without the last sacraments, a disaster in the Catholic communities.[24]

Information on the participation of Silesians in the Civil War is both limited and scattered. With the defeat of the South in 1865, Confederate records were strewn in all directions. This seems to have been particularly true of military records, some of which were kept by individual commanders, some destroyed, others captured by the victorious Union forces, and still others retained by state and local governments. For this reason the story of Silesian activity in the Confederate army remains somewhat sketchy. Union records, on the other hand, have been preserved in better order, and consequently Silesian participation on the northern side in the conflict can be documented more clearly.[25]

The logical place in which to start searching for data on Polish soldiers is in the muster rolls of the military companies raised in the counties where they lived. Because of the reluctance of the Silesians to volunteer for service, however, such lists are disappointing sources. For example, of the several companies raised in Karnes County in the first months of the war, one was actually called the Panna Maria Grays. The name unfortunately is deceptive. On the three preserved muster rolls of this company, only four Silesians were listed on the first roll from 6 July 1861, and only one was left on the third and final roll from 7 February 1862.[26] More Poles are found on the records from Bandera. The one preserved Bandera muster roll from Captain B. Mitchell's Company of Texas State Troops, dated February 1862, bears the names of ten Silesians, whose ages, it is interesting to note, varied from nineteen to forty-nine years.[27] Silesian names are encountered on other local muster rolls, but they are not common.[28]

Existing records suggest that the largest numbers of Silesians found themselves in one or the other of two regiments in the regular Confederate army, the Sixth Texas Infantry and the Twenty-fourth Texas Cavalry. Both of these units were raised in 1862 and in the autumn and winter of that year were ordered to Arkansas, where they joined other Confederate troops defending a reinforced earthen fortress known as the Arkansas Post. After the capitulation of this fort to Union forces in early 1863, most of the Poles in the two regiments were captured and with the other Confederate troops were sent to prisoner-of-war camps in Illinois. Once in the detention centers many of them were offered the opportunity to swear allegiance to the Union and join federal regiments encamped nearby.[29] The story of one of these Silesian soldiers, Peter Kiołbassa, the one about whom the most is known, serves as probably the best illustration of the activities of the others.

Peter Kiołbassa was a twenty-eight-year-old bachelor when in early summer 1861 he swore allegiance to the state of Texas and to the Confederacy and became a member of the Panna Maria Grays. The forty-six-man company, composed almost exclusively of American residents of Karnes County, was raised for home defense against the threats of both potential attacks by Union forces and forays by Indians and renegade Mexicans. Kiołbassa, serving as a bugler, remained with the company for several months, but by early 1862 his name had disappeared from its muster rolls.[30]

The young Silesian next appeared as bugler for Captain B. F. Fly's Company in the Second Regiment of Carter's Brigade in the Texas Mounted Volunteers. He was mustered in at Hempstead, Texas, on 2 April 1862 "for 3 years or the war." At the time he possessed a horse valued at $150 and equipment valued at $40. The name of Kiołbassa's company by the autumn had changed to Company I of Colonel F. C. Wilke's Twenty-fourth Texas Cavalry.[31] At least seven other Silesians served with him in the same unit.[32] The company went in early April as cavalry to Shreveport, Louisiana. From there it went to El Dorado, Arkansas, where the members learned that, because of lack of forage, orders dated 29 July forced them to abandon their horses to other units. This order caused the regiment to be renamed Wilke's Twenty-fourth Texas Dismounted Cavalry. The name change, however, provided little consolation to the disgruntled Texans, who from childhood had ridden horses and who loudly protested the loss of their mounts.[33] The company next was ordered to proceed with all its regiment on foot to the Arkansas Post, which was situated up the Arkansas River from its mouth on the Mississippi. They had arrived at least by October to join other Texas and Arkansas troops in defending the position against possible Union attack.[34]

For about two months the members of Company I of Wilke's Twenty-fourth Texas Dismounted Cavalry stayed at the Arkansas Post. There they occupied their days with drilling and making improvements to the fortifications, but during the evenings they had time for games of checkers, chess, or cards. They apparently were satisfied with their diet of pumpkins, sorghum, and coarse corn bread. Most of the troops lived comfortably; the winter of 1862–1863 had been mild, and when cool weather came, the men had warm quarters in cabins made from logs and covered with split boards.[35]

The peaceful life at the Arkansas Post ended on the night of 9 January 1863, when word reached the fort that Union gunboats were steaming up the Arkansas toward it. The next morning the vessels commenced bombarding the Confederate garrison with cannon fire, while Union troops began landing below the post. Skirmishing had begun by the middle of the day, and the fire from the gunboats continued intermittently into the evening. Late the following morning, 11 January, the federal forces attacked the Arkansas Post from both land and water. Greatly outnumbered and having had almost all their cannon silenced by Union fire, the Confederates knew that they could not resist their blue-clad enemy for any length of time. Thus it happened, in the words of the southern commander, that "white flags were displayed in the Twenty-fourth Regiment Texas Dismounted Cavalry." Federal soldiers took advantage of the situation and crowded upon the lines, forcing the surrender of the fortress. In this manner an unidentified person or group of persons in Peter Kiołbassa's own unit effected the capitulation of the Arkansas Post and the capture of its five thousand defenders.[36]

Immediately after the surrender the Confederates were ordered to stack their arms and proceed to collection points. That night they slept encamped in light snow on the riverbank. Before the battle they had left their warmer clothing in their quarters, not knowing that they would never return for it. On the morning of 12 January the prisoners boarded river transports and were sent down the Arkansas River to the Mississippi and then up the Mississippi past Memphis and Saint Louis to Alton, Illinois. There they were disembarked and placed on railway cars bound for northern prisoner-of-war camps.[37]

Peter Kiołbassa and most of his captured companions from Texas were sent to an internment point at Camp Butler, near Springfield, Illinois. One of the most difficult problems for the prisoners was the change in climate from mild to frigidly cold. One of the men recalled that when they arrived at Camp Butler from Alton, after eleven hours in unheated railway cars, "we were nearly all dead." Kiołbassa and a number of his fellow prisoners, however, were not destined to remain very many days in the wintry prison, though when they arrived they probably had very little hope for the immediate future.[38]

Unknown to the Arkansas Post prisoners, federal officers were considering the release of some of their numbers, particularly foreign-born men who had been compelled to join the Confederate army. As early as 4 February the commander of Camp Butler wrote to one of his superior officers that many of the men then confined were "pressed" into the Confederate service and that they were "anxious to take the oath of allegiance" to the United States and to join loyal

Union regiments then nearby. He added, significantly, that they were "foreigners, Germans, Polanders, &c."[39] At the same time the quartermaster of the camp likewise recommended that the prisoners of war who were believed to be "worthy of confidence" be allowed to enter federal service.[40] In response to these requests the commander of the Department of the Ohio three days later consented to allow the release of the men who had been "forced against their will to serve in the rebel army" in order for them to enter federal regiments. Consequently Peter Kiołbassa and a number of his Polish and German compatriots received the opportunity to leave the prison camp only a few days after they had arrived.[41]

Kiołbassa had already sworn allegiance to the United States government on 4 February. This was the same day that the federal officers at Camp Butler initiated their efforts to free some of their prisoners. Two days after approval was given for the plan, Kiołbassa was out of detention and had volunteered to enter Company D of the Sixteenth Illinois Cavalry. One reason he chose that regiment was that it had a large number of German members with whom he could communicate in their language. Undoubtedly he was pleased when a month later a countryman, Ignatz Kiołbassa (no relation), who also had been interned at Camp Butler, was released and joined him in the same company.[42]

The Sixteenth Illinois Cavalry remained "home" for Peter Kiołbassa for almost two years. During this period he advanced in rank from corporal to first sergeant, and he participated in the battles of Atlanta, Knoxville, and Nashville. Then on 18 January 1865 at Lexington, Kentucky, Kiołbassa was promoted to the rank of captain and placed in command of Company E of the Sixth U.S. Colored Cavalry. He retained this command, serving in Kentucky and Arkansas, until he left the army in the spring of 1866.[43]

Available documents make it possible to trace the military career of one other Silesian who was captured at the Arkansas Post and then released to join Union forces. This man was Albert Lyssy, of Karnes County. From spring 1862 to early 1863, Lyssy first served as a private in the Twenty-fourth Texas Cavalry and then in the Sixth Texas Infantry among numerous other Poles. Like Peter Kiołbassa and several others he was transported after the fall of the Arkansas Post to the Camp Butler prisoner-of-war detention center and subsequently set free. After his release in spring 1863, nineteen-year-old Lyssy chose to join Company C of the Sixteenth Illinois Cavalry. For a year he served as a private in that company, but on 12 May 1864 he was captured by Confederate forces near Tunnel Hill, in the vicinity of Dalton, Georgia. At the time of his capture Lyssy had received two gunshot wounds, one in a hip and the other shattering the bones just above the wrist of his right hand. A prisoner of war for the second time, the young Silesian remained in rebel hands until almost the end of the war. During this detention he received only indifferent attention to his injuries, and as a result the splintered bones in his right arm and wrist grew together abnormally. Lyssy finally was released by the Confederates in an exchange of prisoners in North Carolina on 26 February 1865. Federal authorities two weeks later sent him to Benton Barracks, Missouri, and from there directed him to rejoin his regiment at Nashville, Tennessee. There he received his military discharge when the unit was mustered out of service on 19 August 1865. He returned to central Texas, but because of his arm injury Lyssy never was able to go back fully to his trade as a carpenter.[44]

Not all the rebels captured at the Arkansas Post stayed in federal hands. Some of them, like the twenty-eight-year-old American William J. Butler, of Karnes County, "escaped after the fall of Ark[ansas] Post." One such now-anonymous Silesian who remained in Confederate service was mentioned in a letter from Charles A. Russell, of Helena, written from Company I of the Twenty-fourth Texas Cavalry in April 1864. He noted that, although his unit had good health at the time, it had "a Polander who is sick but not dangerous. I think it is a cold."[45]

Some Silesians left the Twenty-fourth Texas Cavalry under somewhat clouded circumstances. John Brys, for example, was mustered into Company I of the regiment at Hempstead, Texas, along with a number of his boyhood friends from the Karnes County area. His name appears on the muster roll from March 1862, but it vanishes from later rolls. The remarks on the record state that he "deserted." Brys reappeared later in the same year on the rolls of the Thirty-first Texas Cavalry in the Confederate army, which on 12 November he joined as a private at camp near Van Buren, Arkansas. One wonders what caused him to leave one unit and join another. It may very well have been to collect the bounty offered for volunteers, for his records from the second regiment indicate that he was entitled to such a bounty for joining the unit. Whatever the case, Brys remained in the Thirty-first Texas Cavalry until February 1864, when his name again disappeared from the rolls.[46]

Scattered records remain for a considerable number of Silesian participants on the southern side during the Civil War. Thomas Kolodziejczyk and Jacob Lyssy, both Karnes County Poles who had been drafted with John Brys, also appeared at Van Buren, Arkansas, in fall 1862. There they similarly enlisted in the Thirty-first Texas Cavalry, where the three found a fellow Silesian, Joseph Morawietz, who had been serving for six months. It is not known how Kolodziejczyk and Lyssy happened to be in western Arkansas at the time, but it was probably more than a coincidence that they enlisted in the same company on the same day as John Brys.[47] Other Silesians are known to have served in regiments and companies across Texas. Joseph Moczygemba was enrolled in Oakville, Live Oak County, on 23 February 1864, and on the same day was mustered into N. Gussett's Company of Texas State Troops for frontier defense.[48] John Moczygemba, on the other hand, in Goliad on 2 March 1863 joined Captain J. M. Paschall's Company of Volunteers in the state troops.[49] Martin Dugi, Frank Golla, and Anton Wygladacz served in another home-defense company raised by Captain John F. Tom in Atascosa County.[50] Two Silesians who were skilled as masons, John Kush and M. Adamietz, were detailed on 17 September 1863 to leave their positions in Company A of the Thirtieth Battalion of state troops to report for construction duty in San Antonio.[51]

Several Silesians served together in a unit called Willke's Battalion of Light Artillery (this unit should not be confused with Wilke's Twenty-fourth Texas Cavalry, which contained other Poles). The men in the artillery battery included John Adamietz, Frank Knapick, and Thomas Morawietz, of Bandera, and Frank T. Moczygemba, Tom Urbanczyk, and John Urbanczyk, of Panna Maria. Joining the company in September 1862, the men first saw duty for several months on the Rio Grande, as one of them recalled, "keeping back Mexicans and Indians," then for about four months at Corpus Christi, and finally for the remainder of the war in the Galveston area. One of the group, Frank Knapick, apparently had some difficulties conforming to the regimen of military life, for he spent several weeks confined to a military jail near Houston. Commenting on his activities many years later, John Adamietz recollected that Knapick served well, except when he was "under arrest" or "in the guardhouse for misconduct." While off duty in Galveston, the six Silesians were able to visit with another of their Karnes County friends, Anton Jarzombek, who was in the city as a conscript in the Second Texas Cavalry. In later years Tom Urbanczyk's strongest memory of his return from Galveston to Panna Maria at the end of the war was of the taste of the roasting ears that were just ripe in the cornfields.[52]

Other Silesians who saw action on the border area during the war were Joseph Gawlik, Tom Jendrzej, and John T. Moczygemba, all of Karnes County. They joined Captain Wash Brown's Company of Cavalry when it was formed at Helena in 1864. They stayed in the company until the end of the conflict, serving in the vicinity of San Diego, in south Texas, the entire time. When they were released from duty to return home after the Confederate surrender, Tom Jendrzej happened to be ill, and Joseph Gawlik remained with him for three weeks until he was well enough to travel back to his central Texas home.[53]

Considerable numbers of Silesian Poles served singly or in small groups in widespread units of the Confederate army. Anton Anderwald departed Bandera in spring 1863 to enlist as a teamster in the Second Texas Infantry, leaving his brother, Walek, "to protect our homes from the Indians."[54] Adam Skloss left his home in Meyersville in summer 1862 for the Eighth Texas Infantry and duty in southeast Texas.[55] Many of the Poles fought in cavalry units. Joseph Ledwig and John Gregorczyk, of Yorktown, together with Anton Jarzombek, of Panna Maria, served in the Second Texas Cavalry; Charles Korzekwa, of Panna Maria, served in Captain John Littleton's Company of Texas Cavalry; Thomas Kossup, of San Antonio, in Ragsdale's Battalion of Texas Cavalry; Stanisław Woitena, of Wilson County, in Phillips' Cavalry Regiment of Green's Brigade; John Michalski, of Martinez, in the Thirty-second Texas Cavalry; Valentine Gorrell, of San Antonio, in the Thirty-third Texas Cavalry; and Albert Halamuda, of San Antonio, and Joseph F. Pierdolla, of La Vernia, in the Thirty-sixth Texas Cavalry.[56] In circumstances not fully known, Anton Ploch, of Martinez, appeared in Davidson's Battalion of Louisiana Cavalry, where he sustained leg wounds in action.[57] Joseph Dupnik, of Karnes County, on the other hand, "being a mechanic by trade," safely saw the war to its end as a blacksmith at the "Government Post" in San Antonio.[58]

Many other Silesian Poles for whom no complete records have been discovered fought for the southern cause. Among them was Alexander Dziuk, a native of the Silesian village of Płużnica who immigrated with his family to Karnes County.[59] In later life he recalled the war: "At the age of eighteen . . . I was drafted into the Confederate Army and sent to Arkansas. . . . We were badly fed, especially at the beginning, and were armed with old flintlocks. . . . I remained in the Confederate Army until the end of the war and when I got back home even my own mother did not recognize me."[60] Possibly one reason his mother had trouble recognizing him was that during the war he had had such severe lung problems (from which presumably he had lost weight) that he was given a disability discharge from one unit.[61] After returning home from the war, he lived to a ripe old age as one of the wealthiest and most influential farmers at Panna Maria. During the later years one of his pleasures was swapping war stories with Martin Dugi, of the same community. One of the stories still remembered in Karnes County was about his time as a prisoner of war. He related that during the detention he was "kept in a pen" and given "a bucket of water and an ear of corn a day."[62]

Not all the Poles who entered the northern army did so indirectly through capture and subsequent release. At least two men are known to have joined federal service directly. Simon Kolodziej, of Yorktown, while at the Silesian settlements in Franklin County, Missouri, enlisted as a private in Company A of the Fifty-fourth Missouri Militia, which was raised in the town of Washington in 1864. He is noted on the muster roll dated 14 November of that year as having served forty-five days, but soon thereafter he left the company. Almost thirty years later he recalled that he had served for a total of two months. Unfortunately nothing more is known about his Union army activity.[63]

After Peter Kiołbassa the most celebrated Silesian Texan to fight for the Union cause was Joseph Cotulla, the boy immigrant of 1856 for whom the south Texas town of Cotulla later was named. In 1863 he left his home in the Las Gallinas community, in Atascosa County, and with six companions headed for Mexico. They crossed the border and then moved down the Rio Grande to Matamoros, where they divided. Cotulla crossed the river to Brownsville, Texas, which by then was in Union possession, volunteered for the First Texas Cavalry in the Union army, and under orders sailed for New Orleans. He served in that unit for two years, seeing action primarily in Louisiana and receiving his discharge in San Antonio after the close of hostilities.[64]

When the Civil War finally ended in late spring 1865, the Silesians saw it as the act of a merciful God to relieve their long suffering. As one Pole recalled, "At last God took pity on us: The Confederacy was defeated."[65] The end of the fighting did not bring solutions to all the problems, but it did mean the return of most of the Polish soldiers from the battlefields to their families.[66] That probably was the most important thing for the Silesians.

5
Reconstruction

THE years immediately following the Civil War were among the most exciting and important in the history of the Poles in Texas. During those years the immigrants faced severe social and political pressures from the outside, but they overcame them and began for the first time entering the society around them. This decade was probably the most significant of all in molding the Silesian Texans into the people they are today.

During the postwar years the activities of the Silesians were closely tied to the work of a handful of Polish Catholic missionaries who worked among them. These priests were instrumental in shaping and holding together the communities at a time when they were as seriously threatened as at any other time in their existence. The missionaries had strong wills and personalities, as well as staunch faith, which influenced not only their Silesian parishioners but also the Americans.

These clergymen, from the Congregation of the Resurrection, known as Resurrectionists, came to Texas in 1866 through the efforts of Bishop Claude-Marie Dubuis of Galveston. After the war Dubuis, a native Frenchman, returned to Europe searching for both priests and financial assistance for his widespread diocese, which comprised the entire state of Texas. In late summer 1866, while on his way to Lyon, he stopped at Hyères, France, and there chanced to meet Darius and Denise Poniatowski, members of the Polish nobility who had supported the Congregation of the Resurrection. In conversation with them the bishop told of the plight of his Silesian faithful, who had even collected four hundred francs for him to buy Polish prayer books during his European travel. Denise Poniatowski then wrote to the Reverend Alexander Jełowicki, the superior of the mission of the congregation in Paris, concerning the requested books, and in this way she introduced the bishop to the order.[1]

The Congregation of the Resurrection was a relatively new order established in Rome in 1842 after the Polish Insurrection of 1830. After the Russians suppressed the revolt, many of the participants fled to safety abroad. Among these exiles were three men, Bogdan Jański, Peter Semenenko, and Jerome Kajsiewicz, who founded the new Polish religious order. It flourished in the Polish émigré community in western Europe, where Bishop Dubuis discovered it. The principal centers of the congregation were its motherhouse at Rome and its mission to the Poles in France at Paris. The ranks of the order grew considerably after 1863 with more exiles from another unsuccessful Polish insurrection.[2]

With his introduction from Denise Poniatowski, Bishop Dubuis went to confer with the superiors of this little-known order during his visit to Paris. There, after preliminary correspondence, he met on 3 September 1866 with Father Jełowicki. He described the problems of his Silesians, who for three years had been without any permanent priests, and he implored Jełowicki to send Polish-speaking missionaries to them. In the bishop's own words, "If I heard of ten thousand souls outstretching their hands for priests and if I knew their language, I would come to them through fire." After the meeting Jełowicki wrote to Father General Jerome Kajsiewicz in Rome to report the bishop's visit and to recommend that the order consider sending the requested priests. He even went so far as to suggest individuals who might be fitted for such work.[3]

Upon learning of the situation of the Silesian peasants in Texas, Father General Kajsiewicz consented to the establishment of Resurrectionist missions among them. He directed Jełowicki in Paris to draw up an agreement with Dubuis.[4] He also approved the selection of two Resurrectionist priests and one seminarian to go on the mission to Texas. These three men, who soon were to have great influence on the Poles in Texas, were Fathers Adolf Bakanowski and Vincent Barzyński and cleric Felix Zwiardowski.[5]

The Reverend Adolf Bakanowski, who was selected to head the Polish missions in Texas, was born in 1840 in the village of Mohylówka, in Russian Poland. Reared in a substantial gentry family, he was destined from childhood for the clergy. He studied at the Catholic seminary in the town of Kamieniec Podolski, but only a short time after he was ordained a priest on 24 May 1863, he joined a unit that was forming to fight in the Polish Insurrection of 1863. With the suppression of the revolt the young priest fled into Austrian Poland, and from there, after difficulties with the local authorities, he traveled to Rome. In Italy he entered the Congregation of the Resurrection with the intention of continuing his academic studies. When Father Jełowicki wrote from Paris to Rome reporting his consultation with Bishop Dubuis on the subject of sending Resurrectionists to Texas, he did not share Bakanowski's plans but instead recommended that he go because "his study is lost time. . . . he suffers headaches which surely will stop with his apostolic work." Jełowicki added that there was no reason to keep Bakanowski for work in Galicia and that "he is not good enough for Paris." Thus the superiors chose Adolf Bakanowski to head their missions in Texas.[6]

The other full Resurrectionist whom Jełowicki recommended for the American missions was the Reverend Vincent Barzyński, another political exile. Barzyński was born in the village of Sulisławice, near Sandomierz, Russian Poland, in 1838. He studied at the local primary school and then under a private tutor before entering the diocesan seminary at Lublin. After ordination he served as a vicar, or assistant pastor, in three towns before he too was forced in 1863 to flee Russian Poland for his life. The Russians discovered him smuggling guns to the rebel forces in the vicinity of Tomaszów Lubelski. He fled to Kraków, in Austrian Poland, where he hid for six months and then was arrested for illegal entry into the Habsburg empire. Austrian authorities imprisoned him for about a year before releasing him and giving him documents to leave the country. Barzyński first went to Paris, where he learned about the highly nationalistic Congregation of the Resurrection, and then went to Rome, where on 18 September 1866 he took his vows as a Resurrectionist father. A few days before his vows Barzyński was already being considered for missionary duty in Texas. In the same letter in which Jełowicki recommended Bakanowski, he suggested that the "Rev. Barzyński would be very good, because he has apostolic devotion and he is not fastidious."[7]

Of the first Resurrectionist missionaries in Texas the least is known about the early life of cleric Felix Zwiardowski. Unfortunately he wrote no known memoirs, and his preserved correspondence dates from his departure for Texas in 1866. It is known, however, that he was born in Białystok, Russian Poland, on 29 December 1840 and that he studied there. Zwiardowski had made his way to Rome by autumn 1865, because on 9 September of that year he made his profession to enter the Congregation of the Resurrection, but he was not ordained a priest until after his arrival in Texas.[8]

In the second half of September 1866 the three Resurrectionists departed Rome for Paris. In the French capital they met three non-Resurrectionist Polish priests whom the bishop had recruited to go with them to Texas and there to be under their supervision. Together the party departed by train on 27 September for Le Havre. Sailing from the French channel port the next day, they arrived via Brest in New York on 11 October and quickly transferred to another ship bound for Galveston. The second leg of the trip was unusually rough. The force of storms through which they passed not only smashed the doors and windows in the cabins of the ship but even snapped one of its masts in half. Finally the vessel arrived safely in Galveston Harbor on 1 November. After spending four days recuperating in the bishop's house, the missionaries were dispatched to their posts. Superior Bakanowski with cleric Zwiardowski went to Panna Maria, while Vincent Barzyński went to the urban Silesians of San Antonio. The three non-Resurrectionist priests were ordered to Bandera, to Martinez, and to the Czech settlement Praha, in Fayette County.[9]

When the Resurrectionists arrived at what they feared would be desolate missions in Texas, they were relieved and pleased to find warm Polish welcomes from the peasants who had been three years without any permanent Polish-speaking pastors.[10] In the months preceding the arrival of the Resurrectionists there had been an outbreak of cholera among the Silesians, and several of them had died without the last sacraments. With these recent deaths in their thoughts the Poles welcomed the clergymen with all their hearts. Bakanowski wrote from Panna Maria three days after his arrival that all his time had been occupied with confession and other priestly duties. He further related that the parishioners had welcomed him and Zwiardowski with "tears of happiness" so enthusiastically that in their efforts to see the two men they had "destroyed the lock on the door." From San Antonio, Father Barzyński similarly reported the joy of his urban parishioners and said that the "Silesians fell in love with me. They do not want to exchange me for a priest from Silesia who wants to come here."[11]

The conditions in the Silesian settlements, however, were not so idyllic as they first appeared to the missionaries. When they arrived in Texas, in fact, the state was experiencing probably the greatest social and political disorder of its entire history. With the end of the Civil War in the first months of 1865, Confederate administration in Texas had deteriorated to near nonexistence. Conditions became so chaotic, for example, that thieves were able to break into the treasury in Austin and steal the last gold money that the state possessed. The situation was no better in the countryside, where in some areas, particularly on the frontier, law and order collapsed. It was not until 19 June that the first party of federal troops landed in Galveston and declared the authority of the United States over the state. On that day General Gordon Granger initiated the Reconstruction period in Texas by proclaiming all the slaves freed and declaring illegal all the acts of the state government since secession.

By the end of summer 1865 federal troops had occupied Texas and had begun restoring a semblance of order. The next year, under the presidential plan of Reconstruction, Texans elected new officials and adopted a new constitution professing loyalty to the United States. Affairs changed, however, in spring 1867, when the United States Congress took charge of the machinery for the return of the former rebel states to the Union. Under its revised plan the South was divided into five military districts, each supervised by a general, and new elections were ordered in which only Union supporters and freed Negroes were allowed to vote. In Texas the voters in late 1869 adopted another new state constitution and elected a "Radical" Republican, Edmund J. Davis, governor. The fact that he was the fourth governor in as many years suggests the instability of political affairs. Davis served in the statehouse for four years. He was defeated in 1873 by Richard Coke, a Democrat, whose election brought political Reconstruction to a close in Texas.[12]

The defeated white southerners greatly resented the presence of federal troops in Texas. They offered little organized resistance to the new regime only because they had no means to do so. They regarded congressional legislation, especially after 1867, as hostile to their interests and furthermore viewed the loss of voting rights for many whites coupled with enfranchisement of the Blacks as acts of oppression and insult.

The attitude of this majority of the population, together with the general disorder following the war, provided the ideal environment for unrestrained lawlessness. It became exceedingly difficult for authorities to enforce the law even in areas of dense population and often impossible in areas that were sparsely inhabited. Even when the local officials did attempt to make arrests, they frequently failed because of lack of local support. Many offenders who were arrested eventually escaped because they had been placed in insecure jails. Moreover, perhaps because of fear of reprisals, grand juries often failed to find indictments, and petit juries failed to make convictions. Although this situation was not encouraged by most of the whites, their negative attitude toward the Reconstruction governments definitely contributed to the disorder.[13]

The lawless conditions in the post–Civil War years affected all the Silesians in the state. In virtually every community incidents were recorded in which Poles fell victims to robbers, thieves, and even murderers. A classic example of the then common outrages occurred on 24 March 1868 near Martinez. On that day Bill Thompson, brother of the famed Texas badman Ben Thompson, passed through the neighborhood causing trouble. First representing himself as a deputy sheriff, he "arrested" a man on the charge of stealing fence rails and then "arrested" several freedmen and robbed them of their firearms. After this entertainment the outlaw tried to rob an elderly Pole, a man in his eighties. When the old man stubbornly defied the heavily armed Thompson, he responded by shooting him in the arm and side. For the next several days Thompson and a gang of companions terrorized the road from San Antonio to Helena, stopping almost all travel between the two points.[14]

Even in urban San Antonio the Silesians were not safe from the lawlessness. In spring 1868, for example, Jacob Kyrish was attacked and severely injured when he was struck on the back of the head with a whipstock.[15] Early the next year a gang of thieves operated for some time in the Polish Quarter, on the southeast side of San Antonio. The local press warned that they were working "near the Polander church, stealing everything they can get hold of."[16]

In a more brutal incident, on 2 February 1870, a Silesian named Kossup was attacked as he returned from San Antonio to his home in Bandera. He had been in San Antonio selling a load of winter forage from his small wagon and buying supplies to take home. The next morning his body was discovered eight miles from the city on the Bandera road. A thief had shot him through the head with a pistol and robbed him of everything he possessed. The murderer not only took the provisions from the wagon but also cut open the dead man's pockets with a knife to remove their contents. The assailant went so far as to steal his victim's coat.[17]

Later the same month, in yet another occurrence of this nature, an American accidentally became the victim. In the hotel at Helena a man named Bill Reevey began teasing an intoxicated Silesian, who derisively was called "Polander Joe." In response to Reevey's baiting, the Pole made a comment that aroused the southerner, and he drew his pistol. At this moment Reevey's brother-in-law jumped between the two men, and in the fracas that ensued, Reevey fatally discharged the gun into his brother-in-law's abdomen. The newspaper report of the incident added indifferently: "It is not known whether Reevey intended to shoot the Polander or not."[18]

Even though all the Silesians in the state suffered from the general lawlessness during Reconstruction, the Poles of Karnes County endured more serious problems, which had heavy political overtones. The reasons for the trouble were their known Unionist sympathies and their unfortunate geographical location in one of the strongest centers of surviving Confederate sentiment along the entire Texas frontier.[19] As a friendly northern observer noted at the time, "They seem to have settled almost the meanest place in Texas."[20] Resenting their defeat in arms and the loss of their slave property, the southerners took their vengeance on the Unionist Silesians. Father Bakanowski, pastor at Panna Maria at the time, understood the situation clearly:

> They knew very well that we Poles held with the side of the North, so that was why they considered us their enemies.[21]
>
> . . . they began to make every effort to drive them [the Poles] from the

country, even by force of arms. . . . When they saw a Pole without knowledge of the language, a peasant with no education, these southerners looked upon him as they did upon the Blacks, and felt that they had the same right to deny him his human rights as they did the Blacks.[22]

Further endangering the situation of the Karnes County Silesians was the fact that their area had become one of the most lawless in the state. Because of its position on the fringe of settlement it grew into a haven for transients outside the law. One such visiting badman was William Preston Longley, who fled there in 1867 after killing three freedmen in Lee County. Also frequenting the vicinity was Sally Skull, who, with a band of Mexican helpers, traded horses from Texas into Mexico.[23] Conditions deteriorated to such an extent that at least one American family left the county for its own safety.[24] The seriousness of the situation was demonstrated by continuous accounts in the local press of violent crimes in the area.[25]

During the post–Civil War years Helena, the county seat, had the reputation of being particularly rough. A German immigrant who went to Helena in late 1868 said that, although the regular occupation of the inhabitants was cattle raising, they enjoyed most stealing horses and looting the freight wagons that passed along the nearby road from Indianola heading toward inland points. He added significantly that the local authorities "had no power to check this lawlessness."[26] A Union sympathizer characterized Helena as "a mean little Confed town, with 4 stores, 4 whisky mills, and any amount of lazy vagabonds laying around, living by their wits."[27] He added that those inhabitants "own nothing, but have money enough for whisky, tobacco, and occasionally a game of monte."[28]

Preserved records indicate that violence between the southerners and the Poles in Karnes County first flared in the summer of 1867 over the question of voting rights.[29] As mentioned earlier, in the spring of that year the United States Congress had assumed control of Reconstruction, and as part of its plan it allowed only freed Negroes and men loyal to the federal government to vote. In each southern state registrars of voters were appointed in the counties to enroll only voters who could swear an "ironclad" oath that they had never in any way supported the Confederacy. In effect these registrars were disfranchising a great many of the white voters while allowing the former slaves and the detested northern sympathizers to go to the polls. The anger of the southerners was immediate, and frequently the registrars received the brunt of the rage.

Four registrars of voters were appointed in 1867 to serve in Karnes County. One of these men was a Pole, and he became the object of probably the greatest hatred of the local Americans. This man, Emanuel Rzeppa, had come to Texas from the town of Toszek, in Upper Silesia, but little more is known about his early life.[30] He had interests in both San Antonio and Panna Maria.[31] He served as registrar in the latter community. In addition to disfranchising former Confederates and enrolling freedmen and loyal residents, the board of registrars in Karnes County also registered newly naturalized immigrants to vote for the first time. All these "foreigners" swore allegiance to the United States and were considered to be loyal Republicans.[32] It almost goes without saying that this activity incensed the already resentful native southerners.

During registration at Panna Maria in early August 1867 the first of a number of clashes between the Silesians and the Americans occurred. It began when a group of Americans rode on horseback into the Polish village. Once there they not only acted abusively toward the registrars but also went so far as to beat two immigrants who were taking out their naturalization papers. The assailants jeered at the foreigners, who wanted, they said, to make "d——d Yankees" out of themselves. One of the Americans, a man named John Kuhnel, threatened Emanuel Rzeppa's life and pronounced that he would bet any sum of money that after two months no one who showed oaths of allegiance would be left in the place.[33]

Kuhnel played a continuing role among the Silesians throughout Reconstruction. He was an immigrant German who was well liked by the Americans. As early as 1856 he owned property at Panna Maria, and he remained in the community through the Civil War, serving as its Confederate postmaster and as a private in the Panna Maria Grays for home defense. During the conflict, when there was no resident pastor at Panna Maria, he assumed custody of the church property. He seems to have been almost the master of the village during the war years. Father Bakanowski recalled that, when the Resurrectionists arrived in 1866, Kuhnel was "everything: merchant, judge, and counselor." The new missionaries, for the first few weeks after their arrival, took their meals with Kuhnel and his family, for at first it was inconvenient for them to make any other arrangements for meals. During that time, however, Father Bakanowski seems to have developed a personality conflict with Kuhnel, who soon after the priest's arrival was elected justice of the peace for the precinct that included Panna Maria. After only a month of board with the Kuhnel family the priests began taking their meals elsewhere, because they "saw what a disastrous influence" Kuhnel had on the "trusting Poles." Father Bakanowski and Rzeppa quickly became allies against the German judge.[34]

After the registrars for Karnes County were abused and Rzeppa's life threatened, the Silesian immediately lodged formal complaints with the military authorities and requested protection. When General John S. Mason, commander of the federal garrison in San Antonio, received Rzeppa's letters, he forwarded them with favorable endorsements to higher officials, and while he was waiting for a response, he himself led an investigation of the conditions in Karnes County. Most likely he was the officer whom Father Bakanowski described as an "important general from the North" who visited Panna Maria at this time.[35] As a result of Mason's efforts two Americans, one of whom was no less than the county sheriff, were arrested by federal troops and escorted to San Antonio.[36] In the meantime the Office of Civil Affairs of the Fifth Military District in Galveston authorized the San Antonio commander to do whatever was necessary to ensure the safety of Rzeppa and the board of registrars.[37] Mason, through a subordinate, then wrote a stern notice to Kuhnel. In it he stated that the military authorities, having learned that he had uttered "certain threats" against Rzeppa, thereby warned him that "upon the slightest overt act by you directly or indirectly you will be summarily arrested and severely dealt with."[38] Kuhnel, however, continued to represent southern interests among the Silesians, as will be seen.

In the next months the hostility of the southerners against the registrars broadened into general harassment of the Unionist Polish population. Accounts of the incidents suggest that some of them were what the Americans considered to be horseplay, but the Silesian peasants did not interpret them in the same way. On many occasions, for example, the cowboys rode into Panna Maria, firing their guns at the cottages, chasing and roping the Polish children, and shooting at the feet of any peasants they happened to meet. At least once they even rode their horses into the church during mass and conducted themselves in an obscene manner. Uninvited Americans almost always appeared armed at Silesian weddings and parties, where they played pranks on the farmers almost without limits. When Polish men were known to be away from their homes, mounted southerners approached the cottages and "banged on the shutters" to frighten the women and children inside. Some of the troublemakers, seeing women and children outside a cottage cooking or washing over an open fire, would ride up and throw "a handful of bullets" into the fire just to see the foreigners scatter. On one occasion a group of horsemen from Helena rode up to a Polish girl who was milking. Frightening her severely, they threatened to kill her on the spot. Instead, one of them shot the family cow at her side.[39]

It must be recognized that not all the Americans in the Karnes County area engaged in activities hostile to the Poles. Very few writers on the subject, however, either at the time or in later years, made any distinction between the lawless part of the local population and the law-abiding portion. One early-twentieth-century journalist, after interviewing many local settlers, fortunately did note the important difference. He stated clearly that the people who molested the Poles were "the scum of the local society" who had to "drink heavily in order to give themselves courage."[40] A disquieting report published in a contemporary Polish newspaper stated that, according to letters written from Texas, the saddest aspect of the situation was that "some bad Polish settlers joined" the gangs too.[41] All the available sources that bear on this unfortunate episode in Polish Texas history agree that the lawless element attacked and harassed the Silesians confidently, knowing that the local authorities would do nothing to stop them.[42]

Not long after the military investigation of the August 1867 incident involving the registrars at Panna Maria, Father Bakanowski called his parishioners together to plan their strategy for defense. He told them that the church bell would be the alarm signal, and he asked the men to join him with their guns and ride to Helena in a show of force. He ordered his "cavalry" to move as a body and not to fire their guns unless he told them to do so. The group of armed Silesians rode at a trot to the edge of Helena and then galloped back and forth through the sleepy American town to demonstrate to its inhabitants that the Poles were capable of defending themselves. The exercise gave them a measure of self-confidence and the benefit of at least a short time of peace before the next violent clash came that autumn.[43]

The calm lasted a few weeks, but sometime before the middle of November 1867 another party of Americans made its way into Panna Maria looking for trouble. This time they found it, because the Poles were better prepared. The trouble began while Father Adolf, inside the church, was ringing the evening Angelus bell. Hearing noise and the sound of gunfire outside, he rushed out the door of the church to find a party of mounted cowboys shooting at the tower bell. As the priest began running toward the rectory to get his revolver, one of the southerners with his horse barred the way and fired his gun. Undaunted, the clergyman tried to hit the troublemaker in the head with a wooden pole. At this point a group of armed peasants came to the rescue, driving the southerners from the scene. The troublemakers did not fully retreat, however, until they had shot and injured a man and a woman. A band of angry young Silesians pursued the attackers toward Helena as far as Cibolo Creek, where a brief gunfight erupted in the twilight. As the cowboys swam their mounts across the stream, the Poles fired at them. Two of the riders were hit and "sank into the river." The others disappeared into the darkness.[44]

Again the Poles gained a few days of peace, but soon the harassment resumed, and the immigrant farmers began losing hope. By then, however, Union supporters in San Antonio were becoming aware of their plight, and in time this awareness led to help for the Silesians. One of the first Americans to speak up for the Poles was William W. Gamble, a San Antonio stationer who served as county judge of Bexar County and actively participated in local Unionist affairs.[45] In early 1868, Gamble wrote to the Texas secretary of state requesting military protection for the Silesians. He described them as "peaceable & inoffensive" and declared that they were "entirely at the mercy of the lawless desperadoes" who inhabited the area. Gamble further noted that the colony was "in danger of being broken up" and that "the local Civil Authorities appear to connive at their persecution."[46] At about the same time General John S. Mason, who from the Post of San Antonio had visited Karnes County, suggested to his superiors that a company of infantry be transferred to Helena, saying that "there is no more lawless population in the state than that of Karnes."[47] Another year passed, however, before the troops arrived to stay.

A final major incident between the Poles and the Americans occurred in Panna Maria on Easter Sunday, 28 March 1869.[48] As the Silesians left the church on what they considered to be one of the holiest days of the year, they met about eighty mounted cowboys, all armed, waiting to "provoke and make fun" of them. Accompanying the cowboys were several carriages bearing their wives and daughters, who had come along to watch the sport as the foreigners were put in their place. After most of the Poles had left the church, one of the Americans pointed a double-barreled shotgun at a group of peasant women in front of the building and pulled the trigger. Only an apparently malfunctioning percussion cap saved them from injury. When the southern "ladies" broke into "laughter and crazy applause," Father Bakanowski was overcome with rage. After running to get his gun, he went to the second-floor balcony of the newly completed school and shot several times over the heads of the American women. Almost immediately the American party disappeared in a cloud of dust. Quickly the men of Panna Maria gathered at the school to defend the village should the cowboys return. After only a quarter of an hour eight mounted southerners did come back to exchange taunts with the Poles, but they retreated into the brush, convinced that it would be too dangerous to molest the infuriated Silesians further that day.[49]

Father Adolf knew that it was necessary to do something to prevent more such dangerous incidents. He felt that if they continued the settlement might indeed fall apart. The day after the encounter he thought about what to do and decided that a party of Silesians would have to ask the military authorities in San Antonio for protection. Two years earlier a Union army general had visited the settlement and had offered his assistance; if the help ever was needed, it definitely was now. In the next few days Father Adolf gathered the signatures of his parishioners on a petition for protection and tried to recruit peasants to accompany him when he delivered it to the general. Every man he approached was afraid to go for fear of reprisals. One of them answered, "I have a wife and children and the Americans have no mercy. They can take revenge anywhere." Thus in the first week of April 1869, Father Bakanowski and Father Zwiardowski left

Panna Maria by themselves and traveled the back roads on horseback to see the commander in San Antonio.[50]

The two priests arrived in the city about noontime the next day. They went immediately to discuss the situation with the Reverend Vincent Barzyński and there learned that Bishop Dubuis from Galveston happened to be visiting the city. After asking the bishop to join them, the group of clergymen called on the commander.[51] The general received the visitors in his office and, after hearing an account of the difficulties in Karnes County, responded that he already knew of the situation and had made plans to send the army, but not for a month. Father Bakanowski replied, "In a month . . . it could be too late, because during this time they could kill all of us!"[52] At that moment the priest may have been thinking not only of his parishioners but also of himself; about the same time he reported to Rome that, because of his political activities, "the anger of some Americans . . . is so great that they want to kill me."[53] After hearing Father Bakanowski's arguments against delay, the general rang for an orderly to call a certain young cavalry officer, who had already been detailed to establish the post in Karnes County.[54] When he entered the office, the commander asked how soon he could leave with troops. The officer responded that he could be in Helena within a few days. Thus it happened that on 10 April 1869 the United States Army came to Karnes County, at least partly for the protection of the loyal Polish farmers.[55]

When the priests consulted with the general in San Antonio, it is likely that they already knew that several months before plans had been made for the location of an army camp at Helena. Their actual request, in fact, may have been to expedite those plans. As early as 16 January 1869, officers of the Fifth Military District had issued orders for the establishment of a post at Helena as part of an over-all scheme for the division of the state into districts under military commanders. For the avowed purpose of "suppressing insurrection, disorder, and violence," these garrison commanders were invested with the powers of local law-enforcement authorities and with the power to remove civil officials if they failed to execute their duties. This order was printed in the local press and was general knowledge. It provided for several posts, including one at Helena, which would oversee a district embracing Karnes, DeWitt, Gonzales, Bee, Goliad, and Victoria counties, all of which had some Polish settlers. Only a few days after the orders were posted, the newspapers began carrying announcements for bids on the supply of quartermaster stores to the new Post of Helena. The fact that the American population knew of plans for the garrison may explain why some of them reportedly mocked Bakanowski, saying that Texas was "not Europe, where the army protects people."[56]

The troops ordered to Karnes County were not the first federal troops in the area. Throughout the postwar years Union troops had passed through the region. Preserved records show, for example, frequent visits by soldiers in 1867. In the spring of that year a federal marshal requested a military escort to Helena, and in the early autumn soldiers investigated the incident in which the Karnes County registrars were attacked. Later that year an officer from San Antonio returned to Karnes and DeWitt counties with a body of men "to look after these rebel districts." In early 1868 the commander at San Antonio reported that on two occasions his men had traveled to Karnes County to protect the registrars. That spring fifty-nine men and two officers of the Thirty-fifth U.S. Infantry were detailed from Hallettsville, Texas, to Helena, where they bivouacked for almost a month. On at least one occasion before the formal establishment of the Post of Helena, federal troops in the county were fired on by lawless inhabitants. In this encounter the former Confederates ambushed the soldiers as they crossed Hondo Creek on their way to arrest a local resident. With this background of military activity in the area the new troops arrived in Helena in spring 1869 and began setting up a rudimentary camp.[57]

The Post of Helena was physically unimpressive. Situated on a low hilltop adjoining the town, it consisted of tents and temporary rough board shelters. Its quartermaster supplies were not even at the post, but were stored in a rented stone structure in the town. The average strength of the garrison was forty-five men commanded by two or three officers. Despite the unimposing appearance of the camp, however, the men who established it were not ones for the recalcitrant southerners to look down upon. Before coming to Karnes County, they had served at Forts Chadbourne and Concho on the Texas frontier and were seasoned troopers.[58]

The activities of the soldiers stationed at the Post of Helena were varied.[59] Among their earliest duties was posting guard in Panna

Maria, where troops are known to have stood at the church door to deter harassment of the Silesians.[60] In addition to such peaceful duty, some of the men had more excitement serving as guards for the registration of voters and balloting in Karnes and adjoining counties, while others were engaged in apprehending, arresting, and escorting alleged criminals to places of safekeeping.[61] The commanders of the post, in addition to their strictly military duties, also had the responsibility of removing all civil officials who could not swear the "ironclad" oath to the United States and of recommending men to take their places.[62]

The chaotic state of civil affairs in Karnes County at the time of the establishment of the Post of Helena is illustrated by the reports of its young commander, Second Lieutenant William Alexis Thompson. Just after he arrived in Helena, he wrote to a superior that, only shortly before, the sheriff had absconded with four hundred dollars of county funds and that he "was accompanied by the Minister's daughter of this town." Two days later he reported that a killing had occurred in Helena, that the murderer had threatened to shoot anyone who would report the death, and that "there was not a man in the town who had morral [*sic*] courage to inform me of the facts."[63] In a matter of months, however, the troops had successfully restored order in Karnes County. Just over a year after the Post of Helena was established, it was abandoned as no longer necessary, and its surplus government property was sold at public auction.[64]

After the arrival of the United States troops at the Post of Helena, one more potentially violent incident occurred between the Poles and the Americans. This incident involved John Kuhnel, the southern-sympathizing justice of the peace for Panna Maria; Emanuel Rzeppa, the Unionist registrar; and Father Bakanowski. Since the winter of 1866–1867 there had been hard feelings between Kuhnel and Bakanowski, and this continuing antagonism was the basis of the incident. When Bakanowski arrived in late 1866, he began assuming Kuhnel's former dominant role in the village.[65] The resulting competition for control assumed a political cast during the August 1867 encounter between Rzeppa and Kuhnel when the southerners harassed and threatened the registrars.[66] During the intervening two years Kuhnel represented not only the political interests of the Americans in nearby Helena but also opposition to the growing status of Father Bakanowski. When a schismatic Polish cleric, John Frydrychowicz, came to

Texas in 1867, for example, it was Kuhnel who intrigued with him among the parishioners in an attempt to replace Bakanowski with the new arrival.[67] During the same two-year period Rzeppa continued to represent Unionist interests as the registrar of voters. The fact that he assumed Kuhnel's former position as postmaster in April 1868 undoubtedly did little to soothe the upset emotions.[68]

The conflict involving the three men reached its climax in the weeks immediately following the establishment of the Post of Helena. Father Bakanowski complained to the post commander that Kuhnel as justice of the peace constantly provoked arguments among his parishioners so that they would initiate through him legal proceedings against each other and, of course, pay him court costs.[69] The commander replied that under the circumstances he could do little but that if the priest could rouse the German into a dispute he might then "legally" remove him and replace him with an officer more congenial to Father Adolf's tastes. The Polish clergyman wasted no time baiting his rival.

Because Kuhnel had never turned over to the priest the map showing the precise location of church property at Panna Maria, Bakanowski started building a storage barn on what he knew to be Kuhnel's land, which conveniently adjoined that of the church. Kuhnel immediately went to the construction site and ordered the workers to stop. The priest responded that he was doing the work on church land and that the German, on any account, had never given him the map showing church property. Next the judge sent his daughter with a letter stating that the land was his and asking that all work cease. Bakanowski ignored the request. As the work progressed, Kuhnel called on the sheriff to warn the pastor to stop on the threat of being brought to court. Father Adolf told the law officer that to his knowledge the land was his and that he intended to continue. Finally the sheriff returned and delivered the parish priest a summons to court that very day.

At the courtroom, in quick order, the jury convicted Father Bakanowski of building his barn on John Kuhnel's land. At that point the priest for the first time saw on a desk the map showing the location of church property. Examining it, he then finally admitted that the new barn indeed was on the German's land, quickly adding that Kuhnel had refused to give him the map. The pastor concluded, "Now I

. . . know where the boundary is, so I will order everything removed." As the priest turned to leave the courtroom, however, the sheriff stepped up to escort him to jail. Through the window Bakanowski pointed to a menacing crowd of his Polish parishioners and cautioned the law officer that unless he was released immediately "the situation might become very dangerous."

Once outside the courtroom Bakanowski rode at a gallop to the Post of Helena, where he found the commander just sitting down to dinner. Father Adolf hurriedly related the recent events, and without finishing his meal the commander called for his horse and returned with the priest to the court just as the jurors were leaving. Still mounted, the two men met Kuhnel in front of the building, while the other people disappeared behind nearby houses. The frightened Kuhnel attempted to explain what had happened, but before he could finish, the officer ordered him to hand over the papers he held in his hands. When he saw the map showing church lands, the officer asked, "Why do you keep the property of the church?" Then again he interrupted the German's explanations by asking him, "What is your religion?" When Kuhnel replied that he was a Catholic, the commander berated him for his treatment of the parish priest. Finally he declared: "You are no longer a judge. Go home and prepare everything to give your office to someone else."

After consultation Bakanowski and the commander decided that the most appropriate person for the vacant position was Rzeppa. The officer appointed Rzeppa justice of the peace for Karnes County Precinct Two on 4 May 1869, and he qualified for office by swearing the "ironclad" oath nine days later.[70]

Kuhnel made one final bid for power, but Father Bakanowski effectively frustrated it. In the general election held 30 November and 1, 2, and 3 December 1869, the German tried to regain office. Realizing that the Americans of Helena were trying to sway the Polish vote to Kuhnel, Father Bakanowski called a meeting of the parishioners. He discussed the matter with them and then distributed among them slips of paper with the names of the candidates for whom they should vote, including, naturally, Rzeppa. The next day the Poles rode as a body to Helena and voted as a block for their fellow countryman in a total ballot of twenty-nine to six, ensuring Rzeppa's position as their local judge. With his power now completely broken, Kuhnel remained in Panna Maria, where he operated a store for the remaining nine years of his life.[71]

The Silesians were by no means always the victims of harassment and violence. On occasion they themselves were the culprits, as may have been the case in the contrived removal of Kuhnel from office. In another episode in October 1867, for example, two Poles were arrested by military authorities near La Vernia, about seven miles southeast of Martinez, "for cruelly beating and wounding a freedman."[72]

Rzeppa was not the only Silesian to enter local political affairs during Reconstruction. Other Poles were active in Bandera, Bexar, and Karnes counties, as well as farther afield in the state. In Bandera County, John Adamietz served both as county commissioner and as deputy sheriff.[73] Also at Bandera, Albert Adamietz served as county treasurer.[74] In Bexar County, August Krawietz, a loyal Unionist who as early as February 1868 had sworn the "ironclad" oath, held the office of constable.[75] In Karnes County, after Rzeppa initiated Polish participation in local politics, many Silesians entered the field: Alexander Dziuk as county commissioner; Albert Kasprzyk and P. Jurecki as constables; Alexander Dziuk and Emanuel Rzeppa as members of the Karnes County Board of Revision and Appeals; Joseph Kasprzyk as a special guard during the sessions of the board; Joseph Kyrish, John Gawlik, and John Kusar as members of a committee that investigated fire damage to the courthouse; and Joseph Kyrish as a member of the committee that supervised the rebuilding of the courthouse in the early 1870's.[76]

John Moczygemba, of Karnes County, came to West Texas as justice of the peace at Fort Stockton in spring 1870.[77] Fragmentary preserved records indicate that he had little but problems during his tenure of office. Most of these difficulties stemmed from the confusion over the roles of military and civil authorities that accompanied the return of Texas to civil rule in late 1869. As Moczygemba attempted to assume his position, for example, the previous judge appointed under military rule refused to surrender it to him and continued for some time to carry out the duties. After a few weeks the transfer of office did occur, but then difficulties began for the Silesian in earnest.[78]

Moczygemba's troubles as a civil officer were for the most part created by Colonel James F. Wade, the strong-minded military commander of United States troops at Fort Stockton. His first dispute with the commander pertained to a dam constructed on Leon Creek northwest of the town. One George B. Lyles built the structure, which prevented the natural flow of water downstream to land owned by Peter Pleasantier. The latter filed suit in the justice of the peace court to have the dam removed, and on 19 April 1870 the court ruled in his favor, ordering Lyles to remove the dam. When the owner refused to destroy it, Judge Moczygemba on 30 April sent the county sheriff to remove it. A week later Colonel Wade detailed a body of troops to rebuild the dam and then guard it from further tampering. Subsequently, on 9 May, Moczygemba received a complaint from Pleasantier about the reconstruction, and he forwarded a copy of it to Wade.[79]

At the same time another, more serious dispute arose between the civil officer and the military commander. On the night of 30 April 1870, an armed soldier from the post shot and killed one of four sleeping Mexican wood haulers at their camp three miles outside Fort Stockton. When Judge Moczygemba sent a special constable to the army post to request the commander's assistance in an inquest into the death, the colonel cursed him, asking, "What in h——l have you got to do with it?" He then threatened to place the constable in the guardhouse if he pressed the matter further. Despite Wade's noncooperation, on 2 May the inquest was held, and a soldier named Sam Davis was identified as the alleged killer. At this point in the legal proceedings, however, Colonel Wade refused to surrender the trooper to local authorities.[80]

Moczygemba appealed to Governor Edmund J. Davis for assistance in both of these controversies and received mixed results. In the dispute over the building, removal, and reconstruction of the dam, the judge learned that the case was out of his jurisdiction. In the conflict over the surrender of the soldier accused of murder, however, state officials upheld Moczygemba's position as justice of the peace and authorized him to continue his proceedings against the soldier. Known documents do not record the final results in either case. After a period of time, however, John Moczygemba returned to his home in Karnes County, where in his later years he made his living in the much more peaceful occupation of selling and repairing sewing machines.[81]

For the Poles the Reconstruction period was one of the most significant in their history in Texas, because during it they withstood severe attacks from the outside to emerge for the first time as active participants in local affairs. In this manner they proved themselves competent to care not only for their own matters but also for those of concern to other people living around them. It was a major step toward Polish integration into the larger society. Throughout the rest of the nineteenth century and into the twentieth the Poles increased their amicable interaction with the heterogeneous population surrounding them. During this period, however, they also reinforced their Polish identity through religious and educational activities, family and community cooperation, and expansion of their areas of settlement.

6

The Growth and Development of Silesian Institutions and Settlement

As the Silesian Poles emerged from the unfortunate Reconstruction years, they were becoming known by all around them for their ability to take care of their own concerns and those of their neighbors. In all the colonies they were participating in local affairs in unprecedented numbers and were becoming integrated into the larger Texas society. At the same time the Silesians were entering the world around them, however, they also were strengthening their own ethnic and community ties in ways that helped them maintain their distinctive way of life into the twentieth century. The most important elements in preserving Silesian life in Texas were the activities of the Polish Catholic parishes, the expansion of Silesian settlement into new areas, and the establishment and operation of Polish schools. These factors combined to create a cultural framework of ethnicity and religion that in many of the colonies remains intact today.

The Catholic missionaries from the Congregation of the Resurrection who came to Texas in 1866 and who actively worked there for a decade were responsible for building the core of Silesian parishes. These churches, some of which had been founded in the 1850's, provided the nucleus around which later Polish religious activity in the colonies grew. Had the Resurrectionists or other Polish priests not arrived, the Silesian farmers most likely would have merged with the American, Mexican, and German populations around them and would have ceased to exist as distinct entities. The settlers were loyal Catholics, and they were willing to go to churches of any nationality in order to receive the sacraments, although they always preferred Polish clergy, a preference that remains strong to the present day.[1]

When the Resurrectionist missionaries arrived, they found great disorder in the small Texas churches. Seminarian Felix Zwiardowski reported just after he reached Panna Maria that in its sanctuary, "there is almost nothing except one big altar." He regretted that the missionaries had not brought from Europe complete priestly outfits, for the vestments left by the previous pastors were "all ruined by moths." He and Father Bakanowski, having no other place to sleep, spent their nights cramped in a tiny upper-floor room in the church squeezed between the ceiling of the sacristy and the roof above. Writing from the Martinez colony less than a year later, Zwiardowski similarly related that he found things there in "terrible disarray." He reported that the container for consecrated bread was made from a used candle box and that there were "always mice running and eating the communion cloth," while the altar was covered with an ordinary cotton tablecloth. In Panna Maria, Father Bakanowski described the place of worship as "very poor," but he added optimistically, "I hope little by little it will be rich."[2]

Bakanowski and Zwiardowski immediately set about improving the appearance of the church at Panna Maria, the center of the Polish missions. In his first letter from Texas, Father Adolf reported that the parish had only two holy pictures, one of Saint Stanisław and the other, a small one, of the Virgin Mary. He asked his superiors in Europe to have a larger picture of the Virgin painted, even specifying the size that he wanted and offering up to one thousand francs for the work. Several months later, when he sent a draft to cover part of the cost, he requested the fathers in Europe to add a "wide gilded" frame, for such a frame would cost three times as much in Texas. In the meantime the parishioners began building a new altar for the picture. Undoubtedly, as they worked on the altar, they wondered what the new picture would be like. Finally, a year and a half later, in spring 1868, the long-awaited painting arrived in New York, but then Father Adolf learned that he would have to pay two hundred dollars in transportation costs, more than he had paid for the picture. Swallowing his anger, he sent the money, and after a bit more delay it arrived in Panna Maria. Upon seeing the work, which had been painted by Leopold Nowotny, a known Polish religious artist who worked in Rome, Father Bakanowski described it as "full of dignity and majesty." He added, curiously, however, "I do not know what impression it will make on the people . . . but this picture belongs to me, so I care little what they will think about it." The painting was presented to the parishioners on the Day of the Immaculate Conception in 1868, which was one of the most important annual religious holidays at the Panna Maria settlement.[3]

The new painting of the Virgin Mary was only part of the effort by the Resurrectionists to improve the appearance of the church that formed the center of their missions. Less than a year after they arrived, Father Zwiardowski sent to Europe 750 francs, given by the parishioners who did not have children, to pay for the painting of a set of the stations of the cross. Like the picture of the Virgin, they were late in arriving. Shipped in the care of a party of priests journeying across the Atlantic, the crate containing the dozen stations was lost at the port of New York in late 1867. For months nothing was heard of it. The parishioners, becoming more impatient as time passed, even claimed that the missionaries had pocketed the money they had donated. Finally, two years later, the crate appeared, but the priests had to pay two hundred dollars in back shipping charges. The long-awaited stations arrived in early 1870 and were mounted in the church. The celebration that accompanied the mounting of the stations was one of the largest held in the settlement in the nineteenth century. Father Adolf Bakanowski described it in detail to his superiors and even sent a copy of his description to an Upper Silesian newspaper, which published a somewhat altered version. The following excerpt, from two almost identical unsigned, untitled accounts in Adolf Bakanowski's handwriting, provides probably the best single contemporary sketch of festive dress among the Silesian Texans during the post–Civil War years:

> On the day of February 13th [1870], in the state of Texas, in the Polish settlement of Panna Maria, the ceremony of the Way of the Cross [was observed] in the following order:
>
> Little girls, from six to ten years old, carried the stations, two of them to each station. All of them wore white dresses with one band across the shoulder like a sash and another band of the same color worn like a belt. On their heads they wore garlands made from green leaves and white roses. In front of the maidens went others in similar white dresses carrying banners. After them followed three small girls, five years old, dressed in the following manner: The first one had on a violet dress, with the bands and all ornaments in the same color, and she had a crown of thorns on her head and was carrying a cross in her hand. The second one wore a green dress, a laurel crown on her head, and at the side of the green sash hung an anchor. The third one had on a pink

dress, a garland of roses on her head, and at the side of the pink sash hung a heart with golden rays. Farther on in the procession came the girls with the stations. Next came the priests. Behind them came singers, both men and women. Still farther on were fifty riflemen, who celebrated every adoration of the cross with gunshots. At the end walked the people. At the entrance to the church, Rev. Vincent Barzyński heartily welcomed the solemn procession. Inside the church he explained the stations of the cross. . . . He preached for three hours, but we listened with tears in our eyes until the very end.[4]

The devotional aids were not necessary to stimulate the faith of the Silesians at Panna Maria. The missionaries found them, at least in the first months, very receptive to their teachings and plans for the colony. The atmosphere at the time is reflected in young cleric Zwiardowski's description of midnight mass on Christmas Eve 1866. During the nighttime gathering, with the stone church lighted "according to our abilities," Father Bakanowski delivered a moving sermon, and the people, accompanied by Zwiardowski on his barrel organ, sang carols until they became too hoarse to sing any more. In the fields outside the church the farmers fired their guns all night in adoration of the baby Jesus. According to twenty-six-year-old Felix, "The people cried out of happiness that they had lived to see such a day and such a Mass."[5]

Times were not always so joyous at the Panna Maria church. Indeed disaster also struck. On the afternoon of 15 August 1875, well after most of the Resurrectionist missionaries had left Texas for the growing Polish colonies in the North, nature seemed to attack the parish. On this stormy day lightning struck the church, so seriously damaging the structure that it threatened to collapse. After surveying the damage, Father Zwiardowski, who in 1870 had become the superior of the Polish missions, decided that the parishioners would have to build a new place of worship. Though many of the settlers held much sentiment for the old building, the first Polish church in America, it was demolished so that its stone could be used in the newer, larger structure. Only some of the window frames and other woodwork from the old church were incorporated intact into the new building. The members of the parish worked together, raising the walls mostly with their own labor, hauling rock from a quarry on one of their farms, and carrying water from the river for mortar, men, and animals. During a ceremony at which the visiting Father Leopold Moczygemba was a special guest, the cornerstone was blessed on 19 August 1877. Work continued until the church, except for the tower, was completed the next year. Modified and enlarged, it remains today the church of the oldest Polish parish in the United States.[6]

The newly arrived Resurrectionists in late 1866 found conditions less favorable in the other Silesian colonies than in Panna Maria, but they pressed forward in their efforts to develop the Polish parishes. In this way they strengthened the entire Silesian community in the state. At San Antonio, the parish assigned to the Reverend Vincent Barzyński, the Silesians for over a decade had attended services at the old San Fernando Church when traveling Polish priests visited the city. Barzyński found this location altogether unsatisfactory for several reasons. San Fernando was in the heart of the city, while most of the Silesians lived in the Polish Quarter, a mile and a half southeast. When the weather was cold or wet, it was difficult for the parishioners, especially the children and the elderly, to make their way to the church over the unpaved and frequently muddy streets. Furthermore, Father Vincent rented the old church by the hour for the Polish masses, and he was irritated that his time was cut short at both beginning and end by Mexican women who either lingered in the sanctuary or came in early for their own services.[7]

Barzyński's first attempt at solving the problems was to move the Polish services in mid-December 1866 to a temporary location, a former bakery and warehouse in the Polish Quarter. Rented from Emanuel Rzeppa, the Unionist who later engendered the anger of the southerners in Karnes County, the new place of worship was a room measuring sixteen by forty feet. Early the next year the Poles emptied the room, converted it into a chapel, and arranged for the bishop to bless it. The warehouse location, which could not begin to hold the 222 Poles in the parish, proved to be completely unsuitable in the summer. Father Vincent reported that during the hot months "the people say that they cannot breathe."[8]

Early in 1867, Father Barzyński initiated efforts to replace the chapel with a new combined church, school, and rectory. By spring he had gathered fifteen hundred dollars from his parishioners and had purchased from Erasmus Florian four lots in the Polish Quarter as the site for the new structure. All through the summer he collected building materials, and finally on 25 September he could report to Father

Jełowicki in Paris, "Today they started to cut the weeds in the lot we bought for the church . . . and . . . will start to dig the foundation." Work progressed amazingly quickly on the ambitious project. The entire congregation contributed both time and money, each family being assessed specific donations. Their effort was so impressive that it received the commendation of the local American press, which generally said little or nothing about the Polish colony in the city. The new church was completed early in 1868.[9] It was eighty feet long and thirty feet wide. The sanctuary occupied fifty-one feet of the length, and the rectory and school occupied the remainder. Father Bakanowski, as superior of the Polish missions in Texas, blessed the church, which had been built under the patronage of Saint Michael, on 6 January 1868.[10]

Shortly after Father Zwiardowski was transferred from Panna Maria to Martinez in summer 1867, he began planning the construction of a new church for this agricultural colony in Bexar County. For a decade its residents had used the small log church that they had built during the first months of settlement. By the end of summer 1867 the youthful Zwiardowski was collecting money for the new building project. Actual construction began the next spring on land donated by four Silesian parishioners with stone provided by a "rich American." After the blessing of the cornerstone on 25 April 1868, work progressed smoothly, and the structure was completed well before the end of the year.[11] By 1 December, Father Bakanowski was able to report to Rome that Zwiardowski had finished the church at Martinez and that it was "more beautiful than the one in Panna Maria." With two later expansions, this place of worship, erected under the invocation of the Annunciation of the Virgin Mary, remains in use at the settlement today.[12]

In developing the Catholic parish for the Silesians at Martinez, Father Zwiardowski also changed the name of the community. The site had been named for Martinez Creek, which flows through the region. Father Felix apparently misunderstood the origin of the name, because he wrote to Europe that it was named after "a libertine, Martin, who lives six miles from here." Disliking the secular name, particularly with its connotation of a man of loose morals, the good priest set about changing it. In summer 1868 he wrote to one of his superiors asking for advice in the matter. After complaining about the name Martinez, he suggested three new names in its place: Annunciation, "according to the name of the church"; Gabriel, for "the bell will be christened Archangel Gabriel"; or Saint Hedwig, the name of the patron saint of Silesia. The settlers in the rural community revered the saint. The preceding year, because of this feeling, Father Bakanowski had written to Paris for a holy picture of the saint and a stamp with her image, both to be used in the Bexar County parish. The Feast of Saint Hedwig in late October each year was one of the most important festivals in the community. The answer to Father Zwiardowski's question most likely came from the people themselves, because since that time the colony has been known by the name of the Silesian patroness.[13]

Construction of an adequate church for the Poles at Bandera came later than in the other colonies because of the small number of settlers there and their comparative poverty. In 1870, Father Zwiardowski described the colony as "small, only seventeen families, mostly poor." After waiting for several more years, during which time the old log cabin church erected in 1858 deteriorated to such a point that it threatened to fall, Father Felix in spring 1876 initiated efforts to replace it with a new structure. The parishioners worked on the project for a year and a half, finally completing the fresh white-stone building on one of the green hillsides at Bandera in November 1877. The attractive masonry structure serves today as the parish Church of Saint Stanisław and still houses the second-oldest Polish Catholic parish in the United States.[14]

Completing church building in the already established core of Silesian colonies were the efforts at Coleto and Yorktown by the Reverend John Frydrychowicz, a Resurrectionist who arrived in Texas in December 1867. Although most of the time he was at odds with Father Bakanowski and with the bishop on both personal and theological grounds, the headstrong Father John appears to have single-handedly directed the construction of the churches at both places. Father Adolf made several references to his activities at Coleto during spring 1868, commenting about church construction, complaining that Frydrychowicz had enlarged and decorated the church there without his or the bishop's knowledge, and, perhaps in spite of himself, mentioning that Father John had a beautiful church and house at the settlement.

Frydrychowicz after only a short time moved from Coleto to Yorktown, sometime before Easter 1868. There he initiated a more ambitious building campaign. By summer he had enlisted the help of the parishioners in starting a wooden church of his own design. The dozen families agreed among themselves that every day they would send five people to work at the construction site, but soon they regretted their obligation because it prevented them from doing all their own agricultural work. Notwithstanding their grumbling, in September 1868 the people completed a small wooden church with two towers. It was over a year, however, before Father Bakanowski and Bishop Dubuis agreed to visit Yorktown to bless the place of worship built by a priest whom neither of them really liked.[15]

The Silesian community in Texas was strengthened not only by the development of the Polish Catholic parishes within it but also by the expansion of settlement to new areas that before had not been inhabited by Poles. The first and most logical major expansion was of farms up the valley of Cibolo Creek from the initial settlement at Panna Maria. Within forty years Silesian farmers occupied the whole fertile valley all the way through Karnes County and several miles into Wilson County. One reason for the growth of settlement into this area was the comparative cheapness of the land, which in the middle of the nineteenth century cost only about seventy-five cents an acre. Another reason was the proximity to the church at Panna Maria, to which in the first years all the peasants either walked or rode in animal-drawn vehicles at least once a week for religious services.

The first new agricultural community formed in the valley of Cibolo Creek was about five miles above the first colony. By 1873 it had enough population to support a separate school, Saint Joseph's School, which gave the community its name—at the time, it was known as Saint Joe. The school building served the additional function of a chapel, which priests from Panna Maria visited once a month, saving the residents at least one of their weekly trips to the mother colony.

After lightning struck and severely damaged the church at Panna Maria in summer 1875 and Father Felix Zwiardowski initiated his campaign to replace it, the farmers at Saint Joe began to draw away from the Panna Maria residents. They decided that, if a new church was going to be built at Panna Maria, they would be better off to spend their money for their own church at Saint Joe and thus avoid having to go so far to mass. Three local farmers took the initiative. They consulted the residents of the Cibolo Valley for their views on the idea, found them to be favorable, and collected three thousand dollars to begin construction of a new church. With these funds in hand they then conferred with Bishop Dominic Pellicer of the newly established Diocese of San Antonio, asking for his permission to begin construction.

At this point Father Zwiardowski, who was struggling to build a new church at Panna Maria, saw his parish splitting in half. He opposed the project at Saint Joe and tried to convince both the bishop and the people that it would be wiser to concentrate all their efforts in the older Panna Maria settlement. His arguments, however, seem only to have alienated the Saint Joe residents, who resolutely went about their work on a site that had been donated by local people. The peasants gave stone from their fields, hauled the building materials, and donated their labor to the effort. Deciding that they wanted their church to be under the invocation of the Nativity of the Virgin Mary, they named their community Częstochowa, after the site of the greatest Marian shrine in Poland.[16]

The building project was shadowed by hard feelings between the Saint Joe residents, who were becoming known as the Częstochowa residents, and Father Zwiardowski. These feelings flared up when the time came to bless the cornerstone in 1877. Father Felix had been designated to bless the stone, but then rumors spread that he wanted the new Częstochowa church to be under the care of the Resurrectionists. The local settlers strongly opposed this idea, perhaps because of their unpleasant experiences with Zwiardowski's opposition to their project. Father Felix left the ceremony without blessing anything but returned several weeks later to do so under orders from the bishop. Finally, after the church was completed, the farmers in the new parish called on the bishop to consecrate their new place of worship on 11 February 1878. As time passed, the anger of Father Felix and the parishioners who stayed with him at Panna Maria cooled. As a symbol of their fraternal feelings, several months later in an impressive procession accompanied by the firing of guns, they gave the new parish church a large painting of the Virgin of Częstochowa to be placed on the main altar.[17]

Częstochowa today remains an active center of Polish life. Virtually all of the members of the parish are descendants of original Silesian immigrants of the 1850's. In 1973 it commemorated its centenary with a huge celebration that drew visitors from all parts of the state. The old church, now enlarged, is the dominant feature of the landscape, its shining steeple visible for long distances over the Silesian farms that surround it.[18]

Continued expansion of Silesian settlement up the Cibolo Valley led to the establishment in the 1890's of another rural community in Wilson County. It was named Kościuszko, for Tadeusz Kościuszko, the Polish hero of both the American Revolution and the Polish Insurrection against the Russians in 1793. The colony had its inception in 1892 with the construction of a Polish school. Six years later sixty-five families at Kościuszko broke away from the Częstochowa church, six miles distant, and established their own place of worship. They pooled their resources and for two thousand dollars, plus donations of labor and some building materials, were able to erect a wooden church. This Silesian community also has remained active to the present.[19]

Polish settlement in the Cibolo Valley led to the formation of one more Silesian colony in the last years of the nineteenth century. About thirty families settled in the American town Stockdale, ten miles north of Kościuszko. There they erected their own small church, which became a mission of Kościuszko. For a number of years these settlers sent their children to parochial schools at Kościuszko and Panna Maria, but in time the small Silesian community lost most of its Polish identity, even though well into the twentieth century some of its members continued to travel for Polish religious services at the other settlements.[20]

Fertile lands were not the only attraction for the Silesian farmers. In Falls City, for example, a town up the San Antonio River from Panna Maria and about six miles overland from Częstochowa, the appeal was convenient transportation for agricultural products. In 1884 the San Antonio and Aransas Pass Railroad, building between San Antonio and the Gulf of Mexico, placed a railway siding at the theretofore unoccupied site, and the town of Falls City sprang to life. Almost all of its inhabitants were younger Silesians who moved from the Panna Maria and Częstochowa areas. Their movement to the new townsite with railway connections doomed prospects for commercial growth at the two former colonies and relegated them to the status of sleepy rural communities. Initially the residents of Falls City attended religious services in the two older parishes, then for a short time at a new church in nearby Hobson, but after 1902 in their own Polish church. The town became the commercial center for the core of Silesian settlements in Karnes and Wilson counties and is still active today, although twentieth-century paved highways have drawn many of its customers to larger towns.[21]

The Silesians established one colony before World War I outside the general area of Polish settlement. This was the White Deer colony in the Texas Panhandle, forty-three miles northeast of Amarillo on the southern Great Plains. The first Silesians known to have traveled to this portion of the state were five young men from Karnes County who set out on an "adventure" to see the country in late June 1900. They traveled with nine horses and a wagon, and their principal food for the journey consisted of rabbits and other wild game they killed along the way and staples they took from home. By the time the men reached Coleman, they had spent all their money, and they decided to try to raise money to get to Amarillo by selling their horses. Only one of the young men, however, was able to sell his mount, and so he was the only member of the party to reach the destination. The others turned back after one of them received a letter reporting that a large cotton crop was waiting at home to be picked. When the four finally got back to San Antonio, another member of the group found a job, leaving three of them to return home a month after they had left. Although the trip did not immediately stimulate Polish movement to west Texas, it did lay the groundwork by prompting the Silesian farmers to consider the region as an alternative to central Texas and agriculture as practiced there.[22]

The next step toward the establishment of a Polish colony at White Deer occurred when the Anton Urbanczyk family moved from Karnes County to Rhineland, in Knox County. Urbanczyk had come to Texas as a four-year-old from Rozmierz, a village in Upper Silesia. He and his family were among the first immigrants, sailing on the bark *Weser* in 1854. Only a few weeks after the family arrived at Panna Maria, Anton's father, Jacob, died, leaving his widow to care for their seven children. Anton grew to adulthood at Panna Maria, married Mary Czerner, and by her had five children. Probably partly as a result of her hard life on the frontier, his wife died from a miscarriage. Alone with his children, Anton determined to move to new country and for reasons not fully understood chose the Rhineland vicinity. His farm in Knox County became the springboard for the final move to White Deer.[23]

In August 1909 three young men from Panna Maria appeared at the Urbanczyk farm. Henry Czerner, John Krol, and Mat Labus had set out to explore the possibilities of establishing a Silesian agricultural colony in west Texas. At Rhineland the three visited with the Urbanczyk family and learned from them that much productive land was said to be available in the northern region of the Panhandle. When they went on to investigate the prospects, one of Anton Urbanczyk's sons, Ben, joined them to examine the region himself, with the idea that his family might move farther northwest if conditions proved favorable. The four young Poles traveled until they reached Groom, a small German-Catholic settlement. There John Kroll and Mat Labus found work in the wheat harvest and left the others to look for land near the town of Panhandle. The two remaining men saw land in all directions, but all of it was held by stockmen, and they could not learn anything about its availability to farmers. In Panhandle they talked with J. Sid O'Keefe, of the Star Land Company of Iowa, but he was unable to give them an option on a large block of land that they wanted. After this first failure Henry Czerner took a job working on the courthouse under construction at Panhandle, and Ben Urbanczyk returned to Rhineland to help with the harvest.

While Czerner worked on the courthouse, he continued searching for land suitable for a Polish settlement. One day, while traveling by train to Pampa, he saw a sign advertising sixty thousand acres for sale to farmers. He noted that it was available from the White Deer Land Company, and when he arrived in Pampa, he sought out the company agent, Timothy Dwight Hobart. The representative listened as Czerner explained his desire to find a site for a Polish colony and took him to see some of the land available. The two men came to an agreement whereby the company would give the Poles an exclusive option to buy acreage near White Deer. Henry then returned to Rhineland to discuss the news with the Urbanczyk family. They decided that Ben and his father would go immediately to inspect the land and then return to confer again with Czerner, who would wait for them at Rhineland. Coming back as enthusiastic about the possibilities as Henry had been, they decided that White Deer was the place of the future. While some of the Urbanczyks began making plans to leave Rhineland, Henry Czerner returned to Karnes County to spread news about White Deer.

The same year that the Silesians first inspected the site in northern Texas, Henry Czerner's father, Cryspin Czerner, and his family left Panna Maria for the open plains. He was followed in 1910 by John Urbanczyk, of Rhineland, and by Vincent Haiduk and Demas Bednorz, of Panna Maria. The same year two non-Silesian Polish families from Wisconsin, those of William Gordzelik and Jack Juleja, joined the colony. In 1911, Ben and Felix Urbanczyk, of Rhineland, moved to the prairies, as did Sam Bednorz, of Stockdale. The year 1912 saw the arrival of Ladislaus Urbanczyk, from Kościuszko, and John Kotara, from Częstochowa. John Kotara was one of the five young men from Karnes County who had viewed west Texas in 1900 and had brought back tales about it. In 1913 three more families of non-Silesian Poles from Washington State, California, and Nebraska joined the settlements, and in 1915 the Charles Kalka family, from McLean, and the Theodore Mazurek family, from Bandera, arrived. In 1916 the Edmund Jendrush and Edward Kotara families came to White Deer. Since the Poles were slow in coming, however, the White Deer Land Company was unable to hold the land for them any longer. The remaining acreage was put up for public sale, and all of it was sold within six months.[24]

The experiences of the Vincent Haiduk family provide an idea of what it was like to move to White Deer during the early years. Vincent, his wife, and their eight children moved there from Panna Maria in November 1910 in two railway boxcars. To transport their cattle, horses, hogs, furniture, and about 450 bushels of shelled corn, they rented a fifty-foot-long freight car. Their oldest son, Ben, rode by himself in the boxcar to care for the livestock, which had to be watered at each stop. It took the Haiduks and their possessions, traveling in the smaller boxcar, about three and a half days to make the six-hundred-mile journey, but for Ben and the animals it took a week, including a delay to have the cattle dipped in Fort Worth. From there westward he was not allowed to ride in the car with the animals, but was informed that he would have to ride in the caboose, where the only place he could sit or sleep was on a hard wooden bench.

When the Haiduks reached White Deer, they spent the first months with one of their daughters, Rosie, the wife of John Urbanczyk, who had arrived from Rhineland earlier that year. Both families, totaling sixteen people, spent the winter in the only completed building at the Urbanczyk farm, a wooden granary. The weather was unusually cold and bitter for people who were accustomed to the mild central Texas climate. To add to their discomfort, the only entrance to the granary was a north-facing door that let in cold blasts whenever anyone came or went. At night with the beds and pallets laid around the one source of heat, a coal-fired cookstove, it "looked like a hospital," as one of the pioneers recalled. During the day, when the adults were working, the children walked along the nearby railway tracks gathering coal that had fallen from the cars and taking it back to the granary to fuel the stove. In 1910, when the Haiduk family arrived on the treeless plains, there were few visible improvements on the open land—as one of them recalled, "no fences, no roads, no buildings, nothing but cattle." Rosie Haiduk Urbanczyk was not happy with her husband for bringing her to such a barren place. She complained to him, "We have four children and there ain't nothing here." He responded that despite the grim surroundings they were going to stay and "going to make it." The pioneer wife recalled, "So we made it," proudly adding, "We had the first Catholic child born in White Deer."[25]

Only a short time after the Polish settlers began gathering at White Deer, they started planning the establishment of a Polish church. In 1911 they purchased a four-acre tract north of the railroad track in town and began drawing plans for a church building. The colonists adopted the plans in early spring 1913 and almost immediately began construction. Within a few weeks the place of worship was built, and Father C. J. Bier of Amarillo celebrated the first mass there on 30 May 1913. The Catholic parish at White Deer continues to be the center of its Silesian community. Today it is best known through the Texas Panhandle for its annual sausage festival in the autumn after harvest.[26]

Statistics on the population of the Silesian colonies in Texas between the Civil War and World War I are generally based on the numbers of Polish families in the various Catholic parishes. Figures for actual numbers of inhabitants are rare, while the difficulties with the manuscript population schedules of the United States census remain the same for 1870 and 1880 as with the inadequate 1860 schedules. An additional problem with the available statistics is that no one source gives numbers for all the settlements. Limited though the figures are, however, they do give at least a rough idea of the population of the Silesian settlements in Texas during the period.

The population of Panna Maria remained generally stable. It had between 75 and 78 families in 1866 and 1867, 85 families in 1871, and 80 families in 1909.[27]

Bandera, always a small colony, in 1866 and 1867 had 12 families, in 1868 and 1870 it had 17 families, in 1877 it had 26 families, and in 1909 it had 50 families.[28]

The Polish population of San Antonio fluctuated, with a distinct decline in the second half of the nineteenth century. From a high in 1866 and 1867 of between 40 and 44 families it dropped to only 33 in 1876, but by 1900 it had rebounded to 42 households.[29]

Saint Hedwig, or Martinez, profiting from its fertile soil and nearness to markets in San Antonio, had a steadily increasing number of people. In 1866 it had 28 Polish families, in 1867 it had 34, in about 1870 it had 48, in 1897 it had approximately 200, and in 1909 it had 209.[30]

The number of Poles in Yorktown likewise grew substantially. Although in 1867 there were only 13 Silesian households in the town, by 1897 there were about 100, and by 1909 there were 160.[31] Nearby Meyersville, in contrast, could boast only about 50 Silesian families in 1909.

Częstochowa, which began with about 50 households in the 1870's and had about 170 in the early 1880's, lost population to the newer Falls City and Kościuszko settlements. In 1905 it had only 75 families, although by 1909 the number had risen again to 85.[32]

The Catholic parish at Falls City had about 70 families when it was organized in 1902, but in 1909 a writer pointed out that, although in that year 75 families belonged to the parish, only 55 of them were Silesian.[33] The Kościuszko community, when its parish was organized in 1898, had 65 households, and its number increased to between 72 and 75 in 1909.[34] White Deer, the newest of the colonies, on the eve of World War I had between 15 and 20 Polish families.[35]

During the second half of the nineteenth century and the beginning of the twentieth, there was some limited non-Silesian Polish immigration from abroad into the Silesian colonies. Most of these immigrants went to San Antonio, which was a growing metropolitan center offering jobs to the new arrivals.[36] Although most of the immigrants were non-Silesian Poles, there was at least some immigration of people from Upper Silesia.[37] Among the most colorful Poles entering Texas during this period were Polish soldiers who had been transported to Mexico to fight for Emperor Maximilian in the 1860's. A number of these men, who escaped after the fall of the French-backed Austrian ruler in 1867, made their way to Texas.[38] At least one of them settled among the Silesians. This man was Matthew Pilarczyk, who went to Karnes County. Having fled—according to some accounts a firing squad—the fugitive crossed the Rio Grande and made his way to Panna Maria, where he had heard Poles were living. After some time he married into one of the Silesian peasant families and became a substantial member of the Polish community.[39]

Throughout the history of the Silesian settlements in Texas education, and especially religious education, has constituted an important aspect of community life and has contributed significantly to the retention of Slavic culture. At least as early as 1858 there was some limited schooling in Panna Maria.[40] After the Civil War this activity was expanded into teaching conducted in a substantial school by a permanent staff. Because of its distinction as the first Polish school in the United States, the history of Saint Joseph's School deserves more than passing notice.

During the very first days the Resurrectionist missionaries spent at Panna Maria, they initiated plans for the construction of a school building. At the end of November 1866, one of the priests reported to Rome that the farmers already had donated nine hundred dollars for this purpose and that they had begun hauling stone to the construction site.[41] Early the next year Father Adolf Bakanowski wrote that the planned structure was to have two stories, ten rooms, and twenty-four windows, adding optimistically, "In half a year's time everything will be finished."[42] On 27 March 1867 the building committee, composed of Father Adolf, John Kowalik, and the building designers, Frank Biela and Albert Kniejski, signed a contract with the two stonemasons, Joseph Kyrish and John Gawlik. The parishioners obligated themselves to provide stone, lumber, sand, home-burned lime, and water.[43] This last item was of unusual importance, for it had to be hauled from the river at considerable labor, and it cost twenty-five to thirty-five cents a barrel, a high price for that time.[44]

Work on the school did not move as quickly as the overly hopeful Father Adolf had expected. In May 1868 he sadly wrote to Rome that the people had started building the school but that for lack of funds the walls were standing unattended and were "an object of ridicule."[45] The next autumn, however, after a new harvest was in, the farmers returned to the project. They traveled to the coast to buy lumber for the roof, spent many hours working at the site, and finally in January 1869 finished the building. It had two floors; the ground level was devoted to the school, and the upper level served as the rectory. The structure was fifty-seven feet long, forty feet wide, and twenty-two feet high. The ground floor had two large and two small rooms, while the second floor had six rooms. On the front was a small balcony overlooking the village.[46]

Educational activity had not waited for the completion of the school building. In the month the Resurrectionists arrived in Panna Maria, Father Bakanowski reported to Rome that on every Sunday and religious holiday until a school was built he would have "lessons" for the parishioners and that on every Sunday and Thursday he would hold catechism classes for the children. He stated happily, "The children are coming for catechism lessons two hours before the bell."[47] At the end of 1866, Father Zwiardowski wrote, "I am engaged in teaching the children." He went on to say that he had had thirty-two pupils before Christmas and that he expected seventy after the holiday. He continued, "Although the school is not built, we do what we can and we converted a barn for storing corn into a school." This very likely was a partitioned section in John Twohig's old storage barn in the village.[48] A short time later Father Felix apologized to his superiors for writing them such a short letter, explaining, "I do not have the time, because I teach the children and I print the primers myself; my pen is the type and my hand is the press. . . . Thanks to God, the children are making some progress." At that time he had sixty pupils.[49] By spring 1867 the number of children attending classes had grown to seventy-five.[50] Not long thereafter, however, Father Felix was transferred to care for the farmers at Saint Hedwig in Bexar County.[51] With his departure began a period of repeated problems in finding suitable teachers for the school.

The next teacher at Saint Joseph's School was Joseph Barzyński, Sr., the father of the Reverend Vincent Barzyński. He came to Panna Maria in June 1867, the same month that Father Zwiardowski left for Saint Hedwig (which at that time was still known by its old name, Martinez). Father Bakanowski seemed pleased with the fifty-two-year-old Barzyński's effort, writing to Rome: "He is a great help. . . . The school, considering its moral aspects, is good. . . . the children can read, some of them write, and all of them know the four rules of arithmetic. . . . They cry when their parents make them stay home and not go to school or church."[52] The elder Barzyński, nevertheless, had a difficult life at Panna Maria. His home there, a mere lean-to beside the priest's temporary quarters, was made from wooden posts, pieces of scrap lumber, and old barrel staves, with calking in the cracks. In such conditions he remained teacher for only a few months.[53]

Much of the history of Saint Joseph's School is a story of unsuccessful attempts to secure permanent teachers. In light of the difficult physical conditions at the isolated settlement, as well as the low pay, the problem is understandable. Taking the place of Joseph Barzyński in autumn 1868 was Kazimierz Dembowski, a Pole newly arrived from Europe who taught for just a few weeks.[54] Then came sixty-eight-year-old Karol Warenski, who arrived at least as early as spring 1869. Having gained a favorable initial impression of the elderly man, Father Adolf characterized him as having "true zest and calling to be a teacher," while showing "exemplary patience and piety." Warenski taught "only the ABC's," but Bakanowski added, "with the help of God it will come higher" (that is, become more advanced). The pastor reported that several of the children had progressed very well and were learning English, but he regretted that the school did not bring much money; the parents paid monthly tuition of only fifty cents a child.[55] In summer 1869, Father Felix Zwiardowski returned to Panna Maria from Saint Hedwig and again began teaching.[56] The next autumn the boys and girls were separated, Warenski teaching the boys and Zwiardowski teaching the girls. In addition the Resurrectionists employed "one American widow" to instruct the girls in English and sewing.[57]

After Warenski left the Panna Maria school, apparently after some personal conflict with Father Bakanowski, in spring 1870 Peter Kiołbassa returned to Karnes County from the North. His arrival coincided with Bakanowski's preparations for departure to Europe. The two men made an agreement whereby the Silesian, who according to one source already had taught at Panna Maria under Father Anthony Rossadowski in the 1850's, would become teacher and organist. The parishioners, however, protested at the salary that Kiołbassa wanted for his services, and after a few months he returned to Chicago after considerable financial loss. Another reason for his curtailed stay may have been the animosity of the Karnes County southerners, who as defeated Confederates resented the fact that Kiołbassa had changed sides to fight against them, especially as a commander of Negro cavalry.[58]

With Father Adolf away, responsibility for the school at Panna Maria fell on the shoulders of Father Zwiardowski, who succeeded him as superior of the Polish missions. Father Felix first attempted to fill the position with a Polish clergyman, the Reverend Adolf Snigurski, but the parents at the settlement became so "dissatisfied with his conduct toward the children" that they declared that they would no longer send their children to school if Snigurski stayed.[59]

The next teacher at Panna Maria, John Barzyński, the youngest brother of the Reverend Vincent Barzyński, was probably the best received of all the early teachers at Saint Joseph's School. The twenty-one-year-old John, who had drawn the attention of the Russian police while he was a student in Warsaw, departed his homeland for Galveston in spring 1870. He spent his first months in America at San Antonio with his brother, during which time he mastered the English language.[60] In September 1871 he opened the school year at Panna Maria. Father Felix happily reported that Barzyński was conducting the school well and receiving "more and more appreciation from the people." During his tenure as schoolmaster over fifty children attended classes, their parents paying monthly tuition of a dollar a child or seventy-five cents if the family had two or more children in the school.[61] After teaching only one year, however, John left his position in 1872 to move to one of the Silesian settlements in Franklin County, Missouri, where he became editor of a Polish-language newspaper. Again the position of schoolmaster at Panna Maria fell vacant.[62]

School problems were not limited to difficulties in finding and keeping suitable teachers. Another problem came from a most unexpected source, the Unionist justice of the peace, Emanuel Rzeppa. As early as 1867, Father Adolf Bakanowski had written to Europe about the possibilities of Texas state-salaried teachers serving at Panna Maria, and in 1870 he reported that attendance in schools taught by such teachers would be compulsory.[63] Nothing more is recorded for two years in the Resurrectionist correspondence about the subject of secular schools. During the months after John Barzyński left Saint Joseph's School in 1872, Father Felix Zwiardowski added teaching to his many duties as superior of the missions. He found that he simply could not do everything, and he complained that "the most troublesome of all missionary work is schools." Tiring of the seemingly endless searching for teachers who stayed for only a few months at the country school, he tried hiring a German cleric to teach and to play the organ. The people made private arrangements with the German to teach their children, but there were not enough pupils to support him. After the cleric left, angry with Zwiardowski for having brought him there, no school was held at all for several months.

In this vacuum of educational activity Emanuel Rzeppa decided to act. In late June 1872 he arranged for the opening of a public school at Panna Maria. The secular school might not have disturbed the farmers and their pastor too much if it had been conducted by a Catholic teacher approved by them. The problem was the teacher, Miss Navarro Davies, whom Father Felix described as "a harlot, divorcee, and woman of Satan's tongue." According to the priest's biased observations, Rzeppa proceeded to "terrify" the people by mounting posters warning that any man who did not send his children to the "free public common school" would be liable to a fine of twenty-five dollars a child. "Seeing such an injustice," Father Felix announced from the pulpit that if anyone sent his children to the public school he "would be under church censure" and would not receive absolution "even in death." In response to Zwiardowski's declaration Rzeppa brought a complaint against him in the district court. In the case that followed, the judge concluded that if there was no parochial school in the village the public school would have to remain, but if Saint Joseph's School reopened, it could be removed.[64]

After the district judge made this ruling, Father Zwiardowski traveled to Castroville to confer with Mother Saint André, the superior of the Sisters of Divine Providence. During their consultations she agreed to provide three Alsatian nuns to conduct the parochial school. Father Felix was especially pleased that the new sisters were able to support themselves from the proceeds of their teaching. As he bluntly put it, "They do not need much for their lifelihood; they cook and do their own laundry and teach English very well." The order profited in other ways from its presence at Panna Maria; within a matter of months five Silesian girls had entered its convent at Castroville.[65]

What promised to be an ideal situation at Saint Joseph's School was disturbed a few months later by the actions of Mother Saint André. According to Father Zwiardowski, she attempted to arrange with the outgoing Bishop Claude-Marie Dubuis to have all the schools in the German and Polish parishes placed under the direct supervision of her order. Fearing what he saw as Germanization of the Polish parishes, Zwiardowski appealed to the new bishop, the Reverend Dominic Pellicer, to allow instead the formation of a new order of nuns specifically to serve the Silesian parishes. The prelate consented to the request, stating that nuns who were members of the Sisters of Divine Providence could, if they wished, alter their vows and enter the new Polish order. Father Felix wrote in April 1875 that five Polish nuns and two Alsatian nuns had decided to leave the Sisters of Divine Providence and join the new community, the Order of the Immaculate Conception of the Virgin Mary. This was the first congregation of Polish sisters established in America.[66]

Wearing azure-blue habits designed by Father Felix, the Sisters of the Immaculate Conception, commonly known as the "Blue Sisters," served the Silesian communities in Texas for the next half-dozen years. In the summer of 1875 four new Polish girls had entered the novitiate for the order, and in spring 1876 two received habits for the new congregation. The community gradually increased to seventeen members from its original seven.

The Silesian settlers came to prize their nuns. When rumors spread that sisters from Poland were to come to Texas, the farmers called a meeting in Panna Maria to voice their opposition to the coming of "Russian noblewomen" to take the place of their "little angels." Father Zwiardowski was equally happy with the new sisters. He reported, "For this country local nuns are needed who can teach girls and boys. No music or languages other than English, Polish, and German are needed." He continued that the reason for this was that in the

Texas colonies "there are no people of the upper classes, only country people. . . . They learn only how to read and write." Almost immediately the Blue Sisters were divided between the schools at Panna Maria and Saint Hedwig. Later some members of the small congregation also taught in Yorktown and San Antonio. The community existed until 1881, when as a result of various difficulties it was dissolved and its members allowed to enter other orders.[67]

Another problem in operating the school at Panna Maria, as well as later the schools at the other colonies, was the attitude taken by some of the people themselves. Father Bakanowski wrote that on occasion he had to go from house to house asking parents to allow their children to attend classes. Looking back on the situation, he noted: "In Texas people do not care about education. As soon as a child can read, write, and count some, then he says good-by to school." He went on to say that "trade and industry, and here in Panna Maria, agriculture—these bring money." Explaining the status of educated people in the state, he declared: "The educated person, if he were not engaged in a craft, would die of starvation. The skill of a businessman is admired more than [the knowledge of] an educated man."[68] On another occasion he wrote that among the Silesian settlements "a child does not even master the rosary before his father sends him to earn money."[69] Chastising the colonists after hearing of such practices from Father Bakanowski, the Upper Silesian weekly *Zwiastun Górnoszlązki* warned the immigrants, "If you do not teach them [your children] to be wise when they are young, they will teach you when they grow up."[70]

Following the dissolution of the Blue Sisters in 1881, nuns from the Congregation of the Sisters of Charity of the Incarnate Word took over operation of Saint Joseph's School. They remained in charge with a few brief interruptions until the middle of the twentieth century, when the Polish Congregation of the Felician Sisters assumed teaching duties.[71] When he visited the settlement in 1890, Thomas Ruckman noted that large classes were being held in the two-story school building.[72] By the beginning of the twentieth century it had 126 pupils, and by 1909 it had 135. One of the most important things that the children learned was the rudiments of the English language; virtually all of them spoke only Polish at home. During the years around the turn of the century classes were conducted by both Polish-speaking sisters and English-speaking teachers from the public school, an arrangement that gave the children some variety in both teachers and languages of instruction. An observer in 1907 noted that the sister teachers received very low monthly wages, only $12.50 each for all their living costs.[73] A number of years later a Silesian who had attended Saint Joseph's School during this period recalled that he remembered best a public school teacher, Miss Isabelle Zimmerman. Recalling how she had punished him for misbehaving, he declared, "One time she hit me on the head so hard, I had to sleep on my face." Then commenting favorably on what he learned from her, the farmer recalled that the knowledge "she put in my head, she put there good."[74] In 1918 the school was commemorated with a parish celebration of its "golden jubilee" in festivities marked with "joy and devotion." Today the old school building, which was somewhat altered in appearance in 1947, serves as the local historical museum, while Polish sisters still teach in a new public school just east of the church.[75]

Saint Joseph's School at Panna Maria, although it holds the distinction of being the oldest Polish school in America, was but one of many schools begun by Silesian colonists in Texas. The founding of schools closely paralleled the establishment of parishes and in some cases even preceded them.

As early as summer 1867, Father Felix Zwiardowski was teaching children at Saint Hedwig, the next community after Panna Maria to have its own school building. Before the school was constructed, Father Felix taught five hours a day and, in addition, hand-transcribed instructional materials for the pupils. After Father Felix returned to Panna Maria in 1868, the next known teacher at Saint Hedwig was Adolf Snigurski. The parents in the colony became so dissatisfied with his efforts, however, that they expelled him from the parish. This priest was followed by the Reverend Teofil Bralewski, who as pastor gave the children daily lessons during the brief five months he served the parish in 1869.[76] The subsequent recorded educational activity at the settlement was under the guidance of the Reverend Vincent Barzyński, who supervised the construction of a large masonry schoolhouse. The Saint Hedwig parishioners started collecting building materials during the winter of 1872–1873 and began construction the following spring. Work continued under Barzyński's supervision, and in March 1874, Bishop Dubuis blessed the structure. The completed school measured fifty-six by thirty feet and had classrooms on the ground floor and rooms for the teachers on the upper floor. With a certain measure of justifiable pride Father Vincent described it as "very roomy, even impressive."[77] In the early twentieth century the school had 150 children, but by 1936 the number had declined to 65. As at Panna Maria the first sister teachers at Saint Hedwig were members of the Silesian Immaculate Conception Community, followed by Sisters of Charity of the Incarnate Word, and finally by Felician Sisters.[78]

Soon after he arrived in San Antonio in 1866, Father Vincent began suggesting the founding of a school for the Silesian children in the city. Realizing that, "if the children are to be Catholic, they have to go to school," he planned the construction of a classroom as part of the church begun in September 1867. When the building was completed early the next year, the classroom was an integral part of it. There Father Vincent taught thirty "little children" who he reported were learning "to read in Polish" and studying the catechism. He originally planned for the church building to be replaced sometime in the future by another and for the older building to be converted entirely to educational purposes, but the decrease in the size of the Polish parish in the latter part of the century meant that the masonry structure would remain a church into the twentieth century.

After Father Vincent's departure from San Antonio in 1872, his place was taken by his brother, the Reverend Joseph Barzyński, and then by the Reverend Anthony Heinke, who brought Sisters of the Immaculate Conception from Panna Maria to teach. They remained until about 1880, when the school ceased to exist for almost two decades. Then in 1898 Ursuline Sisters from San Antonio erected a school on the grounds of the church in the Polish Quarter and operated it for several years. Beginning with 79 pupils, its enrollment grew to over 200 in the 1930's. The Ursuline Sisters were followed by Sisters of Divine Providence, who continued to serve the San Antonio community, conducting the school until its closing in 1965.[79]

As the years passed, schools proliferated among the Silesian settlements in Texas. As early as 1870 one opened at Yorktown, in DeWitt County, and for a short time it was served by sister teachers from the Immaculate Conception Community at Panna Maria. In 1897 the Sisters of Charity of the Incarnate Word took over operation of the Yorktown facility, which at the time consisted of a long wooden building with two windows on each side and a door at each end. The next year the 121 pupils and their sister teachers happily moved to a new building. An observer at the turn of the century described the school as adjoining the Polish church in "an attractive setting" about a mile from town. Because of the extent of the Yorktown parish, however, it was difficult for the more distant settlers to send their children to the school, and by the third decade of the twentieth century attendance had dwindled to only 60 children. At nearby Meyersville the Silesians shared a school with the local German settlers, and at least one Polish sister taught the Polish language there. It is interesting to note that, of the 60 pupils at Meyersville, 50 were Polish.[80]

Educational activity also began in the 1870's at Bandera. Silesian nuns were teaching there as early as 1877 or 1878, and in 1882, after the dissolution of the Polish order, their position was taken by Sisters of Charity of the Incarnate Word. The school remained active into the twentieth century, and a new, two-story building made from native stone was erected in 1922.[81]

The first organized activity by the farmers at Częstochowa was the construction of a school in 1873. The structure doubled as a chapel for the occasional visits of Polish priests and served as the center of the rural community. It was built on a site donated by two of the settlers, Anthony Jarzombek and Franciszek Mutz. In 1881 the Sisters of Charity of the Incarnate Word assumed operation of the school, as they did at the same time in Panna Maria. Irregular attendance was a particular problem for the Częstochowa school; high water in Cibolo Creek, which divided the settlement, frequently prevented children on the far side from crossing to go to school. Consequently the parishioners built a second school three miles north of the town at a place called Bartole and then a third school at a nearby rural community known as Pulaski. Around the turn of the century each of these schools had about 50 pupils, who were taught by sisters and by one secular teacher who rotated among the three Częstochowa schools and the Panna Maria school. When a visiting Polish traveler recorded his impressions of the Cibolo Valley community in 1907, he noted that the Polish nuns he found teaching there knew only conventional subjects and Polish as a second language, adding that they knew and cared little about world affairs or Polish culture. He related that when he told the children about Adam Mickiewicz, the most famous Polish poet of the nineteenth century, they said that they had never heard of him but assured him that they would ask their teachers to read his works to them. The Sisters of the Incarnate Word remained at Częstochowa until about 1922, when they departed, leaving the parish without nun teachers until 1933, when Benedictine Sisters took charge for a short time. They were replaced in 1934 by Polish Felician Sisters, who in that year operated a school with over 150 children.[82]

Polish educational activity began at Falls City with the construction of Holy Trinity School in 1905. Initially conducted by Sisters of Charity of the Incarnate Word, four years later it was taken by Franciscan Sisters, who taught there until 1913. For the next twelve years the school was without nuns. Then in the mid-1920's, Saint Stanislaus School was built five miles west of the town, and Sisters of the Incarnate Word of the Blessed Sacrament were brought from Victoria to operate both schools. By the 1930's, Holy Trinity School had 100 pupils, and Saint Stanislaus School 57.[83]

The initial community project by the settlers at the Kościuszko community was the erection of a school in 1892. From its beginning, Sisters of Charity of the Incarnate Word conducted the classes. Just a few years after the founding of the first school another was built about two and a half miles away at the Borysownia, or Liberty Hill, community. By the early twentieth century the sister teachers were alternating with a secular teacher at the two schools. When he visited the school at Kościuszko in 1930, the Polish consul general from Chicago, an Upper Silesian, made a number of interesting observations on the children and their education. He described the school as a one-story wooden building and said that he found over seventy children and three nun teachers. The consul characterized the pupils as having "fair hair, bare feet, and eyes—typical Polish childrens' eyes. . . . Looking at these children I feel as if I am in Łaziska Góra, Miechowice, or Królewska Nowa Wieś" (all towns in Silesia). He was particularly impressed by their Polish speech, noting that "the nuns spoke worse Polish than the children" and that obviously the pupils had learned their speech at home. After listening to their prepared program of songs and poems and after talking with some of the pupils, the consul thought to himself that, despite their similar appearance and speech, "there is a noticeable difference between these children and our village children. These were not shy at all. On the contrary, they seemed like little Americans."[84]

As the Silesians continued to become acculturated into general American society in the years between the Civil War and the early twentieth century, they established and strengthened several institutions that maintained their ties with native European peasant culture. The most significant of these institutions were the Polish Catholic parishes, both new ones and original ones that were further developed within the colonies. While this religious activity was going forward in the communities, the Silesian population itself was increasing. This population growth caused the expansion of Silesian settlement into new areas. In all the new rural communities the Silesian farmers soon started their own Polish parishes. Others institutions that the farmers began, probably second in importance only to the churches in maintaining ethnic life, were the Polish schools, which were attended by virtually all Silesian children in the years before World War I. Although the level of Polish culture absorbed by the children in the schools frequently was low, the separate educational system insulated them from the influences to which they would have been exposed in non-Polish schools and reinforced the Silesian culture that they brought from home. These two major elements, church and school, coupled with the increased population and geographic area of settlement, were instrumental in preserving the Silesian folk culture in Texas well into the twentieth century. Moreover, it is because of those institutions that one still can observe the Silesian way of life in some of the colonies today.

7

The Silesian Way of Life in Texas

SEVENTY-FIVE to a hundred years ago life among the Silesians in Texas was distinct from that of the Americans around them. Since the days of Reconstruction the immigrant farmers had participated in local government, and for even longer they had dealt commercially with the Americans, but as late as the years preceding World War I they remained insulated from their neighbors. The Poles spoke their own language, which, of course, was completely unintelligible to the Texans, they went to their own churches and societies, they sent their children to local Polish Catholic schools, and they generally lived apart from the Texans. It is safe to say that in the years before 1915 most of the Silesians were born, were reared, married, bore children, and died within their own communities, little known and even less understood by those who lived around them.[1]

An infant's first weeks of life in a Silesian settlement were surrounded by European traditions alien to most Texans. The mother, for example, was warned by old women that she must cover her head with a scarf for the first six weeks after her child's birth to ward off bad luck. Similarly, the mother had strict injunctions not to hang her baby's freshly washed diapers to dry outside the house either at noon or after dark during the same six-week period. All the Silesians believed strongly that it was inviting disaster for a mother to allow her child to be taken from the house until it was carried to the church for baptism. This religious ceremony usually took place between one and three days after the baby was born. It was customary for the father and the grandmother to leave the mother at home and take the infant to the church, where they met the godparents and then joined the priest who performed the rite.[2]

For decades large families were the rule in the Silesian communities. A Polish observer early in the twentieth century estimated that in the settlements there averaged thirty births and seven weddings to each death. He further judged the annual birthrate in the Kościuszko colony to be 30 to the 200 residents, or the equivalent of 150 births per 1,000 inhabitants. A major reason for such a high birthrate was the economic value of children; from their early years they worked on the farms. The view of children as economic assets dated from the first years of colonization. As early as 1869 one of the Resurrectionist missionaries complained to Europe that his farmer-parishioners considered their children to be "tools to multiply dollars at home." Although the economic necessity for large families declined in the twentieth century, they remained general for many years. Even as late as the 1930's a local priest could relate that it was quite common for him to see four or five children following their mother into church.[3]

Reflecting on the nine children his wife bore during their marriage, John Kotara, of Panna Maria and later of White Deer, recalled, "We never had a doctor when any of them were born." Midwives provided the usual assistance when the time came to deliver children. Kotara recalled that he rode for such help on the occasion of every birth except one, "and my sister was there that time." Each colony had its own women who were skilled as midwives, such as Frances Lyssy at Panna Maria and Josepha Adamietz at Bandera.[4]

Folk medicine was by no means limited to midwifery. Few effective drugs and medicines were available until after the turn of the century, and every Polish mother had to know how to doctor her family. She knew something about how to set and bandage fractured limbs, how to dress wounds, and how to make various poultices and relieve suffering as best she could. Some individuals, such as J. Wiatrek, of Falls City, specialized in their own forms of healing. Wiatrek was described early in this century by a visiting journalist as famous in the vicinity as a setter of broken bones. For many years the old man, who claimed no skill in any other form of curing, set the broken bones of his neighbors. Finally an American physician, reportedly wanting to rid himself of the competition, paid Wiatrek to cease his practice.[5]

Weddings always have been major celebrations in the Silesian colonies. Thomas Ruckman visited one of these feasts at Częstochowa in 1890 and described it in this way:

> Before we get many miles up the west side of the Cibolo, we come upon a wedding party. The whole neighborhood had come together to this jollification. As we stepped in they were at dinner. I didn't have time to take off my hat until I was given a seat at the table, and my plate piled with turkey & everything good to eat and my glass with beer or whatever was good to drink. There was very little prospect for business the rest of the day. They were there for fun, it was a play day. . . . The old ones had a good time over their glasses, and the young ones danced a jolly day away.[6]

Preparations for such weddings, which often took several weeks, involved butchering cattle and hogs, making sausage, baking pastries, and cooking various other foods. When the day of the ceremony arrived, all attended the rites at the parish church and then repaired to the community hall or a private home for the festivities. Furniture was pushed back against the walls to accommodate the guests, and a huge meal was served. Following the dinner, music by local musicians began filling the air, and dancing and eating continued well into the night. After such a day the cleaning up was no small job.[7]

Today many of the old Silesian wedding customs are still observed. Marriage banns are announced in the churches several weeks before the ceremonies, but not before the arrangements have begun for the wedding feast.[8] Animals are slaughtered, food is purchased in bulk, relatives and family friends promise to help prepare and serve the meal, giant kegs of beer are ordered, and a contract is agreed upon with a band to provide dance music. Well before the day of the wedding a notice is printed in the local newspapers, and on occasion the wedding dance is announced in paid advertisements with the note "Everybody invited." After the church ceremony, which is usually held in the afternoon, the guests congregate at a community hall for eating and dancing. The bride and groom and their families sit at the head table during the meal, while the guests, frequently numbering in the hundreds, sit at long tables. At one such celebration, held in Częstochowa in 1973, which had been announced and advertised in the newspaper, approximately eleven hundred guests enjoyed a dinner of beef, sausage, beans, salads, and pastries and then danced until after midnight.[9]

As recently as 1936, the pastor of the church at Panna Maria could write with probable accuracy that there was little intermarriage of Silesians with non-Poles and that there had been only one marriage between a Silesian and a non-Catholic in the history of the settlement. In the years since, however, this pattern has changed dramatically. The shift is demonstrated clearly in a sociological study, prepared by a Catholic priest, of marriage patterns among the Silesians at Yorktown from 1872 to 1959. The study shows that up to World War I the parishioners married almost exclusively within their ethnic group. During this time less than 10 percent of the Poles married non-Poles, but thereafter the percentage soared to a high of 62.2 percent of the men and 57.1 percent of the women married in the final year of the study. Similarly, marriage with non-Catholics remained low before World War I, generally less than 5 percent. After the war, however, it rose to a high in 1959 of 19.8 percent for men and 21.6 percent for women. Thus it is evident from the Yorktown data that in the last fifty years there has been an increasingly high degree of dilution of the old Silesian ethnic and cultural stock.[10]

Although the pastor at Panna Maria declared in 1936 that divorce had "never been heard of" in the area twenty-five miles north and west of his parish, separation of married couples was indeed occurring among the Silesians. The Yorktown study indicates that in the first thirty years of the twentieth century about 1 percent of the Polish males and about 0.5 percent of the Polish females married in the community had been either separated or divorced. In the next three decades, from 1930 to 1959, the percentage for men rose to 3.5 percent and for women to over 5 percent. During the decade of the 1950's, however, the average divorce rate of 4.17 percent for Polish married couples in the parish was far below the average of 39.12 percent for white married couples in the state.[11]

The Silesians seem always to have had a reputation for strict sexual morality. As early as 1866, Father Adolf Bakanowski characterized the Polish girls in Karnes County as "maidens . . . so decent and modest, such as one can find very rarely in Poland, probably only in convents." He went on to declare that "one can find modesty and naïve simplicity in all of them." Another Polish writer half a century later reported that the people were "very moral" and that no illegitimate children were to be found among them. He related that there were more men than women in the colonies and that consequently the women were very particular about the men they chose to marry and expected them "to be as pure as they are."[12] This perhaps idyllic view is not a complete picture of the Silesians. Father Bakanowski revealed the "other side" of his parishioners when in 1868 he wrote from Bandera that "a very sad and painful incident" had brought him there. He continued that the local pastor, who had been under his supervision, "on the night of the 17th of June escaped with a Polish girl from his parish." Another glimpse of this side of the Silesians comes from the Yorktown study, which shows that as early as the 1880's an illegitimate child had been born of Polish parents in that parish and that during the period examined in the study the parish averaged approximately one illegitimate child per decade born to Polish parents.[13]

As in most other aspects of life, funerary rites among the Silesian immigrants had their own distinctive character. At the Panna Maria settlement, for example, upon the death of a parishioner all the church bells were rung after the Angelus until the funeral had taken place. To outsiders this gave the impression almost of joy rather than of sadness. When the rites were held, virtually all the people in the parish came to pay their last respects. In all the communities well into the twentieth century families arranged the burial of their dead, frequently providing homemade coffins. When Frank T. Moczygemba, an immigrant of 1855 and veteran of the Civil War, died at Panna Maria in summer 1917, his son noted in an application for mortuary funds under his father's Confederate pension that there was "no undertaker" but that the family had buried his father in a coffin made "at home out of Boards." It remained common into this century for grave markers to be inscribed solely in Polish or in both Polish and English, a custom that gives the cemeteries a striking appearance.[14]

For many years the Silesians retained the system of inheritance they had brought from Europe. In Upper Silesia it was customary for a man, upon reaching old age, to divide all his property among his children and then live with the children until his death.[15] In Texas the Polish immigrants continued to distribute their property among their children before either death or feebleness prevented them from doing so. This was the case, for example, of John and Franciszka Pyka, who had come to Texas in 1854 from the village of Sucho Daniec, in Strzelce County, and who were among the first settlers at Bandera. In 1888 they allocated their property, consisting of land, houses, and livestock, to their children, "so that we will not lack anything" in old age. Thomas Urbanczyk, of Częstochowa, who had emigrated as a boy from Rozmierz, in Strzelce County, in 1854, similarly divided his earthly possessions. In 1913, while confined to his bed with a serious illness, he gave his children both his personal property and his 395 acres of farmland near Częstochowa, keeping for himself only two horses. Yet another instance of this practice, this time from the mid-twentieth century, was the settlement made by John Kotara, of White Deer. After explaining that he had discovered not oil but natural gas on his land, he recalled, "I kept the gas but gave part and sold part of the land to my sons like my Papa did. I gave the girls the cash from the land just as Papa did his daughters."[16]

From the time the Silesians began arriving in Texas, hunting and fishing have been among their most popular pastimes. As early as 1856 one of the immigrants wrote back to Upper Silesia that the hunting in Texas was without restrictions and that very often the settlers enjoyed eating wild game. He also wrote that the fishing was so good that it was possible to have fish every day if one desired. Father Bakanowski, who in the 1860's occasionally participated in these outdoor activities with his male parishioners, wrote, "In Texas hunting may be considered the most enjoyable entertainment."[17] To Europeans accustomed to government regulation of firearms, he reported that anyone in the new land could possess a gun and carry it with him in order to display his skill as a hunter. The priest then enumerated deer, wolves, panthers, bears, coyotes, and rabbits as possible game. He also listed ducks and turkeys, the latter on the San Antonio River being "almost twice as large" as those in Silesia. The method settlers used to shoot the turkeys, according to Bakanowski, was first, during the day, to find the trees in which the fowls roosted and then, after dark, to conceal themselves below. There the hunters waited quietly until all the turkeys arrived and then picked them off by shooting up into the branches. The priest assured his readers that the birds were so frightened that they did not fly away.

When people wanted to catch fish, Bakanowski reported, they attached large fishing poles to the trees beside the river and left them holding lines in the water overnight. Returning the next morning, according to Father Adolf, the immigrants usually found twenty- to forty-pound fish on the ends of their lines, but, he added, they sometimes found alligators instead.[18]

Another form of recreation enjoyed by the Silesian settlers was the fellowship of meetings of the various societies that sprang into existence in the colonies. For the first seventy-five years of settlement these associations were almost exclusively under church sponsorship. The first known Polish organization in Texas was the Society of the Immaculate Conception, begun by twenty-nine of the Reverend Vincent Barzyński's parishioners at San Antonio in 1866. This short-lived body was followed in 1868 by the organization of Saint Adalbert's Benevolent Society, a mutual-aid association that provided its members with sickness and death benefits. This pioneer society has been credited with being Barzyński's prototype for the Polish Roman Catholic Union, which he was instrumental in founding later in Chicago. Saint Adalbert's Society possessed its own meeting hall adjacent to Saint Michael's Church, held programs presented by local Polish priests and other speakers, and into the twentieth century remained the most popular organization in San Antonio among the old-stock Silesian immigrants and their descendants. Other religious associations that arose in San Antonio during the period were the Polish Young Men's Union, Saint Stephen's Singing Society, and a chapter of the Saint Vincent de Paul Society.[19]

Although San Antonio had the earliest Polish organizations in Texas, other towns also organized similar groups. Falls City had its Catholic Daughters and Holy Trinity School Club; Saint Hedwig had Rosary, Sacred Heart, and Children of Mary groups; and Panna Maria had Rosary, Scapular, and Apostleship of Prayer societies, not to mention an early Brotherhood of the Sacred Heart, formed in 1879.[20]

Secular organizations did not become popular among the Silesians until after the beginning of the twentieth century. Probably the earliest non-Catholic Polish organization with Silesian membership was the Woodrow Wilson Society, begun as a chapter of the Polish National Alliance at San Antonio in 1929. This association, however, had primarily non-Silesian members, and because of its secular outlook frequently was condemned by the old immigrants. The opposition went as far as public name-calling. When the Polish consul general, visiting San Antonio in 1930, was asked to speak before a meeting of the alliance chapter, the chairman of the Catholic St. Adalbert's Society asked the official, "What did they want from you? . . . they're Bolsheviks," a criticism that certainly was not true. With the passage of time, however, such extreme attitudes changed, and today several active chapters of the Polish National Alliance are scattered among the Silesian communities.[21]

The immigrants' social life was by no means limited to the meetings of societies. They gathered frequently at homes, wedding celebrations, and community dances. During the first years of settlement such social events remained under some religious supervision. During the time of Father Bakanowski's tenure in Panna Maria, for example, all festivities in the parish had to be approved by the priest and had to end by a certain hour, usually midnight. As the years passed, however, these restrictions relaxed, and the parties, the wedding feasts, and, for the women, the feather-stripping parties and quilting bees, went on for hours and hours. The latter were two of the favorite wintertime entertainments for the women and girls, who met to work on feather beds and quilts and to gossip until late into the night. Many women in the colonies today still proudly use comforters, pillows, and quilts that date from those evenings during their own or their mothers' girlhoods.[22]

Horseback riding, a necessity during the first years of settlement, later provided an additional pastime for the Silesian men. Concerning this form of recreation, John Kotara recalled from his youth that always, "when I had a good horse with good feet, I'd run her." While he was courting his future wife, Veronica Jarzombek, in Karnes County during the 1890's, her family lived on the other side of a creek from his family, and he generally rode to her house when he went to see her. A wooden bridge spanned the stream and bore a painted sign: "$25.00 Fine to Race Horse or Trot Wagon." Liking to ride fast and taking the warning as a challenge, one night, after visiting the Jarzombek home, young Kotara raced across the bridge. The hooves of his horse made a surprisingly loud clatter that resounded through the quiet of the evening. The next morning his father, who in warm weather always slept on the porch, remarked at breakfast: "Some darn fool went over that bridge wide open last night and woke me up. I thought every board would come out of that bridge."

It was no wonder the elder Kotara was awakened. In fact, he was probably not the only person disturbed by his son's noise, because it was common for the Silesians to sleep outdoors during the hot months of the year. As early as June 1867, one of the Resurrectionist missionaries reported to Europe: "Nearly all the people sleep outdoors or inside the house with the windows and doors open. . . . I slept outside several times and I liked it." This is yet another practice that many of the Poles continued into the twentieth century.[23]

Music played a significant role in the lives of the Silesian farmers and their families. Much of the music was religious and originated in the churches. Not only did the people sing Polish hymns during the services, but the priests sang the liturgy of the mass, which was not always an easy task. Father Stanisław Wojciechowski, of San Antonio, commented about this fact in 1876, writing that his parishioners willingly paid him for his efforts but that they required his "singing of High Mass" as well as weekly sermons, adding, "I do not have such strength." As early as the 1860's the Polish churches were beginning to have organs, simple though they were, and it usually fell the lot of the schoolteachers to play them. In 1866, Felix Zwiardowski wrote from Panna Maria about one of these instruments, "I play the organ . . . but you must understand that the organ fits the player—it's only a little larger than a street organ that one can carry on his back." The most popular secular instruments were violins, and some of the Silesians, like Charlie Haiduk of Bandera, became such proficient fiddlers that they were in great demand by the Americans. From the secular world almost every child learned the patriotic songs "Boże coś Polskę" (God Save Poland) and "Jeszcze Polska nie zginęła" (Poland Is Yet Alive). The singing of Polish songs remained popular in the colonies into the twentieth century, and Polish Christmas carols are still frequently heard during the Yuletide season.[24]

An element of Silesian folk culture that remained alive in Texas for several decades was wood carving. The craft probably reached its height in Częstochowa, where one of the parishioners in the last years of the nineteenth century carved all three of the large altars in the church. Described in such terms as "very fine workmanship" and "carved in minute detail," they were the work of Albert Pawełek. Examples of his art in the form of crucifixes made from such native woods as pecan and mesquite have been exhibited both at the Institute of Texan Cultures and at the Witte Memorial Museum in San Antonio.[25]

As did all other immigrant groups who came to Texas, the Silesian peasants through their own hard work advanced both socially and financially in the open society they found in the New World. Their economic progress began within their first decade and a half in Texas. A study of fourteen Silesians whose property holdings can be traced in the manuscript population schedules of the censuses of 1860 and 1870 shows that their financial worth increased from an average of $295.00 in 1860 to $503.37 a decade later. Some individuals found success in agriculture, while others sought their fortunes in other pursuits. Life was not easy for the people who chose to stay on the farms. They worked long hours for low pay. Farm laborers after the Civil War earned only a dollar a day plus board, and the landowners themselves usually received only four hundred to five hundred dollars for their crops for an entire year of labor. Hard work on the farm, however, was profitable to many Poles. By the turn of the century dozens of them owned several hundred acres apiece. Other kinds of employment were open to Silesians who wanted to avoid what they considered to be the drudgery of rural life. Some of them worked as teamsters, hauling goods from place to place, especially from the coastal ports to San Antonio before the arrival of the railroad in 1877. The teamsters hitched five or six oxen to their wagons and with them could carry three to four thousand pounds on each trip. In the 1870's they earned one to three dollars per hundredweight, depending on the season of the year. Other Silesians who had learned English and who knew some arithmetic sought escape to the towns by working as clerks for merchants, sometimes earning as much as forty to seventy dollars a month.[26]

One of several Silesians who were particularly successful both socially and financially during the second half of the nineteenth century was Edward Kotula. Born in Prussian Poland in 1844, he was ten years old when he immigrated with his family to Panna Maria. Within a year his father died, and his widowed mother with her children moved to San Antonio. Since the family had little money, Edward worked for his living from adolescence. His first job was as a teamster hauling stone. He was seventeen years old when the Civil War broke out, and during the conflict he secured a position as a mail carrier between San Antonio and Boerne and then later between San Antonio and Victoria.

After the close of the war Kotula began working as a clerk in the San Antonio mercantile establishment of D. and A. Oppenheimer. Advancing rapidly within the business, he left it in 1868 to open his own store with a capital of fifteen hundred dollars. The venture, initially housed in a humble adobe building, was a financial success, and Kotula continued to expand his commercial dealings in various locations until he moved his operation to a large building on Military Plaza. As the years passed, he began several other business endeavors, including ranching, real estate, and wool marketing. He became so prominent in the last, in some years handling over half a million dollars' worth of the product, that he was called "the wool king of Texas." Kotula continued operating his mercantile outlet on Military Plaza until 1893, when he turned to his other interests exclusively, actively engaging in them until his death in 1907, a revered citizen of the city.[27]

By no means all of the Silesians were as successful as Edward Kotula, but most of them profited from the upward social mobility they found possible. Jacob Anthony Mazurek, of Bandera, provides a good example. A descendant of the original 1855 settlers, he was born on a farm near Bandera and in 1917 moved with his parents, brothers, and sisters to San Antonio. There his father secured employment as a carpenter in a box factory, and each of the sons found his own job. Working his way up in his chosen field, Jacob was able to advance from clerk in a tire store to owner of the store.[28]

Although the stereotype of the Silesians is that of hard-working, peace-loving farmers and artisans industriously attempting to advance themselves, that image is not correct for all the Poles. At least one of their number, Martin Mróz, a young man from the Saint Hedwig community, rebelled against the restraints imposed by society and became a hunted outlaw. He was described as "a big, rough, blue-eyed blond who wore neither underwear nor boots, but went about in a pair of brogan shoes." He appeared in the Pecos Valley around what is now Carlsbad, New Mexico, in the early 1890's. In a short time he gathered about himself a gang of cattle thieves, married a buxom, fair-haired prostitute in the saloon town of Phenix, New Mexico, and stole enough cattle to become notorious in the neighborhood. With the passage of time and the disappearance of more livestock the local cattlemen's association offered a reward for his arrest, and in spring 1895, Mróz fled across the Mexican border to Juárez with a pocketful of money from his illicit dealings. He subsequently was arrested but later released by the Mexican authorities. Then, on the night of 29 June 1895, while attempting to cross a railway bridge over the Rio Grande to El Paso to visit with his wife, the Silesian badman was ambushed by American lawmen, who killed him for the reward. His unmarked pauper's grave is in the Concordia Cemetery in El Paso beside that of the better-known gunfighter John Wesley Hardin.[29]

Relations between the Silesians and the Americans should not be judged by those of Mróz with the Pecos Valley ranchers. After the nervous days of Reconstruction the two groups settled down to a peaceful though generally separate existence. Occasionally the Americans came to the aid of the Poles, as one did in the construction of the church in Saint Hedwig in 1867 by donating the stone. In another manifestation of good will toward the Silesians, in 1879 three times as many Americans attended the funeral of the Reverend Bronislaus Przewłocki at Bandera as did Poles at the settlement. The natives generally had good opinions of the Silesians, considering them moral, honest, and temperate, but with notable exceptions they remained somewhat distant from the immigrants in all but official or commercial dealings until well into the twentieth century.[30]

After the first excitement of Republican political activity following the Civil War, the Silesians gradually backed away from politics. With the return of the state and local affairs to the Democratic party in the second half of the 1870's, the Silesians also became predominately Democrats and for the most part lost interest in all but local matters. An American observer noted in 1909 that they were little concerned with politics and that, "if they are not strongly urged by the contesting candidates[,] they remain at home on election day to work in the fields." A Polish visitor in the next decade reported that "the Polish population is not involved in the political struggles of the Americans" and that, although most of them were registered voters, they seldom used their franchise. It was not that the Silesians were completely apathetic, the observer explained, but rather that they realized that, as long as almost all Texans voted for the Democratic party, they were too small a group to exert any influence. Despite such general feelings, some Silesians nevertheless did participate in local affairs. Among them were Bernard Kiołbassa, who was elected to a two-year term as county commissioner of Bexar County in 1888, and Alex Mihalski, who served as an election judge at Adkins in the Saint Hedwig parish for the Democratic primary election in 1910.[31]

Similarly to their relations with the Americans, the Polish immigrants got along reasonably well with the other ethnic groups among whom they lived. They were especially indebted to freed Negro slaves, who popularized the cultivation of cotton among them in the years immediately after the Civil War. The Silesians hired some blacks as temporary laborers during the postwar period. Unfortunately not all relations with blacks were filled with understanding. At La Vernia, in Wilson County, in summer 1910 a black youth seriously injured a Pole named Roma Pierdolla when he slashed him across the chest with a razor during a fight.[32]

Contact with Mexicans dated from the first weeks of Polish immigration to Texas, when the colonists hired Mexican teamsters to transport their belongings from the coast to central Texas. Furthermore, a Mexican, Andreas Coy, was among the first persons to give the new arrivals food during the terrible drought of 1856–1857. Soon the association between the two groups became more intimate, and during the initial years of settlement at least one Silesian, a brother of the Reverend Leopold Moczygemba, married into a Mexican family. The Poles always lived near Spanish-speaking people, often having them in their churches, and the cultural exchange between the two groups reached a very high level. Many Silesians learned Spanish as a second language before learning English as a third language. One Polish anthropologist in 1930 even went so far as to suggest that the Mexicans had influenced Silesian culture in Texas to an even greater extent than had the Americans.[33]

The Silesians also lived among other European ethnic groups. The most numerous of these were the German immigrants, and generally the two groups associated with each other on good terms. It was not unusual for Germans to have shops in the Polish communities, such as the one that operated in Saint Hedwig around the turn of the century, but most of the Germans were wise enough to employ Polish clerks. The only known instance of active hostility between the two groups occurred in Meyersville, where they clashed over the language to be used in the parish church. A similar conflict was narrowly avoided in San Antonio during the 1860's. At that time the German Catholics in the city attempted to persuade the Silesians to join them in their parish church, but the Silesians flatly refused. Their highly nationalistic pastor, Vincent Barzyński, declared, "The Germans are great for giving advice and ruling the Poles . . . but we . . . do not want to change our faith for theirs, because we Poles have our own saints in heaven."[34]

The one group with whom the Silesians never made peace was the warlike Indians, who continued to raid frontier settlements until the mid-1870's. In one of these incidents the attackers broke the windows of the Catholic rectory in Bandera and shot arrows through the openings at the pastor, Father Snigurski. The good priest, a veteran of the Polish Insurrection of 1863, was undaunted and began firing his rifle in self-defense, continuing to shoot until his parishioners came to the rescue. As late as 1873, Father Zwiardowski complained about the dangers of attack in the Bandera area. The last recorded encounter between Silesians and Indians occurred in 1874, when Gabe Anderwald, of Bandera, who as a boy had been one of the original immigrants to the town in 1855, had his horses stolen while he was cutting shingles near the hill-country settlement.[35]

Until after World War I one of the strongest ties holding the Silesian communities together was the nearly universal use of the Polish language. Almost every visitor who recorded his impressions of the colonies made some observations on this phenomenon. One traveler, who arrived by train in San Antonio one day in 1907, remarked that "even in the station you can hear Polish spoken." Another visitor about the same time commented that in Yorktown, although the farmers could speak English, "they use only Polish and do not corrupt it in the slightest with foreign expressions."[36] The language used by the colonists, however, was not pure literary Polish but rather the archaic dialect of Upper Silesia, which had been cut away from the Polish state for centuries. Perhaps unconsciously the peasant immigrants realized that their speech was not standard, because the books they wanted most from the Resurrectionist missionaries in the 1860's were prayer books and hymnals "from Opole" in their own dialect.[37]

The use of the Polish language has declined through the years, although probably most of the Silesians now over the age of fifty still can read and speak it. The decline in usage began surprisingly early, at least by the 1860's, in the urban environment of San Antonio. Father Barzyński sadly reported to Rome just after his arrival in San Antonio in 1866 that, although all his adult parishioners spoke Polish, "the children know only English well." He explained that, because the parents were workers or craftsmen, they could not care for their children at home, and consequently they played with American children in the streets and learned English from them. In another letter he described the unhappy situation in which "very often a mother speaks to her child in Polish, it answers in English, and neither can understand the other." After two years in the city he wrote despairingly, "The Polish language does not have any strength for the younger generation, because they think, feel, and even sin in English."[38] The decline in the use of the Polish language followed in later years at the other colonies, especially during the intervals when the parishes were without Polish priests. It is remarkable today, after a century and a quarter of decreasing language use, that one can visit the rural communities and walk into country stores to find only Silesian Polish being spoken and find well-attended Polish-language masses in the churches.[39]

One factor in the maintenance of the Polish language among the Silesian immigrants was a continued although limited contact that they maintained with Poland. Throughout the nineteenth century most of the settlements had priests from the mother country who maintained the Polish language in church affairs. Too, many of the Silesians corresponded with relatives in Upper Silesia well into the twentieth century. On very rare occasions colonists in Texas made visits to Poland. The American Poles, however, read with interest both overseas and American Polish-language newspapers to which they subscribed.[40]

For a short time the Silesians in Texas had their own Polish-language newspaper. The journal *Nowiny Texaskie* appeared in San Antonio in late 1913 and was produced until after the close of World War I by the Texas Polish New Publishing Company. Though it was printed in San Antonio and appealed to Silesian readers, curiously the editorial staff of the paper consisted almost exclusively of non-Silesian Poles. Although no copies of the newspaper are known to exist today, in 1967 a researcher from the Institute of Texan Cultures in San Antonio photographed two now destroyed copies that had survived up to that time. These issues, from late 1914 and early 1915, featured front-page articles on the war in Europe and current events in both Poland and the United States. This newspaper, which ceased publication in 1918, was the sole venture in Polish-language journalism in the state.[41]

Until after World War I the most important economic activity of the Silesians in Texas remained agriculture. With the spread of cotton cultivation among them following the Civil War, this fiber became their most important crop. It had been a useful crop for some time; as one visiting writer related at the turn of the century, it gave them "the cash that they wanted."[42] The large crops just after the war were profitable, but the situation soon changed. Prices plummeted to as low as three cents a pound, and then, even worse, the boll weevil began annually destroying thousands of acres of cotton in the fields. In Karnes County, where Silesians constituted virtually all of the farming population, 44 percent of the 1887 crop was destroyed by the pests. Fortunately, not all the years were so bad. The year 1889 proved to be a good one for the Poles, some of whom made as much as a bale of cotton to the acre and had very good corn harvests. The next year Thomas Ruckman described the Cibolo Valley near Częstochowa as "a magnificent picture of great fields of corn & cotton, sorghum, and . . . oats." He went on to depict orchards, vineyards, and "great rows of bee stands," closing his description of the Polish farmers' property with the declaration: "The Emperor of Prussia is not more independent nor near so happy."[43]

The only systematic examination of Silesian agriculture in Texas was conducted just after World War I by an official sent from the office of the Polish consul general in New York. He reported that among the Silesians the average farm had two hundred acres and that he had visited one large Polish landholding of twelve hundred acres. The normal ratio of cultivated land to pasture was three-fourths to one-fourth, but in areas with poor soil the proportion changed to allow more stock raising. In the Kościuszko area, for example, half the land was under the plow, and the remainder was devoted to cattle grazing. On good soil about three-fourths of the cultivated land was planted in cotton and one-fourth in corn and other livestock feedstuffs, while on the less fertile soils, where the percentage of land devoted to cattle was higher, the farmers had to raise more feed for their animals. By World War I mechanical cultivation with agricultural implements was normal, but power was provided by draft animals rather than by tractors, which did not become common among the Polish farmers until the 1930's. During the nineteenth century oxen had been phased out of use, and mules and horses pulled the plows, implements, and farm vehicles.[44]

Most observers agreed that the Silesian farmers produced more cotton than their American neighbors did under the same conditions. There are two complementary reasons for this situation. First, the Poles themselves worked hard in the fields, while the native Americans ordinarily employed blacks to do the work. The blacks, not owning the land and receiving only a percentage of the crops, frequently lacked the motivation of the Silesians, who were working their own land for their personal benefit. Second, the Polish women and children joined the men in the fields, thus more than doubling the work force without any added labor cost. The Polish consul general from New York observed in 1920 that, because of this circumstance, "a large family places the Polish farmer in an advantageous economic position," considering that at the time a Mexican laborer in the San Antonio area demanded $7.50 a day during the cotton harvest.[45]

For a time at the beginning of the twentieth century it appeared that the Poles would find a new cash crop in onions. Farmers who owned stream bottomlands rushed to install steam-powered irrigation pumps and dig canals to their fields to provide water for this wonder crop that promised them riches. One of these men was John Gawlik, of Częstochowa, who pumped water to his onions from Cibolo Creek. The only Pole who entered this venture on a truly large scale was William Dobrowolski, a real estate promoter from San Antonio who had come to Texas as a boy in 1855. With a partner he developed and operated a twenty-five-hundred-acre commercial farm on the Rio Grande at Eagle Pass, Texas. The enthusiasm for onions, however, passed almost as quickly as it had come, and by World War I most of the farmers had returned to the more familiar cotton cultivation.[46]

Agriculture for the Silesians who went to White Deer was unlike what they had known before. Even the land was different, almost perfectly level and covered with virgin soil. In the first years the farmers were unable to plant large crops because they had only their horses and mules for power to break the difficult sod for cultivation. Their principal crops were wheat and feed grains. Harvests in the early days did not go quickly. In the 1919 harvest it took two weeks for the members of the Vincent Haiduk family to cut and bind their wheat crop and another two weeks for a threshing-machine crew to separate the grain from the sheaves. These large machines were operated by teams of fifteen to twenty men, and while they worked on a farm, the family was obligated to feed them. One of the White Deer pioneers recalled from her younger years that it "was a job to fix so much food" three times a day but that "the harvest men were always surprised at the food we had and wondered where we got it all." At night, she said, "the men layed [*sic*] on the floor like sardines." This was indeed a different life from that of farmers in central Texas.[47]

No matter where they farmed, the Silesians were at the mercy of the weather. Although they had many good harvests, the weather frequently caused them serious problems. Among the times when the Polish farmers of central Texas suffered most severely from the elements were the strong wind and hailstorm that struck in May 1868, the great Texas floods of summer 1869, drought in the early 1870's, and the recurring drought in the mid-1890's.[48] The farmers were not, of course, the only ones hurt by these agricultural disasters; everyone in the communities suffered either directly or indirectly. After a year of drought, for example, the pastor at Panna Maria was forced to write to Rome in February 1872 that his income had stopped because the people could no longer contribute to the church and that he was forced to buy everything on credit until the next harvest.[49]

One of the most interesting social aspects of agriculture among the Silesians is the high level of cooperation the farmers achieved. The most natural forms of cooperation were within families, such as a father and his sons working together haying or harvesting. This kind of teamwork was very evident among the Urbanczyk brothers, John, Felix, and Ben, who moved from Rhineland to White Deer in 1910 and 1911. The two younger brothers, Felix and Ben, bought many things together: cattle, land, Fordson tractors, and even automobiles. They also joined in drilling their first water well. After buying the drilling rig, they sunk the well halfway between their houses. As agricultural machinery became more easily available, the three Urbanczyk brothers bought their own threshing equipment and worked together in harvesting, Ben running a Rhumley steam engine, Felix operating the threshing machine, and John overseeing the hauling of the grain with wagons and horses.

Another form of cooperation in the Silesian communities was that among neighbors, most often among age groups. The men who as boys had played and hunted together helped each other with their farm work. This mutual assistance was not a precise exchange of day for day of labor but general trading of working time. The farmers of one vicinity, for example, met at a farm to harvest a crop of corn and then simply moved on to the next farm and so on until they had completed the job. With increasing farm mechanization in the twentieth century the exchanges among same-age groups became less important. Instead, as one farmer bought a hay baler, another a corn picker, and others their own machines, they contracted for work with their neighbors. In this way with a minimum outlay of capital whole neighborhoods were able to become fully mechanized.[50]

Many of the Polish farmers in Texas felt an overriding compulsion to buy land. A Polish observer noted just after World War I that American merchants and farmers who lived around the Silesians had stressed to him that the characteristic goal of their Polish neighbors was to purchase farmland. From the early days of settlement, in fact, the immigrants were accustomed to lending each other money for this purpose. Another early-twentieth-century writer gave the opinion that the desire to possess real property was a distinctively Polish trait, explaining that throughout the centuries in Poland political rights had been connected with land ownership. He reported that nothing would make the Silesians sell their acreage; rather, they wanted to buy more and more. He concluded, "There are peasants [in Texas] whose land is worth 50,000 rubles [$25,000], but who are as poor as when they arrived."[51]

With the expansion of Silesian agriculture into new areas and the increase of population within the colonies, transportation between the communities became increasingly important during the latter part of the nineteenth century. In the years immediately following the Civil War travel between the settlements was at the most dangerous and at the least adventurous. When the Resurrectionist missionaries arrived in 1866, they were amazed at the lack of roads. One of them wrote back to Europe, "Travel to Panna Maria seemed strange for us, because here there are plains like those in Siberia." He marveled at the ability of their stagecoach driver to find his way "through brush, gorges, and canyons . . . before we reached Panna Maria."[52] The luxury of coach travel, however, was only for the occasional visitor. The Silesian farmers during these years used animal-drawn wagons and horses as their principal means of transportation.[53]

The main roads between the colonies were in fact mere trails

The Reverend Felix Zwiardowski as a young man. (Photograph courtesy Archdiocese of San Antonio.)

Cibolo Creek at a point between Panna Maria and Helena. This was the approximate location of the gunfight between Poles and southerners in fall 1867. (Photograph by the author, 1978.)

The abandoned Protestant church at Helena, the former county seat of Karnes County, four miles from Panna Maria. (Photograph by the author, 1971.)

St. Hedwig, the patroness of Silesia, who was greatly revered by the early Polish immigrants to Texas. The community of St. Hedwig in Bexar County was named for her. (Illustration from Bitschnau, *Żywoty świętych pańskich*.)

Joseph Moczygemba, brother of the Reverend Leopold Moczygemba, born in the village of Płużnica in 1819, and an immigrant to Texas in 1854, seated beside his second wife, Carolina Szyguda. This photograph is one of the very few showing a Silesian woman in folk costume in Texas. This style of dress was commonly worn in Upper Silesia during the second half of the nineteenth century. (Photograph courtesy the John F. Dziuk family, Hobson, Texas.)

The John Dugosh family making molasses at Bandera, ca. 1900–1915. (Photograph courtesy C. M. Dugosh and the St. Stanislaus Museum, Bandera, Texas.)

Philip Kowalik, a Polish cattle buyer at Kościuszko, Texas, ca. 1915. (Photograph courtesy B. Kotara, Kościuszko, Texas.)

Four generations of the Tom Morawietz family at Bandera, Texas, ca. 1900–1915. (Photograph courtesy Mrs. W. C. Allen and the St. Stanislaus Museum, Bandera, Texas.)

A hog slaughtering at Falls City, Texas, in 1921. (Photograph courtesy Mr. and Mrs. Ray Pollok, Falls City, Texas.)

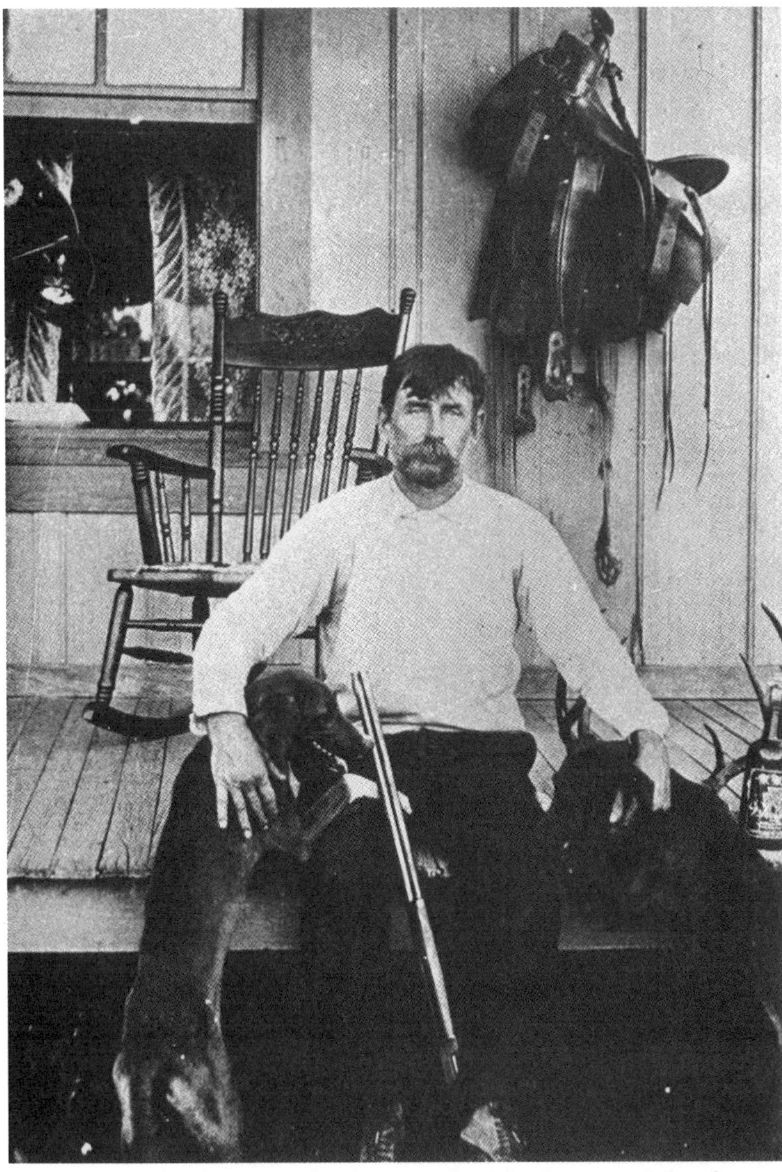

Pete Kaczmarek relaxing on the front porch of his house with his dogs at La Vernia, Wilson County, Texas, in 1914. (Photograph courtesy Mrs. Frank Katzmarek, San Antonio, Texas.)

Members of St. Adalbert's Society, one of the most prominent Polish societies in Texas during the latter years of the nineteenth century. (Photograph courtesy Mr. Ted Deming, San Antonio, Texas.)

Henry Czerner and Ben Urbanczyk, two of the young men responsible for the location of a Polish colony at White Deer in the Texas Panhandle. (Photograph courtesy the Square House Museum, Panhandle, Texas.)

Threshing wheat at the White Deer Polish colony early in the twentieth century. (Photograph courtesy the Square House Museum, Panhandle, Texas.)

A crowd on the street in Falls City waiting for cold beer that has been brought on the train from San Antonio, ca. 1910. (Photograph courtesy Mr. and Mrs. Ray Pollok, Falls City, Texas.)

Members of the Kaczmarek family on an excursion probably near St. Hedwig in Bexar County, ca. 1915–1918. (Photograph courtesy Mrs. Frank Katzmarek, San Antonio, Texas.)

NOWINY TEXASKIE

Z Wojny Europejskiej.

STATE BANK & TRUST CO.

Przegląd najgłówniejszych wypadków w r. 1914

Ogłaszamy się w "Nowinach Texaskich" ponieważ

$4\frac{1}{2}\%$ od wpłaconych depozytów dopisywany kwartalnie

West Texas Bank & Trust Company

Czy to małe czy wielkie

An issue of *Nowiny Texaskie*, photographed by a researcher from the Institute of Texan Cultures in 1967, but subsequently lost. (Photograph courtesy Institute of Texan Cultures, San Antonio, Texas.)

The grave of August Moczygemba, one of the four brothers of the Reverend Leopold Moczygemba who immigrated to Texas in 1854, as it appears with Polish-language inscription at the cemetery at Panna Maria. (Photograph by the author, 1971.)

Participants in a religious procession during the rites for the reinterment of the remains of the Reverend Leopold Moczygemba at Panna Maria, Texas, in October 1974. (Photograph by the author, 1974.)

through the sparsely settled ranching country. For long distances horseback riding was the preferred mode of travel. Describing the journey between Saint Hedwig and Panna Maria, one Pole wrote that, although it was forty-five miles "through forests and steppes," it was always better to ride a horse than to go in a wagon, which took two days "on unpleasant roads."[54] The same writer noted in another description of Texas travel, "The roads here are very disagreeable . . . and one has to have a compass as if he were at sea."[55] Another Polish observer in the mid-nineteenth century characterized the route he took between Saint Hedwig and Panna Maria as going through "dark and brushy forests on the narrow trails made by cattle."[56] Because the area they traversed was virtually uninhabited, travelers had to carry with them all the necessary camp equipment, food, and cooking utensils. This cumbersome outfit did nothing to speed their journeys.[57]

Father Adolf Bakanowski left a personal description of one of his trips from Panna Maria to San Antonio that gives a detailed view of frontier travel just after the Civil War. He left early one morning with Joseph Barzyński, Sr., the father of the Reverend Vincent Barzyński. The day before, they had prepared their supplies of bread, butter, meat, chicken, eggs, pots, and pans. The two men left the Silesian colony after morning mass and breakfast, traveling in a horse-drawn cart that carried, in addition to the passengers and their supplies, the priest's dog. Father Adolf recalled that "the morning was fresh and nice" as they watched cattle wandering in search of new grass and the Silesian farmers working in their fields. Riding out of the village, the men listened as they passed a peasant girl singing the pious Polish hymn "Already from the Morning," as she led ducks and geese to a pond near the farmhouse where she lived.

Soon they were beyond the Polish settlements. They traveled eighteen miles without a stop until they came to a resting place in a motte of mesquite trees, which the Poles, from the name of the trees, called Muszkieciny. There about half-past eleven they took a lunch break. Already the day had grown warm. They unhitched and hobbled the horses to let them graze while they built a fire for their meal of bacon, sausage, chicken, and coffee. After eating, the priest took a nap in the shade of one of the brushy trees, while his elderly companion set out to shoot some rabbits for their dinner. Time passed quickly, and it was four in the afternoon before Barzyński returned with meat for the evening meal. The two travelers hurried to catch up with a party of farmers who had left the day before in wagons loaded with corn to sell in San Antonio. By the time that the two travelers reached the camping place, it was dark, and they had some trouble finding the Silesians among the other groups who were spending the night there. "At last we found the fire of our camp because the greatest noise was there." They unharnessed their animals and fastened them to trees with long ropes for the night, joining the farmers to cook their dinner over the campfire. The next morning after breakfast the entire Polish group left together for San Antonio, which they finally saw in the distance. The Polish Quarter was on their side of town, and soon they could see Saint Michael's Church, as Father Adolf recalled, "and the doors of the rectory were open. They were waiting for us."[58]

Not all travel in Polish Texas was so pleasant as this almost idyllic journey. Father Felix Zwiardowski, who almost always described things in a down-to-earth manner, wrote to Europe in 1879 that he had one problem after another on a trip from San Antonio to Bandera. First, he wrote, "I was hounded by millions of ticks, which bit without mercy." Next, "I sprained my leg while getting down from the wagon" during a rest break. Then he took off his shoes "on the prairie" to care for his horses and pull off the "ticks by the handfuls," but in the process he chilled his extremities, and he complained, "Now I am lame."[59] Zwiardowski also described more serious dangers that threatened travelers between the Silesian settlements. On one occasion he reported that he had just ridden on horseback from San Antonio to Saint Hedwig because it had been raining so heavily that it was impossible for him to go by carriage. He declared, "This is not a joke," because, he explained, after only twenty minutes of heavy rainfall flash floods could fill stream valleys so high that they could carry away men and horses.[60]

Because of the Indian raids that continued to the mid-1870's, the route between San Antonio and Bandera was the most dangerous of the roads connecting Silesian colonies. Father Bakanowski related that when the Polish missionaries traveled there they tried to take "at least one Pole" to accompany them. The Silesians went either on horseback or in carts "with all possible guns, especially rifles." When camping in the forest on the way to or from Bandera, the travelers tied their horses to trees to graze and then lay under their wagons to rest, usually without any campfire for fear of exposing their location. On a trip alone in December 1869, Father Zwiardowski was disturbed just after making camp by what sounded like a person crawling through the brush. After taking cover behind a big oak tree, he fired his rifle twice into the air, frightening away his would-be attacker. Afraid to leave in the dark, he remained standing "the whole night with rifle and rosary in hand." The next morning he hurriedly rode the remaining twenty-five miles to Bandera without stopping, and there he learned that near his camp the night before an eleven-member war party had killed a Mexican "in a terrible way."[61]

With the passage of years travel between the Silesian settlements became easier, especially for colonies like Falls City and Saint Hedwig that had convenient railway lines. Elsewhere the trails of the mid-nineteenth century simply changed into unpaved, rutted country roads. A visitor to the Silesian colonies in Karnes and Wilson counties in 1907 left a vivid description of his eight-mile journey from Falls City to Panna Maria. Having arrived at Falls City by train, he went to the local livery stable but found that no horses were available. "I asked if I could get there [to Panna Maria] on foot and they just laughed at the idea." Finally he did get a horse and a farmer to guide him, and they left in late afternoon. "On the way we saw neither people nor houses, only some plowed fields, but not very often." The solitude of the Texas countryside made an impression on the traveler, who was accustomed to the city noises of Warsaw: "The sun went down and you could hear only the sound of horseshoes. Besides this there was complete silence. We met no one." His legs stiffened in the uncomfortable Mexican saddle, unlike any that he had ever seen before. "It seemed as if we would travel forever. . . . finally we arrived. In the silence the sound of the horseshoes was heard from a distance, so the Rev. . . . ran out to the porch to meet us." In the next days the visitor went from Panna Maria to Częstochowa to Kościuszko. He described the way between the last two communities as "a wide road, almost as wide as the street Aleje Jerozolimskie [in Warsaw]," adding that to keep back the cattle the road was "fenced with barbed wire on both sides." The earth was still drying from a rain, and the thin wheels of the carriage in which he was riding "often were half hidden in the mud."[62] Another visitor to the Silesian colonies two years later said that the road from San Antonio to Saint Hedwig for the first ten miles was "excellent, something rarely experienced in America," but that after that it disappointingly deteriorated.[63]

Transportation for the Silesians at White Deer posed special problems, for the land there was treeless and flat with virtually no landmarks. During the first years the children from the Polish colony had to go five miles across the prairie to attend a public school. At first they had to walk, for a horse was valued as highly as a hired man; the animal was too important in the farm work to be used merely to carry children to school. On foggy days they became lost. Since there were no fences, the cattle would chase them—or so the frightened children thought. After the new arrivals were able to set up their farmsteads, the younger members of the families finally received horses, mules, or donkeys to ride to classes, but that did not solve all the problems. The lack of landmarks in the years before country roads took the place of trails posed a difficulty for all travelers. Often when people were away and expected to return after dark, another member of the family would "hang a lantern on a windmill so they could find their way home."[64]

Slowly the material manifestations of the twentieth century began appearing in the Silesian communities. A Polish visitor who arrived at Falls City in 1907, having viewed its wooden false-front buildings, several saloons, and unpaved main street, told a group of loungers that he wanted to go to Panna Maria. To his amazement they advised him to call the pastor there on the telephone. "So there are telephones in this desert!" he thought to himself. Then, as he went to the other settlement, he noticed telephone wires at the side of the road. Not long after this incident, the automobile, another herald of the new century, appeared in the quiet little Polish towns. One of the first Silesian families in Karnes County to own an automobile was the Valentine Yanta family. They lived on a farm on Ecleto Creek and used their Jackson automobile primarily to drive the twelve miles back and forth to church in Panna Maria.[65]

Not everyone accepted the changes that the twentieth century was bringing. The increasingly rapid transition from the Silesian way of life was painful to many of the older people who had been born in Poland, could not understand the new ways, and longed for the motherland. One of these was Joseph Moczygemba, the brother of the Reverend Leopold Moczygemba, who had been born in the village of Płużnica in 1819. He was married and the father of six children when he and his family left their home in green Upper Silesia in 1854. Either during the voyage or just after their arrival in Texas, Joseph's wife died, leaving him a widower with a family to care for. Perhaps because of this responsibility he remarried a year later at the age of thirty-six. By his second wife he had five more children.

Moczygemba became a successful farmer at Panna Maria, actively participated in local church affairs, and was a respected member of the community. As he aged, however, he became increasingly feeble and infirm. When he was ninety-one years old, his son Jacob plaintively wrote to the family in Poland that the old man's physical and mental health had deteriorated to the unfortunate point that he was unable to recognize his own children. He was losing his ability to speak and had to have someone to care for him at all times. Sadly the son wrote: "Mother is afraid that he will go mad because he is thinking about the old country, about his Fathers, even though they've been lying in their graves for a long time. . . . he is sitting and thinking day and night . . . and desires death."[66] One cannot help but reflect upon how many of the young immigrants who had come to America with such great expectations must have ended their lives in this way.

8

The Twentieth Century

THE years around World War I provided a turning point in the history of the Silesians in Texas. The dramatic changes that the conflict began forcing on society filtered down to the predominantly rural Polish settlements and in time brought them into the mainstream of American life. From that period onward greater numbers of Silesians left the settlements to live among the Americans, spoke Polish less regularly, and felt themselves more and more a part of the larger society around them. They were becoming Americanized. At the same time, however, many of them held tenaciously to their European culture, preserving many of its elements to the present day. Even now the visitor to the settlements senses differences in atmosphere that make him aware that he is among Silesians.

For the Poles in Texas, World War I began with the American entry into the conflict in 1917. While in other parts of the country men struggled with exemption papers and mothers agonized over the conscription of their sons, in the Polish communities the quotas for soldiers were quickly filled with volunteers. Many of the young Silesians went overseas, men like Onufry Zaiontz, who fought at the Meuse and in the Argonne Forest; Adolph Kiołbassa, who participated in a number of engagements with the American Expeditionary Forces; and Wladyslaw Zaiontz, who fought Germans in the Puvenelle Sector of the Western Front. Some of the recruits, like Elias J. Moczygemba of Panna Maria, entered the army too late to participate in the war. By the time they had finished their training in the United States, the fighting was over. Others were not so lucky. As one writer observed in the 1930's: "On the walls of many a quiet old farm home along the Cibolo there hang pictures of big, shy Polish boys in American khaki and trench cap. And in some homes the picture is all they have left of the boy."[1]

A significant immediate effect of the war on the Silesian farmers was the temporary prosperity it brought to them. The high wartime prices for cotton and other agricultural products gave them a few years of comparative affluence. One Pole recalled from his childhood that, as a result of dry weather in 1917, only a few areas had good cotton harvests but that DeWitt County was one of the exceptions and that its "small farmers lost track of all the bales of cotton" they hauled to the gins. Later, rains came, and throughout the Polish settlements "many a farmer wallowed in money." The same Silesian recalled that, although white sugar and flour were available in only limited quantities, trade in other merchandise was heavy, and "nice new cars were in vogue." The prosperity unfortunately was short-lived, and with the 1920's came an agricultural depression that preceded by almost a decade the general depression of the 1930's.[2]

In the years immediately following the war, despite the fact that many Silesians had fought side by side with Americans during the hostilities, the Polish Texans faced one of the most severe periods of social discrimination of their entire history in America. Those were the years when nativist organizations like the Ku Klux Klan campaigned against everything they identified as "non-American," including anything foreign or Roman Catholic. One Silesian recalled that for a time in the early 1920's families from the Panna Maria settlement were reluctant and even afraid to go to nearby Karnes City, fearing physical or verbal abuse. He remembered that, as a boy, when he went to the town, he was "sort of pushed around and laughed at" and called "a damned Polander and a God-damned Catholic." The words stuck in his mind. Even in later years it was difficult for Silesian children in the schools of nearby American towns to receive proper recognition for their achievements. One Pole recalled, "To receive any honor at school you would have to have a certain name," adding significantly, "certainly not Polish." He continued that, if you were both Catholic and Polish in Karnes City, "you were looked upon as a low-class and ignorant person." The situation was probably the most severe at White Deer, in the Texas Panhandle, where the Poles constituted a relatively small but striking exception to the Anglo-American population. There the Polish-speaking children received the brunt of the discrimination. At the predominately Anglo-American public school they had daily fights with the other pupils, who had learned from their parents to call the newcomers

"Polocks and damn Catholics." The Silesian children could scarcely understand English and certainly could not comprehend why they were being mistreated. The virulent discrimination passed away, but it left invisible marks. It is impossible today to calculate the possible psychological damage that the children especially may have suffered. Now they are adults, but the hurt and fear that they felt probably explains why most older Silesian Texans in conversations today want to stress their friendship with the Americans, not telling everything that they remember about the past.[3]

Directly affecting the Silesians for a longer time than the discrimination of postwar years was the long agricultural depression of the 1920's and 1930's. The economic situation of the farmers during this period was even more difficult than it might have been because many of them were victims of the crop-lien system. In this common economic scheme a farmer who did not have money bought all his supplies on credit from a local merchant until his harvest came, and then he was obligated to pay back the indebtedness by selling his crops to the merchant. These businessmen, as creditors, naturally charged interest on their loans. Because of the nature of the principal crop, cotton, the farmers furthermore had to pay a percentage of their harvests to the ginners for cleaning and removing the seeds from the fiber. Even if a farmer was not indebted to a local merchant, he could not successfully sell his crop directly to the major cotton markets but had to sell it to the local buyers, who then passed it on with their own charges. Every person between the farmers and the textile mills received a percentage of the profit, frequently leaving the rural producers with the least.

Cotton was not the only crop that the Silesians raised. In fact, it was because they devoted some of their land to feed grains, pasturage, and gardens that they were self-sufficient enough to survive the hard times. As one Pole recalled: "The depression was pretty bad, but a farmer never starves if he works. You got your chickens, your eggs, a pig or two. . . . There is nothing to buy but a little flour and coffee." Some of the farmers tried to make money from their old wonder crop, onions, but it, like the other cash crops, often failed them. In 1936 a priest from the northern states saw a Silesian with a three-horse team plowing under a beautiful field of onions between Częstochowa and Kościuszko. The visitor asked him why he was destroying it. The man replied bitterly that the market price for onions had dropped to below ten cents a bushel and that he would rather plow under his harvest than sell it at such a low price. Making the plight of the central Texas farmers even worse were weather problems, which included a severe hailstorm in spring 1929 and a large flood in summer 1935.[4]

It was during the period of economic difficulties that the government of the newly established Republic of Poland attempted to organize the export of cotton from the Polish farms in Texas to textile mills in Poland. This effort, which surprised almost everyone in Texas who heard about it, was initiated by a secretary from the Polish consulate general in New York in spring 1920. The secretary, Leon Orłowski, traveled to Texas, visiting most of the Silesian colonies, to investigate the prospects for such trade. According to his official reports, still preserved in Warsaw, Orłowski estimated that the Silesian farmers in a normal year could produce thirty thousand bales of cotton, which would be available for export to Polish mills if it was properly marketed. As time passed, however, other Polish bureaucrats pushed the proposal aside because the textile industry lacked the dollar credits to cover its initiation. The idea, nevertheless, stayed alive. A decade later another Polish official, this time the consul general from Chicago, Alexander Szczepański, visited the Polish colonies to investigate anew the possibilities of securing cotton supplies for the motherland. He discussed the plan with cotton factors in New Orleans, San Antonio, Houston, and Galveston and went to the Polish farmers themselves to seek their opinions on the proposal. When he talked with the country people, "their eyes lighted up," but the farmers lacked the organization to create the cooperatives necessary to begin collecting cotton for export. Szczepański lamented that they just kept saying how good it would be if someone came and helped them sell their cotton to Poland. Thus the plan for exporting cotton from the Polish farms in Texas remained only a dream. The growers in Texas were unable to coordinate their production and marketing, while the textile magnates in Poland lacked the funds to buy the fiber even if it should become available.[5]

Agricultural conditions were no better for the Silesians at White Deer than for the families who had remained in central Texas. Weather conditions on the plains created even more problems for them. One of the settlers recalled, "We never did make a crop every year," adding, "It's hard [at White Deer] to make a crop two years in succession." The Poles were able to continue their farming despite dry years and hail, but when the great dust storms of the 1930's began, some of them thought that it was "the end of the world." The settlement was in the portion of the Great Plains then known as the Dust Bowl, and its residents suffered through several consecutive years of very severe sand and dust storms. Often the people could see the clouds of dust approaching in the distance, and they immediately covered all the windows in their homes with bed sheets to keep out the heaviest particles. After a day of such blowing wind, however, dust covered everything in the houses. One of the women remembered with distaste that the dust was "black and greasy" and that "you could hardly wash it off the windows. . . . when it blew, you couldn't see anything."[6]

As a result of the economic difficulties of the depression, many of the Silesians sought escape from their problems. Some of them found this release by following the exploits of one of their favorite sons, Fabian Kowalik, whom they fondly called "Mayor of Falls City." Coming from that Polish town, Kowalik became well known as a pitcher for the Chicago Cubs baseball team. Members of the Silesian communities thought to themselves that things in the colonies were not really quite so bad as they had believed when, after playing in the 1935 World Series, the prominent professional athlete, whose activities they watched closely, began investing some of his earnings in local real estate.[7]

A handful of Silesian farmers and their families took direct action to improve their economic conditions by moving to the Lower Rio Grande Valley and founding a new Polish settlement. Among the earliest settlers moving to the vicinity of McCook, in Hidalgo County, were the families of Urban Kotzur and his two sons, from Kościuszko. Kotzur bought his land in south Texas in August 1925, and in the next months his family prepared to leave their homes in Wilson County. Like the earlier settlers who went to White Deer, they hired a railway boxcar to transport their household goods and agricultural implements. In November 1926 the three families moved. One of the women later remembered, "We brought our canned and pickled foods, bedding and furniture, . . . a few chickens and a pet dog." Unlike the people who had gone to White Deer, however, the Kotzur family did not transport its livestock by rail. Instead four men on horseback drove the animals overland from Kościuszko to McCook, a two-hundred-mile journey requiring several days. For the first months the extended family lived in barns and sheds, cooking their meals over a temporary stove that the grandfather had made from bricks. The south Texas weather, almost always mild, allowed them to live in the open much of the time, even though they arrived in the winter. The first major work was clearing the land, which was so thickly covered with brush that "you could not see any direction but up." During the first months the men cleared seventy acres, and in 1927 they planted their first crops. As time passed, they cleared the remainder of their land, built permanent homes, and became substantial farmers. By 1936 twenty Silesian families from Karnes and Wilson counties had moved to the McCook area, and by 1950 enough Poles were living there that they were able to establish their own Catholic church.[8]

The most important celebration among the Silesian settlements between the two world wars was the 1929 commemoration of the seventy-fifth anniversary of the founding of the Panna Maria colony. The parishioners organized this observance, which included an outdoor mass under the spreading oak where the immigrants first gathered in late 1854, a huge banquet, and a historical parade. Six thousand persons watched the afternoon procession of early pioneers, an ox-drawn wagon, and families carrying relics from the early days of settlement. The event provided a last opportunity for many of the old settlers to see each other. Unfortunately not all the aspects of growing old in the colonies were so pleasant as this reunion.[9]

The last years of the surviving Civil War veterans in the Polish communities were not always happy. This is a portion of Silesian Texas history that the present generation has largely forgotten. The old veterans, who had shared the dangers and hardships of a war that only a few people in the 1920's and 1930's could remember, had only a decreasing circle of friends with whom they could exchange memories. By that time they were the only people who either remembered or cared about places they had known, such as Arkansas Post, San Diego, and Camp Butler. Few people wanted to listen to the stories they repeated over and over. These veterans or their widows were entitled to pensions from the state or federal governments for their military service. For some this was virtually the only source of income, and every check was needed, especially in the hard times of the depression. Thus it was a serious matter when Mrs. John Kowalik, of Falls City, wrote to the state comptroller to report that she had lost her November 1939 check when her neighbor, "who is suffering from insanity for 20 Yrs. . . . took the mentioned Check and destroyed it." Securing approval for a Civil War pension was not an easy matter; the applicants had to prove their service to the government, either with documents or with sworn testimony from people who knew them at the time, as well as prove their financial need. When Joseph F. Pierdolla, of La Vernia, a veteran of the Thirty-sixth Texas Cavalry, applied for his pension in 1930, he described from a hospital bed his unfortunate situation: "I had my Leg and Arm broken and I was very sick here a year ago or so and it took all I had. . . . [I] was uprooted and I am in need of help." After he had secured his pension, the destitute Adam Skloss, of Yorktown, who had fought in the Eighth Texas Infantry, wrote to the state capital, "Words cannot express our deep [gratitude] that wee [*sic*] feel toward our good Government and also to the Almighty God."[10]

The first half of the twentieth century saw a surprisingly large number of visitors to the Silesian colonies in Texas, both from Poland and from other parts of the United States. Some came to satisfy their curiosity about the oldest Polish colonies, some to explore commercial ties with them, and still others to collect data for scholarly or journalistic publications. Almost all of them left records of their visits.[11]

Among the early travelers to the Silesian colonies was a noted Polish philosopher, Vincent Lutosławski, who came to Texas in 1907 out of a desire to see what the oldest Polish colonies in America were really like. After spending several days in Falls City, Panna Maria, Częstochowa, and Kościuszko, he described his experiences in an article for a popular Warsaw weekly magazine. There he expressed his opinion that the Silesians in Texas, having been separated from their German rulers in Europe and living in the free society of the New World, were growing to be increasingly conscious of their Polish ethnicity.[12] Another visitor about the same time was the pioneer American sociologist Emily Greene Balch. In her major work on Slavic immigrant life in America, *Our Slavic Fellow Citizens*, she left her impressions of the Silesian settlements. Her description of the oldest Polish colony is especially vivid:

> The pictures that I carry away from Panna Marya [*sic*] are of the group of children learning their catechism in the cool stone church, the girls in pink, blue and red sunbonnets, the boys bareheaded and barefooted; of the priest's house with its veranda and flower beds; of the store, a typical country store, with a saddled horse hitched under the live oak before it; of the big, bare schoolrooms in which the children were being taught in English . . . the whole making an impression of the quiet . . . life of men still close to the European peasant, yet by no means untouched by America.[13]

The next important visitors to the Polish settlements came in 1909. They were a field researcher for the United States Immigration Commission and a Polish journalist named Stefan Nesterowicz. During the summer the federal agent visited the communities in Karnes and Wilson counties, collecting information to be used by the commission in recommending changes in United States immigration policies. Although much of his data came from published sources rather than from actual interviews in the countryside, his observations from the American perspective provide an interesting view of the lives of the farmers.[14] The second visitor, the Polish journalist, who was collecting material for his column in a Polish-American newspaper in Ohio, left a detailed account of his journey among the Silesians. Published later as part of his book *Notatki z podróży* (Travel Notes), this report constitutes one of the most valuable sources of information on the Poles in the state at the beginning of the century.[15]

One important Pole came to the Silesian settlements during World War I. This visitor, the Reverend Wacław Kruszka, was the author of the first comprehensive account of the Poles in America, *Historja polska w Ameryce* (Polish History in America). He traveled to Texas in December 1917 to gather materials for his historical writings and to hear confessions from Polish soldiers who were preparing to leave for the Great War.[16] Three years after Father Kruszka's visit, Leon Orłowski, the secretary from the Polish consulate general in New York, came to investigate the possibilities of arranging cotton exports from Texas. His visit, mentioned earlier, stirred the expectations of the Silesian farmers but in the end produced little more than his typewritten reports, which are, however, of considerable historical interest.[17]

The next prominent traveler among the Silesians was Franciszek Niklewicz, a Polish editor and publisher from Green Bay, Wisconsin, who came to Texas in March 1926 to collect data for his publications on the Polish Catholic parishes in the United States. He had a memorable encounter with a party of Silesian school children he met walking from Panna Maria to Częstochowa. Niklewicz greeted them in English, asking if they were Polish. A twelve-year-old Silesian lad answered, "Yes, we are all Polish. . . . There is nothing but Polish people living around here." Then the stranger asked if they could speak Polish, and the same boy responded, "Sure, every one of us can talk Polish." The writer was amazed to find the children of the third and fourth generations fluent in the language of their antecedents' distant motherland.[18]

Following Niklewicz three years later in 1929 came the anthropologist Bolesław Rosiński, a priest from the University of Lwów, who spent several weeks conducting research in the colonies. Some of his results appeared the next year in the Polish ethnographic journal *Ziemia*.[19] Four years after Rosiński came Consul General Alexander Szczepański, again investigating the possibilities of arranging cotton exports to Polish textile mills, as had Leon Orłowski before him. The consul's description of Kościuszko, Texas, included in his book of impressions of his stay in America, is probably the best ever written of the community:

> The first settlement we came to was Kościuszko. This farming community consists of church, rectory, school, and a store where you can buy salt, coffee, lemons, straw hats, artificial fertilizers, small agricultural tools, soap, lamp oil, and . . . ice cream. . . .
>
> In the meantime we began to hear the sound of motors. From time to time Fords and sometimes Chevrolets or Buicks were coming and bringing people in long trousers, white shirts, and big sombreros or light felt hats. They were the local farmers. . . . Soon they surrounded me and their rough hands shook mine. Their smiling faces were familiar Silesian faces, as were their names: Mika, Moczygemba, Zając, Przybysz. . . .
>
> Having the sky and sun above, it was easy to make friends. We talked for a while and then they asked me to tell them about Poland. So we retired to Mika's store and there, sitting on a chest of dried plums, I had my talk.[20]

The next important visitor to the Silesian colonies was the Reverend Joseph Gawlina, a Polish bishop born in Upper Silesia in 1891, who in 1935 visited the United States in his position as chaplain of the Polish army. Arriving in San Antonio in the summer for a visit of several days, he celebrated a Polish mass in the city, was the honored guest at a banquet in one of its largest hotels, and visited the rural Silesian parishes.[21]

The year 1936, the year of the Texas Centennial celebrations, saw a number of visitors among the Silesians. One of these was the Reverend Stanisław Iciek, a Polish-American priest from Connecticut, who later described his visit in one of his books on his travels. Driving through the settlements, he generally was unimpressed by what he viewed from the window of his station wagon. Commenting on Panna Maria, which he saw in the depths of the economic depression as deserted and forgotten, he declared, "This oldest Polish settlement must be the last one so far as progress is concerned." Father Iciek obviously failed to appreciate the charm that most other visitors discovered.[22]

Also visiting Texas during the Centennial year was a delegation of Polish Boy Scouts from Katowice, in Silesia. Their destination was the great Centennial Fair in Dallas, where they had been invited to participate in Polish Day activities. During the special day, featuring music, Polish folk dancing, and a Polish film shown to the public, the contingent of scouts placed a wreath on a memorial plaque at the fairgrounds dedicated to Felix Wardziński, the Polish hero of the Battle of San Jacinto in 1836. The group then met with representatives from the Silesian colonies, and thus the "old" immigrants were able to see and talk with boys from their former home.[23] These scouts were the last important visitors to the Texas Silesians for several years, because three years later World War II broke out with Hitler's invasion of Poland. For the duration of the war there was almost no communication with the homeland.

The visits of Poles to the Silesian settlements in Texas had not been the sole contact between the settlers and their country of origin. Well into the twentieth century the Silesians read Polish-language books and publications imported from Europe. Furthermore, a considerable correspondence continued between the Texans and their relatives across the sea. In these letters the relations discussed primarily their family situations, economic problems, and local news. One Polish correspondent wrote to Karnes County, for example, asking his relatives to send him a group photograph, "so I could see . . . the faces of all my family in that faraway America." Commenting on events at the time of Bishop Gawlina's visit to Texas in 1935, a writer in Poland reported to his kin on the other side of the Atlantic that he knew all about it from his local Polish newspapers.[24]

For most of the twentieth century the Polish press has kept its readers remarkably well informed about the Silesian settlements in Texas. Newspapers and magazines in Poland have published probably more articles about the colonies than have their American counterparts. Polish coverage of the subject has varied from the most superficial accounts to detailed discussions of narrow topics. Occasionally the authors have visited the Texas communities, but most often they have drawn their articles from standard secondary accounts.[25] Despite the limitations of the journalistic treatment the Poles of Poland are much more familiar with the story of the Silesian immigrants than are most other Americans living in Texas. I have been amazed by the number of times people from all levels of society in Poland, upon learning of my Texas origin, have asked me, "Have you been to Panna Maria?"[26]

World War II came to the Silesians in Texas with the Japanese attack on Pearl Harbor in December 1941. Once the United States had actively entered the hostilities, the Poles in Texas were able to come to the aid of both their original and their adopted motherlands. The war provided an opportunity in which many of them demonstrated their bravery in the face of danger. One of the heroes from the Silesian colonies was Gervase A. Gabrysch, of Falls City. He was born there in 1914 and grew up in the peaceful rural community. He attended the local schools, graduating from the high school in nearby Karnes City in 1931. Then in the mid-1930's he entered the United States Navy. During World War II, after serving in New London, Connecticut, where he married in 1942, Gabrysch was transferred to the Pacific to Submarine Chaser No. 151. While he was serving on this vessel, it was bombed and sunk by the Japanese. Gabrysch escaped to Australia to continue fighting. After the war, maintaining his naval career, he was able to return to the area of his birth as navy recruiter in Victoria,

Texas, and as engineman chief at the Corpus Christi Naval Air Station.[27]

The decades that have followed World War II have been years of further Americanization for the Silesians in Texas, coupled with increasingly strong ethnic institutional activity. Among the most important Polish undertakings during these years have been the preparations of periodic large-scale celebrations of anniversaries of historic events. One of these came in 1954, with the centennial of the founding of the Panna Maria colony. In a day of festivities at the rural community in May of that year, a large crowd of visitors witnessed a field mass concelebrated by several priests, heard sermons in both Polish and English, listened to music performed by a combined men's choir from five parishes, and enjoyed an all-day barbecue.[28] A dozen years later the Silesians organized an even larger observance to mark the millennium of Polish Christianity. Again staged at Panna Maria, the event included the official dedication of a mosaic of the Virgin of Częstochowa, the patron of Poland, which President Lyndon B. Johnson presented to the colony. The day also included an outdoor mass and barbecue dinner, both of which by this time had become customary at major Silesian celebrations.[29] Another feature of the 1966 activities was the construction and dedication in San Antonio of a large masonry grotto in honor of the Virgin of Częstochowa. This shrine is visited by almost all Polish visitors to the city.[30]

During the years the large observances were held, equally significant institutional ethnic work was progressing elsewhere. In the decades after World War II well-known organizations such as the Polish National Alliance and the Polish Roman Catholic Union have continued their work and expanded it into the rural communities. New associations have also arisen. The most important of these is the Polish American Congress of Texas, established in 1971 by a group of Poles concerned about lack of communication among the colonies. It has become the major statewide Polish organization and today is probably the most influential of all secular Polish bodies in Texas. Another new organization is the Polish American Priests Association, with its headquarters in San Antonio, which works to unify the Polish clergy in the state. The Polish American Center in San Antonio for many years has served its role as a meeting place and social center.[31]

The Poles in Texas organized two significant ventures in the 1970's. The first of these was the visit of a delegation of fifty-four Texas Poles, most of them Silesians, to Poland in 1973. The trip was planned and executed by the Polish American Congress of Texas and included visits to Kraków, Warsaw, and the mountain resort of Zakopane. The most memorable portion of the trip, however, was a return to the Upper Silesian villages from which the original immigrants to Texas had come in the 1850's. The visitors were divided into small groups and were the guests for several days of Silesian farm families. Where possible, the Texas Poles stayed in the very villages from which their ancestors had come, renewing family ties that had been lost through the passage of time. The reception the Texans found in Silesia was warm and generous, exemplified by their welcome to Płużnica. There a Polish band greeted the guests, little children gave each of them flowers, and the bishop of Opole welcomed them with a special homecoming mass in the parish church.[32]

A second major project of the Texas Poles was the return to the state of the remains of the Reverend Leopold Moczygemba from his original 1891 burial place in Detroit. This effort was prompted by the apparent lack of concern among Poles in the northern states properly to recognize the priest as the initiator of Polish mass immigration to the United States. When in 1972 the pastor of one of the Silesian colonies made a pilgrimage to Detroit to view the grave, not one of the Polish American priests whom he met there was able to take him to the site. Feeling that the founder of their colonies had been slighted by the northerners, the Silesians quickly set to work to transfer Father Leopold's remains from Michigan to Texas. They obtained the consent of traceable relatives, secured a court order, and received approval from church authorities for the unusual disinterment. The remains were moved to Texas in summer 1974 and then on 13 October of that year reinterred beside the church that Mocyzgemba had founded at Panna Maria. The observance included a field mass for several thousand visitors, including priests from Upper Silesia, the reburial ceremony, and a huge banquet for the guests. Plans were made immediately for the erection of a suitable memorial at the new grave, which lies under the same oak where the missionary first said mass for the immigrants at Christmastime 1854.[33]

Contact with Poland remained strong among the Silesian colonies through the 1970's. In 1974 a television crew from Warsaw visited the settlements to make a documentary film as one of sixteen on immigrant life to be shown on both American and Polish television during the 1976 American Revolution Bicentennial Year. The popularity of historical subjects during the Bicentennial, in fact, seemed to bring increased contact between Polish Americans in Texas and Poles in Europe. During summer 1976, for example, the Silesian bishop of Katowice traveled to Panna Maria and Częstochowa to participate in local religious observances. Throughout the year exhibits and presentations about Tadeusz Kościuszko and Casimir Pułaski, the best-known Polish generals in the American Revolution, proliferated wherever Silesians gathered for special events.[34]

The future of Silesian culture in Texas is uncertain. It is likely that the rural Polish communities will remain islands of Slavic culture in a sea of American, Hispanic, and Germanic culture in the foreseeable future. Despite their proximity to the San Antonio metropolitan area, the farming families retain much of their traditional way of life. Although industrial development in the vicinity of the colonies is possible, it is economically more promising for industry to locate either in San Antonio or along the Gulf Coast. For this reason agriculture will remain the major economic activity in the area, and with it will stay the Silesian family farms. Because most of the landholdings are too small to be divided among all the children in a family, frequently one child remains at home while the others go to the cities for higher education and employment. There, in the urban milieu of the much larger general American culture, participation in Polish religious and secular organizations and activities presents the only hope for preserving the ethnic heritage.[35]

9

The Significance of the Silesians in Texas

THE Silesian immigrants and their descendants in Texas possess significance on several different levels. Since their arrival in 1854 they obviously have contributed a hardworking, stable segment to the agricultural population of the state. But their importance reaches much farther than their contribution as dependable tillers of the soil. The Silesians have produced or have influenced considerable numbers of people who have become important leaders both in Texas and in the Polish American community as a whole. From the perspective of European history the immigrants present a unique case study in the Polish consciousness of nineteenth-century Upper Silesian peasants. Finally, in terms of the over-all Polish experience in America, the Silesians were the forerunners, the initiators, of Polish migration to America.

From their first months in Texas the Silesians have been productive farmers. Soon after their arrival they began adapting themselves to the new environment by accepting and cultivating cotton and corn, the main crops of Texas at the time. Before long they began surpassing the native Americans in raising not only these staples but also food crops. After only a decade, for example, the farmers at Panna Maria were feeding both themselves and the Americans in the nearby county seat, Helena. By the early twentieth century Silesian cotton production had reached such proportions that the Polish government considered organizing its export to the Polish textile industry in Europe. The love the immigrants felt for the land was demonstrated by the care they gave it. For over a century the farms of the Silesians in Texas have been noted for their prosperous appearance and high productivity. As an agricultural expert seventy-five years ago declared to his American readers,

"They constitute an element of thrifty, God-fearing people who are . . . a valuable asset to any state."[1]

The Silesian colonies have produced or have influenced a large number of leaders who have gone on to work either in Texas affairs or in Polish American communities in the northern United States. In the nineteenth century probably the best known of these leaders was Peter Kiołbassa, the native of Świbie, in Upper Silesia, whose father had served as a deputy in the Prussian national parliament in 1848. After Peter's immigration to America in 1855 and services to both the Confederate and the Union armies during the Civil War, he settled permanently in Chicago. There he worked as a customs collector and as a policeman, but he soon achieved financial success in real estate and insurance. That was not enough for the ambitious Silesian, and he busied himself in helping establish the first Polish-Catholic church in Chicago. Soon thereafter he entered local politics. His first major office was as representative of his district in the Illinois state legislature in 1877, a position in which he was acclaimed as the first Polish-born state legislator in America. Kiołbassa then held several minor positions before being elected city treasurer of Chicago in 1891. He demonstrated his integrity by being the first treasurer in the history of the city not to keep for himself and his political party the interest earned by the city funds in his custody. Kiołbassa continued to hold other municipal positions until his widely mourned death in 1905.[2]

One of the commanding figures in Polish American life during the second half of the nineteenth century was the Reverend Vincent Barzyński. Coming to America as a Resurrectionist missionary in 1866, he first served eight formative years as a young priest among the Silesians at San Antonio, Saint Hedwig, and Panna Maria before leaving for the northern states in 1874. He built Saint Stanislaus Kostka Church of Chicago into the largest Catholic parish in the United States, while directing the establishment of twenty-five other Polish parishes. He either founded or helped found Polish-Catholic newspapers and publishing houses, orphanages, and religious societies, as well as Saint Stanislaus Kostka College, in Chicago. Today Barzyński is best remembered as the chief cofounder and later reorganizer of the Polish Roman Catholic Union, the largest and most influential Polish-Catholic association in the United States.[3]

Also prominent in Polish American affairs in the second half of the century was the founder of the Silesian colonies, the Reverend Leopold Moczygemba. For most of his later years he worked among Poles in the northern states, founding a number of Polish parishes and helping establish both the Polish Roman Catholic Union and Saints Cyril and Methodius Seminary in Detroit, the major Polish seminary in the United States.[4]

One of the best-known Silesian business leaders in the first years of the twentieth century was Edward Przybysz. Born into a Silesian immigrant family at Panna Maria in 1887, he made his fortune in Chicago, the city that exerted such an attraction for other Poles. There as an attorney he became an officer of the North-Western Trust and Savings Bank, and in this role he exerted considerable influence in the Polish American community. Przybysz was active in ethnic affairs and almost always ready to give both personal help and financial assistance to Polish political, social, and economic undertakings. It was he, for example, who made the initial contacts through his business associates for the meetings of Polish Consul General Szczepański with major cotton buyers during his trip to Texas in 1930.[5]

Another Silesian, the Reverend Thomas J. Moczygemba, was the leading Polish clergyman in Texas during the first half of the twentieth century. He was born at Panna Maria in 1863 to one of the four Moczygemba brothers who had immigrated a decade before. Upon his ordination in 1891 he was the first native-born American elevated to the priesthood in the Diocese of San Antonio. Ministering to the Silesians at Panna Maria and Yorktown until 1912, he then moved to Saint Michael's Church in San Antonio, where he served until his death in 1950. Described by all who knew him as a stern but patient pastor, his memory is still revered among the Silesians in the state.[6]

The middle years of the twentieth century brought many Silesians into prominent positions. It is impossible to enumerate all these individuals. They are active at every level of society and are found in all professions. The church still calls many of them, but no more strongly than do secular careers. Today one finds Silesian Texans in government, religion, business, agriculture, and virtually all the other fields of modern society.[7]

For Europeans what is probably most significant about the Silesians in Texas is that they represent an independent index of the level of Polish national consciousness of mid-nineteenth-century Upper Silesian peasants. Even though their home region had been separated from the Polish state for over five hundred years, the peasants who lived there in the 1850's possessed a remarkably high level of Polish identity. Only shortly after the immigrants left, however, Bismarck initiated a policy of forced Germanization that continued in all of Upper Silesia until after World War I and in areas retained by Germany after the Versailles Peace Conference until the close of World War II. Use of the Polish language in public was all but eliminated, and all manifestations of Polish culture were discouraged if not prohibited. The immigrants who had moved to Texas before the Germanization, however, lived in a comparatively isolated environment, where their folk culture remained little changed for many years. They clearly were free of the great pressures exerted on their relatives who had stayed behind in Europe. For that reason the Silesian Texans can serve as a measure of the Polish national consciousness of Upper Silesian peasants before denationalization was forced on many of them by their Prussian overlords.[8]

The first evidence of the Polish character of the Silesian immigrants comes, ironically, from German sources. As early as October 1854 a member of the German-operated Central Emigration Society for Silesia noted in one of its meetings that members of "the Polish population of Upper Silesia" had begun leaving for Texas. Early the next year a Prussian official at Olesno complained to his superiors that the people leaving his district could speak only Polish. This complaint was repeated by the Prussian consul at Bremen, who in spring 1855 wrote to Opole that emigrants from Upper Silesia who spoke "only Polish" were passing through the port. The German immigrant press in Texas similarly noted that the people arriving in the San Antonio area in 1854 were Polish immigrants, in its words, "*polnische emigranten*."[9]

The Polish press in the Austrian Empire also viewed the Silesian emigrants as Poles. In September 1855, *Gwiazdka Cieszyńska*, across the border from Prussian territory, reported that new groups consisting "exclusively of Polish peasants" were planning to leave soon for America. A few weeks later the same newspaper noted that a group of

"Polish peasants" had just passed through Wrocław on its way to Texas. A writer in *Czas* at Kraków bemoaned the fact that the Silesians were settling in central Texas rather than along the Gulf Coast. He feared that, living in the highly mixed population of central Texas, they would lose their Polish identity. After a Polish press temporarily reappeared in Prussian Upper Silesia, *Zwiastun Górnoszlazki* in 1870 admonished the immigrants in Texas: "Do not forget that you are Poles. Respect and preserve the good traditions of your fathers."[10]

The Americans who encountered the Silesians in Texas uniformly described them as Polish. Frederick Law Olmsted, writing about his saddle trip through Texas in the mid-1850's, made a clear distinction between the Poles and the much larger German population of the state when he pointed out Panna Maria specifically as a "colony of Silesian Poles." He made a similar general observation later in the book when he wrote of "the Silesian peasant" who started "from the Polish frontier." Later in the nineteenth century Thomas Ruckman recorded that among the settlers at Częstochowa "the old spirit of Kosiusko [*sic*] . . . lurks in their blood & bones, and I honor them for it." As recently as 1966 President Johnson recognized the Silesian settlers as Poles with the gift to Panna Maria of the mosaic of the Virgin of Częstochowa mentioned earlier.[11]

The letters the Silesian immigrants sent back to Europe provide additional evidence of their consciousness of their Polish nationality. The letters prove that the peasant immigrants used the Polish language in their day-to-day life, rather than German or English. The correspondence furthermore has characteristic predetermined composition with roots in Polish folk tradition. Almost all the letters begin with the greeting, "Praised be Jesus Christ," to which the reader is supposed to reply silently, "For centuries and centuries, Amen." This salutation demonstrates unity within the same religious and moral community. Then follows information that the writer, with God's help, is in good physical health and is succeeding in life. Finally there are greetings from all the members of the writer's family to all those of the reader's family. This form of letter, which serves as a manifestation of solidarity within the group, is distinct from correspondence originating in the realm of German culture.[12]

The language the Silesian immigrants spoke was Polish, despite years of German domination. The Resurrectionist missionaries who came to Texas in 1866 sent their superiors in Europe detailed information on the speech of their parishioners. Father Vincent Barzyński in San Antonio, knowing that Silesia had been cut away from Poland, feared that he might have difficulty communicating with his new congregation. He was relieved to be able to write, "The language of my parishioners is not broken with German. . . . not only do we understand each other very well, but they say that I speak better Polish than they do, because I know the Polish language they have in books." He added, "the spirit of my parishioners is still Polish, because the strength of tradition is smoldering."[13] Father Adolf Bakanowski wrote from Panna Maria that the old people living there were "such stubborn Poles" that they did not want to learn English, "the foreign language," and that, even though they had been settled in Texas for fifteen years, many of them spoke only Polish. He added that "nearly all the Americans and Germans who live in Panna Maria speak Polish."[14] Writing about this same phenomenon, Felix Zwiardowski explained that in Panna Maria "both the Germans and the Americans learn Polish, and particularly the family of German Catholics with whom we eat [the family of John Kuhnel], where the youngest to the oldest all speak Polish."[15]

Later Polish visitors to the Silesian settlements also had revealing observations on the Polish language they heard. Franciszek Niklewicz discovered on his visit to the communities in 1926 that "everybody speaks Polish here." He wrote for his northern readers, "There is probably no colony in America where you could find people who are more attached to their fathers' language."[16] Leon Orłowski noted in 1920 that in Yorktown "children, both older and younger, can speak Polish very well. The latter hardly know English before they go to school."[17] Anthropologist Bolesław Rosiński recorded during his stay that the farmers at Panna Maria eagerly spoke Polish, "or as they said, they spoke 'in Silesian.'"[18] In 1930, Consul Alexander Szczepański could find no writing whatever in English at the church in Saint Hedwig. When he talked with the parishioners there, he felt as if he were "in the area of Cracow or Poznan" in Poland.[19]

Probably the most important measure of Polish nationality among the Silesian immigrants was the way the people viewed themselves.

As early as 1855, John Moczygemba subconsciously revealed his inner feelings when he wrote to his relatives in Płużnica to give them practical suggestions on how to choose an agent to arrange their travel across the sea. He advised them to "take a good German," showing that in his mind the Upper Silesian peasants were not Germans. Father Leopold Moczygemba emphatically expressed his beliefs concerning the nationality of Upper Silesians when he wrote to Rome in 1875, "As a Silesian I have more Polish feelings than I can express."[20]

One of the most moving examples of the Polish consciousness of the Silesian Texans was recorded in 1936 by Jacek Wnęk, the leader of the Polish Boy Scout delegation that visited the state to participate in the Texas Centennial celebration in Dallas. During the special Polish Day program at the fairgrounds, an elderly gray-haired man took the scout leader aside from the crowd. Wnęk related that the stranger wanted to say something but could not. At last he asked in Polish in a low and broken voice, "Are they from Katowice?" pointing toward the Silesian scouts. "I wanted my son to see them. . . . He was born here. . . . He has never seen anyone from Poland." The old man continued after a pause: "How is it in our Poland? . . . I will probably never see our country. . . . I'm too old . . . eighty-three. . . . Surely I will not see it. . . . Oh, no." The gray-haired man stood silent, thinking to himself, and then placed his arm around the scout leader's shoulders and asked, ". . . but, when you come back to Poland, kiss the blessed soil and greet all my beloved Silesia. . . ." He was so affected that he was unable to utter the last few words that he wanted to say. He had to turn his tanned face away from the scouts to dry the tears that had appeared, while his son, a man about forty, stood helpless and unable to say a word. After a moment the scouts saw the old man turn again and ask, "And you won't forget to say hello to Silesia for me, will you?"[21]

The Silesians who came to Texas were the precursors of the masses of Polish immigrants who followed them to America in the next half century. Although they settled in a different part of the continent from that chosen by most of the later arrivals, their life in Texas has exhibited in microcosm many of the problems, disappointments, and successes that the later immigrants found in the New World. They have constituted an important segment of the Texas population, adding to its economic prosperity and giving it a more varied culture; they have produced many individuals who have contributed significantly to the larger society in which they live; and they have preserved some aspects of their ethnic culture that have disappeared in Europe or have become modified there. But, above all, the Silesian Texans will be remembered as the pioneers who led the way for the thousands of Polish peasants who came after them to what they hoped would be the land of opportunity.

Notes

Chapter 1. The Upper Silesian Origins

1. Royal Landrat Scheider, Rosenberg [Olesno, Regency of Opole, Prussia], to [Royal Administration, Opole, Regency of Opole], 28 February 1855, Kingdom of Prussia, Regency of Opole, Department of the Interior, Die Auswanderung nach den Amerikanisches Staaten—Concesirung von Vereinen u. Agenturen zur Beförderung der Auswanderer [Emigration to the American States—Concessions of Societies and Agents for Transporting Emigrants], vol. 1 (15 May 1847–13 September 1855), p. 564.

2. T. Lindsay Baker, *The Early History of Panna Maria, Texas*; Andrzej Brożek, "Najstarsza polska szkoła w Stanach Zjednoczonych Ameryki" [The Oldest Polish School in the United States of America], *Przegląd Historyczno-Oświatowy* 14 (1971): 60–73; Andrzej Brożek, *Ślązacy w Teksasie: Relacje o najstarszych polskich osadach w Stanach Zjednoczonych* [Silesians in Texas: Accounts of the Oldest Polish Settlements in the United States]; Edward J. Dworaczyk, *The First Polish Colonies of America in Texas*; Martynian Możejewski [Rev. M. M.], "Stany Zjednoczone Ameryki Północnej: Najpierwsza parafia i kościół polski w Ameryce" [United States of America: The First Polish Parish and Church in America], *Przegląd Katolicki* (Warsaw, Russian Empire) 34 (16 January 1896): 43–47; Maria Starczewska, "The Historical Geography of the Oldest Polish Settlement in the United States," *Polish Review* 12 (Spring 1967): 11–40.

3. T. Lindsay Baker, "Panna Maria and Płużnica: A Study in Comparative Folk Culture," in *The Folklore of Texan Cultures*, ed. Francis Edward Abernethy, pp. 218–226.

4. W. F. Reddaway, J. H. Pinson, O. Halecki, and R. Dyboski, *The Cambridge History of Poland*, 2:123; William John Rose, *The Drama of Upper Silesia*, p. 11. I have used current Polish place names in the text, while using nineteenth-century place names as cited in original documents in the footnotes and bibliography (together with current place names when they add to clarity).

5. Andrzej Brożek, *Emigracja zamorska z Górnego Śląska w II połowie XIX wieku* [Overseas Emigration from Upper Silesia in the Second Half of the Nineteenth Century], pp. 3–4; Rose, *Drama of Upper Silesia*, pp. 88–93. Portions of the valuable Brożek monograph have been translated into English and are available as Andrzej Brożek, "The Roots of Polish Migration to Texas," *Polish American Studies* 30 (Spring 1973): 20–35.

6. Bolesław Reiner, "Polityczno-administracyjne podziały Górnego Śląska w XIX i XX wieku" [Political-Administrative Divisions in Upper Silesia in the Nineteenth and Twentieth Centuries], *Studia Śląskie* 21 (1972): 41–47.

7. Felix Triest, *Topographisches Handbuch von Oberschlesien* [Topographical Handbook of Upper Silesia], pp. 48, 206, 261, 427, 473. This work contains one of the

most comprehensive descriptions of the agricultural, commercial, industrial, and social conditions in Upper Silesia for the middle years of the nineteenth century. Similarly valuable works on this topic are J. G. Knie, *Alphabetisch-Statistich-Topographische Uebersicht der Dörfer, Flecken, Städte und Andern Orte der Königl. Preuss. Provinz Schlesien* [Alphabetical-Statistical-Topographical Overview of the Villages, Localities, Cities, and Other Places in the Royal Prussian Province of Silesia]; Th. Schück, *Oberschlesien: Statistik des Regierungs-Bezirks Oppeln mit Besonderer Beziehung auf Landwirtschaft, Bergbau, Hüttenwesen, Gewerbe und Handel nacht Amtlichen Quellen* [Upper Silesia: Statistics of the Regency of Opole with Special Attention to Agriculture, Mining, Foundries, Industry, and Commerce from Official Sources].

It should be noted that there was some limited German immigration to Texas from Upper Silesia concurrent with that of the Poles, such as that of Julius Lichtorn and Friedrich Bannowski, of Karlsruhe (Pokój), Opole County, to La Grange, Texas, in 1859, but this movement was completely separate from that of the Poles and is outside the scope of this work. Kingdom of Prussia, Regency of Opole, Opole County, Passport Journal of the Landrat of Opole County 1858–1861, entries 1210, 1272.

8. Triest, *Topographisches Handbuch*, p. 305.

9. *Times* (London), 13 September 1854, p. 7.

10. Brożek, *Emigracja zamorska*, pp. 9–10; *Czas* (Kraków, Austrian Empire), 14 February 1856, p. 1.

11. Members of the Moczygemba family have spelled their surname in various ways. The three most common forms have been Moczygęba, Moczigemba, and Moczygemba. I have used the last of these forms, which became the most common in America and is used today by the family. When different forms were found in manuscript sources, I have retained the original spellings in footnote citations. The same guideline has been followed for other surnames that have varied spellings in the source materials.

12. St. Stanisław Church, Płużnica, Opole Voivodeship, Poland, Baptismal Records (26 December 1812–2 June 1833), pp. 149–150. For a detailed study of the history and genealogy of the Moczygemba family, see T. Lindsay Baker, "The Moczygemba Family of Texas and Poland: Initiators of Polish Colonization in America," *Stirpes, Texas State Genealogical Society Quarterly* 15 (December 1975): 124–138. The one available biography of the Rev. Leopold Moczygemba is Joseph Swastek, *Priest and Pioneer: Rev. Leopold Moczygemba*.

13. *Katolik* (Królewska Huta [Königshütte], German Empire), 28 November 1881, [lv. 2 of unpaged text]; *Katolik* (Bytom [Beuthen], German Empire), 17 April 1891, [lv. 1 of unpaged text]; Wacław Kruszka, *Historja polska w Ameryce* [Polish History in America], p. 361; "Album des Gymnasiums in Oppeln 10 Oktober 1843 ab bis 31 Dezember 1878" [Album from the Gymnasium in Opole 10 October 1843 to 31 December 1878], p. 9, entry 122.

14. Friars Minor Conventual, Province of the Marches, Urbino Convent, "Conteggio de Zagotti, e Professi del Convento di Urbino" [Financial Accounts of the Professed of the Convent of Urbino]; Friars Minor Conventual, Province of the Marches, "Verbali delle Affigliazioni di Conventi 1828–1858" [Minutes of the Affiliates of the Convents 1828–1858]; "Memoire del P. Moczigemba," in "Notes for a History of the Province Collected by Very Rev. Fr. Othmar Hellmann," comp. and ed. Othmar Hellmann, p. 411; [Note concerning dispensation for Bonaventure Moczygemba dated 8 June 1847], Hellmann, "Notes," p. 221; Swastek, *Priest and Pioneer*, pp. 3–4.

15. Sister Mary Carmelita Glennon, "History of the Diocese of Galveston, 1847–

1874" (master's thesis, University of Texas, 1943), p. 53; Bishop J[ean-] M[arie] Odin, Munich, to Rev. Bonaventure Keller and Rev. Leopoldo Mozigemba [*sic*], [Schönau], 17 February 1852, item no. IX-Tex-I-A, Friars Minor Conventual, Archives of the General Curia; Bishop J[ean-] M[arie] Odin, Gemeunden, [Bavaria], to My Reverend Father [Rev. Robert Zahradniczek, location?], 22 February 1852, Hellmann, "Notes," p. x.

16. Friars Minor Conventual, Argentine Province, Oggersheim Convent, "Chronik" [Chronicle] (3 May 1845–26 May 1898), p. 23; Friars Minor Conventual, Argentine Province, Schönau Convent, "Chronik" [Chronicle] (1791–December 1914), unpaged; Rev. Bonaventure Keller, Schönau, to Honorable Commissary General [Rev. Robert Zahradniczek, location?], 20 February 1852, Hellmann, "Notes," pp. vii–ix; Rev. Bonaventure Keller, Schönau, to Reverend Minister General [Rev. Giacinto Gualerni, Rome], 8 March 1852, item no. IX-Tex-I-A, Archives of the General Curia; [Rev. Leopold] Moczygemba, [Oggersheim], to [Rev. Robert] Zahradniczek, [location?], 16 April 1852, Hellmann, "Notes," p. 345; [Rev. Robert] Zahradniczek, Schönau, to [Rev. Leopold] Moczygemba, [Oggersheim], 30 April 1852, Hellmann, "Notes," p. 345.

17. Rev. [Eugeniusz] Lockay, Wischnitz [Wiśnicze, Regency of Opole], to [Rev. Robert] Zahradniczek, [location?], 26 August 1851, Hellmann, "Notes," p. 334; [Rev. Leopold] Moczygemba, Dudenhofen (Pfalz), to [Rev. Robert] Zahradniczek, [location?], 3 March 1858, Hellmann, "Notes," p. 333; [Rev. Leopold] Moczygemba, Gross Pluschnitz bei Tost [Płużnica near Toszek, Regency of Opole], Prussia, to [Rev. Robert] Zahradniczek, [location?], 28 August 1851, Hellmann, "Notes," p. 335; [Note concerning letter of Rev. Bonaventure Keller, Oggersheim, to Commissary General Rev. Robert Zahradniczek, location? 1851], Hellmann, "Notes," p. 333.

18. Mathias Krawietz, [location? Regency of Opole], to [Rev. Robert] Zahradniczek, [location?], 9 March 1852, Hellmann, "Notes," p. 345; Leopold Moczygemba [Sr.] and Ewa Moczygemba, Gr. Pluschnitz bei Tostin [Płużnica near Toszek, Regency of Opole], to [Rev. Robert] Zahradniczek, [location?], 1 November 1851, Hellmann, "Notes," p. 333; [Rev. Robert] Zahradniczek, [location?], to Mathias Krawietz, [location?, Regency of Opole], 29 March 1852, Hellmann, "Notes," p. 345.

19. Leon Greulich and Othmar Hellmann, *Album Fratrum Minorum S. Francisci Conventualium in Statibus Foederatis Americae pro Anno 1917* [Album of the Friars Minor Conventual in the United States of America for the Year 1917], pp. 86–87; Rev. Bonaventure [Keller], Le Havre, [France], to Reverend Father General [Rev. Giacinto Gualerni, Rome], 2 July 1852, item no. IX-Tex-I-B, Archives of the General Curia.

20. Greulich and Hellmann, *Album Fratrum Minorum*, pp. 86–87; Oscar Haas, *History of New Braunfels and Comal County, Texas, 1844–1946*, p. 301; Rev. Leop[old] Bonav[entura] M[aria] Moczygęba, Castroville, Texas, to Dear Father General [Rev. Giacinto Gualerni, Rome], 24 March 1854, item no. IX-Tex-I-G, Archives of the General Curia; Bishop Jean-Marie Odin, San Antonio, Texas, to Rev. Bonaventure Keller, [location?], 14 September 1852, Hellmann, "Notes," pp. 111, 298; St. Louis Church, Castroville, Texas, Combined Parish Records, vol. 1; Sts. Peter and Paul Church, New Braunfels, Texas, Baptismal Records (20 January 1847–19 December 1893), pp. 20–38.

21. For a description by an American of the life in the German settlements in Texas, including New Braunfels and Castroville, in 1853 and 1854, see Frederick Law Olmstead, *Journey through Texas*.

22. Dworaczyk, *First Polish Colonies*, p. 1; Kruszka, *Historja polska w Ameryce*,

pp. 362–363; Możejewski, "Stany Zjednoczone," p. 44; Stefan Nesterowicz, *Notatki z podróży po północnej i środkowej Ameryce* [Travel Notes through Northern and Middle America], pp. 199–200.

23. Rev. Leop[old] B[onaventura] M[aria] Moczygęba, Panna Maria, [Texas], to Dear Parents, [Płużnica, Regency of Opole], 18 June 1855, Kingdom of Prussia, Regency of Opole, Department of the Interior, Die Auswanderung nach den Amerikanischen Staaten—Concesirung von Vereinen u. Agenturen zur Beförderung der Auswanderer, vol. 2 (1 October 1855–end December 1867), pp. 65–66. This letter, in Polish, appears in Andrzej Brożek and Henryk Borek, *Pierwsi Ślązacy w Ameryce: Listy z Teksasu do Płużnicy z roku 1855* [The First Silesians in America: Letters from Texas to Płużnica in the Year 1855] and in English translation in T. Lindsay Baker, trans. and ed., "Four Letters from Texas to Poland in 1855," *Southwestern Historical Quarterly* 77 (January 1974): 388–389.

24. *Schlesische Zeitung* (Breslau, Kingdom of Prussia), 22 September 1857, p. 2296; Julius Heinr[ich] Schüler, Oppeln [Opole, Regency of Opole] to Highly Esteemed Royal Administration, [Opole, Regency of Opole], 30 December 1856, Prussia, Auswanderung, 2:301–302.

25. Moczygęba to Dear Parents, 18 June 1855, Prussia, Auswanderung, 2:66.

26. Royal Landrat Graf Strachwitz, Kamienitz [Kamień, Regency of Opole], to Police Administration, [Opole, Regency of Opole], 30 August 1855, Prussia, ibid., 2:20.

27. Emily Greene Balch, *Our Slavic Fellow Citizens*, pp. 47–50, 54–56; Brożek, *Emigracja zamorska*, pp. 3–4.

28. Brożek, *Emigracja zamorska*, p. 7; *Czas*, 29 September 1855, p. 2, 21 November 1855, p. 1; *Gwiazdka Cieszyńska* (Cieszyn, Austrian Empire), 1 September 1855, p. 287; Kingdom of Prussia, Regency of Opole, President, Reports to the King for 1851–1854, lv. 234.

29. Kingdom of Prussia, Regency of Opole, President, Reports to the King for 1855–1858, lvs. 25, 86.

30. *Czas*, 29 August 1855, p. 1, 29 September 1855, p. 2, 21 November 1855, p. 1.

31. *Gwiazdka Cieszyńska*, 1 September 1855, p. 287.

32. Ibid., 26 July 1856, p. 236; Scheider to [Royal Administration], 28 February 1855, Prussia, Auswanderung, 1, 564; *Zwiastun Górnoszlązki* (Piekary, Kingdom of Prussia), 8 July 1869, p. 228.

33. *Schlesische Zeitung*, 6 July 1854, p. 1343, 27 June 1855, p. 1294, 24 October 1856, p. 2370.

34. *Czas*, 21 November 1855, p. 1; *Schlesische Zeitung*, 6 July 1854, p. 1343, 24 October 1856, p. 2370.

35. *Czas*, 14 February 1856, p. 1; Prussia, Reports to the King for 1851–1854, lv. 140; *Schlesische Zeitung*, 2 February 1856, p. 233.

36. Brożek, "The Roots," p. 23.

37. Brożek, *Emigracja zamorska*, pp. 5–6; *Czas*, 10 August 1855, p. 2, 29 August 1855, p. 1, 21 November 1855, p. 1; *Schlesische Zeitung*, 17 August 1855, p. 1672, 19 August 1855, p. 1689, 23 August 1855, p. 1720, 24 August 1855, p. 1728, 31 August 1855, p. 1782, 18 September 1855, p. 1918.

38. For typical daily reports of cholera deaths from the president of the police in Wrocław, see *Schlesische Zeitung*, 22 August 1855, p. 1713, 23 August 1855, p. 1723, 2 September 1855, p. 1799, 8 September 1855, p. 1843, 26 September 1855, p. 1984, 27 September 1855, p. 1992.

39. Ibid., 16 September 1855, p. 1909.

40. Prussia, Reports to the King for 1851–1854, lvs. 232–235; *Schlesische Zeitung*, 24 August 1854, p. 1686, 25 August 1854, p. 1694, 28 August 1854, p. 1723, 30 August 1854, p. 1732, 31 August 1854, p. 1740, 1 September 1854, pp. 1748–1749; *Times* (London), 13 September 1854, p. 7.

41. *Schlesische Zeitung*, 9 September 1854, p. 1869, 14 September 1854, p. 1847; *Times* (London), 13 September 1854, p. 7, 19 September 1854, p. 8.

42. *Czas*, 14 February 1856, p. 1; *Gwiazdka Cieszyńska*, 27 September 1856, p. 308.

43. [Editors], *Zwiastun Górnoszląki*, [Piekary, Regency of Opole], to Our Brothers in Christ Who Live in Texas, [24 March 1870], *Zwiastun Górnoszlązki*, 24 March 1870, pp. 95–96.

44. Adolf Bakanowski, *Moje wspomnienia 1840-1863-1913* [My Memoirs 1840-1863-1913], p. 50.

45. Dworaczyk, *First Polish Colonies*, pp. 8, 97; Zdzisław Grot, *Działalność posłow polskich w sejmie pruskim (1848–1850)* [The Activities of Polish Deputies in the Prussian Parliament (1848–1850)], pp. 42–43, 70, 74, 76–77, 138, 325; Kazimierz Popiołek, *Polska "Wiosna Ludów" na Górnym Śląsku* [The Polish "Spring of Peoples" in Upper Silesia], pp. 24, 27–28, 32, 37; *Rosenberg-Creutzberger Telegraph* (Rosenberg [Olesno], Kingdom of Prussia), 20 February 1849, p. 57; *Schlesische Zeitung*, 13 December 1848, p. 3310; Zdzisław Surman, "Wyniki wyborów do pruskiego konstytucyjnego zgromadzenia narodowego i izby posłów sejmu pruskiego na Śląsku w latach 1848–1918" [The Results of Elections to the Prussian Constituent National Assembly and to the Chamber of Deputies of the Prussian Diet from Silesia in 1848–1918], *Studia i Materiały z Dziejów Śląska* 7 (1966): 20, 125; *A Twentieth Century History of Southwest Texas*, 1:189.

46. Lockay to Zahradniczek, 26 August 1851, Hellmann, "Notes," p. 334; Moczygemba to Zahradniczek, 28 August 1851, ibid., p. 335; Kruszka, *Historja polska w Ameryce*, p. 361.

Stanisław Kiołbassa was born at Świbie in the Wiśnicze parish on 7 May 1809, was married in the parish on 21 February 1832, and was the father of seven children born there between 1833 and 1852. Trinity Church, Wiśnicze, Katowice Voivodeship, Poland, Baptismal Records (1 January 1801–30 December 1812), p. 101, Baptismal Records (1 January 1832–9 December 1852), pp. 54–55, 132–133, 186–187, 338–339, 530–531, 706–707, Marriage Records (23 January 1822–25 November 1855), pp. 76–77. For a general study of the Kiołbassa family, see T. Lindsay Baker, "The Kiołbassa Family of Illinois and Texas," *Chicago Genealogist* 5 (Spring 1973): 78–82.

47. Bakanowski, *Moje wspomnienia*, p. 50; *Czas*, 29 September 1855, p. 2; *Times* (London), 5 July 1859, p. 8.

48. Balch, *Our Slavic Fellow Citizens*, p. 54; Moczygęba to Dear Parents, 18 June 1855, Prussia, Auswanderung, 2:65.

49. Prussia, Reports to the King for 1855–1858, lvs. 82–83; Scheider to [Royal Administration], 28 February 1855, Prussia, Auswanderung, 1:564; Strachwitz to Police Administration, 30 August 1855, Prussia, ibid., 2:20.

50. *Gwiazdka Cieszyńska*, 26 July 1856, p. 236; *Schlesische Zeitung*, 22 September 1857, p. 2296; Schüler to Royal Administration, 30 December 1856, Prussia, Auswanderung, 2:301–302.

51. Johan Moczigemba, [Panna Maria, Texas], to My Dear Uncles, [Płużnica, Regency of Opole, 1855]; Johann [*sic*] Moczigemba, Panna Maria, to [Friends and Rela-

tives, Płużnica, Regency of Opole], 13 May 1855; Thomas Moczigemba and Johan Dziuk, [Panna Maria], to [Friends and Relatives, Płużnica, Regency of Opole, 1855]; Moczygęba to Dear Parents, 18 June 1855, Prussia, Auswanderung, 2:53–57, 60, 65–66. These four letters appear in Brożek and Borek, *Pierwsi Ślązacy*, and Andrzej Brożek and Henryk Borek, *Jeszcze jeden list z Teksasu do Płużnicy z 1855 roku* [One More Letter from Texas to Płużnica in the Year 1855], and in English translation in Baker, "Four Letters," pp. 383–389.

52. Moczigemba to [Friends and Relatives], 13 May 1855, Prussia, Auswanderung, 2:56.

53. Moczigemba to My Dear Uncles, [1855], Prussia, ibid., 2:57.

54. Feirer, Patschkau [Paczków, Regency of Opole, Prussia], to Royal Administration, Oppeln [Opole, Regency of Opole], 12 May 1852, Prussia, ibid., 2:201–202; A. W. Berger, Berlin, to Highly Esteemed Royal Administration, Oppeln [Opole, Regency of Opole], 7 September 1855; Gontzki, Mouillard, and Raabe, Royal Administration, Oppeln [Opole, Regency of Opole], to [unidentified addressee, Royal Administration, Opole, Regency of Opole], 12 November 1852; Heidsel, Royal Administration, Oppeln [Opole, Regency of Opole], to Highly Esteemed Royal Administration, Oppeln [Opole, Regency of Opole], 21 September 1855; J[ulius] H[einrich] Schüler, Oppeln [Opole, Regency of Opole], to Highly Esteemed Royal Administration, [Opole, Regency of Opole], 23 February 1855, Prussia, ibid., 1:220–222, 572–573, 843–848.

55. Minister of Commerce, Trade, and Public Works, Berlin, to [lower administrative officials, Kingdom of Prussia], 28 March 1854, Prussia, ibid., p. 454.

56. *Czas*, 1 May 1855, p. 3; *Gwiazdka Cieszyńska*, 14 July 1855, p. 231; E[manuel] Rzeppa, [location?], to Dear Mr. [illegible, location?, n.d.], Prussia, Auswanderung, 2:31.

57. Rzeppa to Dear Mr., [n.d.], Prussia, ibid., pp. 31–32.

58. C. Krawietz, Bremerhaven, to F. Czerner, Tost [Toszek, Regency of Opole], 2 October [1855], Prussia, ibid., p. 33.

59. Moczigemba and Dziuk to [Friends and Relatives, 1855], Prussia, ibid., p. 60.

60. Balch, *Our Slavic Fellow Citizens*, pp. 52–53.

61. *Gwiazdka Cieszyńska*, 14 July 1855, p. 231, 13 October 1855, pp. 334–335.

62. Rev. Adolf [Bakanowski] and Br[other] Felix [Zwiardowski], Panna Maria, to Our Dearest Father Superior [Rev. Jerome Kajsiewicz, Rome], 1 March 1867, Bakanowski Letters no. 9336; [Rev. Adolf Bakanowski], Panna Maria, Texas, to [*Zwiastun Górnoszlązki*, Piekary, Regency of Opole], 6 June 1870, *Zwiastun Górnoszlązki*, 7 July 1870, p. 215; *Czas*, 1 May 1855, p. 3; *Gwiazdka Cieszyńska*, 14 July 1855, p. 231; Kruszka, *Historja polska w Ameryce*, pp. 361–363, 375.

63. Consul Delius, Royal Prussian High Ministry for Foreign Affairs, Bremen, to [Royal Administration, Opole, Regency of Opole], 30 March 1855, Prussia, Auswanderung, 1:755–757.

64. *Czas*, 22 May 1856, p. 2.

65. Bakanowski, *Moje wspomnienia*, pp. 29–30.

Chapter 2. Founding the First Polish Colonies

1. *Czas*, 29 August 1855, p. 1, 22 May 1856, p. 2; Scheider to [Royal Administration], 28 February 1855, Kingdom of Prussia, Regency of Opole, Department of the Interior, Die Auswanderung nach den Amerikanisches Staaten—Concesirung von Vereinen u. Agenturen zur Beförderung der Auswanderer, 1:564–565; *Schlesische Zeitung*, 14 October 1854, p. 2068.

2. Emily Greene Balch, *Our Slavic Fellow Citizens*, pp. 37, 42–44.

3. *Schlesische Zeitung*, 6 July 1854, p. 1343.

4. Scheider to [Royal Administration], 28 February 1855, Prussia, Auswanderung, 1:564–565.

5. Kingdom of Prussia, Regency of Opole, President, Reports to the King for 1855–1858, lv. 83.

6. *Czas*, 9 October 1855, p. 1, 19 October 1855, p. 1; *Gwiazdka Cieszyńska*, 13 October 1855, p. 334, 26 July 1856, p. 236, 27 September 1856, p. 308.

7. *Zwiastun Górnoszlązki*, 8 July 1869, p. 228.

8. For the lists of passengers on the ships carrying the first immigrants, together with somewhat confused information on their home villages, see *Galveston Zeitung* (Galveston, Texas), 9 December 1854, p. 2; *Neu-Braunfelser Zeitung* (New Braunfels, Texas), 22 December 1854, p. 2, 12 January 1855, p. 3.

9. *Czas*, 3 October 1854, p. 3; *Gwiazdka Cieszyńska*, 7 October 1854, p. 555.

10. Free Port of Bremen, "Ausgabe der in Monat October [1854] Aufgegebene Spedition von Auswanderere" [Edition of the Departures of Emigrants in the Month of October 1854]; *Galveston Zeitung*, 9 December 1854, p. 2; *Neu-Braunfelser Zeitung*, 22 December 1854, p. 3, 12 January 1855, p. 3; U.S., Department of State, Secretary, *Letter of the Secretary of State Transmitting a Statement of the Commercial Relations of the United States with Foreign Nations*, p. 280.

The bark *Weser*, which carried the first Polish immigrants to Texas, was launched in 1853 and finally broken up in 1879. Throughout the period of Silesian immigration to Texas the vessel was a frequent carrier of new European settlers to the state. Free Port of Bremen, Registry Documents for Bremen Bark *Weser*, item nos. 2-R.11.p.4, Bd. 24, 30, 50; *San Antonio Weekly Herald*, 12 June 1855, p. 2; U.S., Department of the Treasury, Copies of Lists of Passengers Arriving at the Port of Galveston, 1846–1871.

11. *Galveston Weekly News*, 5 December 1854, p. 3; *Galveston Zeitung*, 9 December 1854, p. 2; R. M. Silas, "Plan of Property Belonging to the Galveston Wharf Co. 1859 as Contained, on Pages 10 & 11, in the Volume Known as 'The History of the Galveston Wharf Company,' in the Files of the Galveston Wharf Company's Main Office, R. M. Silas Chief Engineer January 12, 1926"; U.S., Department of State, Secretary, *Letter from the Secretary of State Transmitting the Annual Report of Passengers Arriving in the United States*, pp. 34–35.

12. Method C. Billy, *Historical Notes on the Order of Friars Minor Conventual*, p. 62; Leon Greulich and Othmar Hellmann, *Album Fratrum Minorum S. Francisci Conventualium in Statibus Foederatis Americae pro Anno 1917*, pp. 86–87; Joseph Swastek, *Priest and Pioneer: Rev. Leopold Moczygemba*, p. 6.

13. *Czas*, 12 May 1858, p. 2; Wacław Kruszka, *Historja polska w Ameryce*, p. 365; Bolesław Rosiński, "Polacy w Texasie" [The Poles in Texas], *Ziemia* (Warsaw, Poland) 15 (1 December 1930): 475.

Since the publication of Rev. Edward J. Dworaczyk's history of the Poles in Texas in 1936, many historians and writers have repeated his statement that the initial Silesian immigrants after arrival in Galveston traveled by oxcart down the Gulf coastal plain to Indianola and thence inland to San Antonio. This interpretation generally disagrees with the sources published before the Dworaczyk book. These materials, including a newspaper article drawn from an interview with the Rev. Leopold Moczygemba in 1858, state that the peasants were "transported" or "carried" from Galveston to Indianola before their overland trek began. For the Dworaczyk version and later accounts apparently based on his seemingly mistaken interpretation, see T. Lindsay Baker, *The Early History of Panna Maria, Texas*, p. 14; Maksymilian Berezowski, "Swojacy wśród kowbojów: Podróż do Teksasu" [Countrymen in the Midst of Cowboys: A Journey to Texas], *Trybuna Ludu* (Warsaw, Poland), nos. 7493–7494 (1–2 November 1969), p. 5; Edward J. Dworaczyk, *The First Polish Colonies of America in Texas*, p. 2; S. A. Iciek, *Samochodem przez stany południowe* [By Automobile through the Southern States], p. 232; Dorothy Moczygemba, "My People Came," *Junior Historian of the Texas State Historical Association* 16 (December 1955): 19; John Ruckman, "Freedom and a Piece of Bread," *San Antonio Express Magazine*, 31 July 1949, p. 4; Swastek, *Priest and Pioneer*, p. 6; Melchior Wańkowicz, *Atlantyk–Pacyfik* [Atlantic–Pacific], p. 205; Sister Jan Maria Wozniak, "St. Michael's Church: The Polish National Catholic Church in San Antonio, Texas, 1855–1950" (master's thesis, University of Texas, 1964), p. 6.

14. Dworaczyk, *First Polish Colonies*, pp. 2–4; Wacław Kruszka, *Historja polska w Ameryce*, p. 365; Moczygemba to [Friends and Relatives], 13 May 1855, Prussia, Auswanderung, 2:56; *Neu-Braunfelser Zeitung*, 29 December 1854, p. 3; Maria Starczewska, "The Historical Geography of the Oldest Polish Settlement in the United States," *Polish Review* 12 (Spring 1967): 17; Swastek, *Priest and Pioneer*, pp. 6–7.

15. Dworaczyk, *First Polish Colonies*, p. 1; Kruszka, *Historja polska w Ameryce*, p. 369; Rosiński, "Polacy w Texasie," p. 475; U.S., Immigration Commission, *Immigrants in Industries (in Twenty-Five Parts); Part 24; Recent Immigrants in Agriculture (in Two Volumes)*, 2:364. For a more detailed examination of Father Moczygemba's plans for the Cracow community, see Jacek Przygoda, "New Light on the Poles in Texas," *Polish American Studies* 27 (Spring–Autumn 1970): 81–83; Jacek Przygoda, *Texas Pioneers from Poland: A Study in the Ethnic History*, pp. 33–36.

Although there is no comprehensive biography of John Twohig, the following sources contain elements of his life story: Charles Merritt Barnes, *Combats and Conquests of Immortal Heroes*, p. 196; Gussie Scott Chaney, *The Breadline Banker of St. Mary's Street*; Jimmy Combs, "John Twohig: Texan by Adoption," *Junior Historian of the Texas State Historical Association* 6 (March 1946): 1–2; *Dallas Morning News*, 14 October 1891, p. 2; W. H. Jackson and S. A. Long, *The Texas Stock Directory*, p. 185; Vinton Lee James, *Frontier and Pioneer Recollections of Early Days in San Antonio and West Texas*, p. 138; Mrs. Perry Kallison, "Our Historical Homes and the People Who Called Them Home," *Witte Museum Quarterly* 4 (1966): 9–13; "Memorial Tablet to John Twohig," *Frontier Times* 1 (August 1924): 27; *San Antonio Daily Herald*, 6 May 1874, p. 1; *San Antonio Express*, 17 July 1867, p. 3, 8 September 1867, p. 2, 14 October 1867, p. 3, 22 February 1868, p. 3, 18 March 1869, p. 3, 26 May 1869, p. 2, 27 July 1869, p. 3, 18 March 1870, p. 3, 19 January 1871, p. 5, 2 July 1911, pp. 9–11, 11 April 1920, p. 1A.

16. Adolf Bakanowski, *Moje wspomnienia 1840-1863-1913*, pp. 28–29; [Bakanowski] and [Zwiardowski] to Our Dearest Father Superior, 1 March 1867, Bakanowski Letters no. 9336; Balch, *Our Slavic Fellow Citizens*, pp. 228–229; Dworaczyk, *First Polish Colonies*, pp. 4–6; Kruszka, *Historja polska w Ameryce*, pp. 365–368; Martynian Możejewski [Rev. M. M.] "Stany Zjednoczone," *Przegląd Katolicki* 34 (16 January 1896): 44.

17. Paul Fox, *The Poles in America*, p. 58; *Gwiazdka Cieszyńska*, 26 July 1856, p. 236; Możejewski, "Stany Zjednoczone," pp. 44, 46–47; George R. Steward, *American Place-Names: A Concise and Selective Dictionary for the Continental United States of America*, p. 357.

18. Dworaczyk, *First Polish Colonies*, p. 6; Hilda Graef, *Mary: A History of Doctrine and Devotion*, 2:79–82; Kruszka, *Historja polska w Ameryce*, p. 366.

19. *Czas*, 12 May 1858, p. 2.

20. Dworaczyk, *First Polish Colonies*, p. 6; *Katolik* (Bytom [Beuthen], German Empire), 5 June 1888, [lv. 1 of unpaged text]; Kruszka, *Historja polska w Ameryce*, p. 366.

21. Amasa Gleason Clark, *Reminiscences of a Centenarian*, pp. 48–49; *Czas*, 12 May 1858, p. 2; J. Marvin Hunter, "The Founding of Bandera," *Frontier Times* 3 (May 1926): 40–44; J. Marvin Hunter, "When the Polish People Came to Bandera," *Frontier Times* 25 (May 1948): 191–195; Kruszka, *Historja polska w Ameryce*, pp. 375–376; Frederick Law Olmstead, *Journey through Texas*, p. 270; *Przegląd Poznański* (Posen, Kingdom of Prussia), July 1858, p. 86; *San Antonio Weekly Herald*, 21 August 1855, p. 3.

Probably because of the difficulty in finding nineteenth-century historical materials on the Polish colony at Bandera, several misconceptions have arisen concerning its founding. One of these errors centers on stories of its establishment by Rev. Felix Zwiardowski, who first came to Texas as a young seminarian in 1866 with missionaries of the Congregation of the Resurrection. Born on 29 December 1840, he was only fourteen years old when the Bandera colony was founded on the other side of the world. Edward T. Janas, *Dictionary of American Resurrectionists 1865–1965*, pp. 77–79; [Cleric] Felix [Zwiardowski], Port Brest, France, to Dear Father, [location?], 28 September 1866, Zwiardowski Letters no. 34688. For examples of the Zwiardowski-Bandera tale, see Marion Moore Coleman, "The Polish Origins of Bandera, Texas," *Polish American Studies* 20 (January–June 1963): 23; *St. Stanislaus Parish, Bandera, Texas: Centennial History, 1855–1955*, pp. 28–30. A second twentieth-century misconception about the settlement at Bandera is that the Silesian peasants who located there came in a different ship from that of the founders of Panna Maria. See Przygoda, "New Light," p. 80. All of the first colonists came together on the same two vessels. *Galveston Zeitung*, 9 December 1854, p. 2; *Neu-Braunfelser Zeitung*, 22 December 1854, p. 3, 12 January 1855, p. 3.

22. [Rev.] Vincent [Barzyński], San Antonio, to Dearest Fathers, Dear Colleagues, and Dear Brothers, [Rome], 19 December 1866, Barzyński Letters no. 8946; *Czas*, 12 May 1858, p. 2; Dworaczyk, *First Polish Colonies*, p. 90; J. M. Gilbert, *Archdiocese of San Antonio, 1874–1849*, p. 31; Chester Thomas Kochan, "The Polish People of San Antonio, Texas, 1900–1960: A Study in Social Mobility" (master's thesis, University of Texas, 1970), pp. 12–14; Stefan Nesterowicz, *Notatki z podróży po północnej i środkowej Ameryce*, p. 177; Wozniak, "St. Michael's Church," pp. 12–15.

23. *Czas*, 12 May 1858, p. 2; *Przegląd Poznański*, July 1858, p. 86; Przygoda, *Texas Pioneers*, pp. 86–87; *San Antonio Daily Herald*, 20 February 1867, p. 4, 21 June 1867, p. 1; *San Antonio Weekly Herald*, 27 December 1862, p. 2, 24 January 1863, p. 2, 25 April 1863, p. 1; *San Antonio Express*, 16 July 1867, p. 1, 26 March 1868, p. 2, 31 March 1868, p. 2, 3 April 1869, p. 3; Aleksander Szczepański, *Drapacze i śmietniki: Wrażenia amerykańskie* [The Skyscrapers and the Dumps: American Impressions], p. 183.

24. Scheider to [Royal Administration], 28 February 1855, Prussia, Auswanderung, 1:564–565; *Czas*, 1 May 1855, p. 3, 14 July 1855, p. 231; *Gwiazdka Cieszyńska*, 1 September 1855, p. 287; *Neu-Braunfelser Zeitung*, 4 January 1856, p. 3; Prussia, Reports to the King for 1855–1858, lv. 82.

25. Carl Hagenmeister, Tost [Toszek, Regency of Opole], sworn statement in case

of Joseph Krauss v. [Julius Heinrich] Schüler of Opole, 29 August 1855; Joseph Krauss, Tost [Toszek, Regency of Opole], sworn legal complaint against [Julius Heinrich] Schüler of Opole, 21 August 1855; Magistrate Reuther, Tost [Toszek, Regency of Opole], transcript of legal proceedings in case of Merchant Joseph Krauss v. Merchant [Julius Heinrich] Schüler of Opole, 23 August 1855; J[ulius] H[einrich] Schüler, Oppeln [Opole, Regency of Opole], to Highly Esteemed Royal Administration, [Opole, Regency of Opole], 23 February 1855; Julius Heinrich Schüler, Oppeln [Opole, Regency of Opole], to [Royal Administration, Opole, Regency of Opole], 14 September 18[55], Prussia, Auswanderung, 1:572–573, 819–826, 829–832, 835–842, 850–857; [Julius Heinrich] Schüler, Oppeln [Opole, Regency of Opole], to Highly Esteemed Royal Administration, [Opole, Regency of Opole, late 1855 or early 1856], Prussia, ibid., 2:49–50.

26. *Czas*, 29 August 1855, p. 1; Delius to [Royal Administration], 30 March 1855, Prussia, Auswanderung, 1:754–757; *Gwiazdka Cieszyńska*, 1 September 1855, p. 287; Moczygęba to Dear Parents, 18 June 1855, Prussia, ibid., 1:66.

27. Moczigemba to [Friends and Relatives], 13 May 1855, Prussia, ibid., 2:56.

28. Free Port of Bremen, *Bremens Schifffahrt von der Weser in Jahre 1855 von und nach Aussereuropäischen Plätzen und Gewässern* [Bremen Shipping on the Weser (River) in the Year 1855 to and from Non-European Places and Waters]; Kruszka, *Historja polska w Ameryce*, p. 370; Nesterowicz, *Notatki z podróży*, p. 200; *Neu-Braunfelser Zeitung*, 4 January 1856, p. 3. Although no precise information is available about it, one sizable contingent of emigrants from Strzelce County arrived in Bremen in late 1854 or early 1855. Unable to find a ship there bound for Texas, they went to Hamburg, where they found passage via Liverpool. Other scattered groups of Silesians found their way to ports other than Bremen, but they were a small minority of the total number. Free Port of Hamburg, Auswanderungsamt, VIII A 1, vol. 8, lvs. 23, 47, 201–202; *Czas*, 22 May 1856, p. 2; Delius to [Royal Administration], 30 March 1855, Prussia, Auswanderung, 1:756–757.

29. *Czas*, 9 October 1855, p. 1. For other comments on the passage of this contingent of emigrants, see *ibid.*, 19 October 1855, p. 1; *Gwiazdka Cieszyńska*, 13 October 1855, p. 334.

30. *Bremens Schifffahrt von der Weser in Jahre 1855*; Dworaczyk, *First Polish Colonies*, p. 109; John A. Joyce, *Our Polish Pioneers*, pp. 8–9; Kruszka, *Historja polska w Ameryce*, p. 377; Nesterowicz, *Notatki z podróży*, p. 181; *Neu-Braunfelser Zeitung*, 4 January 1856, p. 3; Rosiński, "Polacy w Texasie," p. 475.

According to one of the original settlers, the names of the first heads of households at the new settlement were F. Tudyk, M. Tudyk, Adam Pierdoła, Martin Pierdoła, Frank Kosub, Anton Kosub, Jacob Zając, Martin Cybis, Valentine Anioł, Paul Kaczmarek, Walter Stanuś, Joseph Michalski, and Thomas Krawiec. Dworaczyk, *First Polish Colonies*, pp. 108–109; Nesterowicz, *Notatki z podróży*, p. 181. Other pioneer settlers in the Bexar County community included Nicholas Tudyk, Lawrence Ploch, James Anioł, Ludwig Zając, and James Zając. P. F. Parisot and C. J. Smith, *History of the Catholic Church in the Diocese of San Antonio, Texas*, p. 127.

31. Andrzej Brożek, *Ślązacy w Teksasie: Relacje o najstarszych osadach polskich w Ameryce*, p. 138; Dworaczyk, *First Polish Colonies*, p. 107; Iciek, *Samochodem*, p. 225; Joyce, *Our Polish Pioneers*, p. 8; Nesterowicz, *Notatki z podróży*, pp. 180–181; Parisot and Smith, *Catholic Church in the Diocese of San Antonio*, p. 127; Przygoda, *Texas Pioneers*, pp. 16–17, 119–121; U.S., Census of 1860, Texas, Manuscript Popula-

tion Schedules, Bexar County; Rev. Felix [Zwiardowski], St. Hedwig, [Texas], to Dear Father Adolf [Bakanowski, Rome], 17 August 1875, Zwiardowski Letters no. 34747.

32. *Czas*, 22 May 1856, p. 2; *Gwiazdka Cieszyńska*, 26 July 1856, p. 236.

33. Schüler to Royal Administration, 30 December 1856, Prussia, Auswanderung, 2:301.

34. Copies of Lists of Passengers Arriving at the Port of Galveston, 1846–1871; Joseph Cotulla, "Cornbread and Clabber Made a Good Meal," *The Trail Drivers of Texas*, p. 317; *A Twentieth Century History of Southwest Texas*, 2:345; U.S., Department of the Interior, Bureau of Pensions, Pension record file of Joseph Cotulla for service in the First Texas Cavalry.

35. *Czas*, 22 May 1856, p. 2.

36. Hunter, "When the Polish People Came," p. 192; Kingdom of Prussia, Regency of Opole, Strzelce County, Release document for the obligations of Prussian subjects for the family of Johann Pycka [John Pyka], 31 July 1854.

37. *Czas*, 1 May 1855, p. 3; Prussia, Reports to the King for 1855–1858, lv. 82; *Zwiastun Górnoszlązki*, 8 July 1869, p. 228.

38. *Bedingungen der Ueberfahrt von Bremen nach den Vereiningten Staaten von Nord-Amerika, das Handelungshaus Carl Pokrantz & Comp. in Bremen Passagiere Annimmt und Mit Vorzüglich Guten Schiffen Befördert* [Conditions for Passage from Bremen to the United States of North America under Which the Trade House of Carl Pokrantz and Company Accepts Passengers and Transports Them on Exceptionally Good Ships], handbill, 1 lv., in Prussia, Auswanderung, 1:827–828; Andrzej Brożek, *Emigracja zamorska z Górnego Śląska w II połowie XIX wieku*, p. 10. For a typical timetable for the railway line from Mysłowice to Wrocław, crossing the southern portion of the area sending emigrants to Texas, see *Schlesische Zeitung*, 24 October 1856, p. 2372.

39. *Czas*, 29 August 1855, p. 1, 22 May 1856, p. 2, 12 May 1858, p. 2; Delius to [Royal Administration], 30 March 1855, Prussia, Auswanderung, 1:757; Hamburg, Auswanderungsamt, VIII A 1, vol. 8, lvs. 23, 47, 201–202; interview, Rev. John W. Yanta, San Antonio, Texas, 9 August 1973 (unless otherwise indicated, interviews were conducted by the author).

40. *Bedingungen der Ueberfahrt von Bremen*; Delius to [Royal Administration], 30 March 1855, Prussia, Auswanderung, 1:754–757; Krawietz to Czerner, 2 October [1855], Prussia, Auswanderung, 2:33–34.

41. *Bedingungen der Ueberfahrt von Bremen*; Hunter, "When the Polish People Came," p. 192.

42. Moczygęba to Dear Parents, 18 June 1855, Prussia, Auswanderung, 2:65.

43. Moczigemba to [Friends and Relatives], 13 May 1855, Prussia, ibid., 2:54.

44. Moczigemba and Dziuk to [Friends and Relatives, 1855], Prussia, ibid., p. 60.

45. Moczygęba to Dear Parents, 18 June 1855, Prussia, ibid., pp. 65–66.

46. Moczigemba to [Friends and Relatives], 13 May 1855, Prussia, ibid., p. 56.

47. Hunter, "When the Polish People Came," p. 192.

48. Arthur L. Finck, Jr., "The Regulated Emigration of the German Proletariat with Special Reference to Texas" (master's thesis, University of Texas, 1949), p. 109; H. H. McConnell, *Five Years a Cavalryman; or, Sketches of Regular Army Life on the Texas Frontier, Twenty Odd Years Ago*, p. 32; Ferdinand Roemer, *Texas, with Particular Reference to German Immigration and the Physical Appearance of the Country*, trans. Oswald Mueller, p. 135.

49. Brożek, *Emigracja zamorska*, pp. 15–16; *Czas*, 21 November 1855, p. 1, 14 February 1856, p. 1; *Gwiazdka Cieszyńska*, 12 January 1856, pp. 14–15, 27 September 1856, pp. 307–308; Lawrence Schofer, *The Formation of a Modern Labor Force: Upper Silesia, 1865–1914*, pp. 39–77. For examples of the "Prussian California" designation of Upper Silesia, see *Schlesische Zeitung*, 25 July 1855, p. 1501, 21 September 1855, p. 1943, 29 November 1855, p. 2518.

Chapter 3. Polish Life on the Frontier

1. Moczigemba to [Friends and Relatives], 13 May 1855, Kingdom of Prussia, Regency of Opole, Department of the Interior, Die Auswanderung nach den Amerikanischen Staaten—Concesirung von Vereinen u. Agenturen zur Beförderung der Auswanderer, 2:53.

2. Thomas Ruckman, "The Census Taker: A Complete Description of the County of Karnes—in South West Texas—by Thos. Ruckman June 1890," p. 39, Thomas Ruckman Papers.

3. Rev. Adolf [Bakanowski], San Antonio, to Our Dear Father Alexander [Jełowicki, Paris], 7 July 1868, Bakanowski Letters no. 9358.

4. Adolf Bakanowski, *Moje wspomnienia 1840-1863-1913*, pp. 53–56.

5. Stefan Nesterowicz, *Notatki z podróży po północnej i środkowej Ameryce*, pp. 180–181.

6. *Czas*, 12 May 1858, p. 2.

7. Edward J. Dworaczyk, *The First Polish Colonies of America in Texas*, p. 117; S. A. Iciek, *Samochodem przez stany południowe*, p. 225.

8. [Bakanowski] and [Zwiardowski] to Our Dearest Father Superior, 1 March 1867, Bakanowski Letters no. 9336; Emily Greene Balch, *Our Slavic Fellow Citizens*, pp. 228–229; Dworaczyk, *First Polish Colonies*, pp. 5–6; *Gwiazdka Cieszyńska*, 26 July 1856, p. 236; Wacław Kruszka, *Historja polska w Ameryce*, pp. 366–368; Martynian Możejewski, "Stany Zjednoczone Ameryki Północnej: Najpierwsza parafia i kościół polski w Ameryce," *Przegląd Katolicki* 34 (16 January 1896): 44; Franciszek Niklewicz, *Dzieje pierwszych polskich osadników w Ameryce i przewodnik parafij polskich w Stanach Zjednoczonych* [History of the First Polish Settlers in America and Guide around the Polish Parishes in the United States], p. 5; Bolesław Rosiński, "Polacy w Texasie," *Ziemia* 15 (1 December 1930): 476.

9. Bakanowski, *Moje wspomnienia*, pp. 28–29.

10. [Bakanowski] and [Zwiardowski] to Our Dearest Father Superior, 1 March 1867, Bakanowski Letters no. 9336; Bakanowski, *Moje wspomnienia*, p. 29; Kruszka, *Historja polska w Ameryce*, p. 368; interview, LeRoy Moczygemba, San Antonio, Texas, 6 December 1974; Możejewski, "Stany Zjednoczone," p. 44; Rosiński, "Polacy w Texasie," p. 476.

11. Moczigemba to My Dear Uncles, [1855], Prussia, Auswanderung, 2:57.

12. Moczigemba to [Friends and Relatives], 13 May 1855, Prussia, Auswanderung, 2:54–55.

13. Nesterowicz, *Notatki z podróży*, pp. 181–182.

14. Bakanowski, *Moje wspomnienia*, pp. 56, 169; "A Bandera County Pioneer," *Frontier Times* 1 (July 1924): 13; [Barzyński] to Dearest Fathers et al., 19 December 1866, Barzyński Letters no. 8946; J. Marvin Hunter, "When the Polish People Came to Bandera," *Frontier Times* 25 (May 1948): 193; Jo Stewart Randel and Carson County Historical Survey Committee, eds., *A Time to Purpose: A Chronicle of Carson County*,

2:145; T. U. Taylor, "Pioneer Engineering in Texas," *Frontier Times* 15 (October 1937): 31–32.

15. Dworaczyk, *First Polish Colonies*, pp. 5–6; Kruszka, *Historja polska w Ameryce*, pp. 366–368; Dorothy Moczygemba, "My People Came," *Junior Historian of the Texas State Historical Association* 16 (December 1955): 19–20; Nesterowicz, *Notatki z podróży*, pp. 198–201; Sister Jan Maria Wozniak, "St. Michael's Church: The Polish National Catholic Church in San Antonio, Texas, 1855–1950," pp. 6–7.

16. To judge from a letter written by a Silesian colonist to Boronów, in Lubliniec County, from which some material was drawn for a contemporary newspaper article, the peasants at first found the Texas climate favorable. *Gwiazdka Cieszyńska*, 26 July 1856, p. 236. For a few weather statistics for the area of Polish settlement, specifically for New Wied and Austin, in 1854 and 1855, see U.S., Department of the Interior, Patent Office, Commissioner, *Report of the Commissioner of Patents for the Year 1854: Agriculture*, pp. 444–445; U.S., Department of the Interior, Patent Office, Commissioner, *Report of the Commissioner of Patents for the Year 1855: Agriculture*, pp. 376, 387.

17. Moczigemba to [Friends and Relatives], 13 May 1855, Prussia, Auswanderung, 2:55.

18. Bakanowski, *Moje wspomnienia*, p. 29.

19. Moczigemba to [Friends and Relatives], 13 May 1855, Prussia, Auswanderung, 2:53.

20. Ibid., pp. 53, 56.

21. Dworaczyk, *First Polish Colonies*, pp. 5, 110; John A. Joyce, *Our Polish Pioneers*, p. 9; Kruszka, *Historja polska w Ameryce*, pp. 366, 368; Rosiński, "Polacy w Texasie," p. 476; U.S., Immigration Commission, *Immigrants in Industries (in Twenty-five Parts); Part 24: Recent Immigrants in Agriculture (in Two Volumes)*, 2:364.

22. Bakanowski, *Moje wspomnienia*, p. 29. Such "cellar houses" continued to be used, in very rare instances, into the 1970's in Upper Silesia. Interview, Jacek Michałowski, staff photographer, Museum of the Opole Countryside, Bierkowice, Opole Voivodeship, Poland, 8 July 1972 (Krystyna Baker assisted with this interview; hereafter cited as [KB]); Nesterowicz, *Notatki z podróży*, p. 201.

23. Ruckman, "Census Taker," p. 45.

24. Moczigemba to [Friends and Relatives], 13 May 1855, Prussia, Auswanderung, 2:56.

25. *San Antonio Weekly Herald*, 17 April 1855, p. 3.

26. Rev. Adolf Bakanowski, Panna Maria, to Our Dearest Father Superior [Rev. Jerome Kajsiewicz, Rome], 13 November 1966, Bakanowski Letters no. 9330; Dworaczyk, *First Polish Colonies*, pp. 21–22.

27. Moczigemba to [Friends and Relatives], 13 May 1855, Prussia, Auswanderung, 2:53–54.

28. Rev. Teofil Jan Bralewski, Martinez, [Texas], to Reverend Father [Rev. Peter Semenenko, Rome], 14 March 1869, Bralewski Letters no. 41202.

29. Bakanowski to Our Dearest Father Superior, 13 November 1866, Bakanowski Letters no. 9330.

30. T. Lindsay Baker, "Panna Maria and Płużnica: A Study in Comparative Folk Culture," pp. 219–220; interview, Mrs. Mary Mika, Panna Maria, 11 August 1973 (KB); interview, Elias J. Moczygemba, Panna Maria, 10 August 1973 (KB); U.S., Department of the Interior, National Park Service, Historic American Buildings Survey, Number

Tex-311 (Urbanczyk House, Panna Maria, Karnes County, Texas, 1936), Number Tex-312 (Moczygemba Houses, Panna Maria, Karnes County, Texas, 1936), Number Tex-314 (Pawelek House, near Cestohova [*sic*], Karnes County, Texas, 1937). In summer 1972 and in academic years 1975–1976 and 1976–1977, my wife and I visited the villages in Upper Silesia from which the immigrants of the 1850's came, taking many notes and photographs. Some of the architectural comparisons in this paragraph are based on those field observations.

31. Rev. Adolf Bakanowski, Panna Maria, to Our Dearest Father Peter [Semenenko, Rome], 28 June 1867, Bakanowski Letters no. 9344; Viktor Bracht, *Texas in 1848*, trans. Charles Frank Schmidt, p. 135; Arthur L. Finck, Jr., "The Regulated Emigration of the German Proletariat with Special Reference to Texas," p. 64; Ferdinand Roemer, *Texas, with Particular Reference to German Immigration and the Physical Appearance of the Country*, trans. Oswald Mueller, p. 93.

32. Henry Lyman Brightman Russell, *Granddad's Autobiography*, p. 4.

33. *Dallas Morning News*, 24 January 1932, sec. 4, p. 1. For additional information on the folk dress worn by Upper Silesian peasants, see Stanisław Bronicz, "Materiały i uwagi do zagadnienia strojów ludowych na Śląsku Opolskim" [Materials and Comments on the Subject of Folk Dress in Opole Silesia], *Opolski Rocznik Muzealny* (Opole, Poland) 2 (1966): 185–198; Albert Kretchmer, *Deutsche Volkstrachten* [German Folk Dress], pp. 27–28, plate 16.

34. Moczygęba to Dear Parents, 18 June 1855, Prussia, Auswanderung, 2:66.

35. Interview, Franz Karkosz and Maria Karkosz, Płużnica, Opole Voivodeship, Poland, 23 June 1972 (KB); interview, Mary Mika, 11 August 1973 (KB); Alma Oakes and Margot Hamilton Hill, *Rural Clothing: Its Origin and Development in Western Europe and the British Isles*, p. 155.

36. Moczigemba to [Friends and Relatives], 13 May 1855, Prussia, Auswanderung, 2:55.

37. A. Evans, B. E. Edwards, and H. B. Landry, San Antonio, Texas, to E. M. Pease, [Austin], 1 September 1855; J. A. Robins et al., Goliad, [Texas], to [E. M.] Pease, [Austin], 13 September 1855, Dorman H. Winfrey, ed., *Texas Indian Papers 1846–1859*, pp. 231–234, 238–240; *San Antonio Weekly Herald*, 4 September 1855, p. 2.

38. Hunter, "When the Polish People Came," pp. 193–194; Nesterowicz, *Notatki z podróży*, pp. 204–205; *San Antonio Weekly Herald*, 11 September 1855, p. 2.

39. *Galveston Zeitung*, 9 December 1854, p. 2; *Neu-Braunfelser Zeitung*, 22 December 1854, p. 3.

40. Hunter, "When the Polish People Came," p. 194; Randel et al., *Time to Purpose*, 2:145.

41. Amasa Gleason Clark, *Reminiscences of a Centenarian*, p. 61; J. Marvin Hunter, *A Brief History of Bandera County*, p. 74. In Hunter's version of this incident he states that it occurred in summer 1872.

42. Andrew Jackson Sowell, *Early Settlers and Indian Fighters of Southwest Texas*, pp. 828–829.

43. Hunter, "When the Polish People Came," p. 194; *San Antonio Weekly Herald*, 17 April 1855, p. 2. In a similar incident the next year a Silesian and two Americans were attacked on the road from San Antonio to Bandera. Clark, *Reminiscences*, pp. 52–54.

44. Dworaczyk, *First Polish Colonies*, p. 110; Moczigemba to [Friends and Rela-

tives], 13 May 1855, Prussia, Auswanderung, 2:55–56; Nesterowicz, *Notatki z podróży*, p. 182.

45. *Czas*, 12 May 1858, p. 2; *Gwiazdka Cieszyńska*, 26 July 1856, p. 236.

46. Iciek, *Samochodem*, p. 226; Moczigemba to [Friends and Relatives], 13 May 1855, Prussia, Auswanderung, 2:56; Nesterowicz, *Notatki z podróży*, p. 182.

47. *San Antonio Weekly Herald*, 17 April 1855, p. 3.

48. S. G. Dailey, Helena, Texas, to John C. Brightman, Goliad, Texas, 3 May 1858, Correspondence 1849–1935, Henry Lyman Brightman Russell Papers.

49. The thirteen residents of Karnes County definitely identified as Poles in the 1860 census of agriculture are the following: F. Bela [Biela], J. Beula [Biela], Jos Calckha [Kalka], A. Duge [Dugi or Dluge], J. Duck [Dziuk], John Gavalik [Gawlik], A. Labas [Labus], J. Mosakimber [Moczygemba], Jno. Moskimber [Moczygemba], Thos. Moskimber [Moczygemba], J. Rabstein, M. Urbangik [Urbanczyk], and Simin [Simon] Yanta. U.S., Census of 1860, Texas, Manuscript Agriculture Schedules, Karnes County.

50. Ibid.

51. Ibid.; Kruszka, *Historja polska w Ameryce*, p. 370; interview, Mary Mika, 11 August 1973 (KB); Nesterowicz, *Notatki z podróży*, pp. 182, 201; *Zwiastun Górnoszląski*, 8 July 1869, p. 228.

52. Bakanowski, *Moje wspomnienia*, p. 31; Hunter, "When the Polish People Came," p. 194; Iciek, *Samochodem*, p. 226; Moczigemba to [Friends and Relatives], 13 May 1855, Prussia, Auswanderung, 2:54, 56; Nesterowicz, *Notatki z podróży*, p. 182.

53. Moczigemba to [Friends and Relatives], 13 May 1855, Prussia, Auswanderung, 2:53–54, 56. "Maranuses" is a Polonized spelling for the Spanish word *marranas*, "swine."

54. Bakanowski, *Moje wspomnienia*, pp. 35–36, 48, 61; interview, M. Mika, 11 August 1973 (KB).

55. *Gwiazdka Cieszyńska*, 26 July 1856, p. 236.

56. Bakanowski, *Moje wspomnienia*, pp. 33–34, 37–39, 47–50; Hunter, "When the Polish People Came," p. 193; Rosiński, "Polacy w Texasie," p. 476; Ruckman, "Census Taker," p. 39; Rev. Felix [Zwiardowski], Bandera, [Texas], to Reverend Father General [Rev. Jerome Kajsiewicz, Rome], 9 May 1870, Zwiardowski Letters no. 34705.

57. Bakanowski to Our Dearest Father Peter, 28 June 1867, Bakanowski Letters no. 9344.

58. Dworaczyk, *First Polish Colonies*, pp. 7, 18–19, 110; Moczigemba to [Friends and Relatives], 13 May 1855, Prussia, Auswanderung, 2:55–56; Nesterowicz, *Notatki z podróży*, p. 201; Rosiński, "Polacy w Texasie," p. 476; Lillie Terrell Shaver and Willie Williamson Rogers, *Flashlights on Texas*, p. 138.

59. Bakanowski to Our Dearest Father Peter, 28 June 1867, Bakanowski Letters no. 9344; [Rev. Adolf Bakanowski], Panna Maria, to [*Zwiastun Górnoszlązki*, Piekary, Regency of Opole, Spring 1870], *Zwiastun Górnoszlązki*, 14 April 1870, p. 120; Bakanowski, *Moje wspomnienia*, p. 31; *Gwiazdka Cieszyńska*, 26 July 1856, p. 236; Moczigemba to [Friends and Relatives], 13 May 1855, Prussia, Auswanderung, 2:55; *San Antonio Express*, 25 July 1868, p. 4; *Zwiastun Górnoszlązki*, 8 July 1869, p. 229.

60. Bakanowski, *Moje wspomnienia*, p. 31; *Texas Almanac for 1867*, p. 126; *Texas Almanac for 1871*, p. 124.

61. *Texas Alamanac for 1859*, p. 216.

62. Dworaczyk, *First Polish Colonies*, pp. 10, 110; Iciek, *Samochodem*, p. 226; Karnes County, Texas, Deed Records, B: 553–554, C: 3–9, 31, 563–564, H: 363–365; Kruszka, *Historja polska w Ameryce*, p. 369; Nesterowicz, *Notatki z podróży*, p. 201; *Zwiastun Górnoszląski*, 8 July 1869, p. 228.

63. Karnes County, Texas, Deed Records, H: 363–365; Kruszka, *Historja polska w Ameryce*, p. 369; Rev. Leop[old] Bonav[entura] M[aria] Moczygęba, Castroville, Texas, to Dear Father General [Rev. Giacinto Gualerni, Rome], 16 July 1855, item no. IX-Tex-IV-C, Archives of the General Curia; Nesterowicz, *Notatki z podróży*, p. 200; Joseph Swastek, *Priest and Pioneer: Rev. Leopold Moczygemba*, p. 9. The form of land division employed by Twohig and Moczygemba at Panna Maria, unusual by Texas standards, was the form best known to the Upper Silesian immigrants. The two men cut the land into long, narrow strips fronting on the San Antonio River and Cibolo Creek and stretching back toward the settlement. These narrow fields are still visible at Panna Maria. Most other places in Texas—the Felix Mika farm, for example—would be considered exceptional. It is only 600 feet wide but a mile long. Nesterowicz, *Notatki z podróży*, p. 201; Robert H. Thonhoff, "A History of Karnes County" (master's thesis, Southwest Texas State College, 1963), p. 113. For a study of this system of land tenure in Texas, see Terry G. Jordan, "Antecedents of the Long-Lot in Texas," *Annals of the Association of American Geographers* 64 (March 1974): 70–84.

64. *Texas Almanac for 1861*, p. 219.

65. *San Antonio Express*, 22 August 1869, p. 2; *Texas Almanac for 1867*, p. 126; Edward Young, *Special Report on Immigration*, p. 170.

66. *Texas Almanac for 1871*, p. 124; Texas, Department of Insurance, Statistics, and History, *The Resources, Soil, and Climate of Texas*, p. 170.

67. Texas, Department of Agriculture, Insurance, Statistics, and History, *First Annual Report of the Agricultural Bureau, 1887–88*, p. 122; *Second Annual Report of the Agricultural Bureau, 1888–89*, p. 139; *Fifth Annual Report of the Agricultural Bureau, 1891–92*, p. 174; *Sixth Annual Report of the Agricultural Bureau, 1892–93*, p. 182; *Ninth Annual Report of the Agricultural Bureau, 1895*, p. 149.

68. *Texas Almanac and State Industrial Guide 1904*, p. 303.

69. *San Antonio Weekly Herald*, 26 December 1855, p. 2, 9 January 1856, p. 2, 23 January 1856, p. 2, 30 January 1856, p. 3, 6 February 1856, pp. 2–3, 23 February 1856, p. 2, 8 March 1856, p. 2; *Texas Almanac for 1858*, p. 135.

70. *San Antonio Weekly Herald*, 9 August 1856, p. 2, 16 August 1856, p. 2, 30 August 1856, p. 2.

71. Anne Blasig, *The Wends of Texas*, p. 42; Dworaczyk, *First Polish Colonies*, p. 16; Nesterowicz, *Notatki z podróży*, p. 203; Theophilus Noel, *Autobiography and Reminiscences of Theophilus Noel*, p. 42; *Texas Almanac for 1861*, p. 136.

72. Blasig, *Wends of Texas*, p. 42; Joshua F. Lovejoy, [location?], to [unidentified addressee, location?], 24 March 1858, cited in Walter McCausland, Buffalo, N.Y., to S. W. Geiser, Dallas, 12 October 1946, in H. Bailey Carroll, ed., "Texas Collection," *Southwestern Historical Quarterly* 50 (January 1947): 388; Nesterowicz, *Notatki z podróży*, p. 203; Ruckman, "Census Taker," p. 39; *San Antonio Weekly Herald*, 6 February 1856, p. 2.

73. Dworaczyk, *First Polish Colonies*, p. 16; *Gwiazdka Cieszyńska*, 26 July 1856, p. 236; Nesterowicz, *Notatki z podróży*, p. 203; Ruckman, "Census Taker," p. 39; [Cleric] Felix Zwiardowski, Panna Maria, Texas, to Our Dear Reverend Father [Rev. Alexander Jełowicki, Paris], 28 December 1866, Zwiardowski Letters no. 34692;

Zwiastun Górnoszlązki, 8 July 1869, p. 229. For the touching story of a Silesian girl who died of a fever while working for an American family at this time, see *Dallas Morning News*, 24 January 1932, sec. 4, p. 1.

It is interesting to note that one way in which news of the end of the Texas drought reached people in Silesia was through the Silesian press. *Schlesische Zeitung*, 22 September 1857, p. 2296.

74. [Bakanowski] and [Zwiardowski] to Our Dearest Father Superior, 1 March 1867, Bakanowski Letters no. 9336; [Bakanowski] to [*Zwiastun Górnoszlązki*], 6 June 1870, *Zwiastun Górnoszlązki*, 7 July 1870, p. 215; Bakanowski, *Moje wspomnienia*, pp. 28–29; Możejewski, "Stany Zjednoczone," pp. 44–45.

75. Kruszka, *Historja polska w Ameryce*, pp. 366–367; interview, E. J. Moczygemba, 10 August 1973 (KB); Nesterowicz, *Notatki z podróży*, pp. 203–204; interview, Ben P. Urbanczyk, Panna Maria, 10 August 1973 (KB).

76. Rev. Leop[old] Bonav[entura] M[aria] Moczygęba, Castroville, Texas, to Dear Father General [Rev. Giacinto Gualerni, Rome], 13 December 1854, item no. IX-Tex-IV-A, Archives of the General Curia; Rev. Leop[old] B[onaventura] M[aria] Moczygęba, Panna Maria, Texas, to Dear Father General [Rev. Giacinto Gualerni, Rome], 28 August 1855, item no. IX-Tex-IV-F, Archives of the General Curia; Rev. Leop[old] B[onaventura] M[aria] Moczygęba, Panna Maria, Texas, to Dear Father General [Rev. Giacinto Gualerni, Rome], 18 September 1855, item no. IX-Tex-IV-G, Archives of the General Curia; Rev. Leopold Bonav[entura] M[aria] Moczygęba, [Texas], to Eminence, [Leopoldine Society, Vienna, Austria, ca. 1856], Friars Minor Conventual, Immaculate Conception Province, Correspondence; Swastek, *Priest and Pioneer*, pp. 12–14.

77. Rev. Leop[old] B[onaventura] M[aria] Moczygęba, Panna Maria, Texas, to Dear Father General [Rev. Giacinto Gualerni, Rome], 12 March 1856, item no. IX-Tex-IV-E, Archives of the General Curia.

78. [Bakanowski] and [Zwiardowski] to Our Dearest Father Superior, 1 March 1867, Bakanowski Letters no. 9336; Kruszka, *Historja polska w Ameryce*, p. 367; Nesterowicz, *Notatki z podróży*, pp. 203–204.

79. [Bakanowski] and [Zwiardowski] to Our Dearest Father Superior, 1 March 1867, Bakanowski Letters no. 9336; *Katolik*, 10 April 1891, [1v. 1 of unpaged text], 17 April 1891, [1v. 1 of unpaged text]; Kruszka, *Historja polska w Ameryce*, pp. 272–273; "Ksiądz Leopold Moczygemba i polskie kolonie w Ameryce" [Rev. Leopold Moczygemba and the Polish Colonies in America], *Missyonarz Katolicki* (Mikołów, German Empire) 1 (1 September 1891): 262–264; Nesterowicz, *Notatki z podróży*, pp. 203–204; St. Louis Church, Castroville, Combined Parish Records, vol. 1; Sts. Peter and Paul Church, New Braunfels, Baptismal Records (20 January 1847–19 December 1893), p. 61; Swastek, *Priest and Pioneer*, pp. 12–30.

80. Rev. Vincent [Barzyński], San Antonio, to Dearest Most Reverend Father [Rev. Peter Semenenko, Rome], 14 March 1874, Barzyński Letters no. 9004; Dworaczyk, *First Polish Colonies*, p. 49; Rev. Leopold B[onaventura] M[aria] Moczygemba, Terre Haute, Indiana, to Dear Father General [Rev. Antonio Adragna, Rome], 11 May [18]74, item no. IX-5-E, Archives of the General Curia.

81. *Czas*, 12 May 1858, p. 2; Marion A. Habig, *San Antonio's Mission San Jose*, p. 146; Joyce, *Our Polish Pioneers*, p. 9; *Katolik*, 5 June 1888, [1v. 1 of unpaged text]; Edmund L. Kowalczyk, "Jottings from the Polish American Past," *Polish American Studies* 9 (July–December 1952): 86; Kruszka, *Historja polska w Ameryce*, pp. 373–374;

[Note concerning obedience for Rev. Anthony Rossadowski to travel to Texas, dated Rome, 1 May 1856], Othmar Hellmann, comp. and ed., "Notes for a History of the Province Collected by Very Rev. Fr. Othmar Hellmann," p. 139.

82. [Bakanowski] and [Zwiardowski] to Our Dearest Father Superior, 1 March 1867, Bakanowski Letters no. 9336; Rev. Leop[old] B[onaventura] M[aria] Moczygęba, Castroville, Texas, to Dear Father General [Rev. Giacinto Gualerni, Rome], 1 April 1857, item no. IX-Tex-V-I, Archives of the General Curia.

83. Edward J. Dworaczyk, *Church Records of Panna Maria, Texas*, pp. 30–57, 60–64; Dworaczyk, *First Polish Colonies*, pp. 19–20, 22–23, 110–111; Friars Minor Conventual, Immaculate Conception Province, Necrology, printed card index; *Katolik*, 5 June 1888, [1v. 1 of unpaged text]; Kruszka, *Historja polska w Ameryce*, pp. 373–378; Niklewicz, *Dzieje pierwszych*, pp. 7–8; *Przegląd Poznański*, July 1858, p. 86.

84. [Bakanowski] and [Zwiardowski] to Our Dearest Father Superior, 1 March 1867, Bakanowski Letters no. 9336; Rev. Adolf [Bakanowski], Panna Maria, to Our Honorable Father General [Rev. Jerome Kajsiewicz, Rome], 9 April 1868, Bakanowski Letters no. 9352; Rev. Adolf [Bakanowski], Panna Maria, to Our Honorable Father General [Rev. Jerome Kajsiewicz, Rome], 21 April 1868, Bakanowski Letters no. 9353; Rev. Adolf [Bakanowski], Panna Maria, to Our Honorable Father General [Rev. Jerome Kajsiewicz, Rome], 21 September 1868, Bakanowski Letters no. 9360; Rev. Adolf [Bakanowski], Panna Maria, to Honorable Father General [Rev. Jerome Kajsiewicz, Rome], 1 December 1868, Bakanowski Letters no. 9363; Dworaczyk, *First Polish Colonies*, pp. 7, 118–126; John Iwicki, *The First One Hundred Years: A Study of the Apostolate of the Congregation of the Resurrection in the United States 1866–1966*, pp. 44–45; Rev. Joseph A. Koenig, Victoria, Texas, to Most Highly Esteemed Archbishop, [Munich], 12 December 1859, Ludwig-Missionsverein, Papers and Letters Received Concerning the Diocese of Galveston, Texas; Kruszka, *Historja polska w Ameryce*, pp. 374–375, 506, 617–618; Nesterowicz, *Notatki z podróży*, pp. 210–214; Frederick Law Olmstead, *Journey through Texas*, p. 270; P. F. Parisot and C. J. Smith, *History of the Catholic Church in the Diocese of San Antonio, Texas*, p. 187; Rosiński, "Polacy w Texasie," p. 478; Rev. Felix [Zwiardowski], Panna Maria, to Honorable Reverend Father Superior, [location?], 24 September 1868, Zwiardowski Letters no. 34703.

85. [Bakanowski] and [Zwiardowski] to Our Dearest Father Superior, 1 March 1867, Bakanowski Letters no. 9336; [Bakanowski] to Our Honorable Father General, 9 April 1868, Bakanowski Letters no. 9352; Visus Barzy [Rev. Vincent Barzyński], San Antonio, to Dear Father Adolf [Bakanowski, Chicago], 19 June 1871, Barzyński Letters no. 8976; Koenig to Most Highly Esteemed Archbishop, 12 December 1859, Ludwig-Missionsverein, Papers and Letters Received Concerning the Diocese of Galveston, Texas; Kruszka, *Historja polska w Ameryce*, p. 621; Rev. Felix [Zwiardowski], San Antonio, Texas, to Honorable Father Adolf [Bakanowski, Paris], 2 March 1876, Zwiardowski Letters no. 34751; Rev. Felix Zwiardowski, Panna Maria, to Dear Father Adolf [Bakanowski, location?], 12 September 1878, Zwiardowski Letters no. 34771.

86. Jacek Przygoda, "New Light on the Poles in Texas," *Polish American Studies* 27 (Spring–Autumn, 1970): 85–86; Jacek Przygoda, *Texas Pioneers from Poland: A Study in the Ethnic History*, pp. 72–73; St. Francis Church, St. Francisville, Texas, Cemetery Grave Inscriptions; *Texas Catholic Herald* (Houston), 6 December 1968, p.2.

87. Visus Barzy [Barzyński] to Dear Father Adolf, 19 June 1871, Barzyński Letters no. 8976; Dworaczyk, *First Polish Colonies*, p. 150; Joseph Cotulla, "Cornbread and Clabber Made a Good Meal," in *The Trail Drivers of Texas*, ed. J. Marvin Hunter,

pp. 317–318; Iwicki, *First One Hundred Years*, p. 45; Kruszka, *Historja polska w Ameryce*, p. 621; Przygoda, *Texas Pioneers*, p. 73.

88. Dworaczyk, *First Polish Colonies*, p. 16; Kruszka, *Historja polska w Ameryce*, p. 370; Nesterowicz, *Notatki z podróży*, p. 203; John Rothensteiner, *History of the Archdiocese of St. Louis*, 2:416–417; U.S., Immigration Commission, *Recent Immigrants in Agriculture*, 2:370–371. Among the heads of households who have been identified as moving from Texas to Missouri were Franz Mikosz, Casimir Szeguda, Christian Gasz, Paul Labus, Nicholas Krawiec, Ignatz Hutch, and Joseph Gomula. Dworaczyk, *Church Records of Panna Maria*, pp. 30, 58; Dworaczyk, *First Polish Colonies*, p. 7; *Galveston Zeitung*, 9 December 1854, p. 2; Kruszka, *Historja polska w Ameryce*, p. 370; *Neu-Braunfelser Zeitung*, 22 December 1854, p. 3; St. Gertrude Church, Krakow, Mo., Death Records (25 May 1862 to 3 March 1972), unpaged.

89. Rev. Adolf [Bakanowski], Panna Maria, Texas, to Our Dearest Father General [Rev. Jerome Kajsiewicz, Rome], 18 February 1870, Bakanowski Letters no. 9375; Rev. Adolf [Bakanowski], Panna Maria, Texas, to Our Dearest Father General [Rev. Jerome Kajsiewicz, Rome], 29 March 1870, Bakanowski Letters no. 9376; Rev. Adolf [Bakanowski], Bandera, Texas, to Our Dearest Father General [Rev. Jerome Kajsiewicz, Rome], 9 May 1870, Bakanowski Letters no. 9378; Rev. Adolf [Bakanowski], Panna Maria, Texas, to Our Dearest Father General [Rev. Jerome Kajsiewicz, Rome], 5 July 1870, Bakanowski Letters no. 9382; T. Lindsay Baker, "Nation's Second Oldest Polish Newspaper Was Founded in Washington in 1870," *Washington Missourian* (Washington, Mo.), 26 September 1974, sec. B, p. 1; John Barzyński, Union, Missouri, to Reverend Father General [Rev. Jerome Kajsiewicz], Rome, 10 June 1872, John Barzyński Letters no. 45298; Rev. Vincent [Barzyński], San Antonio, to Most Reverend Father General [Rev. Jerome Kajsiewicz], Rome, 2 March 1872, Barzyński Letters no. 8986; Rev. V[incent] Barzyński, San Antonio, to Most Reverend Father General [Rev. Jerome Kajsiewicz, Rome], 17 March 1872, Barzyński Letters no. 8987; *History of Franklin, Jefferson, Washington, Crawford, and Gasconade Counties, Missouri*, p. 317; Eugene P. Willging and Herta Hatzfeld, "Nineteenth Century Polish Catholic Periodical Publications in the United States," *Polish American Studies* 13 (January–June 1956): 25–27; Stanisław Zieliński, *Bibljografja czasopism polskich zagranicą, 1830–1934* [Bibliography of Polish Periodicals Abroad, 1830–1934], pp. 92, 95; Rev. Felix Zwiardowski, San Antonio, to Reverend Father General [Rev. Jerome Kajsiewicz, St. Mary, Ky.], 19 August 1871, Zwiardowski Letters no. 34714; Rev. Felix Zwiardowski, Panna Maria, to Reverend Father [Rev. Jerome Kajsiewicz, St. Mary], 30 August 1871, Zwiardowski Letters no. 34716; Rev. Felix [Zwiardowski], Panna Maria, to Reverend Father General [Rev. Jerome Kajsiewicz, Rome], 2 October 1871, Zwiardowski Letters no. 34719; [Rev. Felix Zwiardowski], Panna Maria, to Reverend Father General [Rev. Jerome Kajsiewicz, Rome], 13 March 1873, Zwiardowski Letters no. 34724.

90. Rev. Adolf [Bakanowski], Galveston, Texas, to Our Dearest Father General [Rev. Jerome Kajsiewicz, Rome], 25 July 1870, Bakanowski Letters no. 9383; Rev. Adolf [Bakanowski], Chicago, to Dearest Father General [Rev. Jerome Kajsiewicz, Rome], 18 August 1870, Bakanowski Letters no. 9384; James L. Miller, Missourian Publishing Company, Washington, Mo., to Baker, Lubbock, 29 July 1974.

91. *Czas*, 12 May 1858, p. 2; *Przegląd Poznański*, July 1858, p. 86; U.S., Census of 1860, Texas, Population Schedules, Bandera, Bexar, DeWitt, and Karnes counties. It is interesting to note that the average family size of 4.66 persons computed from the manuscript population schedules of the census of 1860 is close to the average of

five members per family among the Texas Poles estimated by an official of the Polish Consulate General early in this century. [Leon Orłowski], "Polacy w Texasie" [The Poles in Texas], [New York, May 1920], typescript, p. 5, Republic of Poland, Ministry of Foreign Affairs, Embassy in Washington, Document Registration no. 1493, File no. 979, Embassy of the Republic of Poland in Washington Collection, Archives of Contemporary Documents, Warsaw.

92. Przygoda, *Texas Pioneers*, pp. 7–8, 113–125, 133–149, 154–159; U.S., Census of 1860, Texas, Population Schedules, Bandera, Bexar, DeWitt, and Karnes counties. It should be noted that the census of 1860 recorded only approximately 800 Silesians in the state.

93. [Bakanowski] and [Zwiardowski] to Our Dearest Father Superior, 1 March 1867, Bakanowski Letters no. 9336.

94. *Czas*, 3 October 1854, p. 3, 9 October 1855, p. 1, 22 May 1856, p. 2; *Gwiazdka Cieszyńska*, 26 July 1856, p. 236.

95. Dworaczyk, *Church Records of Panna Maria*, p. 27; Moczigemba to [Friends and Relatives], 13 May 1855, Prussia, Auswanderung, 2:54; Leop[old] B[onaventura] M[aria] Moczygęba, Panna Maria, Texas, to Dear Father General [Rev. Giacinto Gualerni, Rome], 28 August 1855, item no. IX-Tex-IV-F, Archives of the General Curia. For a more detailed examination of the construction of the first Polish church in America at Panna Maria in 1855–1856, see T. Lindsay Baker, *The Early History of Panna Maria, Texas*, pp. 19–21, 24, 47.

96. Dworaczyk, *First Polish Colonies*, pp. 8–10; Karnes County, Texas, Deed Records, H: 363–365; Kruszka, *Historja polska w Ameryce*, pp. 368–369; Nesterowicz, *Notatki z podróży*, pp. 200–201.

97. Dworaczyk, *First Polish Colonies*, p. 10; *Katolik*, 5 June 1888, [lv. 1 of unpaged text]; Theodore Roemer, "Bavaria Helps America," *The Commonweal* 21 (11 January 1935): 312–313; Swastek, *Priest and Pioneer*, p. 9.

98. Rev. Leop[old] Bonav[entura] M[aria] Moczygęba, Castroville, Texas, to Dear Father General [Rev. Giacinto Gualerni, Rome], 24 March 1854, item no. IX-Tex-I-G, Archives of the General Curia; Rev. Leop[old] Bonaventura [Maria] Moczygęba, Castroville, Texas, to Dear Father General [Rev. Giacinto Gualerni, Rome], 4 May 1854, item no. IX-Tex-II-C, Archives of the General Curia; untitled financial accounts, Ludwig-Missionsverein, Papers and Letters Received Concerning the Diocese of Galveston, Texas; Theodore Roemer, *The Ludwig-Missionsverein and the Church in the United States (1838–1918)*, Catholic University of America Studies in American Church History, 26:29–30, 80–81; Theodore Roemer, *Ten Decades of Alms*, pp. 148–149; [Rev. Robert] Zahradniczek, Würzberg, to Minister General [Rev. Giacinto Gualerni, Rome], 29 August 1854, Hellmann, "Notes," p. 127.

99. T. Lindsay Baker, "The Early Years of Rev. Wincenty Barzyński," *Polish American Studies* 32 (Spring 1975): 40; Dworaczyk, *First Polish Colonies*, pp. 101, 110; J. M. Gilbert, *Archdiocese of San Antonio 1874–1949*, p. 76; Joyce, *Our Polish Pioneers*, p. 9; Kruszka, *Historja polska w Ameryce*, pp. 377, 504; Nesterowicz, *Notatki z podróży*, pp. 182, 185; Parisot and Smith, *Catholic Church in the Diocese of San Antonio*, p. 127; *Przegląd Poznański*, July 1858, p. 86.

100. *Czas*, 12 May 1858, p. 2; *Przegląd Poznański*, July 1858, p. 86.

101. *Katolik*, 5 June 1888, [lv. 1 of unpaged text].

102. Andrzej Brożek, "Najstarsza polska szkoła w Stanach Zjednoczonych Ameryki," pp. 60–73; Dworaczyk, *First Polish Colonies*, pp. 21, 38–42.

103. Ruckman, "Census Taker," p. 39.

104. Bakanowski, *Moje wspomnienia*, p. 29.

105. Dworaczyk, *First Polish Colonies*, pp. 18–19; interview, E. J. Moczygemba, 10 August 1973 (KB); Shaver and Rogers, *Flashlights on Texas*, p. 138.

106. *San Antonio Weekly Herald*, 12 June 1855, p. 3, 14 August 1855, p. 2, 9 January 1856, p. 3, 16 January 1856, p. 2, 23 February 1856, p. 3.

107. [Bakanowski] to [*Zwiastun Górnoszlązki*], 6 June 1870, *Zwiastun Górnoszlązki*, 7 July 1870, p. 215; Bakanowski, *Moje wspomnienia*, p. 29; Balch, *Our Slavic Fellow Citizens*, p. 229; Cotulla, "Cornbread and Clabber," p. 317; Kruszka, *Historja polska w Ameryce*, pp. 367–368; Niklewicz, *Dzieje pierwszych*, p. 6.

108. *Zwiastun Górnoszlązki*, 8 July 1869, pp. 228–229.

Chapter 4. The Civil War

1. Zwiardowski to Our Dear Reverend Father, 28 December 1866, Zwiardowski Letters no. 34692.

2. [Bakanowski] to [*Zwiastun Górnoszlązki*], 6 June 1870, *Zwiastun Górnoszlązki*, 7 July 1870, p. 215.

3. U.S., Census of 1860, Texas Manuscript Slave Schedules, Bandera, Bexar, DeWitt, and Karnes counties.

4. Adolf Bakanowski, *Moje wspomnienia 1840-1863-1913*, p. 50; *Czas*, 29 September 1855, p. 2.

5. *San Antonio Weekly Herald*, 25 January 1862, p. 1. The minimum age for conscription subsequently was lowered to seventeen years. Ibid., 7 June 1862, p. 1.

6. Ibid., 7 June 1862, p. 1.

7. Ibid., 20 December 1862, p. 2.

8. Ibid., 18 July 1863, p. 2.

9. [Bakanowski] to [*Zwiastun Górnoszlązki*], 6 June 1870, *Zwiastun Górnoszlązki*, 7 July 1870, pp. 215–216.

10. Interview, Ben P. Urbanczyk, 10 August 1973 (KB).

11. *San Antonio Weekly Herald*, 31 May 1862, p. 1. Emphasis in the original.

12. Ibid., 23 May 1863, p. 2.

13. [Anonymous], Helena, Texas, to Dear Uncle, [location?], 25 September 1863, Charles A. Russell Papers.

14. [Bakanowski] to [*Zwiastun Górnoszlązki*], 6 June 1870, *Zwiastun Górnoszlązki*, 7 July 1870, pp. 215–216; *San Antonio Weekly News*, 13 September 1862, p. 2.

15. Henry Lyman Brightman Russell, "Autobiography of Henry Lyman Brightman Russell," p. 14, Henry Lyman Brightman Russell Papers; *San Antonio Weekly Herald*, 2 August 1862, p. 2, 13 September 1862, p. 2, 11 October 1862, p. 2, 30 May 1863, p. 2.

16. Russell, "Autobiography," pp. 13–14; interview, Urbanczyk, 10 August 1973 (KB).

17. Karnes County, Texas, Petition no. 40, Citizens of Karnes County Ask That a Company Be Formed for the Protection of Karnes and Other Counties, 8 December 1863.

18. Russell, "Autobiography," p. 12; *San Antonio Weekly Herald*, 29 March 1862, p. 2, 5 July 1862, p. 2, 2 May 1863, p. 2, 9 May 1863, p. 2, 30 May 1863, p. 1, 27 June 1863, p. 2; Robert H. Thonhoff, "A History of Karnes County," pp. 148–150, 157–165.

19. Annunciation of the Blessed Virgin Mary Church, St. Hedwig, Texas, Combined Parish Records, vol. 1, unpaged; John A. Joyce, *Our Polish Pioneers*, pp. 9–10; Wacław Kruszka, *Historja polska w Ameryce*, pp. 376–378.

20. Edward J. Dworaczyk, *The First Polish Colonies of America in Texas*, p. 23; Joyce, *Our Polish Pioneers*, pp. 9–10; Kruszka, *Historja polska w Ameryce*, pp. 376–378.

21. [Bakanowski] and [Zwiardowski] to Our Dearest Father Superior, 1 March 1867, Bakanowski Letters no. 9336.

22. Rev. Felix Zwiardowski, Martinez, to Dearest Reverend Father Alexander [Jełowicki, Paris], 27 August 1867, Zwiardowski Letters no. 34698.

23. [Bakanowski] and [Zwiardowski] to Our Dearest Father Superior, 1 March 1867, Bakanowski Letters no. 9336; Bakanowski, *Moje wspomnienia*, pp. 58, 171; Annunciation of the Blessed Virgin Mary Church, Combined Parish Records, vol. 1, unpaged; Joyce, *Our Polish Pioneers*, p. 10; interview, Emil A. Kosub, St. Hedwig, Texas, 27 November 1971; Kruszka, *Historja polska w Ameryce*, pp. 377–378; Franciszek Niklewicz, *Dzieje pierwszych polskich osadników w Ameryce i przewodnik parafij polskich w Stanach Zjednoczonych*, p. 8; Zwiardowski to Dear Reverend Father Alexander, 27 August 1867, Zwiardowski Letters no. 34698.

24. Bakanowski to Our Dearest Father Superior, 13 November 1866, Bakanowski Letters no. 9330; [Bakanowski] to Honorable Father General, 1 December 1868, Bakanowski Letters no. 9363; Bakanowski, *Moje wspomnienia*, p. 31; Dworaczyk, *First Polish Colonies*, pp. 23–24; Kruszka, *Historja polska w Ameryce*, p. 481; Niklewicz, *Dzieje pierwszych*, p. 8.

25. *Harvard Guide to American History*, pp. 125–127.

26. Texas, Militia, Muster Roll of Capt. J. A. Tivey's Company of Mounted Riflemen, 5 August 1861; Texas, Militia, Muster Roll of the Panna Maria Grays, 9 July 1861; Texas, Militia, Muster Roll of the Panna Maria Greys, 7 February 1862. The four Silesians listed as members of the Panna Maria Grays were Peter Kiolbassa [Kiołbassa], Thomas Kiolbassa [Kiołbassa], R. T. Rzeppa, and Valentine Polack. The term *muster roll* as used in this work denotes a register of the officers and men in a military unit.

Since the publication of a 1932 article by Gertrude Harris Cook on Panna Maria in the *Dallas Morning News*, stories have been reprinted concerning a company supposedly consisting "entirely of Polanders" raised in Karnes County during the Civil War. The author of the newspaper article cited as her source an interview with Lyman Brightman Russell, a boyhood resident of Karnes County in the late 1850's and early 1860's, but neither Russell's published nor manuscript autobiographies mention such a company. Furthermore, no primary documents from the period have been found to substantiate the assertion that the company existed. *Dallas Morning News*, 24 January 1932, sec. 4, p. 1; Dworaczyk, *First Polish Colonies*, pp. 26–27; Edmund L. Kowalczyk, "Jottings from the Polish American Past," *Polish American Studies* 11 (January–June 1954): 38; Edward C. Rozanski, "Civil War Poles of Illinois," *Polish American Studies* 23 (July–December 1966): 112–113; Russell, "Autobiography"; Henry Lyman Brightman Russell, *Granddad's Autobiography*.

27. Texas, Militia, Muster Roll of Captain B. Mitchell['s] Company, Bandera County, [Frontier] Dist. no. 3, Texas State Troops, February 1862. The names and ages of the Silesians listed on this muster roll are as follows: Albert Adamitz [Adamietz] (19), W. Anderwald (28), John Dugosz [Dlugosz] (46), Albert Hiduke [Haiduk] (49), Casper Kalka (49), Joseph Kalka (28), Thos. Mazouriek [Mazurek] (46), Joseph Moravitz [Morawietz] (32), Antone Pika [Anton Pyka] (43), and F. Woclawczyk [Waclawczyk] (39). Serving with the Silesians was one non-Silesian Pole, Paul Martin (64), who lived at Bandera.

28. Texas, Militia, Muster Roll of Capt. Harrison Gregg's Company C Infantry, 24th Brigade, 18 August 1863; Texas, Militia, Muster Roll of J. H. Paschal's Company of Volunteers, 29th Brigade, Texas State Troops, 2 March 1863; Texas, Militia, Muster Roll of Capt. John F. Tom's Company, T[exas] S[tate] T[roops], 3d Frontier District, 20 February 1864; Texas, Militia, Muster Roll of N. Gussett's Company, 3d Frontier District, T[exas] S[tate] T[roops], 26 March 1865.

29. *San Antonio Weekly Herald*, 23 May 1863, p. 2; U.S., Department of War, *The War of Rebellion: A Compilation of the Official Records of the Union and Confederate Armies*, ser. 1, vol. 17, pt. 1, pp. 698–796. Silesian Poles identified as having served in the 6th Texas Infantry are F. Killasa [Kiołbassa], Ignatz Kielbasa [Kiołbassa], T. Goschko [Josko], John Rzeppa, T. Breppa [Rzeppa], T. Opulla [Opiela], John Opiella [Opiela], A. Lesse [Lyssy], James Musiol, John Golla, T. Golla, Joseph Dlugosch [Dlugosz], Anton Kosielsky, Simon Kolodzey [Kolodziej], T. Katrmaeigk [Kaczmarek], and John Katzmark [Kaczmarek]. C.S., Department of War, Army, 6th Texas Infantry, Compiled Military Records, Compiled Military Service Records; *San Antonio Weekly Herald*, 23 May 1863, p. 2.

Silesians identified as having served in the 24th Texas Cavalry are John Brys, Joseph Jasko [Josko], Joseph Kaczmarch [Kaczmarek], Peter Kiolbassa [Kiołbassa], Joseph Kolodeyczyk [Kolodziejczyk], Albert Leyssy [Lyssy], Frank Moczyjsba [Moczygemba], and J. Opiela. C.S., Department of War, Army, 24th Texas Cavalry, Compiled Military Records, Compiled Military Service Records.

30. Muster Roll of Capt. J. A. Tivey's Company of Mounted Riflemen, 5 August 1861; Muster Roll of the Panna Maria Grays, 9 July 1861; Muster Roll of the Panna Maria Greys, 7 February 1862. Peter Kiołbassa, son of parliamentary Deputy Stanisław Kiołbassa, was born in the village of Świbie in Upper Silesia on 13 October 1838. T. Lindsay Baker, "The Kiołbassa Family of Illinois and Texas," pp. 78–82; Trinity Church, Wiśnicze, Poland, Baptismal Records (1 January 1832–9 December 1852), pp. 186–187.

31. 24th Texas Cavalry, Compiled Military Records, Peter Kiolbassa [Kiołbassa] Compiled Military Service Record.

32. 24th Texas Cavalry, Compiled Military Records, Compiled Military Service Records.

33. R. A. Cameron, near Helena, Arkansas, to Brigadier-General Hovey, Helena, Arkansas, 29 October 1862, *War of Rebellion*, ser. 1, vol. 13, p. 770; 24th Texas Cavalry, Compiled Military Records, Company I Captions and Record of Events, Field and Staff Captions and Record of Events, and Regimental Captions and Record of Events.

34. P. O. Hébert, San Antonio, Texas, to H. H. Sibley, San Antonio, Texas, 8 August 1862, *War of Rebellion*, ser. 1, vol. 9, pp. 729–731; S. S. Anderson, Headquarters, Trans-Mississippi Department, Little Rock, Arkansas, Special Orders no. 39, 28 September 1862, *War of Rebellion*, ser. 1, vol. 13, pp. 884–885.

35. L. V. Caraway, "The Battle of Arkansas Post," *Confederate Veteran* 14 (March 1906): 127; 24th Texas Cavalry, Compiled Military Records, Regimental Captions and Record of Events.

36. Caraway, "Battle of Arkansas Post," pp. 127–128; T. J. Churchill, Richmond, Virginia, to T. H. Holmes, Little Rock, 6 May 1863, *War of Rebellion*, ser. 1, vol. 17, pp. 780–782; C. H. Smith, Mobile, [Ala.], to [unidentified addressee, location?], 24 February 1863, *San Antonio Weekly Herald*, 4 April 1863, p. 2. For the official reports on the Battle of Arkansas Post, see *War of Rebellion*, ser. 1, vol. 17, pp. 698–796.

37. Caraway, "Battle of Arkansas Post," p. 128.

38. Ibid.; 24th Texas Cavalry, Compiled Military Records, Peter Kiolbassa Compiled Military Service Record; *San Antonio Weekly Herald*, 23 May 1863, p. 2.

39. W. F. Lynch, Camp Butler, Illinois, to [N. H. McLean, location?], 4 February 1863, *War of Rebellion*, ser. 2, vol. 5, p. 240.

40. George Sawin, Headquarters, Department of the Ohio, to Adjutant General, Department of the Ohio, 4 February 1863, *War of Rebellion*, ser. 2, vol. 5, p. 240.

41. *San Antonio Weekly Herald*, 23 May 1863, p. 2; 24th Texas Cavalry, Compiled Military Records, Peter Kiolbassa [Kiołbassa] Compiled Military Service Record; 6th Texas Cavalry, Compiled Military Records, Ignatz Kielbassa [Kiołbassa], John Rzeppa, Albert Lesse [Lyssy], John Opiella [Opiela], James Musiol, John Golla, Joseph Dlugosch [Dlugosz], Anton Kosiesky, Simon Kolodzey [Kolodziej], and John Katzmark [Kaczmarek] Compiled Military Service Records; U.S., Department of War, Army, 16th Illinois Cavalry, Compiled Military Records, Peter Kiolbassa [Kiołbassa], Ignatz Kiolbassa [Kiołbassa], and Albert Lyssy Compiled Military Service Records; H. G. Wright, Cincinnati, Ohio, to Commissary General of Prisoners, [location?], 7 February 1863, *War of Rebellion*, ser. 2, vol. 5, p. 241.

42. Helen Busyn, "Peter Kiołbassa: Maker of Polish America," *Polish American Studies* 8 (July–December 1951): 69–70; Helen Busyn, "The Political Career of Peter Kiolbassa," ibid. 7 (January–June 1950): 8; Kowalczyk, "Jottings," pp. 37–38; Rozanski, "Civil War Poles," pp. 112–113; 16th Illinois Cavalry, Compiled Military Records, Peter Kiolbassa and Ignatz Kiolbassa Compiled Military Service Records; 24th Texas Cavalry, Compiled Military Records, Peter Kiolbassa Compiled Military Service Record; U.S., Department of the Interior, Bureau of Pensions, Pension record files of Peter Kiolbassa [Kiołbassa] and Ignatz Kiolbassa [Kiołbassa] for service in the 16th Illinois Cavalry.

Although at least two secondary accounts state that Ignatz Kiołbassa was Peter's brother, Ignatz was born into a different family, in the village of Jemielnica, on 29 July 1839. Ascension of the Blessed Virgin Mary Church, Jemielnica, Opole Voivodeship, Poland, Baptismal Records (8 August 1831–30 December 1842), p. 215; Kowalczyk, "Jottings," pp. 37–38; Jacek Przygoda, *Texas Pioneers from Poland: A Study in the Ethnic History*, p. 155; Rozanski, "Civil War Poles," pp. 112–113.

43. Busyn, "Peter Kiołbassa," pp. 69–71; Busyn, "Political Career," pp. 8–9; 16th Illinois Cavalry, Compiled Military Records, Peter Kiolbassa Compiled Military Service Record; U.S., Department of War, Army, 6th U.S. Colored Cavalry, Compiled Military Records, Peter Kiolbassa [Kiołbassa] Compiled Military Service Record.

Except for brief trips back to Texas, Peter Kiołbassa remained in the North. Living in Chicago, he became a realtor and entered local politics, later becoming prominent in Chicago affairs. A. T. Andreas, *History of Chicago*, 3:563–564; Busyn, "Peter Kiołbassa," pp. 65–84; Busyn, "Political Career," pp. 8–22; Rev. Felix Zwiardowski, Częstochowa, Texas, to Most Reverend and Dear Father, [location?], 3 April 1889, Zwiardowski Letters no. 34783.

44. U.S., Department of the Interior, Bureau of Pensions, pension record file of Albert Lyssy for service in the 16th Illinois Cavalry; 16th Illinois Cavalry, Compiled Military Records, Albert Lyssy Compiled Military Service Record; 24th Texas Cavalry, Compiled Military Records, Albert Leyssy [Lyssy] Compiled Military Service Record; 6th Texas Infantry, Compiled Military Records, Albert Lesse [Lyssy] Compiled Military Service Record.

For information on the fighting around Tunnel Hill, Georgia, on 12 May 1864, in which Lyssy was injured and captured, see *War of Rebellion*, ser. 1, vol. 38, pt. 4, pp. 146–160.

45. C[harles] A. Russell, Camp Patterson, to Dear Children, [Helena, Texas], 17–18 April 1864, Charles A. Russell Papers; 24th Texas Cavalry, Compiled Military Records, William J. Butler Compiled Military Service Record.

46. C.S., Department of War, Army, 31st Texas Cavalry, Compiled Military Records, John Brys Compiled Military Service Record; 24th Texas Cavalry, Compiled Military Records, John Brysch [Brys] Compiled Military Service Record.

47. Texas, Comptroller of Public Accounts, Mrs. Eva Lyssy Texas Confederate Pension Application no. 35561, 21 October 1918; Mrs. Mary Moravitz [Morawietz], Texas Confederate Pension Application no. 51059, 19 December 1932; Stefan Nesterowicz, *Notatki z podróży po północnej i środkowej Ameryce*, p. 209; 31st Texas Cavalry, Compiled Military Records, Thomas Kolodziejczyk, Jacob Lyssy, and Joseph Morawietz Compiled Military Service Records.

48. Muster Roll of N. Gussett's Company, 3d Frontier District, T[exas] S[tate] T[roops], 26 March 1865.

49. Muster Roll of J. H. Paschal's Company of Volunteers, 29th Brigade, Texas State Troops, 2 March 1863.

50. Martin Dugi, Texas Confederate Pension Application no. 47794, 3 October 1930; Mrs. Martin Dugi, Texas Confederate Pension Application no. 51897, 19 January 1939; Muster Roll of Capt. John F. Tom's Company, T[exas] S[tate] T[roops], for Frontier Defense, 3d Frontier District, 20 February 1864.

51. *San Antonio Weekly Herald*, 10 October 1863, p. 2.

52. Mrs. John Adamietz, Texas Confederate Pension Application no. 30874, 13 March 1915; C.S., Department of War, Army, Capt. H. Willke's Battalion Light Artillery (6th Texas Field Battery), Compiled Military Records, Frank Knapick and Thom. Morawitz [Morawietz] Compiled Military Service Records; C.S., Department of War, Army, Dege's (formerly Willke's) Battalion Light Artillery (8th Texas Field Battery), Compiled Military Records, John Urbanczyk, John Adamitz [Adamietz] and Thomas Morawitz [Morawietz] Compiled Military Service Records; Anton Jarzombek, Texas Confederate Pension Application no. 29897, 20 November 1914; Mrs. Frances Knapick, Texas Confederate Pension Application no. 35099, 18 April 1918; Frank Knapick, Texas Confederate Pension Application no. 19484, 10 September 1910; F. T. Moczygemba, Texas Confederate Pension Application no. 19812, 31 October 1910; Mrs. Frances Morawitz [Morawietz], Texas Confederate Pension Application no. 33896, 12 March 1917; Tom Moravietz [Morawietz], Texas Confederate Pension Application no. 18820, 11 July 1910; Tom Urbanczyk, Texas Confederate Pension Application no. 30514, 18 January 1915; Mrs. Tom Urbanczyk, Texas Confederate Pension Application no. 32242, 22 November 1915.

53. Joseph Gawlik, Texas Confederate Pension Application no. 47709, 22 September 1930; Mrs. Joseph Gawlik, Texas Confederate Pension Application no. 49729, 4 May 1931; Mrs. Francisca Jendrzey [Jendrzej], Texas Confederate Pension Application no. 50654, 7 March 1932; Tom Jendrzey [Jendrzej], Texas Confederate Pension Application no. 49318, 25 September 1930; Mrs. John T. Moczygemba, Texas Confederate Pension Application no. 47952, 6 November 1930.

54. Anton Anderwald, Texas Confederate Pension Application no. 18819, 4 July 1910; Mrs. Katherine Anderwald, Texas Confederate Pension Application no. 35821, 30 April 1919; C.S., Department of War, Army, 2d Texas Infantry, Compiled Military Records, Anton Anderwald Compiled Military Service Record.

55. C.S., Department of War, Army, 8th Texas Infantry, Compiled Military Records, Adam Skloss Compiled Military Service Record; Adam Skloss, Texas Con-

federate Pension Application no. 18921, 27 July 1910; Mrs. Adam Skloss, Texas Confederate Pension Application no. 51837, 7 January 1938.

56. Anton Jarzombek, Texas Confederate Pension Application no. 29897, 20 November 1914; Joseph Ledwik, Texas Confederate Pension Application no. 15048, 17 March 1909; Charles Korzekwa, Texas Confederate Pension Application no. 47749, 23 September 1930; C.S., Department of War, Army, Ragsdale's Battalion Texas Cavalry, Compiled Military Records, Thomas Kossup Compiled Military Service Record; Mrs. Anna Kossup, Texas Confederate Pension Application no. 51751, 4 November 1936; Mrs. Mary Woitena, Texas Confederate Pension Application no. 38335, 18 May 1922; S[tanisław] Woitena, Texas Confederate Pension Application no. 11700, 22 November 1904; Mrs. Anna Michalski, Texas Confederate Pension Application no. 28782, 18 August 1914; C.S., Department of War, Army, 33d Texas Cavalry, Compiled Military Records, Valentine Gorrell Compiled Military Service Record; C.S., Department of War, Army, 36th Texas Cavalry, Compiled Military Records, Albert Halamuda and Joseph F. Piedolla [Pierdolla] Compiled Military Service Records; Mrs. Frances Halamuda, Texas Confederate Pension Application No. 11711, 5 February 1904; J. F. Pierdolla, Texas Confederate Pension Application no. 47845, 3 October 1930.

57. Mrs. Kate Ploch, Texas Confederate Pension Application no. 37694, 2 September 1921.

58. Mrs. Annie Dupnik, Texas Confederate Pension Application no. 25283, 17 November 1913.

59. St. Stanisław Church, Płużnica, Poland, Baptismal Records (20 June 1833–14 April 1858), pp. 137–138.

60. Alexander Dziuk to Stefan Nesterowicz, interview at Panna Maria, 1909, cited in Nesterowicz, *Notatki z podróży*, p. 209.

61. According to Dziuk's medical discharge certificate he suffered as follows: "Phthisis Pulmonation Consumption—the said soldier has a deformed Breast—Never was fit for the Service—Never has been on duty more than two months—Since he was enlisted is an expense to the Government—and I do think he ought to be discharged from the forces." 31st Texas Cavalry, Compiled Military Records, Alexander Dziuk Compiled Military Service Record.

62. Mrs. Alexander Dziuk, Texas Confederate Pension Application no. 47601, 23 September 1930; Nesterowicz, *Notatki z podróży*, pp. 208–209; interview, Urbanczyk, 10 August 1973 (KB).

63. Missouri, Militia, 54th Regiment Enrolled Missouri Militia, Compiled Military Records, Simeon Kolecki [Simon Kolodziej] Compiled Military Service Record; U.S., Census of 1890, Texas, Manuscript Schedules Enumerating Union Veterans and Widows of Union Veterans of the Civil War, DeWitt County. Curiously the 1890 special census schedules list no Silesians in Karnes, Bandera, or Bexar counties.

64. Bureau of Pensions, pension record file of Joseph Cotulla for service in the 1st Texas Cavalry; Joseph Cotulla, "Cornbread and Clabber Made a Good Meal," in *The Trail Drivers of Texas*, ed. J. Marvin Hunter, pp. 317–318; Jacek Przygoda, "New Light on the Poles in Texas," *Polish American Studies* 27 (Spring–Autumn, 1970): 83; *A Twentieth Century History of Southwest Texas*, 2:345; U.S., Department of War, Army, 1st Texas Cavalry, Compiled Military Records, Joseph Cotulli [Cotulla] Compiled Military Service Record.

65. [Bakanowski] to [*Zwiastun Górnoszlązki*], 6 June 1870, *Zwiastun Górnoszlązki*, 7 July 1870, p. 215.

66. The only identified soldier dying in the war who could be Silesian was John

Novack [Nowak?], who served in Company I of the 24th Texas Cavalry with a number of Poles. He was among the troops captured at the Battle of Arkansas Post, but later in 1863 he was paroled from internment and allowed to return to the South. Though he had sworn an oath not to take up arms against the United States, he returned to his regiment, but soon thereafter was sent to a military hospital for treatment of diarrhea. The last item in Novack's compiled military service record is an abstract from a "Register of Effects of Deceased Soldiers," which stated that upon his death his personal possessions had a total value of only ten cents. Although Novack served among Silesians like Peter Kiołbassa and Albert Lyssy, it still has not been documented that he himself was a Silesian. 24th Texas Cavalry, Compiled Military Records, John Novack Compiled Military Service Record.

Chapter 5. Reconstruction

1. John Iwicki, *The First One Hundred Years: A Study of the Apostolate of the Congregation of the Resurrection in the United States 1866–1966*, p. 25; Wacław Kruszka, *Historja polska w Ameryce*, pp. 483–484.

2. "Congregation of the Resurrection," *The Catholic Encyclopedia*, 12:794; [Leonard Long], *For God and Man, 1842–1942: A Short History of the Congregation of the Resurrection*, pp. 4–36.

3. Rev. [Alexander] Jełowicki, [Paris], to Rev. [Jerome] Kajsiewicz, Rome, 4 September 1866, cited in Paweł Smolikowski, "Historia Zgromadzenia Zmartwychwstania Pańskiego" [History of the Congregation of the Resurrection], vol. 8, chap. 9, pp. 52–55. This letter also is quoted at length in Kruszka, *Historja polska w Ameryce*, pp. 484–486.

4. For the original text of this agreement dated 28 September 1866, see Bishop Claude-Marie Dubuis Letters no. 39460–39461.

5. Iwicki, *First One Hundred Years*, pp. 26–28; [Denise Poniatowski], Lyon, [France], to [Rev. Jerome Kajsiewicz, Rome], 18 October 1866, Poniatowski Letters no. 55590; Smolikowski, "Historia," vol. 8, chap. 9, pp. 55–66. It should be pointed out that Bishop Dubuis grossly overestimated the population of the Silesians in Texas in his negotiations with Jełowicki and in this sense lured the Resurrectionists to his diocese under false pretenses. See Bishop C. M. Dubuis, Paris, to My Dear Reverend Father [Rev. Alexander Jełowicki, Paris], 3 July 1866, Dubuis Letters no. 39457.

6. Adolf Bakanowski, *Moje wspomnienia 1840-1863-1913*, pp. 1–17, 24, 112–115; Edward T. Janas, *Dictionary of American Resurrectionists 1865–1965*, pp. 4–5; Jełowicki to Kajsiewicz, 4 September 1866, Smolikowski, "Historia," vol. 8, chap. 9, p. 54, and Kruszka, *Historja polska w Ameryce*, p. 485.

7. Janas, *Dictionary of American Resurrectionists*, pp. 6–7; Jełowicki to Kajsiewicz, 4 September 1866, Smolikowski, "Historia," vol. 8, chap. 9, p. 54, and Kruszka, *Historja polska w Ameryce*, p. 485; St. Mary Church, Sulisławice, Tarnobrzeg Voivodeship, Poland, Baptismal Records (8 January 1826–30 December 1838), p. 182; Stanisław Siatka, *Krótkie wspomnienia o życiu i działalności ks. Wincentego Barzyńskiego, C.R.* [A Brief Résumé of the Life and Works of Father Vincent Barzyński, C.R.], pp. 7–10. For a detailed study of the early life of the Rev. Vincent Barzyński in Europe and in America, see T. Lindsay Baker, "The Early Years of Rev. Wincenty Barzyński," *Polish American Studies* 32 (Spring 1975): 29–52.

8. Janas, *Dictionary of American Resurrectionists*, p. 77; Rev. Felix Zwiardowski, San Antonio, to Dear Reverend Father Alexander [Jełowicki, Paris], 12 June 1867, Zwiardowski Letters no. 34696.

9. Bakanowski, *Moje wspomnienia*, pp. 18–24; Bishop C. M. Dubuis, Lyon, France, to Superior [Jerome] Kajsiewicz, Rome, 19 September 1866, telegram, Dubuis Letters no. 39459; Iwicki, *First One Hundred Years*, p. 28; Kruszka, *Historja polska w Ameryce*, pp. 487–488; [Zwiardowski] to Dear Father, 28 September 1866, Zwiardowski Letters no. 34688; [Cleric] Felix [Zwiardowski], Panna Maria, Texas, to Dear Reverend Father, [location?], 12 November 1866, Zwiardowski Letters no. 34690.

10. One Polish-speaking priest, Rev. Anthony Zielinski (sometimes de Zielinski), had visited some of the Silesian parishes in 1865–1866 before the arrival of the Resurrectionists, but the extent of his ministrations was limited. He is best known for his activities in subsequent years, when he was instrumental in establishing the first permanent Polish settlement in Brazil. [Bakanowski] and [Zwiardowski] to Our Dearest Father Superior, 1 March 1867, Bakanowski Letters no. 9336; [Bakanowski] to Honorable Father General, 1 December 1868, Bakanowski Letters no. 9363; Andrzej Brożek, *Emigracja zamorska z Górnego Śląska w II połowie XIX wieku*, pp. 19–20; Edward T. Dworaczyk, *The First Polish Colonies of America in Texas*, p. 23; Stefan Nesterowicz, *Travel Notes*, trans. and ed. Marion Moore Coleman, p. 117; Rev. Wojciech Sojka, Erie, Pennsylvania, to Rev. John W. Yanta, San Antonio, Texas, 1 June 1974; Rev. Antonio de Zielinski, Santiago, Cuba, to Illustrious Bishop of New Orleans [Rev. Jean-Marie Odin, New Orleans, La.], 3 June 1865, Louisiana Papers.

11. Bakanowski to Our Dearest Father Superior, 13 November 1866, Bakanowski Letters no. 9330; Rev. Adolf Bakanowski, Panna Maria, to Our Dearest Father Peter [Semenenko, Rome], 20 November 1866, Bakanowski Letters no. 9331; [Bakanowski] to Honorable Father General, 1 December 1868, Bakanowski Letters no. 9363; Rev. Vincent Barzyński, San Antonio, Texas, to Rev. Father General [Rev. Jerome Kajsiewicz], Most Reverend Fathers Superior, Future Missionaries, and All Brothers, Rome, last days of 1866 and first days of 1867, Barzyński Letters no. 8945; [Barzyński] to Dearest Fathers et al., 19 December 1866, Barzyński Letters no. 8946; Kruszka, *Historja polska w Ameryce*, p. 488; [Zwiardowski] to Dear Reverend Father, 12 November 1866, Zwiardowski Letters no. 34690.

12. Reconstruction in Texas generally followed the pattern in the other southern states. Still the best summary of this period is Charles W. Ramsdell, *Reconstruction in Texas*.

13. For a moderate Unionist description of Reconstruction lawlessness in Texas and of the attitudes of the white southerners, see E. M. Pease, Austin, Texas, to Wm. G. Mitchell, Secretary of Civil Affairs, [location?], 17 January 1868, U.S., Department of War, Secretary, *Report of the Secretary of War, 1868*, pp. 268–271.

14. *San Antonio Express*, 27 March 1868, p. 3. For additional information on Bill Thompson, who was using the alias Tope in the Martinez vicinity, see *San Antonio Express*, 25 April 1868, p. 1, 4 May 1868, p. 3, 12 May 1868, p. 2, 11 June 1868, p. 1.

15. Ibid., 7 May 1868, p. 3. In the original article the surname of the Silesian was misspelled Kriesh.

16. Ibid., 14 January 1869, p. 3.

17. Ibid., 3 February 1870, p. 3. In the original article the surname of the Silesian was spelled Kossups, one of the several ways it was spelled in Texas.

18. Ibid., 3 March 1869, p. 2.

19. Ibid., 29 August 1867, p. 2, 31 August 1867, p. 2, 2 September 1867, p. 2, 19 November 1867, p. 3, 18 February 1868, p. 2.

20. Bejareno, Helena, Texas, to Dear Sir [*San Antonio Express*], 16 July 1868, ibid., 25 July 1868, p. 4.

21. Bakanowski, *Moje wspomnienia*, p. 63.

22. Ibid., pp. 30–31.

23. Robert H. Thonhoff, "A History of Karnes County," pp. 168–169.

24. Henry Lyman Brightman Russell, "Autobiography of Henry Lyman Brightman Russell," pp. 18–19, Henry Lyman Brightman Russell Papers.

25. *San Antonio Express*, 30 August 1867, p. 2, 4 October 1867, p. 2, 3 March 1869, p. 2.

26. M. Krueger, *Pioneer Life in Texas*, pp. 54–55.

27. Bejareno to Dear Sir, 16 July 1868, *San Antonio Express*, 25 July 1868, p. 4.

28. Bejareno, Helena, Texas, to [*San Antonio Express*], 17 July 1868, ibid., 25 July 1868, p. 4. The "Helena duel," which the lawless inhabitants of the town engaged in, exemplifies the reputation Helena had in the second half of the 1860's. In this duel the left hands of the two combatants were strapped together with deerskin thongs. Each of the duelists was provided with a short-bladed knife, and then the two men were given a spin and told to begin the fight. The knives had short blades to prevent the duelists from striking any vital organs, and consequently the two fought until one of them bled to death. Krueger, *Pioneer Life in Texas*, pp. 54–55. For a completely different contemporary view of Helena and Karnes County written by one of its law-abiding inhabitants, see C[harles] A. Russell, "Karnes County," *Texas Almanac for 1867*, pp. 125–126.

29. Relations between the Silesians and the Americans in Karnes County appear to have remained relatively calm up to the summer of 1867, because in late June of that year Father Adolf Bakanowski reported to Rome that the residents of Panna Maria slept at night with the windows and doors of their houses open because "nobody is afraid of thieves as there are none here." Bakanowski to Our Dearest Father Peter, 28 June 1867, Bakanowski Letters no. 9344.

30. St. Catherine Church, Toszek, Katowice Voivodeship, Poland, Baptismal Records (1 October 1846–28 May 1867), pp. 270–271, Marriage Records (27 January 1835–22 November 1853), pp. 292–293. The original Polish spelling of Emanuel Rzeppa's Christian name is followed in this work in place of the English Emmanuel or Immanuel.

31. Emanuel Rzeppa was a property owner in San Antonio, and it is known that in 1865 he received his mail there. In 1867 he rented a former bakery and warehouse to the Polish-Catholic parish in the city as a place of worship, and later he contributed to the construction of a new Polish church there. In Panna Maria he was also active, serving in 1868 and 1869 as postmaster. Dworaczyk, *First Polish Colonies*, p. 89; W. H. Jackson and S. A. Long, *The Texas Stock Directory*, p. 220; John A. Joyce, *Our Polish Pioneers*, pp. 12–13; P. F. Parisot and C. J. Smith, *History of the Catholic Church in the Diocese of San Antonio, Texas*, p. 179; *San Antonio Express*, 27 November 1867, p. 2; *Texas Almanac for 1869*, p. 230; *Texas Almanac for 1870*, p. 217.

32. One such Silesian who took out his naturalization papers, swearing the "ironclad" oath, and registered to vote was the illiterate Simon Yainta [Yanta]. Simon Yainta, Oath of Allegiance to the United States of America, 25 November 1869, manuscript in possession of the Rev. John W. Yanta, San Antonio.

33. Emanuel Rzeppa, [Panna Maria], to J[ohn] S. Mason, San Antonio, Texas, [August 1867], U.S., Department of War, Army, Fifth Military District, Office of Civil Affairs, Register of Letters Received (16 April 1867–28 May 1869), p. 530, entry 62 R 28; [Emanuel] Rzeppa, Pan[n]a Maria, to [John S. Mason], San Antonio, Texas, 10 August 1867, Fifth Military District, Office of Civil Affairs, Register of Letters Received (16

April 1867–28 May 1869), p. 531, entry 62 R 35; *San Antonio Express*, 30 August 1867, p. 2.

34. Bakanowski, *Moje wspomnienia*, pp. 26–27; interview, Mrs. Richard E. Bensmiller, Panna Maria, 27 November 1971; Jackson and Long, *Texas Stock Directory*, p. 74; Karnes County, Texas, Deed Records, A: 274; interview, Fletcher B. Kuhnel, Sr., Karnes City, Texas, 24 November 1971; Texas, Militia, Muster Roll of Capt. J. A. Tivey's Company of Mounted Riflemen, 5 August 1861; Texas, Militia, Muster Roll of the Panna Maria Grays, 9 July 1861; Texas, Militia, Muster Roll of the Panna Maria Greys, 7 February 1862; Grover C. Ramsay, *Confederate Postmasters in Texas*, p. 48; C[harles] A. Russell, San Antonio, Texas, to Emilene [C. Russell, Helena], 16 December 1863, Charles A. Russell Papers; Texas, Secretary of State, Election Register 1866–1870.

35. Rzeppa to Mason, [August 1867], Fifth Military District, Office of Civil Affairs, Register of Letters Received (16 April 1867–28 May 1869), p. 530, entry 62 R 28; Rzeppa to [Mason], 10 August 1867, Fifth Military District, Office of Civil Affairs, Register of Letters Received (16 April 1867–28 May 1869), p. 531, entry 62 R 35; [John S. Mason], San Antonio, Texas, Endorsement on Affidavit of Emanuel Rzeppa of Pan[n]a Maria, Texas, 30 August 1867, U.S., Department of War, Army, Post of San Antonio, Texas, Endorsements Sent (21 December 1866–11 October 1867), p. 147, entry 312; Rev. Adolf [Bakanowski], Panna Maria, to Our Dearest Father Alexander [Jełowicki, Paris], 11 September 1867, Bakanowski Letters no. 9346; Jno [*sic*] Mason, San Antonio, Texas, to W. S. Abert, Galveston, Texas, 14 August 1867, U.S., Department of War, Army, Post of San Antonio, Texas, Letters Sent (21 December 1866–13 March 1868), pp. 91–92, entry 149.

36. Mason to Abert, 14 August 1867, Post of San Antonio, Letters Sent (21 December 1866–13 March 1868), pp. 91–92, entry 149; *San Antonio Express*, 10 August 1867, p. 3.

37. W. Prince, Galveston, Texas, to J[ohn] S. Mason, [San Antonio], 11 September 1867, U.S., Department of War, Army, Fifth Military District, Office of Civil Affairs, Endorsements Sent (16 April 1867–8 May 1868), p. 88, entry 287.

38. Chas. P. Smith, San Antonio, Texas, to John Kuhnel, Pan[n]a Maria, Texas, 21 September 1867, Post of San Antonio, Letters Sent (21 December 1866–13 March 1868), p. 105, entry 172.

39. [Bakanowski] to [*Zwiastun Górnoszlązki*], 6 June 1870, *Zwiastun Górnoszlązki*, 7 July 1870, pp. 215–216; Bakanowski, *Moje wspomnienia*, p. 63; Adolf Bakanowski, "Pamiętniki" [Recollections], cited in Smolikowski, "Historia," vol. 8, chap. 9, p. 88; Dworaczyk, *First Polish Colonies*, pp. 33–34; Kruszka, *Historja polska w Ameryce*, p. 489; Stefan Nesterowicz, *Notatki z podróży po północnej i środkowej Ameryce*, p. 205; interview, Ben P. Urbanczyk, 10 August 1973.

40. Nesterowicz, *Notatki z podróży*, p. 205.

41. *Zwiastun Górnoszlązki*, 8 July 1869, p. 229. The article in which this information appears begins with the statement that it was written to discourage emigration from Silesia, but its contents in general are not overly biased.

42. [Bakanowski] to [*Zwiastun Górnoszlązki*], 6 June 1870, *Zwiastun Górnoszlązki*, 7 July 1870, p. 216; Bakanowski, *Moje wspomnienia*, pp. 31, 63; Dworaczyk, *First Polish Colonies*, p. 36; Kruszka, *Historja polska w Ameryce*, p. 489; Nesterowicz, *Notatki z podróży*, p. 205.

43. Bakanowski, *Moje wspomnienia*, p. 64.

44. Rev. Adolf Bak[anowski], Panna Maria, to Our Dear Father Alexander

[Jełowicki, Paris], 18 November 1867, Bakanowski Letters no. 9347; Bakanowski, *Moje wspomnienia*, pp. 64–65; Bakanowski, "Pamiętniki," cited in Smolikowski, "Historia," vol. 8, chap. 9, p. 88.

45. Jackson and Long, *Texas Stock Directory*, p. 41 of advertising section; *San Antonio Express*, 8 November 1867, p. 2; W[illiam] W. Gamble, San Antonio, Texas, to [Post of San Antonio], 28 October 1869, U.S., Department of War, Army, Post of San Antonio, Texas, Office of Civil Affairs, Register of Letters Received (6 February 1869–30 April 1870), p. 76, entry G 21; W[illia]m W. Gamble, San Antonio, Texas, to [Post of San Antonio], 14 November 1869, Post of San Antonio, Office of Civil Affairs, Register of Letters Received (6 February 1869–30 April 1870), p. 77, entry G 26; W[illiam] W. Gamble, San Antonio, Texas, to [Office of Civil Affairs, Fifth Military District, Austin], 21 December 1869, U.S., Department of War, Army, Fifth Military District, Office of Civil Affairs, Register of Letters Received (20 October 1869–31 August 1870), p. 41, entry 65 B 16; *San Antonio Express*, 21 August 1869, p. 3.

46. W[illia]m W. Gamble, San Antonio, Texas, to W. C. Phillips [*sic*], Secretary of State, [Austin], 18 February 1868, Texas, Secretary of State, Letters Received.

47. Jno. S. Mason, San Antonio, Texas, to C[harles] E. Morse, Austin, Texas, 17 January 1868, Post of San Antonio, Letters Sent (21 December 1866–13 March 1868), p. 139.

48. Both Kruszka and Niklewicz incorrectly state that this incident occurred at Easter 1868. Kruszka, *Historja polska w Ameryce*, p. 490; Franciszek Niklewicz, *Dzieje pierwszych polskich osadników w Ameryce i przewodnik parafij polskich w Stanach Zjednoczonych*, p. 11.

49. Bakanowski, *Moje wspomnienia*, pp. 65–66; Bakanowski, "Pamiętniki," cited in Smolikowski, "Historia," vol. 8, chap. 9, pp. 88–89. The version of the confrontation given here, taken from Father Adolf Bakanowski's published and unpublished memoirs, is probably the most accurate. For other variations in the story see Dworaczyk, *First Polish Colonies*, pp. 35–36; Kruszka, *Historja polska w Ameryce*, pp. 490–491; Nesterowicz, *Notatki z podróży*, p. 205; Niklewicz, *Dzieje pierwszych*, p. 11.

50. [Bakanowski] to Our Dearest Father Alexander, 11 September 1867, Bakanowski Letters no. 9346; Rev. Adolf Baka[nowski], Panna Maria, Texas, to Our Dearest Father Peter [Semenenko, Rome], 23 May 1870, Bakanowski Letters no. 9380; Bakanowski, *Moje wspomnienia*, p. 66; Bakanowski, "Pamiętniki," cited in Smolikowski, "Historia," vol. 8, chap. 9, pp. 88–90; Mason to Abert, 15 August 1867, Post of San Antonio, Letters Sent (21 December 1866–13 March 1868), pp. 91–92, entry 149.

51. Bakanowski, *Moje wspomnienia*, p. 66; Bakanowski, "Pamiętniki," cited in Smolikowski, "Historia," vol. 8, chap. 9, p. 90. Although no minutes or records of this meeting have been found in manuscript army records in the National Archives, other materials from both Rev. Adolf Bakanowski and military sources suggest that the officer visited by the four priests was General John S. Mason, commander of the Post of San Antonio, who had seen conditions in Karnes County, had recommended the stationing of troops in the area, and apparently already knew Bakanowski. Bakanowski, *Moje wspomnienia*, p. 66; [Bakanowski] to Our Dearest Father Alexander, 11 September 1867, Bakanowski Letters no. 3946; Baka[nowski] to Our Dearest Father Peter, 23 May 1870, Bakanowski Letters no. 9380; Mason to Abert, 14 August 1867, Post of San Antonio, Letters Sent (21 December 1866–13 March 1868), pp. 91–92, entry 149; Mason to Morse, 17 January 1868, Post of San Antonio, Letters Sent (21 December 1866–13 March 1868), p. 139.

52. Bakanowski, *Moje wspomnienia*, p. 66.

53. [Bakanowski] to Our Dearest Father General, 5 July 1870, Bakanowski Letters no. 9382.

54. Bakanowski, *Moje wspomnienia*, pp. 66–67. The young officer chosen to establish the U.S. Army post in Karnes County was Second Lieutenant William Alexis Thompson. Francis B. Heitman, *Historical Register and Dictionary of the United States Army*, 1:954; U.S., Department of War, Army, Post of Helena, Texas, Post Returns (10 April–1 May 1869).

55. Bakanowski, *Moje wspomnienia*, pp. 66–67; Post of Helena, Post Returns (10 April–1 May 1869).

56. Bakanowski, *Moje wspomnienia*, p. 67; *San Antonio Express*, 22 January 1869, p. 2, 23 January 1869, p. 3, 5 February 1869, p. 2; U.S., Department of War, Army, Fifth Military District, General Orders no. 4, 16 January 1869.

57. Joseph Burke, San Antonio, Texas, to [Post of San Antonio], 26 April 1867, U.S., Department of War, Army, Post of San Antonio, Texas, Register of Letters Received (22 December 1866–15 May 1867), p. 19; Krueger, *Pioneer Life in Texas*, pp. 56–57; Mason to Abert, 14 August 1867, Post of San Antonio, Letters Sent (21 December 1866–13 March 1868), pp. 91–92, entry 149; Jno. S. Mason, San Antonio, Texas, to C[harles] E. Morse, Austin, Texas, 13 March 1868, U.S., Department of War, Army, Post of San Antonio, Texas, Letters Sent (13 March 1868–9 April 1869), pp. 3–4; *San Antonio Express*, 19 November 1867, p. 3; Post of Helena, Post Returns (5–31 March 1868).

58. [George H. Crossman], Inspecting Officer, Helena, Texas, to Assistant Adjutant General, Fifth Military District, Austin, Texas, 2 October 1869, U.S., Department of War, Army, Post of Helena, Texas, Letters Sent (15 August 1869–22 May 1870), p. 17; Krueger, *Pioneer Life in Texas*, pp. 57–58; *San Antonio Express*, 24 March 1870, p. 2; Post of Helena, Post Returns (10 April 1869–30 April 1870); U.S., Department of War, Secretary, *Report of the Secretary of War, 1867*, pp. 470–471; *Report of the Secretary of War, 1868*, pp. 706, 710.

59. Company H of the 4th U.S. Cavalry established the Post of Helena on 10 April 1869, and it was joined there by Company G of the 10th U.S. Infantry on 12 August 1869. The two companies remained there until Company H, 4th Cavalry, left the post for Austin on 15 January 1870. Company G, 10th Infantry, remained at Helena until 23 May 1870, when the post was formally abandoned. Geo. H. Crossman, Helena, Texas, to A[ssistant] A[djutant] G[eneral], Dep[artmen]t of Texas, 22 May 1870, Post of Helena, Letters Sent (15 August 1869–22 May 1870), p. 51; Post of Helena, Post Returns (10 April 1869–30 April 1870); H. Clay Woods, Austin, Texas, to George G. Huntt, Helena, Texas, 3 January 1870, telegram, George G. Huntt Papers.

60. Bakanowski, *Moje wspomnienia*, p. 67; Dworaczyk, *First Polish Colonies*, p. 36.

61. Post of Helena, Post Returns (1 November to 31 December 1869); C. L. Bell, Belmont, Texas, to Comdg. Officer, San Antonio, Texas, 24 August 1869, *San Antonio Express*, 27 August 1869, p. 2; C. S. [*sic*] Bell, Helena, Texas, to C[harles] E. Morse, [Austin], 8 August 1869, U.S., Department of War, Army, Fifth Military District, Office of Civil Affairs, Letters Received, item no. 63 H 108; Geo. H. Crossman, Helena, Texas, to [James] Callahan, [Helena], 19 September 1869, Post of Helena, Letters Sent (15 August 1869–22 May 1870), p. 14; Louis Peyton, Helena, Texas, to George M. Harris, Helena, Texas, 11 August 1869, Fifth Military District, Office of Civil Affairs, Letters Received, item no. 63 H 108; W[illia]m A[lexis] Thompson, Helena, Texas, to L. V. Coziard, Austin, Texas, 15 April 1869, U.S., Department of War, Army, Post of Helena,

Texas, Letters Received; [William Alexis Thompson], Helena, Texas, to A. N. Jenkins, [Helena], 7 June 1869, Post of Helena, Letters Received; Post of Helena, Post Returns (1 May–31 July 1869).

A typical outlaw apprehended and delivered for safekeeping by federal troops at the Post of Helena was Oscar Rose, for whose capture there was a three-hundred-dollar reward from McLennan County, Texas, and who was arrested by Lieutenant George W. Smith in the summer of 1869. W. C. Philips, Austin, Texas, to Geo. W. Smith, Helena, 13 August 1869, Texas, Secretary of State, W. C. Philips Public Letterbook (23 August 1867–21 January 1870), p. 435, in *Records of the United States of America*; W. C. Philips, Austin, Texas, to Geo. W. Smith, Helena, 14 September 1869, W. C. Philips Public Letterbook, p. 438.

62. C[harles E.] Morse, Austin, Texas, to Commanding Officer, [Helena], 26 April 1869, Post of Helena, Letters Received; *San Antonio Express*, 20 April 1869, p. 1; [unidentified writer], Helena, Texas, to C[harles] E. Morse, Austin, Texas, [spring or summer 1869], Post of Helena, Letters Received. The file of Letters Received at the Post of Helena contains from the first four months of its existence the preliminary drafts of many letters that were sent from the post but not recorded in the bound volume of Letters Sent, which begins with 15 August 1869. This situation explains why some footnote citations for letters actually sent are noted in the file of Letters Received.

63. W[illia]m [Alexis] Thompson, Helena, Texas, to L. V. Cazaire, [Austin], 12 April 1869, Post of Helena, Letters Received; W[illia]m [Alexis] Thompson, Helena, Texas, to L. V. Coziard [*sic*], [Austin], 14 April 1869, Post of Helena, Letters Received.

64. Geo. H. Crosman [*sic*], Helena, Texas, to A[ssistant] A[djutant] G[enera]l, [Austin], 22 May 1870, Post of Helena, Letters Sent (15 August 1869 to 22 May 1870), p. 51; *San Antonio Express*, 24 March 1870, p. 2, 25 March 1870, pp. 2–3. Father Adolf Bakanowski was the source of the frequently repeated information that the U.S. Army during its stay at Helena captured and executed 150 to 300 outlaws (sometimes called "rebels") in the Karnes County area. The exaggerated claim of 300 first appeared in his letter to Rome of 23 May 1870 and that of 150 in his letter to *Zwiastun Górnoszlązki* of 6 June 1870. The earlier statement was reprinted verbatim in the editor's notes to Bakanowski's published memoirs in 1913. The figure 150 next appeared in Bakanowski's manuscript "Pamiętniki" [Recollections], subsequently reprinted in Kruszka's history of the Poles in America, and then presented in somewhat altered form in Dworaczyk's history of the Poles in Texas. Manuscript records from the Post of Helena fail to substantiate such large numbers of apprehended individuals. Baka[nowski] to Our Dearest Father Peter, 23 May 1870, Bakanowski Letters no. 9380; [Bakanowski] to [*Zwiastun Górnoszlązki*], 6 June 1870, *Zwiastun Górnoszlązki*, 7 July 1870, p. 216; Bakanowski, *Moje wspomnienia*, p. 182; Bakanowski, "Pamiętniki," cited in Smolikowski, "Historia," vol. 8, chap. 9, p. 91; Dworaczyk, *First Polish Colonies*, p. 37; Kruszka, *Historja polska w Ameryce*, p. 491.

65. Bakanowski, *Moje wspomnienia*, pp. 26–27, 63, 67. The Rev. Vincent Barzyński, in San Antonio, wrote to Rome in the winter of 1866–1867 that the initial falling out between Kuhnel and Bakanowski was over the German's handling of parish financial matters in the interval before the coming of the Resurrectionists. Rev. Vincent Barzyński, San Antonio, to Most Reverend Father General [Rev. Jerome Kajsiewicz], Most Reverend Father Superior, Dear Priest Friends, All Dearest Future Missionaries, and Dearest Brothers, [Rome], last days of 1866 and beginning of 1867, Barzyński Letters no. 8947.

66. Rzeppa to Mason, [August 1867], Fifth Military District, Office of Civil Affairs,

Register of Letters Received (16 April 1867–28 May 1869), p. 530, entry 62 R 28; Rzeppa to [Mason], 10 August 1867, Fifth Military District, Office of Civil Affairs, Register of Letters Received (16 April 1867–28 May 1869), p. 531, entry 62 R 35.

67. [Cleric] John Frydrychowicz, Panna Maria, Texas, to Dearest Father, [location?], 15 December 1867, Frydrychowicz Letters no. 35765; [Cleric] John Frydrychowicz, Panna Maria, Texas, to Beloved and Dearest Father [Rev. Alexander Jełowicki, Paris], 15 December 1867, Frydrychowicz Letters no. 35766; Rev. J[ohn] Frydrychowicz, Maulbery [*sic*], Texas, to Beloved and Dearest Father General [Rev. Jerome Kajsiewicz, Rome], 10 November 1868, Frydrychowicz Letters no. 35767; [Zwiardowski] to Honorable Reverend Father Superior, 24 September 1868, Zwiardowski Letters no. 34703.

68. Dworaczyk, *First Polish Colonies*, p. 89; Morse to Commanding Officer, 26 April 1869, Post of Helena, Letters Received; C[harles] E. Morse, Austin, Texas, to E[manuel] Rzeppa, [Panna Maria], 26 February 1868, Fifth Military District, Office of Civil Affairs, Endorsements Sent (16 April 1867–8 May 1868), p. 237, entry 783; Cha[rle]s E. Morse, Austin, Texas, to E[manuel] Rzeppa, Helena, Texas, 8 March 1870, U.S., Department of War, Army, Fifth Military District, Office of Civil Affairs, Letters Sent (8 November 1869–22 March 1870), pp. 527–529, entry 2351; E[manuel] Rzeppa, Panna Maria, Texas, to Commanding Officer, Helena, Texas, 4 December 1869, Fifth Military District, Office of Civil Affairs, Letters Received, item no. 65 K 12; *Texas Almanac for 1869*, p. 230; *Texas Almanac for 1870*, p. 217.

69. Father Adolf Bakanowski had a criticism of long standing of Kuhnel's handling of the court at Panna Maria. As early as autumn 1867 he wrote to Rome that Silesians came to him "from tens of miles" to settle disputes among them "because they cannot find any justice in the courts." Rev. Adolf [Bakanowski], Panna Maria, to Our Most Honorable Father General [Rev. Jerome Kajsiewicz, Rome], 10 September 1867, Bakanowski Letters no. 9345; Bakanowski, *Moje wspomnienia*, p. 63.

70. Bakanowski, *Moje wspomnienia*, pp. 67–70; Texas, Secretary of State, Election Register 1866–1870; [unidentified writer], Helena, Texas, to C[harles] E. Morse, Austin, Texas, [n.d.], Post of Helena, Letters Received. Emanuel Rzeppa has been called the first Polish judge in America. Kruszka, *Historja polska w Ameryce*, pp. 491–493.

71. Bakanowski, "Pamiętniki," cited in Smolikowski, "Historia," vol. 8, chap. 9, p. 91; Bensmiller to Baker, interview, 27 November 1971; Kruszka, *Historja polska w Ameryce*, pp. 492–493; "Return of an Election Ordered by General Orders no. 174, Headquarters Fifth Military District, Austin, Texas, October 1, 1869, under the Reconstruction Acts of Congress, in the County of Karnes[,] State of Texas, for Election of 'Justices of the Peace' for Said County, (Second Precinct)," 4 December 1869, U.S., Department of War, Army, Fifth Military District, Office of Civil Affairs, Manuscript Returns of Texas Election Held 30 November and 1, 2, 3 December 1869. The Rev. Adolf Bakanowski and John Kuhnel seem never to have become reconciled to each other. Just before the priest left Texas in 1870, reviewing his accomplishments as a missionary for four years among the Silesians, he coldly wrote that Kuhnel had opposed him from the start but that "I drove him out of his office and everything else." Rev. Adolf [Bakanowski], Panna Maria, Texas, to Our Dearest Father General [Rev. Jerome Kajsiewicz, Rome], 16 May 1870, Bakanowski Letters no. 9379.

72. *San Antonio Express*, 18 October 1867, p. 3.

73. Jno. S. Mason, San Antonio, Texas, Endorsements on Oaths of Office of John Adam[ie]tz as County Commissioner of Bandera County and of R. J. Farr as County Clerk of Kerr County, 9 April 1869, U.S., Department of War, Army, Post of San

Antonio, Texas, Endorsements Sent Relating to Civil Affairs (31 January 1869–28 April 1870), p. 26, entry 27; Cha[rle]s E. Morse, Austin, Texas, to Geo. B. Taylor, Bandera, Texas, 17 January 1870, Fifth Military District, Office of Civil Affairs, Letters Sent (8 November 1869–22 March 1870), p. 244, entry 1751.

74. W. P. Bainbridge, Austin, Texas, to Commanding Officer, San Antonio, Texas, 6 August 1869, U.S., Department of War, Army, Fifth Military District, Office of Civil Affairs, Letters Sent (29 May 1869–8 November 1869), p. 242, entry 473; James H. Carleton, San Antonio, Texas, to Charles E. Morse, Austin, Texas, 30 July 1869, U.S., Department of War, Army, Post of San Antonio, Texas, Letters Sent (5 February 1869–4 May 1870), p. 77, entry 210; Saml. Koeningheim, Bandera, Texas, to Jno. S. Mason, [San Antonio], 7 June 1869, Fifth Military District, Office of Civil Affairs, Letters Received, item no. 63 S 28.

75. "Fifth Mil[itary] District," Austin, Texas, to [Office of Civil Affairs, Post of San Antonio, San Antonio], 21 December 1869, Post of San Antonio, Texas, Office of Civil Affairs, Register of Letters Received (6 February 1869–30 April 1870), p. 277, entry F 153; August Krawietz, San Antonio, Texas, to [Office of Civil Affairs, Austin], 15 December 1869, U.S., Department of War, Army, Fifth Military District, Office of Civil Affairs, Register of Letters Received (2 March 1869–15 April 1870), p. 161, entry 64 B 361; *San Antonio Express*, 13 February 1868, p. 4, 10 February 1870, p. 2.

76. Dworaczyk, *First Polish Colonies*, p. 46; Nesterowicz, *Notatki z podróży*, p. 206.

77. J[ohn] Moczygemba, Fort Stockton, Texas, to [Office of Civil Affairs, Fifth Military District, Austin, Texas], 12 March 1870, Fifth Military District, Office of Civil Affairs, Register of Letters Received (29 October 1869–31 August 1870), p. 654, entry 65 P 63. Handwriting analysis indicates that the John Moczygemba who was elected justice of the peace at Fort Stockton, Texas, was not the cousin of Rev. Leopold Moczygemba who wrote the 1855 letters from Panna Maria but was rather the priest's brother, born at Ligota Toszecka (Płużnica parish) in Upper Silesia on 1 June 1833. T. Lindsay Baker, "The Moczygemba Family of Texas and Poland: Initiators of Polish Colonization in America," *Stirpes: Texas State Genealogical Society Quarterly* 15 (December 1975): 132, 137–138; St. Stanisław Church, Płużnica, Poland, Baptismal Records (26 December 1812–2 June 1833), pp. 273–274.

78. John Moczygemba, Fort Stockton, Texas, to Charles E. Morse, Austin, Texas, 12 April 1870, Texas, Governor, Letters Received; [Edmund J. Davis], Austin, Texas, to J[ohn] Moczygemba, Fort Stockton, Texas, 30 April 1870, Texas, Governor, Edmund J. Davis Executive Record Book for 1870, pp. 110–111.

79. Pat[ric]k Cusack, Fort Stockton, Texas, to John Moczygemba, [Fort Stockton], Texas, 21 April 1870; John Moczygemba, Fort Stockton, Texas, to P[atrick] Cusack, Fort Stockton, Texas, 21 April 1870; John Moczygemba, [Fort Stockton], Texas, to Sheriff or Any Other Authorized Officer, Presidio County, Texas, 30 April 1870; John Moczygemba, Fort Stockton, Texas, to James F. Wade, Fort Stockton, Texas, 9 May 1870; Peter Pleasantier, Sworn Statement before Justice of the Peace Court, Precinct 1, Presidio County, Texas, [19 April 1870]; Presidio County, Texas, Justice of the Peace Court, Precinct 1, Writ in Case of Peter Pleasantier vs. George B. Lyles, 19 April 1870. The above cited correspondence and documents are filed with John Moczygemba, Fort Stockton, Texas, to E[dmund] J. Davis, [Austin], Texas, 14 May 1870, Texas, Governor, Letters Received.

80. Moczygemba to Davis, 14 May 1870, Texas, Governor, Letters Received.

81. James P. Newcomb, Austin, Texas, to John Moczygemba, Fort Stockton,

Texas, 31 May 1870, Texas, Governor, Letters Received; interview, LeRoy Moczygemba, San Antonio, Texas, 6 December 1974.

Chapter 6. The Growth and Development of Silesian Institutions and Settlement

1. John Iwicki, *The First One Hundred Years: A Study of the Apostolate of the Congregation of the Resurrection in the United States 1866–1966*, p. 24–25; Jacek Przygoda, "Poles in Texas Today," *Quarterly Review: Official Publication of the American Council of Polish Cultural Clubs* (Washington, D.C.) 21 (October–December 1969): 1; Jacek Przygoda, *Texas Pioneers from Poland: A Study in the Ethnic History*, pp. 18–21.

2. Bakanowski to Our Dearest Father Superior, 13 November 1866, Bakanowski Letters no. 9330; Adolf Bakanowski, *Moje wspomnienia 1840-1863-1913*, pp. 26, 170; [Zwiardowski] to Dear Reverend Father, 12 November 1866, Zwiardowski Letters no. 34690; Zwiardowski to Dearest Reverend Father Alexander, 27 August 1867, Zwiardowski Letters no. 34698.

3. Bakanowski to Our Dearest Father Superior, 13 November 1866, Bakanowski Letters no. 9330; Rev. Adolf Bakanowski, San Antonio, to Dear Father Alexander [Jełowicki, Paris], 14 May 1867, Bakanowski Letters no. 9339; Rev. Adolf Bak[anowski], Panna Maria, to Our Dear Father Alexander [Jełowicki, Paris], 7 June 1867, Bakanowski Letters no. 9341; Bakanowski to Our Dearest Father Peter, 28 June 1867, Bakanowski Letters no. 9344; Rev. Adolf [Bakanowski], Panna Maria, to Dear Father Alexander [Jełowicki, Paris], 20–24 May 1868, Bakanowski Letters no. 9355; Rev. Adolf [Bakanowski], Panna Maria, to Dear Father Alexander [Jełowicki, Paris], 6 November 1868, Bakanowski Letters no. 9362; [Bakanowski] to Honorable Father General, 1 December 1868, Bakanowski Letters no. 9363; [Bakanowski] to [*Zwiastun Górnoszlązki*, Spring 1870], *Zwiastun Górnoszlązki*, 14 April 1870, p. 120; Bakanowski, *Moje wspomnienia*, pp. 42, 158–159; Emmanuel Bénézit, ed., *Dictionnaire Critique et Documentaire des Peintres, Sculpteurs, Dessinateurs et Graveurs* [Critical and Documentary Dictionary of Painters, Sculptors, Designers, and Engravers], new rev. ed., 6:391; Wacław Kruszka, *Historja polska w Ameryce*, p. 499.

4. Rev. Adolf [Bakanowski], Panna Maria, to Our Dearest Father General [Rev. Jerome Kajsiewicz, Rome], 4 January 1868, Bakanowski Letters no. 9349; Rev. Adolf [Bakanowski] and [Rev.] Vincent [Barzyński], Panna Maria, to Our Dear Father Alexander [Jełowicki, Paris], 20 February 1868, Bakanowski Letters no. 9351; Rev. Adolf [Bakanowski], Martinez, to Our Dear Father Alexander [Jełowicki, Paris], 15 May 1868, Bakanowski Letters no. 9354; [Bakanowski] to Honorable Father General, 1 December 1868, Bakanowski Letters no. 9363; Rev. Adolf [Bakanowski], Panna Maria, Texas, to Our Honorable Father General [Rev. Jerome Kajsiewicz, Rome], 22 November 1869, Bakanowski Letters no. 9374; Rev. Adolf [Bakanowski], Panna Maria, Texas, to Honorable and Dear Father Alexander [Jełowicki, Paris], 27 June 1870, Bakanowski Letters no. 9381; Rev. Felix Zwiardowski, Martinez, to Dearest Reverend Father, [location?], 13 September 1867, Zwiardowski Letters no. 34699; Rev. Felix Zwiardowski, Galveston, to Honorable Reverend Father, [location?], 16 December 1867, Zwiardowski Letters no. 34701. For the version of the celebration quoted above, see Bakanowski Letters no. 9367 and Barzyński Letters no. 9130. For other information on the celebration, including the published account, see [Bakanowski] to Our Dearest Father General, 18 February 1870, Bakanowski Letters no. 9375; [Bakanowski] to Our Dearest Father Gen-

eral, 29 March 1870, Bakanowski Letters no. 9376; [Rev. Adolf Bakanowski], Panna Maria, Texas, to [*Zwiastun Górnoszlązki*, Piekary, Regency of Opole, February 1870], *Zwiastun Górnoszlązki*, 24 March 1870, pp. 95–96; [Bakanowski] to [*Zwiastun Górnoszlązki*, Spring 1870], *Zwiastun Górnoszlązki*, 14 April 1870, p. 120; Edward J. Dworaczyk, *The First Polish Colonies of America in Texas*, pp. 42–43.

5. Zwiardowski to Our Dear Reverend Father, 28 December 1866, Zwiardowski Letters no. 34692.

6. Rev. Henry Cichocki, Panna Maria, to Dear Father, [location?], 16 September 1875, Cichocki Letters no. 35215; Edward J. Dworaczyk, *The Centennial History of Panna Maria, Texas*, pp. 35, 77–79, 90; Dworaczyk, *First Polish Colonies*, pp. 13–14, 49–53; Edward J. Dworaczyk, *The Millennium History of Panna Maria, Texas*, pp. 35, 77–79, 97, 99; Rev. Leopold M[oczygemba], Jeffersonville, Ind[.], to My Beloved and Dear Father Vincent [Barzyński, Chicago], 1 September 1877, Moczygemba Letters no. 37371; Felix V. Snoga to Baker, interview at Polish American Historical Association Convention, New Orleans, La., 27 December 1972; Rev. Felix Zwiardowski, San Antonio, Tex[as], to Most Reverend Father, [location?], 1 August 1877, Zwiardowski Letters no. 34768; Rev. Felix Zwiardowski, Panna Maria, to Most Reverend Father, [location?], 6 December 1877, Zwiardowski Letters no. 34770.

7. Barzyński to Most Reverend Father General et al., last days of 1866 and beginning of 1867, Barzyński Letters no. 8947; Rev. Vincent [Barzyński], San Antonio, to Reverend Father General [Rev. Jerome Kajsiewicz], Most Reverend and My Dear Spiritual Father Rev. Peter Semenenko, and Dear Fathers of Our Order, [Rome], Day of the Five Wounds of Our Lord Jesus Christ 1867, Barzyński Letters no. 8949; Rev. Vincent [Barzyński], San Antonio, to Most Reverend Father General [Rev. Jerome Kajsiewicz], Most Reverend Fathers Peter [Semenenko], Alexander [Jełowicki], and Thomas, Dear Brothers, and Dear Fathers, [Rome], 11 April 1867, Barzyński Letters no. 8950.

8. [Barzyński] to Most Reverend Father General et al., Day of the Five Wounds 1867, Barzyński Letters no. 8949; [Barzyński] to Most Reverend Father General et al., 11 April 1867, Barzyński Letters no. 8950; Rev. Vincent [Barzyński], San Antonio, to Our Most Reverend Father Superior, [location?], 9 May 1867, Barzyński Letters no. 8953; Rev. Vincent [Barzyński], San Antonio, Texas, to Most Reverend Father Alexander [Jełowicki, Paris], 25 September 1867, Barzyński Letters no. 8972; Iwicki, *First One Hundred Years*, p. 37; John A. Joyce, *Our Polish Pioneers*, p. 13; Kruszka, *Historja polska w Ameryce*, p. 500; P. F. Parisot and C. J. Smith, *History of the Catholic Church in the Diocese of San Antonio, Texas*, p. 179; *San Antonio Express*, 26 November 1867, pp. 2–3.

9. Several sources state that the church at San Antonio was completed in 1871, but manuscript sources indicate 1868 as the completion date. See Joyce, *Our Polish Pioneers*, pp. 12–13; Sister Jan Maria Wozniak, "St. Michael's Church: The Polish National Catholic Church in San Antonio, Texas, 1855–1950," p. 33.

10. [Bakanowski] to Our Dearest Father General, 4 January 1868, Bakanowski Letters no. 9349; [Barzyński] to Most Reverend Father General et al., Day of the Five Wounds 1867, Barzyński Letters no. 8949; [Barzyński] to Most Reverend Father General et al., 11 April 1867, Barzyński Letters no. 8950; [Barzyński] to Most Reverend Father Alexander, 25 September 1867, Barzyński Letters no. 8972; Rev. Vincent [Barzyński], San Antonio, to Most Reverend Father General [Rev. Jerome Kajsiewicz, Rome], Autumn 1867, Barzyński Letters no. 8951; Rev. Vincent [Barzyński], San Antonio, to Most Reverend Father Superior, All Reverend Fathers, and Dear Brothers

of Our Order, [Rome], 27 February 1869, Barzyński Letters no. 8955; Rev. Vincent [Barzyński], San Antonio, to Most Reverend Father General [Rev. Jerome Kajsiewicz, Romè], 5 August 1868, Barzyński Letters no. 8958; Iwicki, *First One Hundred Years*, p. 37; Joyce, *Our Polish Pioneers*, p. 13; Kruszka, *Historja polska w Ameryce*, p. 500; Parisot and Smith, *Catholic Church in the Diocese of San Antonio*, p. 179; *San Antonio Express*, 17 April 1868, p. 3.

11. Misunderstandings exist concerning the construction of the church at Martinez, as they do about the church in San Antonio. At least two historians have written that the church at Martinez was completed under the pastorates of the Rev. Teofil Bralewski (1869) and the Rev. Vincent Barzyński (visiting from San Antonio, 1869–1872, and resident pastor, 1872–1873), although the correspondence of these two men says nothing about such major church construction. Iwicki, *First One Hundred Years*, pp. 40–41; Kruszka, *Historja polska w Ameryce*, pp. 503–504, 614–615.

12. [Bakanowski] to Our Dearest Father Alexander, 11 September 1867, Bakanowski Letters no. 9346; [Bakanowski] to Our Honorable Father General, 9 April 1868, Bakanowski Letters no. 9352; [Bakanowski] to Our Dear Father Alexander, 15 May 1868, Bakanowski Letters no. 9354; [Bakanowski] to Honorable Father General, 1 December 1868, Bakanowski Letters no. 9363; Rev. Adolf [Bakanowski], Panna Maria, to Our Dearest Father General [Rev. Jerome Kajsiewicz, Rome], 28 January 1869, Bakanowski Letters no. 9367; Dworaczyk, *First Polish Colonies*, pp. 111–116; J. M. Gilbert, *Archdiocese of San Antonio 1874–1949*, p. 76; Stefan Nesterowicz, *Notatki z podróży po północnej i środkowej Ameryce*, pp. 183–184; Parisot and Smith, *Catholic Church in the Diocese of San Antonio*, pp. 127, 129; Przygoda, *Texas Pioneers*, p. 18; Rev. Felix Zwiardowski, Panna Maria, to Dearest Reverend Father Superior, [location?], 16 May 1867, Zwiardowski Letters no. 34695; Zwiardowski to Dearest Reverend Father Alexander, 27 August 1867, Zwiardowski Letters no. 34698; Rev. Felix Zwiardowski, Martinez, to Honorable Reverend Father, [location?], 17 June 1868, Zwiardowski Letters no. 34702.

13. Bakanowski to Dear Father Alexander, 14 May 1867, Bakanowski Letters no. 9339; Bak[anowski] to Our Dear Father Alexander, 7 June 1867, Bakanowski Letters no. 9341; Dworaczyk, *First Polish Colonies*, p. 107; Iciek, *First One Hundred Years*, pp. 224–225; Kruszka, *Historja polska w Ameryce*, p. 377; Parisot and Smith, *Catholic Church in the Diocese of San Antonio*, p. 128; Zwiardowski to Honorable Reverend Father, 17 June 1868, Zwiardowski Letters no. 34702.

14. Kruszka, *Historja polska w Ameryce*, p. 612; Rev. Adolphe [*sic*] Snigurski, Kraków, [Austrian Empire], to Committee of the Propagation of the Faith at Vienna [Leopoldine Foundation], Vienna, Austria, 7 September 1874, Leopoldine Foundation, Letters from the Dioceses in the U.S.A., Box A-G, Diocese of Galveston Folder, Leopoldinen-Stiftung Collection; Rev. Felix Zwiardowski, Bandera, Texas, to Reverend Father General [Rev. Jerome Kajsiewicz, Rome], 31 January 1870, Zwiardowski Letters no. 34704; Rev. Felix Zwiardowski, St. Hedwig, Texas, to Most Reverend Father General [Rev. Peter Semenenko, Rome], 15 February 1876, Zwiardowski Letters no. 34749; [Zwiardowski] to Honorable Father Adolf, 2 March 1876, Zwiardowski Letters no. 34751; Rev. Felix Zwiardowski, Atlantic Ocean, to Most Reverend Father, [location?], 17 July 1876, Zwiardowski Letters no. 34754.

15. [Bakanowski] to Our Honorable Father General, 9 April 1868, Bakanowski Letters no. 9352; [Bakanowski] to Our Honorable Father General, 21 April 1868, Bakanowski Letters no. 9353; Rev. Adolf [Bakanowski], Panna Maria, to Our Dear Father Alexander [Jełowicki, Paris], 27 May 1868, Bakanowski Letters no. 9356; [Baka-

nowski] to Our Honorable Father General, 21 September 1868, Bakanowski Letters no. 9360; Rev. Adolf [Bakanowski] Panna Maria, Texas, to Our Dearest Father General [Rev. Jerome Kajsiewicz, Rome], 20 September 1869, Bakanowski Letters no. 9372; Dworaczyk, *First Polish Colonies*, pp. 121–122; Kruszka, *Historja polska w Ameryce*, pp. 506, 617; Zwiardowski to Honorable Reverend Father, 17 June 1868, Zwiardowski Letters no. 34702; [Zwiardowski] to Honorable Reverend Father Superior, 24 September 1868, Zwiardowski Letters no. 34703.

16. For background on the position of Częstochowa in Polish Catholicism, see Oscar Halecki, "The Place of Czestochowa in Poland's Millennium," *Catholic Historical Review* 52 (January 1967): 494–508. The local non-Silesians call it by the anglicized name Cestohowa. *Karnes City Citation*, 11 July 1974, sec. A, p. 1, 3 February 1977, sec. A, p. 1; *Nixon News* (Nixon, Texas), 23 August 1973, p. 3.

17. Dworaczyk, *First Polish Colonies*, pp. 49–50, 126–130; Joyce, *Our Polish Pioneers*, pp. 6–7; Kruszka, *Historja polska w Ameryce*, pp. 615, 622–624; M[oczygemba] to My Beloved and Dear Father Vincent, 1 September 1877, Moczygemba Letters no. 37371; Nesterowicz, *Notatki z podróży*, p. 191; Franciszek Niklewicz, *Dzieje pierwszych polskich osadników w Ameryce i przewodnik parafij polskich w Stanach Zjednoczonych*, p. 12; Bolesław Rosiński, "Polacy w Texasie," *Ziemia* 15 (1 December 1930): 477; Thomas Ruckman, "The Census Taker: A Complete Description of the County of Karnes—In South West Texas—by Thos. Ruckman June 1890," p. 39, Thomas Ruckman Papers; Rev. Felix Zwiardowski, St. Hedwig, to Dear Father Valerian, [location?], 1 September 1876, Zwiardowski Letters no. 34758.

18. Olgierd Budrewicz, "Częstochowa w Teksasie" [Częstochowa in Texas], *Przekrój* (Kraków), no. 792 (12 June 1960), pp. 5–7; *Karnes City Citation*, 11 July 1974, sec. A, p. 1; Nativity of the Blessed Virgin Mary Church, Częstochowa, Texas, weekly parish news bulletins, mimeographed, 10 January 1971, 21 November 1971, 7 July 1974; *Nixon News*, 23 August 1973, p. 3.

19. Dworaczyk, *First Polish Colonies*, pp. 136–137, 139–141; Niklewicz, *Dzieje pierwszych*, p. 12; Nesterowicz, *Notatki z podróży*, pp. 195–197; Przygoda, *Texas Pioneers*, pp. 52–53; Rosiński, "Polacy w Texasie," p. 478; St. Ann Church, Kościuszko, Texas, *Financial Report for the Year 1970 St. Ann's Church Kosciusko, Texas*, 1 lv.

20. Dworaczyk, *First Polish Colonies*, pp. 140, 150; Przygoda, *Texas Pioneers*, p. 73.

21. Dworaczyk, *First Polish Colonies*, pp. 141–148; Nesterowicz, *Notatki z podróży*, pp. 187–190, 198; Niklewicz, *Dzieje pierwszych*, p. 12; Przygoda, *Texas Pioneers*, pp. 53–55; Rosiński, "Polacy w Texasie," p. 478; Robert H. Thonhoff, "A History of Karnes County," pp. 218, 247–249.

22. Regina Haiduk, "History of the White Deer Polish Settlement," unpaged, Earl Vandale Collection.

23. Dworaczyk, *First Polish Colonies*, pp. 7, 52; *Galveston Zeitung*, 9 December 1854, p. 2; Karnes County, Texas, Deed Records, C: 6–7; Karnes County, Texas, manuscript deed for transfer of land from John Twohig to Francisca Urbanczyk and children, 21 April 1855; *Neu-Braunfelser Zeitung*, 22 December 1854, p. 3; Kingdom of Prussia, Regency of Opole, Strzelce County, release document for the obligations of Prussian subjects for the family of Jacob Urbanczyk, 5 September 1854; Jo Stewart Randel and Carson County Historical Survey Committee, eds., *A Time to Purpose: A Chronicle of Carson County*, 2:329.

24. *Amarillo Sunday News-Globe*, 14 August 1938, sec. F, p. 15; Haiduk, "History of the White Deer Polish Settlement," unpaged; Randel et al., *Time to Purpose*, 2:134–

138, 145–152, 195–197, 328–334; interview (by John Pinkham), Rosie Urbanczyk, White Deer, Texas, 17 June 1974, typescript, pp. 1–2.

25. Randel et al., *Time to Purpose*, 2:146–147; interview, R. Urbanczyk, 17 June 1974, pp. 1–3 (Pinkham).

26. Dworaczyk, *First Polish Colonies*, pp. 152–155; Haiduk, "History of the White Deer Polish Settlement," unpaged; Randel et al., *Time to Purpose*, 1:259–260, 265, 2:146–147, 332, 334; [Sacred Heart Church, White Deer], "Polish Sausage Supper Work List—1973—White Deer, Texas," mimeographed, 1 lv.

27. [Bakanowski] and [Zwiardowski] to Our Dearest Father Superior, 1 March 1867, Bakanowski Letters no. 9336; [Zwiardowski] to Dear Reverend Father, 12 November 1866, Zwiardowski Letters no. 34690; [Cleric] Felix Zwiardowski, Panna Maria, Texas, to Dearest Reverend Father, [location?], 27 November 1866, Zwiardowski Letters no. 34691; Zwiardowski to Our Dear Reverend Father, 28 December 1866, Zwiardowski Letters no. 34692; [Cleric] Felix Zwiardowski, Panna Maria, Texas, to Our Dear Reverend Father [Rev. Alexander Jełowicki, Paris], 17 January 1867, Zwiardowski Letters no. 34693; Rev. Felix Zwiardowski, Panna Maria, to Reverend Father General [Rev. Jerome Kajsiewicz, Rome], 18 July 1871, Zwiardowski Letters no. 34712; U.S., Immigration Commission, *Immigrants in Industries (in Twenty-five Parts); Part 24: Recent Immigrants in Agriculture (in Two Volumes)*, 2:364.

28. [Bakanowski] and [Zwiardowski] to Our Dearest Father Superior, 1 March 1867, Bakanowski Letters no. 9336; Zwiardowski to Our Dear Reverend Father, 28 December 1866, Zwiardowski Letters no. 34692; [Bakanowski] to Our Dear Father Alexander, 7 July 1868, Bakanowski Letters no. 9358; Zwiardowski to Reverend Father General, 31 January 1870, Zwiardowski Letters no. 34704; Kruszka, *Historja polska w Ameryce*, p. 612; Nesterowicz, *Notatki z podróży*, p. 185.

29. [Bakanowski] and [Zwiardowski] to Our Dearest Father Superior, 1 March 1867, Bakanowski Letters no. 9336; Barzyński to Reverend Father General et al., last days of 1866 and first days of 1867, Barzyński Letters no. 8945; [Barzyński] to Most Reverend Father General et al., Day of the Five Wounds 1867, Barzyński Letters no. 8949; Rev. Vincent [Barzyński], San Antonio, to Most Reverend Father General [Rev. Jerome Kajsiewicz], Most Reverend and Dearest Fathers Peter [Semenenko], Alexander [Jełowicki], and Julian, Dear Fathers of Our Order, and Dear Brothers, [Rome], 19 May 1867, Barzyński Letters no. 8952; Kruszka, *Historja polska w Ameryce*, pp. 500, 610; Zwiardowski to Our Dear Reverend Father, 28 December 1866, Zwiardowski Letters no. 34692; Rev. [Stanisław] Wojciechowski, St. Hedwig, to Most Reverend Father, [location?], 13 February 1876, Wojciechowski Letters no. 45090; Chester Thomas Kochan, "The Polish People of San Antonio, Texas, 1900–1960: A Study in Social Mobility," pp. 17–21.

30. Zwiardowski to Our Dear Reverend Father, 28 December 1866, Zwiardowski Letters no. 34692; [Bakanowski] and [Zwiardowski] to Our Dearest Father Superior, 1 March 1867, Bakanowski Letters no. 9336; Kruszka, *Historja polska w Ameryce*, p. 503; Parisot and Smith, *Catholic Church in the Diocese of San Antonio*, p. 128; Nesterowicz, *Notatki z podróży*, p. 184.

31. [Bakanowski] and [Zwiardowski] to Our Dearest Father Superior, 1 March 1867, Bakanowski Letters no. 9336; Parisot and Smith, *Catholic Church in the Diocese of San Antonio*, p. 187; Nesterowicz, *Notatki z podróży*, pp. 191, 210, 214.

32. Dworaczyk, *First Polish Colonies*, p. 132; Nesterowicz, *Notatki z podróży*, pp. 191, 192.

33. Dworaczyk, *First Polish Colonies*, p. 143; Nesterowicz, *Notatki z podróży*, p. 189; U.S., Immigration Commission, *Recent Immigrants in Agriculture*, 2:364.

34. Dworaczyk, *First Polish Colonies*, p. 136; Nesterowicz, *Notatki z podróży*, p. 196; U.S., Immigration Commission, *Recent Immigrants in Agriculture*, 2:364.

35. Randel et al., *Time to Purpose*, 2:245–246.

36. Joyce, *Our Polish Pioneers*, pp. 19, 35–36; Wozniak, "St. Michael's Church," pp. 72–79; Zwiardowski to Reverend Father General, 31 January 1870, Zwiardowski Letters no. 34704.

37. Rev. V[incent] Barzyński, San Antonio, to Most Reverend Father General [Rev. Jerome Kajsiewicz, Rome], 28 March 1872, Barzyński Letters no. 8988; interview, Mary Mika, 11 August 1973 (KB); [Leon Orłowski], "Polacy w Texasie," [New York, May 1920], typescript, p. 16, Republic of Poland, Ministry of Foreign Affairs, Embassy in Washington, Document Registration no. 1493, File no. 979, Embassy of the Republic of Poland in Washington Collection; Wozniak, "St. Michael's Church," pp. 72–74, 77–79.

38. J. W. Baker, *A History of Robertson County, Texas*, p. 397; Edmund L. Kowalczyk, "Jottings from the Polish American Past," p. 39; Nesterowicz, *Notatki z podróży*, pp. 142, 144.

39. *Houston Chronicle*, 13 November 1932, p. 8; interview, Clem Kaczmarek, Panna Maria, Texas, 10 August 1973 (KB); interview, Mrs. Mary Lyssy, Panna Maria, 10 August 1973; interview, F. V. Snoga, 27 December 1972.

40. *Czas*, 12 May 1858, p. 2; *Przegląd Poznański*, July 1858, p. 86.

41. Bakanowski to Our Dearest Father Superior, 13 November 1866, Bakanowski Letters no. 9330; Bakanowski to Dearest Father Peter, 20 November 1866, Bakanowski Letters no. 9331; [Zwiardowski] to Dear Reverend Father, 12 November 1866, Zwiardowski Letters no. 34690.

42. Rev. Adolf Bak[anowski], Panna Maria, to Our Dearest Father Superior [Rev. Jerome Kajsiewicz, Rome], 17 January 1867, Bakanowski Letters no. 9334.

43. Dworaczyk, *First Polish Colonies*, pp. 38–39. The primitive but effective method used by the Silesian peasants to burn lime for mortar is interesting. The farmers dug one or more pits in the ground, eight feet deep and six to ten feet square. In the pits they placed alternating layers of lime-rich caliche rocks and live-oak timbers. After filling the pits, they ignited the wood and allowed it to burn until the embers went out. They then removed the caliche and crushed it to mix with sand to make mortar. Interview, Ben P. Urbanczyk, 10 August 1973 (KB).

44. [Zwiardowski] to Reverend Father General, 9 May 1870, Zwiardowski Letters no. 34705.

45. [Bakanowski] to Dear Father Alexander, 27 May 1868, Bakanowski Letters no. 9356.

46. [Bakanowski] to Dear Father Alexander, 6 November 1868, Bakanowski Letters no. 9362; [Bakanowski] to Honorable Father General, 1 December 1868, Bakanowski Letters no. 9363; Rev. Adolf [Bakanowski], Panna Maria, to Dear Father Peter [Semenenko, Rome]. 16–20 January 1869, Bakanowski Letters no. 9365; [Bakanowski] to [unidentified addressee, location?], 13 February 1869, Bakanowski Letters no. 9367; Rev. Adolf [Bakanowski], Panna Maria, to Our Honorable Father General [Rev. Jerome Kajsiewicz, Rome], 22 May 1869, Bakanowski Letters no. 9369.

47. Bakanowski to Our Dearest Father Peter, 20 November 1866, Bakanowski Letters no. 9331.

48. [Bakanowski] to Honorable Father General, 1 December 1868, Bakanowski Letters no. 9363; Dworaczyk, *First Polish Colonies*, p. 21; Zwiardowski to Our Dear Reverend Father, 28 December 1866, Zwiardowski Letters no. 34692.

49. Zwiardowski to Our Dear Reverend Father, 17 January 1867, Zwiardowski Letters no. 34693.

50. Rev. Felix Zwiardowski, Galveston, to Dearest Father Alexander [Jełowicki, Paris], 23 April 1867, Zwiardowski Letters no. 34694.

51. Zwiardowski to Dearest Reverend Father Superior, 16 May 1867, Zwiardowski Letters no. 34695.

52. Bakanowski to Dearest Father Peter, 28 June 1867, Bakanowski Letters no. 9344; Bakanowski, *Moje wspomnienia*, pp. 160–161; St. Mary Church, Sulisławice, Baptismal Records (8 January 1826–30 December 1838), p. 182.

53. Bakanowski, *Moje wspomnienia*, pp. 27–28; Kruszka, *Historja polska w Ameryce*, pp. 494–495.

54. Rev. Adolf [Bakanowski], Panna Maria, to Dear Father Alexander [Jełowicki, Paris], 15 October 1868, Bakanowski Letters no. 9361; [Bakanowski] to Dear Father Alexander, 6 November 1868, Bakanowski Letters no. 9362; Rev. Adolf [Bakanowski], Panna Maria, to Our Dear Father Alexander [Jełowicki, Paris], 22 January 1869, Bakanowski Letters no. 9366.

55. Rev. Adolf [Bakanowski], Panna Maria, to Our Dear Father Alexander [Jełowicki, Paris], 8 April 1869, Bakanowski Letters no. 9368; [Bakanowski] to Our Honorable Father General, 22 May 1869, Bakanowski Letters no. 9369; Rev. Adolf Baka[nowski], Panna Maria, to Our Dear Father Peter [Semenenko, Rome], 9–13 July 1869, Bakanowski Letters no. 9370.

56. [Zwiardowski] to Honorable Reverend Father Superior, 24 September 1868, Zwiardowski Letters no. 34703.

57. Baka[nowski] to Our Dear Father Peter, 9–13 July 1869, Bakanowski Letters no. 9370; [Bakanowski] to Our Dearest Father General, 5 July 1870, Bakanowski Letters no. 9382.

58. [Bakanowski] to Our Dearest Father General, 9 May 1870, Bakanowski Letters no. 9378; [Bakanowski] to Our Dearest Father General, 5 July 1870, Bakanowski Letters no. 9382; Barzyński to Most Reverend Father General, 17 March 1872, Barzyński Letters no. 8987; Kruszka, *Historja polska w Ameryce*, pp. 496–497.

59. [Cleric] Adolf Snigurski, Bordeaux, [France], to [unidentified addressee, location?], 26 December 1865, Snigurski Letters no. 44626.1; [Cleric] Adolf Snigurski, San Antonio, to Most Reverend Father, [location?], 17 August 1871, Snigurski Letters no. 44630.1; Rev. Felix Zwiardowski, Panna Maria, Tex[as], to Very Reverend Father [Bishop Claude-Marie Dubuis, Galveston], 10 September 1871, Zwiardowski Letters no. 34718.

60. Rev. Vincent [Barzyński], San Antonio, to Most Reverend Father, [location?], 28 July 1869, Barzyński Letters no. 8962; Rev. Vincent [Barzyński], Bandera, to Most Reverend Father Alexander [Jełowicki, Paris], 9 May 1870, Barzyński Letters no. 8966; Rev. Vincent [Barzyński], San Antonio, Texas, to Most Reverend Father General [Rev. Jerome Kajsiewicz, Rome], 5 September 1870, Barzyński Letters no. 8971.

61. Zwiardowski to Reverend Father General, 19 August 1871, Zwiardowski Letters no. 34714; Zwiardowski to Reverend Father, 30 August 1871, Zwiardowski Letters no. 34716; [Zwiardowski] to Reverend Father General, 2 October 1871, Zwiardowski Letters no. 34719.

62. John Barzyński to Reverend Father General, 10 June 1872, John Barzyński

Letters no. 45298; [Barzyński] to Most Reverend Father General, 2 March 1872, Barzyński Letters no. 8986; [Zwiardowski] to Reverend Father General, 13 March 1873, Zwiardowski Letters no. 34724. For an examination of the later life of John Barzyński, see Meroe J. Owens, "John Barzynski, Land Agent," *Nebraska History* 36 (June 1955): 81–91.

63. [Bakanowski] to Our Dearest Father Alexander, 11 September 1867, Bakanowski Letters no. 9346; [Bakanowski] to [*Zwiastun Górnoszlązki*], 6 June 1870, *Zwiastun Górnoszlązki*, 7 July 1870, p. 216.

64. Rev. Felix Zwiardowski, Panna Maria, to Reverend Father General [Rev. Jerome Kajsiewicz, Rome], 2 February 1873, Zwiardowski Letters no. 34723; [Zwiardowski] to Reverend Father General, 13 March 1873, Zwiardowski Letters no. 34724; Rev. Felix Zwiardowski, St. Hedwig, Texas, to Most Reverend Father, [location?], 24 March 1875, Zwiardowski Letters no. 34741.

65. Dworaczyk, *First Polish Colonies*, pp. 46, 48; Zwiardowski to Reverend Father General, 2 February 1873, Zwiardowski Letters no. 34723; [Zwiardowski] to Reverend Father General, 13 March 1873, Zwiardowski Letters no. 34724; Rev. Felix Zwiardowski, Panna Maria, to Dear Father Adolf [Bakanowski, Paris], 20 April 1875, Zwiardowski Letters no. 34743. The five Silesian girls who entered the Divine Providence Convent where Albina Musioł (Sister Maria Kazimierz), Cecylia Felix (Sister Stanisław Kostka), Paulina Urbanczyk (Sister Maria Jadwiga), Kunegunda Krawietz (Sister Maria Bronisława), and Barbara Krawietz (Sister Maria Kunegunda). Zwiardowski to [Bakanowski], 20 April 1875, Zwiardowski Letters no. 34743.

66. Dworaczyk, *First Polish Colonies*, pp. 48–49; Iwicki, *First One Hundred Years*, pp. 34–35; Zwiardowski to Most Reverend Father, 24 March 1875, Zwiardowski Letters no. 34741; Zwiardowski to Dear Father Adolf, 20 April 1875, Zwiardowski Letters no. 34743.

67. Dworaczyk, *First Polish Colonies*, pp. 48–49, 54, 115, 122; Zwiardowski to Most Reverend Father, 24 March 1875, Zwiardowski Letters no. 34741; Rev. Felix Zwiardowski, San Antonio, to Most Reverend Father General [Rev. Peter Semenenko, Rome], 14 April 1875, Zwiardowski Letters no. 34742; Zwiardowski to Dear Father Adolf, 20 April 1875, Zwiardowski Letters no. 34743; [Zwiardowski] to Dear Father Adolf, 17 August 1875, Zwiardowski Letters no. 34747; [Zwiardowski] to Honorable Father Adolf, 2 March 1876, Zwiardowski Letters no. 34751.

68. [Bakanowski] to Our Honorable Father General, 22 May 1869, Bakanowski Letters no. 9369.

69. [Bakanowski] to Dear Father Peter, 16–20 January 1869, Bakanowski Letters no. 9365.

70. [Editor] to Our Brothers in Christ Who Live in Texas, [24 March 1870], *Zwiastun Górnoszlązki*, 24 March 1870, p. 96.

71. Dworaczyk, *First Polish Colonies*, pp. 54–56; Przygoda, *Texas Pioneers*, p. 48.

72. Ruckman, "Census Taker," p. 45.

73. Dworaczyk, *First Polish Colonies*, p. 63; Wincenty Lutosławski, "Odrodzenie Śląska w Texasie" [The Rebirth of Silesia in Texas], *Świat* (Warsaw, Russian Empire) 3 (28 November 1908): 8–9, and (5 December 1908): 13; Nesterowicz, *Notatki z podróży*, p. 192; U.S., Immigration Commission, *Recent Immigrants in Agriculture*, 2:364. The Lutosławski article cited here was reprinted in Wincenty Lutosławski, *Iskierki warszawskie* [Warsaw Sparks], pp. 232–251.

74. Interview, John Kotara, Sr., White Deer, ca. 1965, cited in Randel et al., *A Time to Purpose*, 2:195–196.

75. Dworaczyk, *The Centennial History of Panna Maria, Texas*, p. 90; Dworaczyk, *First Polish Colonies*, pp. 69, 77; Dworaczyk, *The Millennium History of Panna Maria, Texas*, pp. 90, 103; Przygoda, *Texas Pioneers*, p. 48. For a secondary account of St. Joseph's School at Panna Maria, see Andrzej Brożek, "Najstarsza polska szkoła w Stanach Zjednoczonych Ameryki," *Przegląd Historyczno-Oświatowy* 14 (1971): 60–73.

76. Rev. Adolf [Bakanowski], Panna Maria, Texas, to Our Honorable Father General [Rev. Jerome Kajsiewicz, Rome], 4 November 1869, Bakanowski Letters no. 9373; Bakanowski, *Moje wspomnienia*, p. 58; Rev. Felix Zwiardowski, Martinez, to Dearest Reverend Father Alexander [Jełowicki, Paris], 9 July 1867, Zwiardowski Letters no. 34697; Zwiardowski to Very Reverend Father, 10 September 1871, Zwiardowski Letters no. 34718.

77. Rev. Vincent [Barzyński], San Antonio, to Most Reverend Father, Rome, 20 November 1872, Barzyński Letters no. 8992; Rev. Vincent [Barzyński], San Antonio, to Most Reverend General [Rev. Jerome Kajsiewicz], Rome, 10 March 1873, Barzyński Letters no. 8993; Rev. Vincent [Barzyński], San Antonio, to Most Reverend Father, Rome, 31 May 1873, Barzyński Letters no. 8995; Rev. Vincent [Barzyński], Martinez, to Most Reverend Father, Rome, 15 July 1873, Barzyński Letters no. 8996; Rev. Vincent [Barzyński], Martinez, to Most Reverend Father General [Rev. Peter Semenenko, Rome], 27 September 1873, Barzyński Letters no. 8998; Rev. Vincent [Barzyński], San Antonio, to Most Reverend Father General [Rev. Peter Semenenko, Rome], 2 December 1873, Barzyński Letters no. 9000; Rev. Vincent [Barzyński], San Antonio, to Most Reverend and Dearest Father, [location?], 10 January 1874, Barzyński Letters no. 9001; Rev. Vincent [Barzyński], Panna Maria, to Most Reverend and Dearest Father, Rome, 17 January 1874, Barzyński Letters no. 9002; [Barzyński] to Dearest Most Reverend Father, 4 March 1874, Barzyński Letters no. 9004; Rev. Vincent [Barzyński], San Antonio, to Most Reverend Dearest Father, Rome, 10 March 1874, Barzynsi Letters no. 9005; Dworaczyk, *First Polish Colonies*, p. 114; Kruszka, *Historja polska w Ameryce*, pp. 614–615.

78. Dworaczyk, *First Polish Colonies*, pp. 115–117; S. A. Iciek, *Samochodem przez stany południowe*, p. 226; Nesterowicz, *Notatki z podróży*, p. 185.

79. [Barzyński] to Most Reverend Father Alexander, 25 September 1867, Barzyński Letters no. 8972; [Barzyński] to Most Reverend Father General, Autumn 1867, Barzyński Letters no. 8951; [Rev. Vincent Barzyński, location?], to Dearest Father General [Rev. Jerome Kajsiewicz, Rome, ca. 1867], letter misfiled in Bakanowski Letters no. 9350; [Barzyński] to Most Reverend Father General, 5 August 1868, Barzyński Letters no. 8958; [Barzyński] to Most Reverend Father Superior et al., 27 February 1869, Barzyński Letters no. 8955; Dworaczyk, *First Polish Colonies*, pp. 91–94; Joyce, *Our Polish Pioneers*, pp. 23–24; Kruszka, *Historja polska w Ameryce*, p. 610; Nesterowicz, *Notatki z podróży*, p. 179; Parisot and Smith, *Catholic Church in the Diocese of San Antonio*, p. 181; Przygoda, *Texas Pioneers*, p. 26; Wozniak, "St. Michael's Church," pp. 35–36, 45–46.

80. Dworaczyk, *First Polish Colonies*, pp. 120–126; Nesterowicz, *Notatki z podróży*, p. 210.

81. Dworaczyk, *First Polish Colonies*, pp. 104–106; Kruszka, *Historja polska w Ameryce*, p. 612; Rev. Felix Zwiardowski, St. Hedwig, to Dear Father, [location?], 28 December 1876, Zwiardowski Letters no. 34763.

82. Dworaczyk, *First Polish Colonies*, pp. 131–133, 135; Iciek, *Samochodem*, p. 227; Kruszka, *Historja polska w Ameryce*, p. 622; Lutosławski, "Odrodzenie Śląska," p. 13; Nesterowicz, *Notatki z podróży*, p. 192.

83. Dworaczyk, *First Polish Colonies*, pp. 145, 148.

84. Ibid., pp. 136, 139–141; Lutosławski, "Odrodzenie Śląska," p. 13; Nesterowicz, *Notatki z podróży*, pp. 196–197; Aleksander Szczepański, *Drapacze i śmietniki: Wrażenia amerykańskle*, pp. 187–188.

Chapter 7. The Silesian Way of Life in Texas

1. Both Polish and American observers agreed that the Silesians lived in a society apart from their neighbors. Adolf Bakanowski, *Moje wspomnienia 1840-1863-1913*, p. 30; Edward J. Dworaczyk, *The First Polish Colonies of America in Texas*, p. 37; LeRoy Hodges, "The Poles of Texas," *Texas Magazine* 7 (December 1912): 120; LeRoy Hodges, *Slavs on Southern Farms: An Account of the Bohemian, Slovak, and Polish Agricultural Settlements in the Southern States*, p. 11; Bolesław Rosiński, "Polacy w Texasie," *Ziemia* 15 (1 December 1930): 477; U.S., Immigration Commission, *Immigrants in Industries (in Twenty-Five Parts); Part 24: Recent Immigrants in Agriculture (in Two Volumes)*, 2:361.

2. T. Lindsay Baker, "Panna Maria and Płużnica: A Study in Comparative Folk Culture," in *The Folklore of Texan Cultures*, ed. Francis Edward Abernethy, pp. 221–222; Dworaczyk, *First Polish Colonies*, p. 82; interview, Mary Mika, 11 August 1973 (KB); interview, Mrs. Ella Snoga, Panna Maria, 11 August 1973 (KB). For further information on baptismal customs among the Silesians, see Sister Jan Maria Wozniak, "St. Michael's Church: The Polish National Catholic Church in San Antonio, Texas, 1855–1950," pp. 57–58.

3. [Bakanowski] to Dear Father Peter, 16–20 January 1869, Bakanowski Letters no. 9365; [Bakanowski] to Our Honorable Father General, 22 May 1869, Bakanowski Letters no. 9369; Dworaczyk, *First Polish Colonies*, p. 81; Hodges, "Poles of Texas," p. 120; Wincenty Lutosławski, "Odrodzenie Śląska w Texasie," *Świat* 3 (28 November 1908): 8, 13; [Leon Orłowski], "Polacy w Texasie," p. 13.

4. Interview, John Kotara, ca. 1965, cited in Jo Stewart Randel and Carson County Historical Survey Committee, eds., *A Time to Purpose: A Chronicle of Carson County*, 2:195; Jacek Przygoda, *Texas Pioneers from Poland: A Study in the Ethnic History*, p. 159; *St. Stanislaus Parish, Bandera, Texas, Centennial History, 1855–1955*, p. 29.

5. J. Marvin Hunter, "When the Polish People Came to Bandera," *Frontier Times* 25 (May 1948): 194; Stefan Nesterowicz, *Notatki z podróży po północnej i środkowej Ameryce*, p. 189.

6. Thomas Ruckman, "The Census Taker: A Complete Description of the County of Karnes—In South West Texas—by Thos. Ruckman June 1890," pp. 39–40, Thomas Ruckman Papers.

7. Interview, M. Mika, 11 August 1973 (KB); Randel et al., *Time to Purpose*, 2:147, 151; interview, Rosie Urbanczyk, 17 June 1974, p. 6 (Pinkham); Wozniak, "St. Michael's Church," pp. 58–61.

8. Nativity of the Blessed Virgin Mary Church, Częstochowa, Texas, weekly parish news bulletins, mimeographed, 21 November 1971, 7 July 1974; St. Ann Church, Kościuszko, Texas, weekly parish news bulletin, mimeographed, 10 January 1971.

9. *Karnes City Citation*, 12 July 1973, sec. A, p. 4, 29 January 1976, sec. A, p. 4, 5 February 1976, sec. A, p. 4, 8 April 1976, sec. A, p. 2, 17 June 1976, sec. A, p. 4, 1 July 1976, sec. A, p. 5, 8 July 1976, sec. A, p. 5; interview, M. Mika, 11 August 1973 (KB).

10. Dworaczyk, *First Polish Colonies*, p. 81; John William Mullally, "A Study of

Marriage Patterns in a Rural Polish Roman-Catholic Parish from 1872 to 1959" (master's thesis, University of Texas, 1963), pp. 74–84. For evidence that the changes in marriage patterns documented in Yorktown are similar to the patterns in the other Silesian colonies, valuable sources are obituaries that give information on the survivors of the deceased persons. For examples see *Karnes City Citation*, 22 January 1976, sec. A, p. 1, 29 January 1976, sec. A, p. 4, 26 February 1976, sec. A, p. 1, 25 March 1976, sec. A, p. 1, 1 April 1976, sec. A, p. 4.

11. Dworaczyk, *First Polish Colonies*, p. 81; Mullally, "Study of Marriage Patterns," pp. 88–95.

12. Bakanowski to Our Dearest Father Superior, 13 November 1866, Bakanowski Letters no. 9330; Lutosławski, "Odrodzenie Śląska," p. 13.

13. Rev. Adolf [Bakanowski], Bandera, to Our Honorable Father General [Rev. Jerome Kajsiewicz, Rome], 28 June 1868, Bakanowski Letters no. 9357; Mullally, "Study of Marriage Patterns," pp. 84–88, 129.

14. Dworaczyk, *First Polish Colonies*, pp. 81–82; Texas, Comptroller of Public Accounts, F. T. Moczygemba, Texas Confederate Pension Application no. 19812, 31 October 1910; Aleksander Szczepański, *Drapacze i śmietniki: Wrażenia amerykańskie*, pp. 189–190. For photographs of typical Silesian grave markers in Texas, see T. Lindsay Baker, *The Early History of Panna Maria, Texas*, p. 27; Andrzej Brożek, *Ślązacy w Teksasie: Relacje o najstarszych polskich osadach w Stanach Zjednoczonych*, p. 196; Andrzej Brożek, *Jeszcze jeden list z Teksasu do Płużnicy z roku 1855*, plate opp. p. 13; Jan Erdman, "Opisanie Panny Marii, najstarszej osady polskiej w USA" [Description of Panna Maria, the Oldest Polish Colony in the U.S.A.], *Ameryka* (Washington, D.C.), no. 159 (April 1972), p. 41; Przygoda, *Texas Pioneers*, unpaged illustration section.

15. A typical instance of this form of inheritance in Upper Silesia was the father of Rev. Leopold Moczygemba, who when he grew old gave everything that he had to his children and lived with them until his death in 1869. St. Stanisław Church, Płużnica, Poland, Death Records (9 February 1847–27 December 1890), pp. 135–136.

16. *Galveston Zeitung*, 9 December 1854, p. 2; interview, Kotara, ca. 1965, in Randel et al., *Time to Purpose*, 2:196; *Neu-Braunfelser Zeitung*, 22 December 1854, p. 3; Kingdom of Prussia, Regency of Opole, Strzelce County, release document for the obligations of Prussian subjects for the family of Jacob Urbanczyk, 5 September 1854; Kingdom of Prussia, Regency of Opole, Strzelce County, release document for the obligations of Prussian subjects for the family of Johann Pycka [John Pyka], 31 July 1854; John Pyka and Franciszka Pyka, last will and testament, Bandera, Texas, 1 June 1888; Tom Urbanczyk, Texas Confederate Pension Application no. 30514, 18 January 1915.

17. Bakanowski, *Moje wspomnienia*, pp. 37–39; *Gwiazdka Cieszyńska*, 26 July 1856, p. 236.

18. [Bakanowski] to [*Zwiastun Górnoszlązki*], 6 June 1870, *Zwiastun Górnoszlązki*, 7 July 1870, p. 216.

19. Barzyński to Most Reverend Father General et al., last days of 1866 and beginning of 1867, Barzyński Letters no. 8947; Barzyński to Most Reverend Father General, 28 March 1872, Barzyński Letters no. 8988; Dworaczyk, *First Polish Colonies*, pp. 93–96; John A. Joyce, *Our Polish Pioneers*, pp. 13–14, 29; John Iwicki, *The First One Hundred Years: A Study of the Apostolate of the Congregation of the Resurrection in the United States 1866–1966*, pp. 37–38; Nesterowicz, *Notatki z podróży*, p. 179; *The Polish Texans*, p. 14; Przygoda, *Texas Pioneers*, pp. 26–30; Szczepański, *Drapacze i śmietniki*, pp. 180–181; Rev. Felix Zwiardowski, Częstochowa, Texas, to My Most

Reverend and Dearest Father, [location?], 18 April 1888, Zwiardowski Letters no. 34780.

20. Baka[nowski] to Our Dear Father Peter, 9–13 July 1869, Bakanowski Letters no. 9370; Dworaczyk, *First Polish Colonies*, pp. 62–63, 116, 146; Rev. Felix Zwiardowski, Panna Maria, Texas, to Most Reverend and Dear Father, [location?], 27 October 1879, Zwiardowski Letters no. 34776.

21. Przygoda, *Texas Pioneers*, pp. 29, 43, 58; Szczepański, *Drapacze i śmietniki*, pp. 181–183.

22. Bakanowski, *Moje wspomnienia*, p. 32; Wacław Kruszka, *Historja polska w Ameryce*, p. 488; interview, M. Mika, 10 August 1973 (KB); Randel et al., *Time to Purpose*, 2:147; interview, E. Snoga, 11 August 1973 (KB); interview, Urbanczyk, 11 June 1974, pp. 5–6 (Pinkham).

23. Bakanowski to Our Dearest Father Peter, 28 June 1867, Bakanowski Letters no. 9344; interview, Kotara, ca. 1965, in Randel et al., *Time to Purpose*, 2:195; interview, Urbanczyk, 10 August 1973 (KB).

24. Bakanowski, *Moje wspomnienia*, pp. 48, 161; Dworaczyk, *First Polish Colonies*, p. 82; "Hej Kolęda Polish Christmas Carols," mimeographed [Christmas carols sung by church choir at Panna Maria, Texas, 1970]; J. Marvin Hunter, "Old Time Barbecues in Bandera County," *Frontier Times* 19 (June 1942): 326–327; Kruszka, *Historja polska w Ameryce*, pp. 488, 494, 497; Lutosławski, "Odrodzenie Śląska," p. 13; Franciszek Niklewicz, *Dzieje pierwszych polskich osadników w Ameryce i przewodnik parafij polskich w Stanach Zjednoczonych*, pp. 12–13; Orłowski, "Polacy w Texasie," pp. 17–18; Randel et al., *Time to Purpose*, 2:147, 196; Melchior Wańkowicz, *Atlantyk-Pacyfik*, p. 207; Wojciechowski to Most Reverend Father, 13 February 1876, Wojciechowski Letters no. 45090; [Zwiardowski] to Dear Reverend Father, 12 November 1866, Zwiardowski Letters no. 34690; Zwiardowski to Dearest Reverend Father, 27 November 1866, Zwiardowski Letters no. 34691; Zwiardowski to Our Dear Reverend Father, 28 December 1866, Zwiardowski Letters no. 34692.

25. Dworaczyk, *First Polish Colonies*, p. 130; Kruszka, *Historja polska w Ameryce*, p. 624; James P. McGuire, Institute of Texan Cultures, San Antonio, Texas, to T. Lindsay Baker, Wrocław, Poland, 25 March 1976; James P. McGuire, Institute of Texan Cultures, San Antonio, Texas, to T. Lindsay Baker, Wrocław, Poland, 30 September 1976; Rosiński, "Polacy w Texasie," p. 477; Cecilia Steinfeldt and Donald L. Stover, *Early Texas Furniture and Decorative Arts*, pp. 236–237, 260.

26. [Bakanowski] to [*Zwiastun Górnoszlązki*], 6 June 1870, *Zwiastun Górnoszlązki*, 7 July 1870, p. 216; Orłowski, "Polacy w Texasie," p. 12; U.S., Census of 1860, Texas, Population Schedules, Bandera, Bexar, and Karnes counties; U.S., Census of 1870, Texas, Population Schedules, Bandera, Bexar, and Karnes counties; *Zwiastun Górnoszlązki*, 8 July 1869, p. 228. The fourteen Silesians whose economic fortunes were studied were Anton Anderwald, Valentine Anderwald, and Albert Haiduk, of Bandera County; Jacob Halamuda, Anton Moczygemba, and Florian Mushall, of Bexar County; and Albert Czerner, John Gawlik, Frank Josko, Albert Lyssy, Frank Lyssy, Jacob Lyssy, John Lyssy, and John Moczygemba, of Karnes County. These persons were selected by the author as representative individuals who could be traced from one census to the other.

27. Charles Merritt Barnes, *Combats and Conquests of Immortal Heroes*, pp. 130, 134; Frank W. Johnson and Eugene C. Barker, *A History of Texas and Texans*, 3:1237; Joyce, *Our Polish Pioneers*, pp. 13, 29; Jacek Przygoda, "New Light on the Poles in Texas," *Polish American Studies* 27 (Spring–Autumn 1970): 83–84; Przygoda, *Texas*

Pioneers, pp. 26, 30, 90–91; *A Twentieth Century History of Southwest Texas*, 1:191–193. Edward Kotula should not be confused with his contemporary, the south Texas rancher Joseph Cotulla.

28. Chester Thomas Kochan, "The Polish People of San Antonio, Texas, 1900–1960: A Study in Social Mobility," pp. 22–23, 28, 34.

29. For various accounts of the life of Martin Mróz, see J. Evetts Haley, *Jeff Milton: A Good Man with a Gun*, pp. 228–243; Dee Harkey, *Mean as Hell*, pp. 113–133; Leon Claire Metz, *John Selman: Texas Gunfighter*, pp. 161–167; C. L. Sonnichsen, *Pass of the North*, pp. 320–330. Mróz's surname was phonetically spelled several ways by the Americans, but usually as M'Rose or McRose.

30. [Bakanowski] to Our Honorable Father General, 9 April 1868, Bakanowski Letters no. 9352; Hodges, "Poles of Texas," p. 120; U.S., Immigration Commission, *Recent Immigrants in Agriculture*, 2:364–365; Rev. Felix Zwiardowski, Panna Maria, to Most Reverend Father, [location?], 6 February 1879, Zwiardowski Letters no. 34773.

31. Orłowski, "Polacy w Texasie," pp. 21–22; *San Antonio Daily Express*, 14 July 1910, p. 8; *Twentieth Century History*, 1:189–191; U.S., Immigration Commission, *Recent Immigrants in Agriculture*, 2:361.

32. Dworaczyk, *First Polish Colonies*, p. 28; Nesterowicz, *Notatki z podróży*, p. 182; *San Antonio Daily Express*, 7 July 1910, p. 14; *San Antonio Express*, 2 October 1867, p. 3.

33. T. Lindsay Baker, "The Moczygemba Family of Texas and Poland: Initiators of Polish Colonization in Texas," *Stirpes: Texas State Genealogical Society Quarterly* 15 (December 1975): 132; Dworaczyk, *First Polish Colonies*, pp. 12, 18; interview, Rev. Henry Moczygemba, Polish American Historical Association Convention, New Orleans, La., 27 December 1972; interview, LeRoy Moczygemba, 6 December 1974; Mullally, "Study of Marriage Patterns," pp. 10–11; Nesterowicz, *Notatki z podróży*, p. 184; Randel et al., *Time to Purpose*, 2:195; Rosiński, "Polacy w Texasie," p. 477; Lillie Terrell Shaver and Willie Williamson Rogers, *Flashlights on Texas*, pp. 137–138; U.S., Census of 1860, Texas, Population Schedules, Bexar and Karnes counties; interview, Urbanczyk, 10 August 1973 (KB).

34. Barzyński to Most Reverend Father General et al., last days of 1866 and beginning of 1867, Barzyński Letters no. 8947; Dworaczyk, *First Polish Colonies*, pp. 120–121; Nesterowicz, *Notatki z podróży*, pp. 180, 189. It is interesting to note that the Silesians, as a former Prussian subjects, shared the joy of the Texas Germans over the Prussian defeat of France in the Franco-Prussian War. Rev. Felix Zwiardowski, Panna Maria, to Reverend Father General [Rev. Jerome Kajsiewicz, Rome], 17 August 1870, Zwiardowski Letters no. 34706.

35. Bakanowski, *Moje wspomnienia*, p. 56; *Galveston Zeitung*, 9 December 1854, p. 2; J. Marvin Hunter, *A Brief History of Bandera County*, pp. 60–61; *Neu-Braunfelser Zeitung*, 22 December 1854, p. 3; Zwiardowski to Reverend Father General, 2 February 1873, Zwiardowski Letters no. 34723.

36. Dworaczyk, *First Polish Colonies*, p. 82; S. A. Iciek, *Samochodem przez stany południowe*, p. 228; Lutosławski, "Odrodzenie Śląska," pp. 8, 13; Nesterowicz, *Notatki z podróży*, pp. 210, 220–221; Niklewicz, *Dzieje pierwszych*, pp. 12–13; Orłowski, "Polacy w Texasie," pp. 9, 16–18; Rosiński, "Polacy w Texasie," pp. 476–477; Szczepański, *Drapacze i śmietniki*, p. 118; U.S., Immigration Commission, *Recent Immigrants in Agriculture*, 2:364; Jacek Wnęk, "Ślązacy w Texasie" [Silesians in Texas], *Powstaniec* (Katowice, Poland) 11 (15 February 1937): 29.

37. Bakanowski to Dear Father Alexander, 14 May 1867, Bakanowski Letters no.

9339; [Barzyński] to Most Reverend Father General et al., 10 May 1867, Barzyński Letters no. 8952; Rev. Vincent [Barzyński], Panna Maria, to Our Most Reverend Father General [Rev. Jerome Kajsiewicz, Rome], 15 December 1867, Barzyński Letters no. 8954; Rev. Felix Orzechowski, San Antonio, Texas, to Reverend Father, [location?], 15 February 1867, Orzechowski Letters no. 44037. For a rare example of the Silesian-dialect devotional aids of the kind wanted by the colonists, see *Książka modlitewna i kancyonał dla pospolitego ludu katolickiego* [Prayer Book and Hymnbook for Ordinary Catholic People], 10th ed., in Silesian-Wendish Collection, Wrocław University Library, Wrocław, Poland. For recent linguistic studies of the Silesian dialect spoken among the colonists in Texas, see Franciszek Lyra, "English and Polish in Contact" (Ph.D. diss., Indiana University, 1962), pp. 30, 147–148, 276–281; Franciszek Lyra, "Język polski w najstarszych osadach polskich w Stanach Zjednoczonych" [The Polish Language in the Oldest Polish Colonies in the United States], *Zaranie Śląskie* 28 (April–June 1965): 562–566; Reinhold Olesch, "The West Slavic Languages in Texas with Special Regard to Sorbian in Lee County," in *Texas Studies in Bilingualism*, ed. Glenn G. Gilbert, pp. 151–162.

38. Barzyński to Reverend Father General et al., last days of 1866 and first days of 1867, Barzyński Letters no. 8945; Barzyński to Most Reverend Father General et al., last days of 1866 and beginning of 1867, Barzyński Letters no. 8947; [Barzyński] to Most Reverend Father General et al., Day of the Five Wounds 1867, Barzyński Letters no. 8949; [Barzyński] to Most Reverend Father General, 5 August 1868, Barzyński Letters no. 8958.

39. Maksymilian Berezowski, "Swojacy wśród kowbojów: Podróż do Teksasu," *Trybunu Ludu*, nos. 7493–7494 (1–2 November 1969): 5; Olgierd Budrewicz, "Częstochowa w Teksasie," *Przekrój*, no. 792 (12 June 1960), pp. 6–7; Dworaczyk, *First Polish Colonies*, pp. 104–106, 143; Orłowski, "Polacy w Texasie," pp. 2, 8–10, 16–18; Szczepański, *Drapacze i śmietniki*, p. 191; Wańkowicz, *Atlantyk–Pacyfik*, p. 206.

40. Baker, "Moczygemba Family," p. 136; [Bakanowski] to Our Dearest Father General, 29 March 1870, Bakanowski Letters no. 9376; [Bakanowski] to Our Dearest Father General, 9 May 1870, Bakanowski Letters no. 9378; Railway Assistant Wincenty Banduch, Strzebin, Poland, to My Dear Niece Agata, [Panna Maria], 25 October 1935; [Barzyński] to Most Reverend Father, 28 July 1869, Barzyński Letters no. 8962; Rev. V[incent] Barzyński, San Antonio, to Most Reverend Father General [Rev. Jerome Kajsiewicz, Rome], 21 August 1872, Barzyński Letters no. 8991; interview, Karkosz and Karkosz, 23 June 1972 (KB); interview, Rev. Jan Karkosz, Piotrówka, Opole Voivodeship, Poland, 21 June 1972 (KB); *San Antonio Express*, 13 June 1868, p. 2; Kaspar Sohattka, Kg. Neudorf [Bolko], Germany, to Our Dear Friends, [Panna Maria], 1 December 1924; *Zwiastun Górnoszlązki*, 27 January 1870, p. 32, 24 March 1870, pp. 95–96.

41. James P. McGuire, Institute of Texan Cultures, San Antonio, Texas, to Baker, Wrocław, 22 June 1976; *Nowiny Texaskie* (San Antonio, Texas), 31 December 1914, p. 1, 15 January 1915, p. 1; Orłowski, "Polacy w Texasie," p. 21; Przygoda, "New Light," p. 86; Przygoda, *Texas Pioneers*, pp. 28–29; Stanisław Zieliński, *Bibljografja czasopism polskich zagranicą 1830–1934*, p. 87. An English-language newspaper, the *Polish American*, was edited by the Rev. Edward J. Dworaczyk at Panna Maria for a short time in 1939. Edmund L. Kowalczyk, "Jottings from the Polish American Past," p. 38; Przygoda, *Texas Pioneers*, p. 50.

42. Dworaczyk, *First Polish Colonies*, p. 28; Nesterowicz, *Notatki z podróży*, pp. 182, 205–206.

43. [Bakanowski] to [*Zwiastun Górnoszlązki*, Spring 1870], *Zwiastun Górnoszlązki*, 14 April 1870, p. 120; Nesterowicz, *Notatki z podróży*, pp. 205–206, 211–212; Ruckman, "Census Taker," pp. 37–39, 46–47; Texas, Department of Agriculture, Insurance, Statistics, and History, *First Annual Report of the Agricultural Bureau, 1887–88*, p. 122; Texas, Department of Insurance, Statistics, and History, *The Resources, Soil, and Climate of Texas*, p. 169.

44. Interview, Felix Mika, Sr., Panna Maria, 27 November 1971 (KB); Orłowski, "Polacy w Texasie," pp. 10–14; Leon Orłowski, "Produkcya bawełny przez farmerów polaków w Texasie" [The Production of Cotton by the Polish Farmers in Texas], New York, 5 May 1920, Republic of Poland, Ministry of Foreign Affairs, Embassy in Washington, Document Registration no. 1494, pp. 1–14, file no. 979, Embassy of the Republic of Poland in Washington Collection.

45. Hodges, "Poles of Texas," p. 120; Hodges, *Slavs on Southern Farms*, p. 11; Orłowski, "Polacy w Texasie," p. 13; Randel et al., *Time to Purpose*, 2:196, 331; U.S., Immigration Commission, *Recent Immigrants in Agriculture*, 2:361.

46. Nesterowicz, *Notatki z podróży*, pp. 168, 193, 195, 213; *Texas Almanac and State Industrial Guide 1904*, p. 303; *Twentieth Century History*, 1:468–470; Orłowski, "Produkcya bawełny," pp. 1–14.

47. Randel et al., *Time to Purpose*, 2:147; interview, Urbanczyk, 17 June 1974, pp. 4–7 (Pinkham).

48. [Bakanowski] to Dear Father Alexander, 20–24 May 1868, Bakanowski Letters no. 9355; [Bakanowski] to Our Dear Father Alexander, 27 May 1868, Bakanowski Letters no. 9356; *San Antonio Express*, 20 May 1868, p. 3, 21 May 1868, pp. 2–3, 22 May 1868, pp. 2–3, 23 May 1868, pp. 1–2, Baka[nowski] to Our Dear Father Peter, 9–13 July 1869, Bakanowski Letters no. 9370; Bakanowski, *Moje wspomnienia*, pp. 62, 172, 177; Dworaczyk, *First Polish Colonies*, p. 42; *San Antonio Express*, 4 July 1869, p. 3, 6 July 1869, p. 3, 7 July 1869, p. 3, 8 July 1869, p. 3, 9 July 1869, p. 3, 10 July 1869, p. 3, 11 July 1869, p. 3, 13 July 1869, p. 3, 14 July 1869, p. 3, 16 July 1869, p. 2, 17 July 1869, p. 3, 18 July 1869, p. 3, 20 July 1869, p. 2, 21 July 1869, p. 3, 23 July 1869, p. 1, 24 July 1869, p. 1, 25 July 1869, p. 2; Rev. Felix [Zwiardowski], Panna Maria, to Dear Father Adolf [Bakanowski, Chicago] 30 July 1871, Zwiardowski Letters no. 34713; Zwiardowski to Reverend Father General, 19 August 1871, Zwiardowski Letters no. 34714; Rev. Felix Zwiardowski, Częstochowa, Tex[as], to Most Reverend and Dearest Father, [location?], 9 March 1894, Zwiardowski Letters no. 34794; Rev. Felix Zwiardowski, Częstochowa, Texas, to Most Reverend and Dearest Father, [location?], 27 March 1895, Zwiardowski Letters no. 34795.

49. Rev. Felix Zwiardowski, Panna Maria, to Most Reverend Father General [Rev. Jerome Kajsiewicz, Rome], 8–9 February 1872, Zwiardowski Letters no. 34720.

50. Przygoda, *Texas Pioneers*, pp. 39–40; Randel et al., *Time to Purpose*, 2: 329–330.

51. Lutosławski, "Odrodzenie Śląska," p. 13; Orłowski, "Polacy w Texasie," pp. 13–14; U.S., Immigration Commission, *Recent Immigrants in Agriculture*, 2:365.

52. [Zwiardowski] to Dear Reverend Father, 12 November 1866, Zwiardowski Letters no. 34690.

53. Bakanowski, *Moje wspomnienia*, pp. 35–37, 47–54, 56–58, 171; [Zwiardowski] to Reverend Father General, 9 May 1870, Zwiardowski Letters no. 34705.

54. Zwiardowski to Dearest Reverend Father Alexander, 27 August 1867, Zwiardowski Letters no. 34698.

55. Zwiardowski to Our Dear Reverend Father, 17 January 1867, Zwiardowski Letters no. 34693.

56. Bakanowski, *Moje wspomnienia*, p. 58.

57. Ibid., pp. 35, 47–48; [Zwiardowski] to Reverend Father General, 9 May 1870, Zwiardowski Letters no. 34705.

58. Bakanowski, *Moje wspomnienia*, pp. 47–52.

59. Rev. Felix Zwiardowski, Panna Maria, Tex[as], to Dear Father, [location?], 7 April 1879, Zwiardowski Letters no. 34775.

60. Zwiardowski to Dearest Reverend Father, 13 September 1867, Zwiardowski Letters no. 34699.

61. Bakanowski, *Moje wspomnienia*, pp. 53–54; Zwiardowski to Reverend Father General, 31 January 1870, Zwiardowski Letters no. 34704.

62. Lutosławski, "Odrodzenie Śląska," pp. 8–9, 13.

63. Nesterowicz, *Notatki z podróży*, p. 179.

64. Randel et al., *Time to Purpose*, 2:147, 151; interview, Urbanczyk, 17 June 1974, pp. 3–4, 7 (Pinkham).

65. Regina Haiduk, "History of the White Deer Polish Settlement," unpaged, Earl Vandale Collection; Lutosławski, "Odrodzenie Śląska," pp. 8–9; interview, Mary Mika, Panna Maria, Texas, 27 November 1971 (KB); Randel et al., *Time to Purpose*, 2:151–152, 196; interview, Urbanczyk, 17 June 1974, p. 7 (Pinkham).

66. Baker, "Moczygemba Family," pp. 129–131; interview, Elias J. Moczygemba, 10 August 1973 (KB); Jacob Moczygemba, Panna Maria, Texas, to Frau Marie Karkosch, Gros[s] Pluschnitz [Płużnica], Post Tost, O/Sch, [German Empire], 24 July 1910.

Chapter 8. The Twentieth Century.

1. Edward J. Dworaczyk, *The First Polish Colonies of America in Texas*, pp. 65–67, 69, 117; John A. Joyce, *Our Polish Pioneers*, p. 7; Mrs. Anna Kiolbassa, affidavit concerning World War I service of her grandsons, St. Hedwig, Texas, September 1921, in U.S., Department of the Interior, Bureau of Pensions, Pension record file of Ignatz Kiolbassa for service in 16th Illinois Cavalry; interview, Elias J. Moczygemba, 10 August 1973 (KB); Lillie Terrell Shaver and Willie Williamson Rogers, *Flashlights on Texas*, pp. 138–139; Thos. B. Smiley, Karnes City, Texas, to George H. Sheppard, Austin, Texas, 2 October 1930, in Texas, Comptroller of Public Accounts, Joseph Gawlik, Texas Confederate Pension Application no. 47709, 23 September 1930; interview, Rosie Urbanczyk, 17 June 1974, p. 8 (Pinkham).

Many families with members living both in Texas and in Upper Silesia, which was in 1917 still part of Prussia, were divided by the hostilities and not infrequently had members fighting on both sides. For example, the only soldier from Panna Maria who was killed in action was Ignatz Moczygemba, whose family had immigrated to Texas from the village of Płużnica in 1854. By a chance of fate a distant cousin, H. Moczygemba, was one of the eleven soldiers from that village killed in the war fighting in the German army. Dworaczyk, *First Polish Colonies*, p. 69; "Ehrentafel für Unsere in Weltkrieg Gefallenen und Mitkämpfer Gross Pluschnitz" [Roll of Honor for Our Dead and Comrades in the World War from Płużnica], mounted photograph, ca. 1918.

2. Dworaczyk, *First Polish Colonies*, pp. 66–67; Leon Orłowski, "Produkcya bawełny przez farmerów polaków w Texasie," p. 6.

3. Dworaczyk, *First Polish Colonies*, p. 155; Mrs. Mary Lyssy, Karnes City, Texas, to Baker, Wrocław, Poland, 27 June 1976; Jo Stewart Randel and Carson County His-

torical Survey Committee, eds., *A Time to Purpose: A Chronicle of Carson County*, 2:332; interview, Ben P. Urbanczyk, 10 August 1973 (KB); interview, Urbanczyk, 17 June 1974, p. 3 (Pinkham). Within about a decade after World War I the most blatant discrimination against the Silesians had ceased. When the Polish consul general from Chicago delivered a speech at Falls City in 1930, he noted that among the crowd of Silesian farmers were also the local judge, the chairman of the school board, and law-enforcement officials, whom the consul remembered as being "very friendly and approving toward the Poles." Aleksander Szczepański, *Drapacze i śmietniki: Wrażenia amerykańskie*, p. 192.

4. Dworaczyk, *First Polish Colonies*, pp. 75–77; S. A. Iciek, *Samochodem przez stany południowe*, pp. 228–229; interview, John Kotara, ca. 1965, in Randel et al., *Time to Purpose*, 2:196; Orłowski, "Produkcya bawełny," pp. 4–6; Szczepański, *Drapacze i śmietniki*, pp. 185–186.

5. Andrzej Brożek, "Próby organizacji dostaw bawełny do Polski z farm polonijnych w Teksasie (1920–1930)" [Attempts to Organize Cotton Supplies for Poland from the Farms of the Polish Immigrants in Texas (1920–1930)], *Zeszyty Naukowe Wyżwzej Szkoły Pedagogicznej w Opolu* (Opole), History Series 10 (1972): 65–74; Leon Orłowski, "Polacy w Texasie," pp. 1–22; Orłowski, "Produkcya bawełny," pp. 1–14; Szczepański, *Drapacze i śmietniki*, pp. 166–201.

6. Dworaczyk, *First Polish Colonies*, p. 155; interview, Kotara, ca. 1965, in Randel et al., *Time to Purpose*, 2:196; Randel et al., *Time to Purpose*, 2:151; interview, Urbanczyk, 17 June 1974, pp. 7–8 (Pinkham).

7. Dworaczyk, *First Polish Colonies*, p. 148; *Victoria Daily Advocate* (Victoria, Texas), 6 December 1935, p. 3.

8. Dworaczyk, *First Polish Colonies*, pp. 141, 155–156; *Karnes City Citation*, 20 January 1977, sec. A, p. 5; Mrs. Nick Kotzur, [McCook, Texas], to Rev. Jacek Przygoda, [Los Angeles], 25 October 1969, cited in Jacek Przygoda, *Texas Pioneers from Poland: A Study in the Ethnic History*, pp. 74–75.

9. *Dallas Morning News*, 24 January 1932, sec. 4, p. 1; Dworaczyk, *First Polish Colonies*, pp. 70, 72–73, 75; Bolesław Rosiński, "Polacy w Texasie," p. 476.

10. John M. Kinney, comp., *Index to Applications for Texas Confederate Pensions*, pp. v–vi; Mrs. John Kowolik [Kowalik], Texas Confederate Pension Application no. 49044, 11 December 1930; Joseph F. Pierdolla, Texas Confederate Pension Application no. 47845, 3 October 1930; Adam Skloss, Texas Confederate Pension Application no. 18921, 27 July 1910; C.S., Department of War, Army, 36th Texas Cavalry, Compiled Military Records, Joseph F. Piedolla [Pierdolla] Compiled Military Service Record; C.S., Department of War, Army, 8th Texas Infantry, Compiled Military Records, Adam Skloss Compiled Military Service Record; Urbanczyk to Baker and Baker, interview, 10 August 1973.

11. For the best collection of twentieth-century accounts of the Silesians in Texas, see Andrzej Brożek, *Ślązacy w Teksasie: Relacje o najstarszych polskich osadach w Stanach Zjednoczonych*, pp. 125–252.

12. Wincenty Lutosławski, "Odrodzenie Śląska w Texasie," *Świat* 3 (December 1908): 8–9, 13–14.

13. Emily Greene Balch, *Our Slavic Fellow Citizens*, p. 229.

14. U.S., Immigration Commission, *Immigrants in Industries (in Twenty-five Parts); Part 24: Recent Immigrants in Agriculture (in Two Volumes)*, 2:361–362, 364–365.

15. Stefan Nesterowicz, *Notatki z podróży po północnej i środkowej Ameryce*,

pp. 160–215. This work is available in English translation as Stefan Nesterowicz, *Travel Notes*, trans. and ed. Marion Moore Coleman.

16. Wacław Kruszka, *Historja polska w Ameryce*, pp. 364, 375.

17. Orłowski, "Polacy w Texasie," pp. 1–22; Orłowski, "Produkcya bawełny," pp. 1–14. It should be noted that portions of Orłowski's reports were reprinted eight years after they were written. [Leon Orłowski], "Polacy w Teksasie" [The Poles in Texas], *Wychodźca* (Warsaw) 7 (6 May 1928): 2–3; ibid. 7 (13 May 1928): 2–4.

18. Franciszek Niklewicz, *Dzieje pierwszych polskich osadników w Ameryce i przewodnik parafij polskich w Stanach Zjednoczonych*, pp. 3–13, 31; F[ranciszek] Niklewicz, *Polacy w Stanach Zjednoczonych* [The Poles in the United States], pp. 5–6, 34–35.

19. Bolesław Rosiński, "Polacy w Texasie," *Ziemia* 15 (1 December 1930): 473–479.

20. Constantin Symonolewicz, "Polish Travelers and Observers in the U.S.A. (1918–1939)," *Polish American Studies* 2 (January–June 1945): 47–48; Szczepański, *Drapacze i śmietniki*, pp. 166–201.

21. Dworaczyk, *First Polish Colonies*, pp. 135–136; Joyce, *Our Polish Pioneers*, pp. 21–22; Jan Jakub Kowalczyk, "Górnoślązacy w Teksasie" [Upper Silesians in Texas], *Gość Niedzielny* (Katowice, Poland) 15 (31 January 1937): 81.

22. Iciek, *Samochodem*, pp. 221–242; Symonolewicz, "Polish Travelers and Observers," p. 50.

23. Jacek Wnęk, "Ślązacy w Texasie," *Powstaniec* 11 (15 February 1937): 26–30.

24. Banduch to My Dear Niece Agata, 25 October 1935; Moczygemba to Karkosch, 24 July 1910; Sohattka to Our Dear Friends, 1 December 1924; Szczepański, *Drapacze i śmietniki*, p. 187.

25. A listing of Polish newspaper and magazine articles on the Silesian colonies in Texas would be almost endless. The following are typical examples: Andrzej Brożek, "Podróże ze Stanów to Teksasu i z powrotem" [Travel from the States to Texas and Return], *Opole* (Opole) 5 (May 1973): 22–23; Mieczysław Czuma, "Płużnicy dzień powszedni" [Płużnica Every Day], *Przekrój* (Kraków, Poland), no. 1514 (14 April 1974), pp. 4–7; Mieczysław Fiolek, "W stulecie Teksasu i pierwszej emigracji Ślązaków za ocean [On the Centennial of Texas and the First Emigration of Silesians across the Ocean], *Polska Zachodnia* (Katowice, Poland) 11 (5 December 1936): 5; Franciszek German, "Ślązacy w Teksas: Z dziejów osadnictwa polskiego w Ameryce" [Silesians in Texas: From the History of Polish Colonization in America], *Biuletyn dla Polonii Zagranicznej, Zachodnia Agencja Prasowa* (Poznan, Poland), no. 9 (November 1957), pp. 22–40; Karol Jonca, "Z Opolszczyzny do Teksasu: Śladami dawnej emigracji" [From the Opole Region to Texas: On Traces of the Old Emigration], *Trybuna Opolska* (Opole), no. 3445 (9–10 February 1963), pp. 1, 3; Marek Konopka, "Z Płużnicy i Toszka do . . . Teksasu" [From Płużnica and Toszek to . . . Texas], *Trybuna Robotnicza* (Katowice), no. 7935 (9–10 August 1969), pp. 1, 6; Kowalczyk, "Górnoszlązacy w Teksasie," pp. 47–48, 67, 81; Lutosławski, "Odrozenie Śląska," pp. 8–9, 13–14; Robert Małowieski, "Amerykanin wśród Ślązaków" [An American among Silesians], *Opole* 3 (September 1972): 10; Krystyna Murzynowska, "Polscy pionierzy w Teksasie (1854–1880)" [Polish Pioneers in Texas (1854–1880)], *Mówią Wieki, Magazyn Historyczny* (Warsaw) 8 (October 1965): 23–28; Orłowski, "Polacy w Teksasie," *Wychodźca* 7 (6 May 1928): 2–3; ibid. 7 (13 May 1928): 2–4; Marta Pampuch, "Ślązacy w Teksas w drugiej połowie XIX wieku" [Silesians in Texas in the Second Half of the Nineteenth

Century], *Polonia* (Katowice), no. 1403 (15 March 1936), "Kultura i życie" supplement, p. 1; Wincenty Rozmus, "Polacy w Ameryce Północnej" [The Poles in North America], *Głosy z nad Odry* (Mikołów, Germany) 4 (March 1921): 7–9; Marian Szczurek, "Wilkołak przepłynął Atlantyk" [The Werewolf Swam the Atlantic], *Trybuna Odrzańska* (Opole), no. 8016 (20–21 November 1976), pp. 1, 4; Stefan Włoszczewski, "Polacy w Teksasie" [The Poles in Texas], *Tygodnik Kulturalny* (Warsaw) 13 (13 August 1969): 2, 11.

26. This observation is drawn from the author's experience in living and traveling in Poland in 1970, 1972, and 1975–1977.

27. *Karnes City Citation*, 1 April 1976, sec. A, p. 4.

28. Edward J. Dworaczyk, *The Centennial History of Panna Maria, Texas*, pp. 3–7.

29. Edward J. Dworaczyk, *The Millennium History of Panna Maria, Texas*, pp. 5, 99–103; *Everybody Invited to Historic and Significant Celebration Panna Maria, Texas Immaculate Conception Church Sunday, October 23, 1966 Celebrating the Millennium of Polish Christianity*, poster, 1 lv.; Przygoda, *Texas Pioneers*, p. 49.

30. Przygoda, *Texas Pioneers*, p. 52; *Souvenir* [of Our Lady of Częstochowa Grotto, San Antonio, Texas], unpaged.

31. *Karnes City Citation*, 6 November 1975, sec. A, p. 1, 25 December 1975, sec. A, p. 5, 10 June 1976, sec. A, p. 7, 8 July 1976, sec. B, p. 2; [Polish American Congress of Texas], *First Convention Polish American Congress of Texas San Antonio, St. Anthony Hotel—Nov. 5 and 6 Panna Maria Pilgrimage—Nov. 7*; [Polish American Congress of Texas], *Second Convention Polish American Congress of Texas November 3–5, 1972 Houston, Texas*; [Polish American Congress of Texas], *Fourth Convention Polish American Congress of Texas San Antonio, Texas October 25–26, 1974*; "P[olish] A[merican] P[riests] A[ssociation] Newsletter," mimeographed, 11 November 1976; Przygoda, *Texas Pioneers*, pp. 29, 43, 48–49, 58, 76–80.

32. Rev. Rafał Kaczmarczyk, Płużnica, Poland, to Reverend Pastor [Rev. Bernard Goebel, Panna Maria], 29 January 1973; Rev. Rafał Kaczmarczyk, Płużnica, Poland, to T. Lindsay Baker and Krystyna Baker, Lubbock, Texas, 29 June 1973; *Karnes City Citation*, 12 July 1973, sec. A, pp. 1, 4; *Nixon News*, 28 June 1973, p. 3, 30 August 1973, p. 13; Felix V. Snoga, "P[olish] A[merican] C[ongress] Pilgrimage to Poland Diary," typescript, 1973; Rev. John W. Yanta, San Antonio, Texas, to Rev. Kaczmarczyk, Płużnica, Rev. Kocur, Zębowice, Rev. Donarski, Szremrowice, and Rev. Pokora, Radawie, Poland, 3 May 1973.

33. *Houston Chronicle*, 8 September 1974, sec. 1, p. 25; *Karnes City Citation*, 4 March 1976, sec. A, p. 1, 18 November 1976, sec. A, p. 1, 9 December 1976, sec. A, p. 1; *Memorial Homecoming Father Leopold Moczygemba Liturgical Reinterment October 13, 1974 Panna Maria, Texas*; St. Mary Church, Panna Maria, Texas, weekly parish news bulletins, mimeographed, 1 October 1972, 15 October 1972; sworn authorization by surviving next of kin for disinterment of remains of the Rev. Leopold Moczygemba, April 1974.

34. *Karnes City Citation*, 1 April 1976, sec. A, p. 1, 12 April 1976, sec. A, p. 1, 24 June 1976, sec. A, p. 1, 8 July 1976, sec. A, p. 1, sec. B, p. 2, 22 July 1976, sec. A, p. 1; "Warsaw Television Films Segments of Polish Texan History at ITC," *People* (Institute of Texan Cultures, San Antonio, Tex.) 4 (May–June 1974): 5.

35. Si Dunn, "A Visit to Panna Maria," *Scene: The Dallas Morning News Sunday Magazine* 5 (30 June 1974): 16–18, 19; Jan Erdman, "Opisanie Panny Marii, najstarszej osady polskiej w USA," *Ameryka*, no. 159 (April 1972), pp. 40–46; Rev. Bernard

Goebel, Panna Maria, Texas, to Baker, Wrocław, Poland, 5 July 1976; Mary Lyssy to Baker, 27 June 1976; Arthur J. Moczygemba, San Antonio, Texas, to Baker and Baker, Wrocław, Poland, [6 July 1976]; Jacek Przygoda, "Poles in Texas Today," *Quarterly Review: Official Publication of the American Council of Polish Cultural Clubs* 21 (October–December 1969): 1; Maria Starczewska, "The Historical Geography of the Oldest Polish Colony in the United States," *Polish Review* 12 (Spring 1967): 30–32.

Chapter 9. The Significance of the Silesians in Texas

1. Bejareno to Dear Sir, 16 July 1868, *San Antonio Express*, 25 July 1868, p. 4; Andrzej Brożek, "Próby organizacji dostaw bawełny do Polski z farm polonijnych w Teksasie (1920–1930)," *Zeszyty Naukowe Wyższej Szkoły Pedagogiczne w Opolu* 10 (1972): 65–72; LeRoy Hodges, "The Poles of Texas: Their Effect on the State's Agricultural Development," *Texas Magazine* 7 (December 1912): 118–120; Moczigemba to [Friends and Relatives], 13 May 1855, Kingdom of Prussia, Regency of Opole, Department of the Interior, Die Auswanderung nach den Amerikanischen Staaten—Concesirung von Vereinen u. Agenturen zur Beförderung der Auswanderer, 2:55–56; Thomas Ruckman, "The Census Taker: A Complete Description of the County of Karnes—In South West Texas—by Thos. Ruckman June 1890," pp. 37–40, 45–47, Thomas Ruckman Papers.

2. A. T. Andreas, *History of Chicago*, 3:563–564; Helen Busyn, "Peter Kiołbassa: Maker of Polish America," *Polish American Studies* 8 (July–December 1951): 65–84; Helen Busyn, "The Political Career of Peter Kiolbassa," *Polish American Studies* 7 (January–June 1950): 8–22; Franciszek German, "Ludzie ziemi gliwickiej: Piotr Kiełbassa (1838–1905)" [People of the Gliwice Land: Peter Kiołbassa (1838–1905)], *Zeszyty Gliwickie* (Gliwice, Poland) 5 (1967): 153–158; Peter Kiołbassa, Chicago, Illinois, to Very Reverend Sir, [Congregation of the Resurrection, Rome], 17 September 1869, Kiołbassa Letters no. 47746; U.S., Department of the Interior, *Register of Officers and Agents, Civil, Military, and Naval, in the Service of the United States on the Thirteenth of September, 1875*, p. 140; Sygurd Wiśniowski, "Piotr Kiolbassa: Poseł z Chicago" [Peter Kiołbassa: Representative from Chicago], *Tygodnik Illustrowany* (Warsaw, Russian Empire), 3d ser., 3 (9 June 1877): 360, 362.

3. Andreas, *History of Chicago*, 3:777–778; T. Lindsay Baker, "The Early Years of Rev. Wincenty Barzyński," *Polish American Studies* 32 (Spring 1975): 29–52; Mieczysław Haiman, "Michał Wincenty Barzyński," *Polski słownik biograficzny* [Polish Biographical Dictionary], 1:348; John Iwicki, *The First One Hundred Years: A Study of the Apostolate of the Congregation of the Resurrection in the United States 1866–1966*, pp. 26–45, 53–56, 58, 61–108, 118–124, 126, 135, 138, 142, 155–156, 167, 169, 195, 197–205, 227–231, 246, 248, 258, 263; Edward T. Janas, *Dictionary of American Resurrectionists 1865–1965*, pp. 6–10; Stanisław Siatka, *Krótkie wspomnienia o życiu i działalności ks. Wincentego Barzyńskiego, C.R.*, pp. 17–65.

4. Iwicki, *First One Hundred Years*, pp. 47, 74, 78, 118–119, 135, 245; *Katolik*, 10 April 1891, [lv. 1 of unpaged text], 17 April 1891, [lv. 1 of unpaged text]; "Ksiądz Leopold Moczygemba i polskie kolonie w Ameryce," *Missyonarz Katolicki* 1 (1 September 1891): 262–264; Martynian Możejewski, "Stany Zjednoczone Ameryki Północnej: Najpierwsza parafia i kościół polski w Ameryce," *Missye Katolickie* 15 (April 1896): 43–47; Joseph Swastek, *Priest and Pioneer: Rev. Leopold Moczygemba*, pp. 3–30.

5. Francis Bolek, ed., *Who's Who in Polish America*, 3d ed., p. 362; Aleksander Szczepański, *Drapacze i śmietniki: Wrażenia amerykańskie*, pp. 166–167.

6. Bolek, *Who's Who in Polish America*, p. 303; Edward J. Dworaczyk, *The First*

Polish Colonies of America in Texas, pp. 59, 62, 123–124; John A. Joyce, *Our Polish Pioneers*, pp. 14–15, 17; *Karnes City Citation*, 10 June 1976, sec. A, p. 7; Stefan Nesterowicz, *Notatki z podróży po północnej i środkowej Ameryce*, pp. 191–192, 211; Jacek Przygoda, *Texas Pioneers from Poland: A Study in the Ethnic History*, pp. 22–31, 45, 52, 57–58; Sister Jan Maria Wozniak, "St. Michael's Church: The Polish National Catholic Church in San Antonio, Texas, 1855–1950," pp. 38–49.

7. Chester Thomas Kochan, "The Polish People of San Antonio, Texas, 1900–1960: A Study in Social Mobility," pp. 32–38; Prosper A. Mika, Austin, Texas, to Baker and Baker, Wrocław, 31 August 1976; Jacek Przygoda, "Poles in Texas Today," *Quarterly Review: Official Publication of the American Council of Polish Cultural Clubs* 21 (October–December 1969): 1; Przygoda, *Texas Pioneers*, pp. 41–43, 55–56, 80, 93.

8. T. Lindsay Baker, "National Consciousness among the Silesians at the Oldest Polish Colony in America," *Poland and Germany (East and West)* (London) 19 (January–June 1975): 27–36; Andrzej Brożek, "The Most Polish of the Poles in America," ibid. 14 (January–June 1970): 17–24; Andrzej Brożek, "Najbardziej polscy emigranci w Ameryce" [The Most Polish Immigrants in America], *Poglądy* (Katowice, Poland) 7 (1–15 February 1968): 12, 18; Andrzej Brożek, "Trwanie w polskości pierwszych osadników górnośląskich w Teksasie" [The Existence of Polish Consciousness among the First Upper Silesian Settlers in Texas], *Kwartalnik Nauczyciela Opolskiego* (Opole), no. 40 (1968), pp. 3–8. Among the English-language studies that discuss the forced Germanization of the Polish minority in Prussia are the following: Ian F. D. Morrow, "The Prussianization of the Poles," *Slavonic and East European Review* 15 (1936–1937): 153–164; Richard Wonser Tims, *Germanizing Prussian Poland*.

9. Delius to [Royal Administration], 30 March 1855, Prussia, Auswanderung, 1: 754, 757; *Neu-Braunfelser Zeitung*, 29 December 1854, p. 3; Scheider to [Royal Administration], 28 February 1855, Prussia, Auswanderung, 1:565; *Schlesische Zeitung*, 14 October 1854, p. 2068.

10. *Czas*, 22 May 1856, p. 2; *Gwiazdka Cieszyńska*, 1 September 1855, p. 287, 13 October 1855, p. 334; *Zwiastun Górnoszlązki* to Our Brothers in Christ Who Live in Texas, [24 March 1870], *Zwiastun Górnoszlązki*, 24 March 1870, p. 96.

11. Edward J. Dworaczyk, *The Millennium History of Panna Maria, Texas*, pp. 99–103; Frederick Law Olmstead, *Journey through Texas*, pp. 270, 283; Przygoda, *Texas Pioneers*, p. 49; Ruckman, "Census Taker," p. 40.

12. Moczigemba to [Friends and Relatives], 13 May 1855, Moczigemba to My Dear Uncles, [1855], Moczigemba and Dziuk to [Friends and Relatives, 1855], Moczygęba to Dear Parents, 18 June 1855, Prussia, Auswanderung, 2:53–57, 60, 65–66; Moczygemba to Karkosch, 24 July 1910; William I. Thomas and Florian Znaniecki, *The Polish Peasant in Europe and America*, 1:303–304.

13. Barzyński to Most Reverend Father General et al., last days of 1866 and beginning of 1867, Barzyński Letters no. 8947.

14. Bakanowski to Our Dearest Father Superior, 13 November 1866, Bakanowski Letters no. 9330.

15. [Zwiardowski] to Dear Reverend Father, 12 November 1866, Zwiardowski Letters no. 34690.

16. Franciszek Niklewicz, *Dzieje pierwszych polskich osadników w Ameryce i przewodnik parafij polskich w Stanach Zjednoczonych*, pp. 12–13.

17. Leon Orłowski, "Polacy w Texasie," p. 16.

18. Bolesław Rosiński, "Polacy w Texasie," *Ziemia* 15 (1 December 1930): 476.

19. Szczepański, *Drapacze i śmietniki*, p. 195.

20. Moczigemba to [Friends and Relatives], 13 May 1855, Prussia, Auswanderung, 2:56; Rev. Leopold B[onaventura] M[aria] Moczygemba, Jeffersonville, Ind., to Reverend Father General [Rev. Peter Semenenko, Rome], 6 December 1875, Moczygemba Letters no. 37369.

21. Wnęk, "Ślązacy w Texasie," *Powstaniec* 11 (15 February 1937): 29–30.

Bibliography

Archival Materials

"*Album des Gymnasiums in Oppeln 10 Oktober 1843 ab bis 31 Dezember 1878*" [Album of the Gymnasium in Opole, 10 October 1843 to 31 December 1878]. Manuscript. Burggymnasium Collection. Archives of the Voivodeship of Opole, Opole, Poland.

Annunciation of the Blessed Virgin Mary Church, St. Hedwig, Texas. Parish Records. Manuscript. Catholic Archives at San Antonio, Chancery Office, Archdiocese of San Antonio, San Antonio, Texas.

Ascension of the Blessed Virgin Mary Church, Jemielnica, Opole Voivodeship, Poland. Parish Records. Manuscript.

Bakanowski, Adolf. Letters Sent. Manuscript. Archives, Congregation of the Resurrection, Rome, Italy.

Banduch, Railway Assistant Wincenty. Strzebin, Poland, to My Dear Niece Agata, [Panna Maria, Texas], 25 October 1935. Manuscript letter in possession of the Rev. Bernard Goebel, Panna Maria, Texas.

Barzyński, John. Letters Sent. Manuscript. Archives, Congregation of the Resurrection, Rome, Italy.

Barzyński, Vincent. Letters Sent. Manuscript. Archives, Congregation of the Resurrection, Rome, Italy.

Bralewski, Teofil. Letters Sent. Manuscript. Archives, Congregation of the Resurrection, Rome, Italy.

Bremen, Free Port of. "Ausgabe der in Monat October [1854] Aufgegebene Spedition von Auswanderere" [Edition of the Departures of Emigrants in the Month of October (1854)]. Manuscript. Bremen State Archives, Bremen, Federal Republic of Germany. Photocopy provided by Dr. Andrzej Brożek, Katowice, Poland.

———. Registry documents for Bremen bark *Weser*. Manuscript. Bremen State Archives, Bremen, Federal Republic of Germany. Photocopy provided by Dr. Andrzej Brożek, Katowice, Poland.

Cichocki, Henry. Letters Sent. Manuscript. Archives, Congregation of the Resurrection, Rome, Italy.

Compiled Military Records. See specific unit under Confederate States of America, Department of War, Army, or U.S., Department of War, Army.

Confederate States of America, Department of War, Army. Capt. H. Willke's Battalion Light Artillery (6th Texas Field Battery). Compiled Military Records. Manuscript. National Archives, Washington, D.C.

———. Dege's (Formerly Willke's) Battalion Light Artillery (8th Texas Field Battery). Compiled Military Records. Manuscript. National Archives, Washington, D.C.

———. Ragsdale's Battalion Texas Cavalry. Compiled Military Records. Manuscript. National Archives, Washington, D.C.

———. 24th Texas Cavalry. Compiled Military Records. Manuscript. National Archives, Washington, D.C.

———. 31st Texas Cavalry. Compiled Military Records. Manuscript. National Archives, Washington, D.C.

———. 33d Texas Cavalry. Compiled Military Records. Manuscript. National Archives, Washington, D.C.

———. 36th Texas Cavalry. Compiled Military Records. Manuscript. National Archives, Washington, D.C.

———. 2d Texas Infantry. Compiled Military Records. Manuscript. National Archives, Washington, D.C.

———. 6th Texas Infantry. Compiled Military Records. Manuscript. National Archives, Washington, D.C.

———. 8th Texas Infantry. Compiled Military Records. Manuscript. National Archives, Washington, D.C.

Dubuis, Bishop Claude-Marie. Letters Sent. Manuscript. Archives, Congregation of the Resurrection, Rome, Italy.

Fink, Arthur L., Jr. "The Regulated Emigration of the German Proletariat with Special Reference to Texas." Master's thesis, University of Texas, Austin, 1949.

Friars Minor Conventual. Archives of the General Curia, Rome, Italy.

———, Argentine Province. Oggersheim Convent. "Chronik" [Chronicle] (3 May 1845–26 May 1898). Manuscript. Oggersheim Convent, Ludwigshaven-Oggersheim, Federal Republic of Germany.

———. Schönau Convent. "Chronik" [Chronicle] (1791–December 1914). Manuscript. Schönau Convent, Schönau, Federal Republic of Germany.

———, Immaculate Conception Province. Correspondence. Manuscript. Archives, St. Francis Convent, Syracuse, N.Y.

———. Necrology. Printed card index. Archives, St. Francis Convent, Syracuse, N.Y.

———, Province of the Marches. Urbino Convent. "Conteggio de Zagotti, e Professi del Convento di Urbino" [Financial Accounts of the Professed of the Convent of Urbino]. Manuscript. Archives, Urbino Convent, Urbino, Italy. Photocopy provided by Rev. Peter D. Fehlner, O.F.M. Conv., Rensselaer, N.Y.

———. "Verbali delle Affigliazioni de Conventi 1828–1858" [Minutes of the Affiliates of the Convents 1828–1858]. Manuscript. Archives of the Province of the Marches, Anacona, Italy. Photocopy provided by Rev. Peter D. Fehlner, O.F.M. Conv., Rensselaer, N.Y.

Frydrychowicz, John. Letters Sent. Manuscript. Archives, Congregation of the Resurrection, Rome, Italy.

Glennon, Sister Mary Carmelita. "History of the Diocese of Galveston, 1847–1874." Master's thesis, University of Texas, Austin, 1943.

Goebel, Rev. Bernard. Panna Maria, Texas, to T. Lindsay Baker, Wrocław, Poland, 5 July 1976. Manuscript letter in possession of the author.

Haiduk, Regina. "History of the White Deer Polish Settlement." Typescript. Earl Vandale Collection. University of Texas Archives, Austin.

Hamburg, Free Port of. Auswanderungsamt. Manuscript. Hamburg State Archives, Hamburg, Federal Republic of Germany. Selected photocopies provided by Dr. Andrzej Brożek, Katowice, Poland.

Hellmann, Othmar, comp. and ed. "Notes for a History of the Province Collected by Very Rev. Fr. Othmar Hellmann." Typescript. Archives, St. Anthony-on-Hudson Conventual Franciscans, Rensselaer, N.Y.

Huntt, George Gibson. Papers. Microfilm copy. Southwest Collection, Texas Tech University, Lubbock.

Kaczmarczyk, Rev. Rafał. Płużnica, Poland, to Reverend Pastor [Rev. Bernard Goebel, Panna Maria, Texas], 29 January 1973. Photocopy in possession of the author.

———. Płużnica, Poland, to T. Lindsay Baker and Krystyna Baker, Lubbock, Texas, 29 June 1973. Manuscript letter in possession of the author.

Karnes County, Texas. Deed Records. Manuscript. Karnes County Courthouse, Karnes City, Texas.

———. Manuscript deed for transfer of land from John Twohig to Francisca Urbanczyk and children, 21 April 1855. Manuscript in possession of Ben P. Urbanczyk, Panna Maria, Texas.

———. Petition no. 40. Citizens of Karnes County Ask That a Company Be Formed for the Protection of Karnes and Other Counties. 8 December 1863. Manuscript. Archives Division, Texas State Library, Austin.

Kiołbassa, Peter. Letters Sent. Manuscript. Archives, Congregation of the Resurrection, Rome, Italy.

Kochan, Chester Thomas. "The Polish People of San Antonio, Texas, 1900–1960: A Study in Social Mobility." Master's thesis, University of Texas, Austin, 1970.

Leopoldine Foundation. Letters from the Dioceses in the U.S.A. Manuscript. Leopoldinen-Stiftung Collection. Archives, Archdiocese of Vienna, Vienna, Austria.

Louisiana Papers. Manuscript. Archives, University of Notre Dame, Notre Dame, Ind.

Ludwig-Missionsverein. Papers and Letters Received Concerning the Diocese of Galveston, Texas. Manuscript. Archives, Ludwig-Missionsverein, Munich, Federal Republic of Germany.

Lyra, Franciszek. "English and Polish in Contact." Ph.D. diss., Indiana University, Bloomington, Ind., 1962.

Lyssy, Mrs. Mary. Karnes City, Texas, to T. Lindsay Baker, Wrocław, Poland, 27 June 1976. Manuscript letter in possession of the author.

McGuire, James P. Institute of Texan Cultures, San Antonio, to T. Lindsay Baker, Wrocław, Poland, 25 March 1976, 22 June 1976, 30 September 1976. Manuscript letter in possession of the author.

Mika, Prosper A. Austin, Texas, to T. Lindsay Baker and Krystyna Baker, Wrocław, Poland, 31 August 1976. Manuscript letter in possession of the author.

Miller, James L. Missourian Publishing Company, Washington, Missouri, to T. Lindsay Baker, Lubbock, Texas, 29 July 1974. Manuscript letter in possession of the author.

Missouri, Militia. 54th Regiment Enrolled Missouri Militia. Compiled Military Records. Manuscript. Archives, Headquarters Missouri National Guard, Jefferson City, Mo.

Moczygemba, Arthur J. San Antonio, Texas, to T. Lindsay Baker and Krystyna Baker, Wrocław, Poland, [6 July 1976]. Manuscript letter in possession of the author.

Moczygemba, Jacob. Panna Maria, Texas, to Frau Marie Karkosch, Gros[s] Pluschnitz [Płużnica], Post Tost, O/Sch, [German Empire], 24 July 1910. Manuscript. Photographic copy in possession of the author.

Moczygemba, Leopold. Letters Sent. Manuscript. Archives, Congregation of the Resurrection, Rome, Italy.

Mullally, John William. "A Study of Marriage Patterns in a Rural Polish Roman-Catholic Parish from 1872 to 1959." Master's thesis, University of Texas, Austin, 1963.

Muster Rolls. Texas State Troops. See Texas, Militia, under unit captain's name.

[Orłowski, Leon.] "Polacy w Texasie" [The Poles in Texas]. [New York, May 1920]. Typescript. Republic of Poland. Ministry of Foreign Affairs. Embassy in Washington. Document Registration no. 1493. File no. 979. Embassy of the Republic of Poland in Washington Collection. Archives of Contemporary Documents, Warsaw, Poland.

Orłowski, Leon. "Produkcya bawełny przez farmerów polaków w Texasie" [The Production of Cotton by the Polish Farmers in Texas]. New York, 5 May 1920. Typescript. Republic of Poland. Ministry of Foreign Affairs. Embassy in Washington. Document Registration no. 1494. File no. 979. Embassy of the Republic of Poland in Washington Collection. Archives of Contemporary Documents, Warsaw, Poland.

Poniatowski, Denise. Letters Sent. Manuscript. Archives, Congregation of the Resurrection, Rome, Italy.

Prussia, Kingdom of, Regency of Opole. Department of the Interior. Die Auswanderung nach den Amerikanischen Staaten—Concesirung von Vereinen u. Agenturen zur Beförderung der Auswanderer [Emigration to the American States—Concessions of Societies and Agents for Transporting Emigrants] (15 May 1847–end of December 1867). 2 vols. Manuscript. Regency of Opole Collection, sec. 1, vols. 12132–12133. Archives of the City and Voivodeship of Wrocław, Wrocław, Poland.

———. Opole County. Passport Journal of the Landrat of Opole County 1858–1861. Manuscript. Collection of the Landrat of Opole. Archives of the Voivodeship of Opole, Opole, Poland.

———. President. Reports to the King for 1851–1858. 2 vols. Manuscript. Vols. 2.2.1, nos. 16571–16572. German Central State Archives, Historical Section 2, Merseburg, German Democratic Republic.

———. Strzelce County. Release document for the obligations of Prussian subjects for the family of Jacob Urbanczyk, 5 September 1854. Manuscript in possession of Ben P. Urbanczyk, Panna Maria, Texas.

———. Strzelce County. Release document for the obligations of Prussian subjects for the family of Johann Pycka, 31 July 1854. Manuscript in possession of Mrs. Coy F. Ross, Bandera, Texas, on loan to Institute of Texan Cultures, San Antonio.

Pyka, John, and Pyka, Franciszka. Last will and testament. Bandera, Texas, 1 June 1888. Manuscript in the possession of Mrs. Coy F. Ross, Bandera, Texas, on loan to Institute of Texan Cultures, San Antonio.

Ruckman, Thomas. "The Census Taker: A Complete Description of the County of Karnes—In South West Texas—by Thos. Ruckman June 1890." Manuscript. Thomas Ruckman Papers. University of Texas Archives, Austin.

———. Correspondence. Manuscript. Thomas Ruckman Papers. University of Texas Archives, Austin.

Russell, Charles A. Papers. Manuscript. University of Texas Archives, Austin.

Russell, Henry Lyman Brightman. "Autobiography of Henry Lyman Brightman Russell." Manuscript. Henry Lyman Brightman Russell Papers. University of Texas Archives, Austin.

———. Correspondence 1849–1935. Manuscript. Henry Lyman Brightman Russell Papers. University of Texas Archives, Austin.

St. Catherine Church, Toszek, Katowice, Voivodeship, Poland. Parish Records. Manuscript.

St. Gertrude Church, Krakow, Mo. Parish Records. Manuscript.

St. Louis Church, Castroville, Texas. Parish Records. Manuscript.

St. Mary Church, Panna Maria, Texas. Parish Records. Manuscript.

St. Mary Church, Sulisławice, Tarnobrzeg Voivodeship, Poland. Parish Records. Manuscript.

Sts. Peter and Paul Church, New Braunfels, Texas. Parish Records. Manuscript.

St. Stanisław Church, Płużnica, Opole Voivodeship, Poland. Parish Records. Manuscript.

Smolikowski, Paweł. "Historia Zgromadzenia Zmartwychwstania Pańskiego" [History of the Congregation of the Resurrection]. Manuscript. Archives, Congregation of the Resurrection, Rome, Italy.

Snigurski, Adolf. Letters Sent. Manuscript. Archives, Congregation of the Resurrection, Rome, Italy.

Snoga, Felix V. "P[olish] A[merican] C[ongress] Pilgrimage to Poland Diary." Typescript. 1973. Photographic copy in possession of the author.

Sohattka, Kaspar. Kgl. Neudorf [Bolko], Germany, to Our Dear Friends, [Panna Maria, Texas], 1 December 1924. Manuscript letter in possession of the Rev. Bernard Goebel, Panna Maria, Texas.

Sojka, Rev. Wojciech. Erie, Pennsylvania, to Rev. John W. Yanta, San Antonio, Texas, 1 June 1974. Photocopy in possession of the author.

Sworn authorization by surviving next of kin for the disinterment of remains of the Rev. Leopold Moczygemba. April 1974. Manuscript. Photocopy in possession of the author.

Texas. Comptroller of Public Accounts. Texas Confederate Pension Applications. Manuscript. Archives Division, Texas State Library, Austin.

———. Confederate Pension Applications. See entry next above.

———. Governor. Edmund J. Davis Executive Record Book for 1870. Manuscript. Archives Division, Texas State Library, Austin.

———. Governor. Letters Received. Manuscript. Archives Division, Texas State Library, Austin.

———. Militia. Muster Roll of Captain B. Mitchell['s] Company, Bandera County, [Frontier] Dist. no. 3, Texas State Troops, February 1862. Manuscript. Achives Division, Texas State Library, Austin.

———. Militia. Muster Roll of Capt. Harrison Gregg's Company C Infantry, 24th Brigade, 18 August 1863. Manuscript. Archives Division, Texas State Library, Austin.

———. Militia. Muster Roll of Capt. J. A. Tivey's Company of Mounted Riflemen, 5 August 1861. Manuscript. Archives Division, Texas State Library, Austin, Texas.

———. Militia. Muster Roll of Capt. John F. Tom's Company T[exas] S[tate] T[roops] for Frontier Defense, 3d Frontier District, 20 February 1864. Manuscript. Archives Division, Texas State Library, Austin, Texas.

———. Militia. Muster Roll of J. M. Paschal's Company of Volunteers, 29th Brigade, Texas State Troops, 2 March 1863. Manuscript. Archives Division, Texas State Library, Austin.

———. Militia. Muster Roll of N. Gussett's Company, 3d Frontier District, T[exas] S[tate] T[roops], 26 March 1865. Manuscript. Archives Division, Texas State Library, Austin.

———. Militia. Muster Roll of the Panna Maria Grays, 9 July 1861. Manuscript. Archives Division, Texas State Library, Austin.

———. Militia. Muster Roll of the Panna Maria Greys, 9 July 1861. Manu- Manuscript. Archives Division, Texas State Library, Austin.

———. Secretary of State. Election Register 1866–1870. Manuscript. Archives Division, Texas State Library, Austin.

———. Secretary of State. Letters Received. Manuscript. Archives Division, Texas State Library, Austin.

———. Secretary of State. W. C. Philips Public Letterbook (23 August 1867–21 January 1870). Manuscript. In *Records of the United States of America*. Washington, D.C.: Library of Congress Microcopy no. Tex. E.3, reel 4, 1949.

———. State Troops. Muster Rolls. See Texas, Militia, under unit captain's name.

Thonhoff, Robert H. "A History of Karnes County." Master's thesis, Southwest Texas State College, San Marcos, 1963.

Trinity Church, Wiśnicze, Katowice Voivodeship, Poland. Parish Records. Manuscript.

United States. Census of 1860. Texas. Manuscript Agriculture Schedules. National Archives, Washington, D.C. Microfilm.

———. Census of 1860. Texas. Manuscript Population Schedules. National Archives, Washington, D.C. Microfilm.

———. Census of 1860. Texas. Manuscript Slave Schedules. National Archives, Washington, D.C. Microfilm.

———. Census of 1870. Texas. Manuscript Population Schedules. National Archives, Washington, D.C. Microfilm.

———. Census of 1890. Texas. Manuscript Schedules Enumerating Union Veterans and Widows of Union Veterans of the Civil War. National Archives, Washington, D.C. Microfilm.

———. Department of the Interior. Bureau of Pensions. Pension Record Files. Manuscript. National Archives, Washington, D.C.

———. Department of the Interior. National Park Service. Historic American Buildings Survey. Structures nos. Tex-311, Tex-312, Tex-314. Library of Congress, Washington, D.C.

———. Department of the Treasury. Copies of Lists of Passengers Arriving at the Port of Galveston, 1846–1871. Manuscript. Washington, D.C. National Archives and Records Service, Microcopy 755, roll 3, 1964.

———, Department of War. Army. Fifth Military District. General Orders no. 4. 16 January 1869. National Archives, Washington, D.C.

———. Fifth Military District. Office of Civil Affairs. Endorsements Sent (16 April 1867–8 May 1868). Manuscript. National Archives, Washington, D.C.

———. Fifth Military District. Office of Civil Affairs. Letters Received. Manuscript. National Archives, Washington, D.C.

———. Fifth Military District. Office of Civil Affairs. Letters Sent (29 May 1869–8 November 1869). Manuscript, National Archives, Washington, D.C.

———. Fifth Military District. Office of Civil Affairs. Letters Sent (8 November 1869–22 March 1870). Manuscript. National Archives, Washington, D.C.

———. Fifth Military District. Office of Civil Affairs. Manuscript Returns of Texas Election Held 30 November and 1, 2, 3 December 1869. Manuscript. National Archives, Washington, D.C.

———. Fifth Military District. Office of Civil Affairs. Register of Letters Received (16 April 1867–28 May 1869). Manuscript. National Archives, Washington, D.C.

———. Fifth Military District. Office of Civil Affairs. Register of Letters Received (2 March 1869–15 April 1870). Manuscript. National Archives, Washington, D.C.

———. Fifth Military District. Office of Civil Affairs. Register of Letters Received (29 October 1869–31 August 1870). Manuscript. National Archives, Washington, D.C.

———. 1st Texas Cavalry. Compiled Military Records. Manuscript. National Archives, Washington, D.C.

———. Post of Helena, Texas. Letters Received. Manuscript. National Archives, Washington, D.C.

———. Post of Helena, Texas. Letters sent (15 August 1869–22 May 1870). Manuscript. National Archives, Washington, D.C.

———. Post of Helena, Texas. Post Returns (5–31 March 1868 and 10 April 1869–30 April 1870). Manuscript. National Archives, Washington, D.C.

———. Post of San Antonio, Texas. Endorsements Sent (21 December 1866–11 October 1867). Manuscript. National Archives, Washington, D.C.

———. Post of San Antonio, Texas. Endorsements Sent Relating to Civil Affairs (31 January 1869–28 April 1870). Manuscript. National Archives, Washington, D.C.

———. Post of San Antonio, Texas. Letters Sent (21 December 1866–13 March 1868). Manuscript. National Archives, Washington, D.C.

———. Post of San Antonio, Texas. Letters Sent (13 March 1868–9 April 1869). Manuscript. National Archives, Washington, D.C.

———. Post of San Antonio, Texas. Letters Sent (5 February 1869–4 May 1870). Manuscript. National Archives, Washington, D.C.

———. Post of San Antonio, Texas. Office of Civil Affairs. Register of Letters Received (6 February 1869–30 April 1870). Manuscript. National Archives, Washington, D.C.

———. Post of San Antonio, Texas. Register of Letters Received (22 December 1866–15 May 1867). Manuscript. National Archives, Washington, D.C.

———. 16th Illinois Cavalry. Compiled Military Records. Manuscript. National Archives, Washington, D.C.

———. 6th U.S. Colored Cavalry. Compiled Military Records. Manuscript. National Archives, Washington, D.C.

Wojciechowski, [Stanisław]. Letters Sent. Manuscript. Archives, Congregation of the Resurrection, Rome, Italy.

Wozniak, Sister Jan Maria. "St. Michael's Church: The Polish National Catholic Church in San Antonio, Texas, 1855–1950." Master's thesis, University of Texas, Austin, 1964.

Yainta, Simon. Oath of Allegiance to the United States of America. 25 November 1869. Manuscript in possession of Rev. John W. Yanta, San Antonio, Texas.

Yanta, Rev. John W. San Antonio, Texas, to Rev. Kaczmarczyk, Płużnica; Rev. Kocur, Zębowice; Rev. Donarski, Szremrowice; and Rev. Pokora, Radawie, Poland, 3 May 1973. Photocopy in possession of the author.

Zwiardowski, Felix. Letters Sent. Manuscript. Archives, Congregation of the Resurrection, Rome, Italy.

Books

Andreas, A. T. *History of Chicago*. 3 vols. Chicago: A T. Andreas Company, Publishers, 1886.

Bakanowski, Adolf. *Moje wspomnienia 1840-1863-1913* [My Memoirs 1840-1863-1913]. Edited by Tadeusz Olejniczak. Lwów, Austrian Empire: Nakładem XX. Zmartwychwstańców, 1913.

———. *Polish Circuit Rider*. Translated and edited by Marion Moore Coleman. Cheshire, Conn.: Cherry Hill Books, 1971.

Baker, J. W. *A History of Robertson County, Texas*. N.p.: Robertson County Historical Survey Committee, 1970.

Baker, T. Lindsay. *The Early History of Panna Maria, Texas*. Texas Tech University Graduate Studies no. 9. Lubbock: Texas Tech Press, 1975.

———. Research writer. *Poles in Texas Resource Guide, Texas Heritage Unit (Poles)*. Developmental ed. Austin: Ethnic Heritage Studies Program, Southwest Educational Development Laboratory, 1975.

———. Research writer. *Poles in Texas Student Text, Texas Heritage Unit (Poles)*. Developmental ed. Austin: Ethnic Heritage Studies Program, Southwest Educational Development Laboratory, 1975.

———. Research writer. *Poles in Texas Teacher's Guide, Texas Heritage Unit (Poles)*. Developmental ed. Austin: Ethnic Heritage Studies Program, Southwest Educational Development Laboratory, 1975.

Balch, Emily Greene. *Our Slavic Fellow Citizens*. New York: Charities Publication Committee, 1910.

Barnes, Charles Merritt. *Combats and Conquests of Immortal Heroes*. San Antonio: Guessaz & Ferlet Company, 1910.

Bénézit, Emmanuel, ed. *Dictionnaire Critique et Documentaire des Peintres, Sculpteurs, Dessinateurs et Graveurs* [Critical and Documentary Dictionary of Painters, Sculptors, Designers, and Engravers]. New rev. ed. 8 vols. [Paris]: Librarie Gründ, 1966.

Biesele, Rudolph L. *The History of the German Settlements in Texas, 1831–1861*. Austin: Von Boeckmann-Jones, 1930.

Billy, Method C. *Historical Notes on the Order of Friars Minor Conventual.*

Rensselaer, N.Y.: Conventual Franciscan Publications, Saint Anthony-on-Hudson, n.d.

Bitschnau, Rev. O. *Żywoty Świętych pańskich na wszystkie dnie roku.* [The Lives of the Saints for Every Day of the Year]. Mikołów, German Empire: Nakładem Karola Miarki, 1905.

Blasig, Anne. *The Wends of Texas.* San Antonio: Naylor Company, 1954.

Bolek, Francis, ed. *Who's Who in Polish America.* 3d ed. New York: Harbinger House, 1943.

Bracht, Viktor. *Texas in 1848.* Translated by Charles Frank Schmidt. San Antonio: Naylor Printing Company, 1931.

Brożek, Andrzej. *Emigracja zamorska z Górnego Śląska w II połowie XIX wieku* [Overseas Emigration from Upper Silesia in the Second Half of the Nineteenth Century]. Opole, Poland: Inst. Śląski w Opolu, 1969.

———. *Ślązacy w Teksasie: Relacje o najstarszych polskich osadach w Stanach Zjednoczonych* [Silesians in Texas: Accounts of the Oldest Polish Settlements in the United States]. Warsaw, Poland: Państwowe Wydawnictwo Naukowe, 1972.

———, and Borek, Henryk. *Jeszcze jeden list z Teksasu do Płużnicy z 1855 roku* [One More Letter from Texas to Płużnica in the Year 1855]. Opole, Poland: Instytut Śląski w Opolu, 1972.

———, and ———. *Pierwsi Ślązacy w Ameryce: Listy z Teksasu do Płużnicy z roku 1855* [The First Silesians in America: Letters from Texas to Płużnica in the Year 1855]. Opole, Poland: Instytut Śląski w Opolu, 1967.

The Catholic Encyclopedia. 15 vols. New York: Robert Appleton Company, 1911.

Chaney, Gussie Scott. *The Breadline Banker of St. Mary's Street.* San Antonio: San Antonio Public Service Company, 1937.

Clark, Amasa Gleason. *Reminiscences of a Centenarian.* Bandera, Texas: Privately printed, 1930.

Crocchiola, Stanley Francis Louis [F. Stanley]. *The White Deer Texas Story.* Nazareth, Texas: Privately printed, 1974.

Davis, E. E., and Gray, C. T. *A Study of Rural Schools in Karnes County.* University of Texas Bulletin no. 2246. Austin: University of Texas Press, 1922.

Dworaczyk, Edward J. *The Centennial History of Panna Maria, Texas.* N.p.: Privately printed, 1954.

———. *Church Records of Panna Maria, Texas.* Chicago: Polish Roman Catholic Union of America, 1945.

———. *The First Polish Colonies of America in Texas.* San Antonio: Naylor Company, 1936.

———. *The Millennium History of Panna Maria, Texas.* N.p.: Privately printed, 1966.

Fox, Paul. *The Poles in America.* New York: George H. Doran Company, 1922.

Gilbert, J. M. *Archdiocese of San Antonio, 1874–1949*. San Antonio: Schneider Printing Company, 1949.

Graef, Hilda. *Mary: A History of Doctrine and Devotion*. 2 vols. New York: Sheed and Ward, 1965.

Greulich, Leon, and Hellmann, Othmar. *Album Fratrum Minorum S. Francisci Conventualium in Statibus Foederatis Americae pro Anno 1917* [Album of the Friars Minor Conventual in the United States of America for the Year 1917]. Syracuse, N.Y.: Henrici Dick, 1917.

Grot, Zdzisław. *Działalność posłów polskich w sejmie pruskim (1848–1850)* [The Activities of the Polish Representatives in the Prussian Parliament (1848–1850)]. Poznan, Poland: Wydawnictwo Poznańskie, 1961.

Haas, Oscar. *History of New Braunfels and Comal County, Texas, 1844–1946*. Austin: Steck Company, 1968.

Habig, Marion A. *San Antonio's Mission San Jose*. San Antonio: Naylor Company, 1968.

Haiman, Miecislaus. *The Poles in the Early History of Texas*. Chicago: Polish Roman Catholic Union Archive and Museum, 1936.

———. *Polish Past in America, 1608–1865*. Chicago: Polish Roman Catholic Union, 1939.

Haley, J. Evetts. *Jeff Milton: A Good Man with a Gun*. Norman: University of Oklahoma Press, 1949.

Harkey, Dee. *Mean as Hell*. Albuquerque: University of New Mexico Press, 1948.

Harvard Guide to American History. Cambridge, Mass.: Harvard University Press, Belknap Press, 1955.

History of Franklin, Jefferson, Washington, Crawford, and Gasconade Counties, Missouri. Chicago: Goodspeed Publishing Company, 1888.

Hunter, J. Marvin. *A Brief History of Bandera County*. Bandera, Texas: Frontier Times, 1936.

———. *100 Years in Bandera*. [Bandera, Texas]: Privately printed, 1953.

Iciek, S. A. *Samochodem przez stany południowe* [By Automobile through the Southern States]. Ware, Mass.: Ware River News Print, 1937.

Iwicki, John. *The First One Hundred Years: A Study of the Apostolate of the Congregation of the Resurrection in the United States, 1866–1966*. Rome: Gregorian University Press, 1966.

Jackson, W. H., and Long, S. A. *The Texas Stock Directory*. San Antonio: Herald Office, 1865.

James, Vinton Lee. *Frontier and Pioneer Recollections of Early Days in San Antonio and West Texas*. San Antonio: Privately printed, 1938.

Janas, Edward T. *Dictionary of American Resurrectionists 1865–1965*. Rome: [Congregation of the Resurrection], 1967.

Johnson, Frank W., and Barker, Eugene C. *A History of Texas and Texans*. 5 vols. Chicago: American Historical Society, 1914.

Jordan, Terry G. *German Seed in Texas Soil: Immigrant Farmers in Nineteenth Century Texas*. Austin: University of Texas Press, 1966.

Joyce, John A. *Our Polish Pioneers*. San Antonio: St. Michael's School, [1937].

Kinney, John M., comp. *Index to Applications for Texas Confederate Pensions*. Austin: Archives Division, Texas State Library, 1975.

Knie, J. G. *Alphabetisch-Statistich-Topographische Uebersicht der Dörfer, Flecken, Städte und Andern Orte der Königl. Preuss. Provinz Schlesien* [Alphabetical-Statistical-Topographical Overview of the Villages, Localities, Cities, and Other Places of the Royal Prussian Province of Silesia]. Breslau, Kingdom of Prussia: Graf, Barth und Comp., 1845.

Kretchmer, Albert. *Deutsche Volkstrachten* [German Folk Dress]. Leipzig: J. G. Bach's Verlag, n.d.

Krueger, M. *Pioneer Life in Texas*. N.p., n.d.

Kruszka, Wacław. *Historja polska w Ameryce* [Polish History in America]. Rev. ed. Milwaukee: Drukiem Kuryera Polskiego, 1937.

Książka modlitewna i kancyonał dla pospolitego ludu katolickiego [Prayer Book and Hymnbook for Ordinary Catholic People]. 10th ed. Opole, Kingdom of Prussia: Drukiem i Nakładem F. Wellshäusera, 1864.

Kummer, Gertrude. *Die Leopoldinen-Stiftung (1829–1914): Der Älteste Österreichische Missionsverein* [The Leopoldine Foundation (1829–1914): The Oldest Austrian Mission Society]. Vienna, Austria: Wiener Dom-Verlag, 1966.

Leksykon polactwa w Niemczech [Lexicon of the Poles in Germany]. Opole [Oppeln], Germany: Związek Polaków w Niemczech T. z., 1939. Reprint ed. Warsaw, Poland: Państwowe Wydawnictwo Naukowe, 1973.

[Long, Leonard.] *For God and Man, 1842–1942: A Short History of the Congregation of the Resurrection*. [Chicago]: Nordmann Printing Co., [1942].

Lutosławski, Wincenty. *Iskierki warszawskie* [Warsaw Sparks]. Warsaw, Russian Empire: Nakładem Księgarni St. Sadowskiego, 1911.

McConnell, H. H. *Five Years a Cavalryman; or, Sketches of Regular Army Life on the Texas Frontier, Twenty Odd Years Ago*. Jacksboro, Texas: J. N. Rogers & Co., 1889.

Memorial Homecoming Father Leopold Moczygemba Liturgical Reinterment October 13, 1974 Panna Maria, Texas. N.p.: Privately printed, 1974.

Metz, Leon Claire. *John Selman: Texas Gunfighter*. New York: Hastings House, 1966.

Moczygemba, Leopold. *Enchiridion Sacerdotum Curam Animarum Agentium*. Rome: Typius S. Cong. de Propaganda Fide Soc. Eq. Petro Marietti Admin., 1870.

Nesterowicz, Stefan. *Notatki z podróży po północnej i środkowej Ameryce* [Travel Notes through Northern and Middle America]. Toledo, Ohio: A. A. Paryski, 1909.

———. *Travel Notes*. Translated and edited by Marion Moore Coleman. Cheshire, Conn.: Cherry Hill Books, 1970.

Niklewicz, Franciszek. *Dzieje pierwszych polskich osadników w Ameryce i przewodnik parafij polskich w Stanach Zjednoczonych* [History of the First Polish Settlers in America and Guide around the Polish Parishes in the United States]. Green Bay, Wisc.: Drukiem Nowin Polskich, 1927.

———. *Polacy w Stanach Zjednoczonych* [The Poles in the United States]. Green Bay, Wisc.: F. Niklewicz, 1937.

Noel, Theophilus. *Autobiography and Reminiscences of Theophilus Noel.* Chicago: Theo. Noel Company Print, 1904.

Oakes, Alma, and Hill, Margot Hamilton. *Rural Clothing: Its Origin and Development in Western Europe and the British Isles.* New York: Van Nostrand Reinhold Company, 1970.

Olmsted, Frederick Law. *Journey through Texas.* New York: Mason Brothers, 1860.

Parisot, P. F., and Smith, C. J. *History of the Catholic Church in the Diocese of San Antonio, Texas.* San Antonio: Carrico & Bowen, 1897.

[Polish American Congress of Texas.] *First Convention Polish American Congress of Texas San Antonio, St. Anthony Hotel—Nov. 5 and 6 Panna Maria Pilgrimage—Nov. 7.* N.p.: Privately printed, 1971.

———. *Second Convention Polish American Congress of Texas November 3–5, 1972 Houston, Texas.* N.p.: Privately printed, 1972.

———. *Fourth Convention Polish American Congress of Texas San Antonio, Texas October 24–26, 1974.* N.p.: Privately printed, 1974.

———. *Seventh Convention Polish American Congress of Texas Ramada Gondolier Austin, Texas October 21 & 22, 1977.* N.p.: Privately printed, 1977.

The Polish Texans. San Antonio: Institute of Texan Cultures, 1972.

Polski słownik biograficzny [Polish Biographical Dictionary]. Kraków, Poland: Polska Akademia Umiejętności, 1935–.

Popiołek, Kazimierz. *Polska "Wiosna Ludów" na Górnym Śląsku* [The Polish "Spring of Peoples" in Upper Silesia]. Poznan, Poland: Instytut Zachodni, 1948.

Prus, Konstanty, comp. *Spis miejscowości Polskiego Śląska Górnego: Nazwy wszystkich gmin, obszarów dworskich oraz osad i kolonij znaczniejszych* [List of Places in Polish Upper Silesia: Names of All Communities, Manors, Settlements, and More Important Colonies]. Bytom [Beuthen], Germany: Nakładem Polskiego Komisarjatu Plebyscytowego dla Górnego Śląska, 1920.

Przygoda, Jacek. *Texas Pioneers from Poland: A Study in the Ethnic History.* Waco, Texas: Privately printed, 1971.

Ramsay, Grover C. *Confederate Postmasters in Texas.* Waco, Texas: W. M. Morrison, 1963.

Ramsdell, Charles W. *Reconstruction in Texas.* New York: Columbia University Press, 1910.

Randel, Jo Stewart, and Carson County Historical Survey Committee, eds.

A Time to Purpose: A Chronicle of Carson County. 2 vols. N.p.: Pioneer Publishers, 1966.

Reddaway, W. F., Pinson, J. H., Halecki, O., and Dyboski, R. *The Cambridge History of Poland*. Vol. 2: *From Augustus II to Pilsudski (1697–1935)*. Cambridge, England: Cambridge University Press, 1950.

Roemer, Ferdinand. *Texas, with Particular Reference to German Immigration and the Physical Appearance of the Country*. Translated by Oswald Meuller. San Antonio: Standard Printing Company, 1935.

Roemer, Theodore. *The Ludwig-Missionsverein and the Church in America (1838–1918)*. Catholic University of America Studies in American Church History no. 26. Washington, D.C.: Catholic University of America, 1933.

———. *Ten Decades of Alms*. St. Louis: B. Herder Book Co., 1942.

Rose, William John. *The Drama of Upper Silesia*. London: Williams & Norgate, 1936.

Rothensteiner, John. *History of the Archdiocese of St. Louis*. 2 vols. St. Louis: Blackwell Wielandy Co., 1928.

Russell, L. B. *Granddad's Autobiography*. Comanche, Texas: Comanche Publishing Co., [1930].

St. Stanislaus Parish, Bandera, Texas: Centennial History, 1855–1955. N.p.: Privately printed, [1955].

Schofer, Lawrence. *The Formation of a Modern Labor Force: Upper Silesia, 1865–1914*. Berkeley: University of California Press, 1975.

Schück, Th. *Oberschlesien: Statistik des Regierungs-Bezirks Oppeln mit Besonderer Beziehung auf Landwirtschaft, Bergbau, Hüttenwesen, Gewerbe und Handel nacht Amtlichen Quellen* [Upper Silesia: Statistics of the Regency of Opole with Special Attention to Agriculture, Mining, Foundries, Industry, and Commerce from Official Sources]. Iserlohn: Verlag von F. Bädeker, 1860.

Shaver, Lillie Terrell, and Rogers, Willie Williamson. *Flashlights on Texas*. Austin: A. C. Baldwin & Sons, n.d.

Siatka, Stanisław. *Krótkie wspomnienia o życiu i działalności ks. Wincentego Barzyńskiego, C.R.* [A Brief Résumé of the Life and Works of Father Vincent Barzyński, C.R.]. Chicago: Dziennik Chicagowski, 1901.

Sonnichsen, C. L. *Pass of the North*. El Paso, Texas: Texas Western Press, 1968.

Souvenir [of Our Lady of Częstochowa Grotto, San Antonio, Texas]. N.p., [ca. 1966].

Sowell, Andrew Jackson. *Early Settlers and Indian Fighters of Southwest Texas*. Austin: Ben C. Jones & Co., 1900.

Steinbomer, Robert A. *Three Early Polish Houses in Panna Maria Texas*. N.p.: Privately printed, 1977.

Steinfeldt, Cecilia, and Stover, Donald L. *Early Texas Furniture and Decorative Arts*. San Antonio: Trinity University Press for the San Antonio Museum Association, 1973.

Steward, George R. *American Place-Names: A Concise and Selective Directory for the Continental United States of America*. New York: Oxford University Press, 1970.

Swastek, Joseph. *Priest and Pioneer: Rev. Leopold Moczygemba*. Detroit: Conventual Press, 1951.

Szczepański, Aleksander. *Drapacze i śmietniki: Wrażenia amerykańskie* [The Skyscrapers and the Dumps: American Impressions]. Warsaw, Poland: Towarzystwo Wydawnicze "Rój," 1933.

Texas, Department of Agriculture, Insurance, Statistics, and History. *First Annual Report of the Agricultural Bureau, 1887–88*. Austin: State Printing Office, 1889.

———. *Second Annual Report of the Agricultural Bureau, 1888–89*. Austin: State Printing Office, 1890.

———. *Fifth Annual Report of the Agricultural Bureau, 1891–92*. Austin: Ben C. Jones & Co., State Printers, 1893.

———. *Sixth Annual Report of the Agricultural Bureau, 1892–93*. Austin: Ben C. Jones & Co., State Printers, 1894.

———. *Ninth Annual Report of the Agricultural Bureau, 1895*. Austin: Ben C. Jones & Co., State Printers, 1897.

Texas, Department of Insurance, Statistics, and History. *The Resources, Soil, and Climate of Texas*. Galveston: A. H. Belo & Company, 1882.

Texas Almanac and State Industrial Guide 1904. Galveston: A. H. Belo & Co., 1904.

Texas Almanac for 1858. Galveston: Richardson & Co., 1857.

Texas Almanac for 1859. Galveston: Richardson & Co., n.d.

Texas Almanac for 1861. Galveston: W. & D. Richardson, 1860.

Texas Almanac for 1867. Galveston: W. Richardson & Co., 1866.

Texas Almanac for 1869. Galveston: Richardson & Co., 1868.

Texas Almanac for 1870. Galveston: Richardson & Co., 1870.

Texas Almanac for 1871. Galveston: Richardson & Co., 1871.

Thomas, William I., and Znaniecki, Florian. *The Polish Peasant in Europe and America*. 5 vols. Boston: Richard G. Badger, 1918.

Tims, Richard Wonser. *Germanizing Prussian Poland*. New York: Columbia University Press, 1941.

Triest, Felix. *Topographisches Handbuch von Oberschlesien* [Topographical Handbook of Upper Silesia]. Breslau, Kingdom of Prussia: Verlag von Wilh. Gottl. Korn, 1865.

A Twentieth Century History of Southwest Texas. 2 vols. Chicago: Lewis Publishing Company, 1907.

Wańkowicz, Melchior. *Atlantyk–Pacyfik* [Atlantic–Pacific]. Warsaw, Poland: Iskry, 1967.

Winfrey, Dorman H., ed. *Texas Indian Papers, 1846–1859*. Austin: Texas State Library, 1960.

Zieliński, Stanisław. *Bibljografja czasopism polskich zagranicą 1830–1934*

[Bibliography of Polish Periodicals Abroad 1830–1934]. Warsaw, Poland: Nakładem Światowego Związku Polaków z Zagranicy, 1935.

Articles

Bakanowski, Adolf. "My Memoirs—Texas Sojourn (1866–70)." Translated and edited by Marion Moore Coleman. *Polish American Studies* 25 (July–December 1968): 106–124.

Baker, T. Lindsay. "The Early Years of Rev. Wincenty Barzyński." *Polish American Studies* 32 (Spring 1975): 29–52.

———. "The Kiołbassa Family of Illinois and Texas." *Chicago Genealogist* 5 (Spring 1973): 78–82.

———. "The Moczygemba Family of Texas and Poland: Initiators of Polish Colonization in America." *Stirpes: Texas State Genealogical Society Quarterly* 15 (December 1975): 124–138.

———. "National Consciousness among the Silesians at the Oldest Polish Colony in America." *Poland and Germany (East and West)* (London) 19 (January–June 1975): 27–36.

———. "Nation's Second Oldest Polish Newspaper Was Founded in Washington in 1870." *Washington Missourian* (Washington, Mo.), 26 September 1974, sec. B, p. 1.

———. "Panna Maria and Płużnica: A Study in Comparative Folk Culture." In *The Folklore of Texan Cultures*, edited by Francis Edward Abernethy, pp. 218–226. Publications of the Texas Folklore Society, vol. 38. Austin: Encino Press, 1974.

———. "Tecla Rzeppa (1802–1880)." In *Women in Early Texas*, edited by Evelyn M. Carrington, pp. 214–218. Austin: Pemberton Press, 1975.

———, trans. and ed. "Four Letters from Texas to Poland in 1855." *Southwestern Historical Quarterly* 77 (January 1974): 381–389.

———, and Stanisław Rospond, eds. "Z życia śląskich emigrantów w Teksasie: List Jakuba Moczygemby do Polski w 1910 r." [From the Life of the Silesian Emigrants in Texas: The Letter of Jakob Moczygemba to Poland in 1910]. *Kwartalnik Opolski* (Opole, Poland) 23 (1977): 58–75.

"A Bandera County Pioneer." *Frontier Times* 1 (July 1924): 12–14.

Berezowski, Maksymilian. "Swojacy wśród kowbojów: Podróż do Teksasu" [Countrymen in the Midst of Cowboys: A Journey to Texas]. *Trybuna Ludu* (Warsaw, Poland), nos. 7493–7494 (1–2 November 1969), p. 5.

Bronicz, Stanisław. "Materiały i uwagi do zagadnienia strojów ludowych na Śląsku Opolskim" [Materials and Comments on the Subject of Folk Dress in Opole Silesia]. *Opolski Rocznik Muzealny* (Opole, Poland) 2 (1966): 185–198.

Brożek, Andrzej. "The Most Polish of the Poles in America." *Poland and Germany (East & West)* (London) 14 (January–June 1970): 17–24.

———. "Najbardziej polscy emigranci w Ameryce" [The Most Polish Immigrants in America]. *Poglądy* (Katowice, Poland) 7 (1–15 February 1968): 12, 18.

———. "Najstarsza polska szkoła w Stanach Zjednoczonych Ameryki" [The Oldest Polish School in the United States of America]. *Przegląd Historyczno-Oświatowy* 14 (1971): 60–73.
———. "Z najstarszych polskich relacji prasowych o pionierach górnośląskich w Teksasie" [The Oldest Polish Press Accounts of the Upper Silesian Pioneers in Texas]. *Studia Śląskie*, n.s. 20 (1971): 49–63.
———. "Nowe publikacje zagraniczne o początkach osadnictwa polskiego w Ameryce" [New Publications Abroad on the Beginnings of Polish Settlement in America]. *Przegląd Historyczny* 63 (April–June 1972): 306–314.
———. "Początki emigracji z Górnego Śląska do Ameryki w świetle współczesnej prasy polskiej na Śląsku" [The Beginning of Immigration from Upper Silesia to America as Seen from the Viewpoint of the Polish Press in Silesia]. *Kwartalnik Historyczny* 75 (1968): 3–21.
———. "Podróże ze Stanów do Teksasu i z powrotem" [Travel from the States to Texas and Return]. *Opole* (Opole, Poland) 5 (May 1973): 22–23.
———. "Polonia zagraniczna za polskim Śląskiem" [Poles Abroad from Polish Silesia]. *Opole* (Opole, Poland) 2 (May 1971): 5–6.
———. "Próby organizacji dostaw bawełny do Polski z farm polonijnych w Teksasie (1920–1930)" [Attempts to Organize Cotton Supplies for Poland from the Farms of the Polish Immigrants in Texas (1920–1930)]. *Zeszyty Naukowe Wyższej Szkoły Pedagogicznej w Opolu* (Opole, Poland), History Series, 10 (1972): 65–74.
———. Review of "Four Letters from Texas to Poland in 1855," by T. Lindsay Baker. *Acta Polonia Historica* 33 (1976): 177–178.
———. "The Roots of Polish Migration to Texas." *Polish American Studies* 30 (Spring 1973): 20–35.
———. "Trwanie w polskości pierwszych osadników górnośląskich w Teksasie" [The Existence of Polish Consciousness among the First Upper Silesian Settlers in Texas]. *Kwartalnik Nauczyciela Opolskiego* (Opole, Poland), no. 40 (1968), pp. 3–8.
Budrewicz, Olgierd. "Częstochowa w Teksasie" [Częstochowa in Texas]. *Przekrój* (Kraków, Poland), no. 792 (12 June 1960), pp. 5–7.
Busyn, Helen. "Peter Kiołbassa: Maker of Polish America." *Polish American Studies* 8 (July–December 1951): 65–84.
———. "The Political Career of Peter Kiolbassa." *Polish American Studies* 7 (January–June 1950): 8–22.
Caraway, L. V. "The Battle of Arkansas Post." *Confederate Veteran* 14 (March 1906): 127–128.
Carroll, H. Bailey, ed. "Texas Collection." *Southwestern Historical Quarterly* 50 (January 1947): 377–407.
Coleman, Marion Moore. "The Polish Origins of Bandera, Texas." *Polish American Studies* 20 (January–June 1963): 21–27.
Combs, Jimmy. "John Twohig: Texan by Adoption." *Junior Historian of the Texas State Historical Association* 6 (March 1946): 1–2.
Cotulla, Joseph. "Cornbread and Clabber Made a Good Meal." In *The Trail*

Drivers of Texas, edited by J. Marvin Hunter, pp. 317–319. 2d ed. Nashville: Cokesbury Press, 1925.

Czuma, Mieczysław. "Płużnicy dzień powszedni" [Płużnica Every Day]. *Przekrój* (Kraków, Poland), no. 1514 (14 April 1974), pp. 4–7.

Domański, F. "Przyczyny niepowodzenia w życiu ks. Leopolda Moczygemby" [The Causes of the Failures in the Life of Rev. Leopold Moczygemba]. *Sodalis* 36 (January 1955): 8–16.

Dunn, Si. "A Visit to Panna Maria." *Scene, the Dallas Morning News Sunday Magazine* 5 (30 June 1974): 16–18, 20.

Erdman, Jan. "Opisanie Panny Marii, najstarszej osady polskiej w USA" [Description of Panna Maria, the Oldest Polish Colony in the U.S.A.]. *Ameryka* (Washington), no. 159 (April 1972), pp. 40–46.

Fenner, Annette. "The Headless Ghost of Panna Maria." In *Backwoods to Border*, edited by Mody C. Boatright and Donald Day, pp. 140–141. Publications of the Texas Folk-Lore Society, vol. 18. Austin: Texas Folk-Lore Society, 1943.

Fiołek, Mieczysław. "W stulecie Teksasu i pierwszej emigracji Ślązaków za Ocean" [On the Centennial of Texas and the First Emigration of Silesians across the Ocean]. *Polska Zachodnia* (Katowice, Poland) 11 (5 December 1936): 5.

German, Franciszek. "Ludzie ziemi gliwickiej: Piotr Kiełbassa (1838–1905)" [People of the Gliwice Land: Peter Kiołbassa (1838–1905)]. *Zeszyty Gliwickie* (Gliwice, Poland) 5 (1967): 153–158.

———. "Ślązacy w Teksas: Z dziejów osadnictwa polskiego w Ameryce" [Silesians in Texas: From the History of Polish Colonization in America]. *Biuletyn dla Polonii Zagranicznej, Zachodnia Agencja Prasowa* (Poznan, Poland), no. 9 (November 1957), pp. 22–40.

Halecki, Oscar. "The Place of Czestochowa in Poland's Millennium." *Catholic Historical Review* 52 (January 1967): 494–508.

Hodges, LeRoy. "The Poles of Texas: Their Effect on the State's Agricultural Development." *Texas Magazine* 7 (December 1912): 116–120.

Hunter, J. Marvin. "The Founding of Bandera." *Frontier Times* 3 (May 1926): 40–44.

———. "Old Time Barbecues in Bandera County." *Frontier Times* 19 (June 1942): 325–328.

———. "When the Polish People Came to Bandera." *Frontier Times* 25 (May 1948): 191–195.

Iwuc, Antoni. "Panna Maria czy Parisville?" [Panna Maria or Parisville?]. *Sodalis* 36 (January 1955): 6–8.

Janik, Michał. "Ludność polska w Stanach Zjednoczonych Ameryki Północnej" [The Polish People in the United States of America]. *Lud* (Cracow, Austrian Empire) 11 (1905): 249–269.

Jonca, Karol. "Śladami dawnej emigracji" [On the Traces of the Old Emigration]. *Trybuna Opolska* (Opole, Poland), no. 3793 (28–30 March 1964), p. 6.

———. "Z Opolszczyzny do Teksasu: Śladami dawnej emigracji" [From the Opole Region to Texas: On the Traces of the Old Emigration]. *Trybuna Opolska* (Opole, Poland), no. 3445 (9–10 February 1963), pp. 1, 3.

Jordan, Terry G. "Antecedents of the Long-Lot in Texas." *Annals of the Association of American Geographers* 64 (March 1974): 70–84.

Kallison, Mrs. Perry. "Our Historical Homes and the People Who Called Them Home." *Witte Museum Quarterly* 4 (1966): 4–13.

Konopka, Marek. "Z Płużnicy i Toszka do . . . Teksasu" [From Płużnica and Toszek to . . . Texas]. *Trybuna Robotnicza* (Katowice, Poland), no. 7935 (9–10 August 1969), pp. 1, 6.

Koraszewski, Jacek. "Ślązacy w Texas: Pseudonauka niemieckich rewizjonistów w świetle historycznych faktów" [Silesians in Texas: German Revisionist Pseudoscience in the Light of Historical Facts]. *Dziennik Zachodni* (Katowice, Poland), no. 2541 (23 April 1952), p. 4.

Kowalczyk, Edmund L. "Jottings from the Polish American Past." *Polish American Studies* 9 (July–December 1952): 86–96; 11 (January–June 1954): 31–42.

Kowalczyk, Jan Jakub. "Górnoślązacy w Teksasie" [Upper Silesians in Texas]. *Gość Niedzielny* (Katowice, Poland) 15 (17 January 1937): 47–48; 15 (24 January 1937): 67; 15 (31 January 1937): 81.

"Ksiądz Leopold Moczygemba i polskie kolonie w Ameryce" [The Rev. Leopold Moczygemba and the Polish Colonies in America]. *Missyonarz Katolicki* (Mikołów, German Empire) 1 (1 September 1891): 262–264.

Lucille, Sister. "The Causes of Polish Immigration to the United States." *Polish American Studies* 8 (July–December 1951): 85–91.

Lutosławski, Wincenty. "Odrodzenie Śląska w Texasie" [The Rebirth of Silesia in Texas]. *Świat* (Warsaw, Russian Empire) 3 (28 November 1908): 8–9; 3 (5 December 1908): 13–14.

Lyra, Franciszek, "Język polski w najstarszych osadach polskich w Stanach Zjednoczonych" [The Polish Language in the Oldest Polish Colonies in the United States]. *Zaranie Śląskie* (Katowice, Poland) 28 (April–June 1965): 562–566.

Ladomirska, Joanna. "Z dziejów Śląskiej emigracji do Ameryki północnej" [From the History of Silesian Immigration to North America]. *Studia Śląskie*, n.s. 10 (1966): 271–280.

Małowieski, Robert. "Amerykanin wśród Ślązaków" [An American among Silesians]. *Opole* (Opole, Poland) 3 (September 1972): 10.

"Memorial Tablet to John Twohig." *Frontier Times* 1 (August 1924): 27.

Moczygemba, Dorothy. "My People Came." *Junior Historian of the Texas State Historical Association* 16 (December 1955): 19–21.

Morrow, Ian F. D. "The Prussianization of the Poles." *Slavonic and East European Review* 15 (1936–1937): 153–164.

Możejewski, Martynian [Rev. M. M.]. "Pierwsza parafia i kościół polski w Ameryce" [The First Polish Parish and Church in America]. *Missye Katolickie* (Kraków, Austrian Empire) 15 (April 1896): 95–99.

———. "Stany Zjednoczone Ameryki Północnej: Najpierwsza parafia i kościół polski w Ameryce" [United States of America: The First Polish Parish and Church in America]. *Przegląd Katolicki* (Warsaw, Russian Empire) 34 (16 January 1896): 43–47.

Murzynowska, Krystyna. "Polscy pionierzy w Teksasie (1854–1880)" [Polish Pioneers in Texas (1854–1880)]. *Mówią Wieki, Magazyn Historyczny* (Warsaw, Poland) 8 (October 1965): 23–28.

Olesch, Reinhold. "The West Slavic Languages in Texas with Special Regard to Sorbian in Serbin, Lee County." In *Texas Studies in Bilingualism*, edited by Glenn G. Gilbert, pp. 151–162. Berlin: Walter de Gruyter & Co., 1970.

[Orłowski, Leon]. "Polacy w Teksasie" [The Poles in Texas]. *Wychodźca* (Warsaw, Poland) 7 (6 May 1928): 2–3; 7 (13 May 1928): 2–4.

Owens, Meroe J. "John Barzynski, Land Agent." *Nebraska History* 36 (June 1955): 81–91.

Pajewski, Bernard. "The Headless Ghost of Panna Maria." *Polish Folklore* 4 (March 1959): 11–12.

Pampuch, Marta. "Ślązacy w Teksas w drugiej połowie XIX wieku" [Silesians in Texas in the Second Half of the Nineteenth Century]. *Polonia* (Katowice, Poland), no. 4103 (15 March 1936), "Kultura i życie" supplement, p. 1.

Perkowski, Jan L. "A Survey of the West Slavic Immigrant Languages in Texas." In *Texas Studies in Bilingualism*, edited by Glenn G. Gilbert, pp. 163–169. Berlin: Walter de Gruyter & Co., 1970.

Przygoda, Jacek. "New Light on the Poles in Texas." *Polish American Studies* 27 (Spring–Autumn 1970): 80–86.

———. "Poles in Texas Today." *Quarterly Review; Official Publication of the American Council of Polish Cultural Clubs* (Washington) 21 (October–December 1969): 1.

———. "Wracamy do historii Polaków w Teksasie" [We Return to the History of the Poles in Texas]. *Sodalis* 50 (February 1969): 60–61; 50 (March 1969): 88–91; 50 (June 1969): 189–191.

Reiner, Bolesław, "Polityczno-administracyjne podziały Górnego Śląska w XIX i XX wieku" [Political-Administrative Divisions in Upper Silesia in the Nineteenth and Twentieth Centuries]. *Studia Śląskie* 21 (1972): 41–64.

Roemer, Theodore. "Bavaria Helps America." *Commonweal* 21 (11 January 1935): 312–313.

Rosiński, Bolesław. "Polacy w Texasie" [The Poles in Texas]. *Ziemia* (Warsaw, Poland) 15 (1 December 1930): 473–479.

Rozanski, Edward C. "Civil War Poles of Illinois." *Polish American Studies* 23 (July–December 1966): 112–114.

Rozmus, Wincenty. "Polacy w Ameryce Północnej" [The Poles in North America]. *Głosy z nad Odry* (Mikolów, Germany) 4 (March 1929): 7–9.

Ruckman, John. "Freedom and a Piece of Bread." *San Antonio Express Magazine*, 31 July 1949, pp. 3–5.

Starczewska, Maria. "The Historical Geography of the Oldest Polish Settlement in the United States." *Polish Review* 12 (Spring 1967): 11–40.

Stawasz, Jan. "Stuletnia Panna Maria" [Centennial of Panna Maria]. *Sodalis* 36 (January 1955): 17–19.

Surman, Zdzisław. "Wyniki wyborów do pruskiego konstytucyjnego zgromadzenia narodowego i izby posłów sejmu pruskiego na Śląsku w latach 1848–1918" [Results of Elections of the Prussian Constituent National Assembly and to the Chamber of Deputies of the Prussian Diet from Silesia in 1848–1918]. *Studia i Materiały z Dziejów Śląska* (Wrocław, Poland) 7 (1966): 13–167.

Symonolewicz, Constantin. "Polish Travelers and Observers in the U.S.A. (1918–1939)." *Polish American Studies* 2 (January–June 1945): 46–51.

Szczurek, Marian. "Wilkołak przepłynął Atlantyk" [The Werewolf Swam the Atlantic]. *Trybuna Odrzańska* (Opole, Poland), no. 8016 (20–21 November 1976), pp. 1, 4.

Szramek, Emil. Review of *The First Polish Colonies of America in Texas*, by Edward J. Dworaczyk. *Roczniki Towarzystwa Przyjaciół Nauk na Śląsku* (Katowice, Poland) 6 (1938): 398–400.

"Śląskie osady w Texas" [The Silesian Settlements in Texas]. *Dziennik Polski* (Cieszyn, Czechoslovakia) 4 (4 April 1937): 4.

Taylor, T. U. "Pioneer Engineering in Texas." *Frontier Times* 15 (October 1937): 31–37.

"Warsaw Television Films Segments of Polish Texan History at ITC." *People* (Institute of Texan Cultures, San Antonio) 4 (May–June 1974): 5.

Willging, Eugene P., and Hatzfeld, Herta. "Nineteenth Century Polish Catholic Periodical Publications in the United States." *Polish American Studies* 13 (January–June 1956): 19–35.

Wiśniowski, Sygurd. "Piotr Kiolbassa: Poseł z Chicago" [Peter Kiołbassa: Representative from Chicago]. *Tygodnik Illustrowany* (Warsaw, Russian Empire), 3d ser. 3 (9 June 1877): 360, 362.

Włoszczewski, Stefan. "Polacy w Teksasie" [The Poles in Texas]. *Tygodnik Kulturalny* (Warsaw, Poland) 13 (31 August 1969): 2, 11.

———. "Z historii emigracji Ślązaków do Teksasu" [From the History of Silesian Emigration to Texas]. In *W jedności z macierzą: Referaty i materiały z sesji poświęconej łączności Śląska z macierzą* [In Unity with the Motherland: Papers and Materials from the Session Devoted to the Connection of Silesia with the Motherland], edited by Tadeusz Cieślak, pp. 96–101. Katowice, Poland: Wydawnictwo "Śląsk," 1965.

Wnęk, Jacek. "Ślązacy w Texasie" [Silesians in Texas]. *Powstaniec* (Katowice, Poland) 11 (1 February 1937): 25–29; 11 (15 February 1937): 26–30.

Newspapers

Amarillo Sunday News-Globe (Amarillo, Texas), 1938.
Czas (Kraków, Austrian Empire), 1854–1858.
Dallas Morning News (Dallas, Texas), 1891, 1932.
Galveston Weekly News (Galveston, Texas), 1854.
Galveston Zeitung (Galveston, Texas), 1854.
Gwiazdka Cieszyńska (Cieszyn, Austrian Empire), 1854–1858.
Houston Chronicle (Houston, Texas), 1932, 1974.
Karnes City Citation (Karnes City, Texas), 1973–1977.
Katolik (Królewska Huta [Königshütte] and Bytom [Beuthen], German Empire), 1881, 1888, 1891.
Neu-Braunfelser Zeitung (New Braunfels, Texas), 1854–1856.
Nixon News (Nixon, Texas), 1973.
Nowiny Texaskie (San Antonio, Texas), 1914–1915.
Przegląd Poznański (Posen, Kingdom of Prussia), 1858.
Rosenberg-Creutzburger Telegraph (Rosenberg [Olesno], Kingdom of Prussia), 1849.
San Antonio Daily Express (San Antonio, Texas), 1910.
San Antonio Daily Herald (San Antonio, Texas), 1867, 1874.
San Antonio Express (San Antonio, Texas), 1866–1871, 1911, 1920.
San Antonio Weekly Herald (San Antonio, Texas), 1855, 1861–1864.
Schlesische Zeitung (Breslau, Kingdom of Prussia), 1848, 1854–1857.
Texas Catholic Herald (Houston, Texas), 1968.
Times (London), 1854, 1859.
Victoria Daily Advocate (Victoria, Texas), 1935.
Zwiastun Górnoszląski (Piekary, Kingdom of Prussia), 1869–1870.

Published U.S. Government Documents

Heitman, Francis B. *Historical Register and Dictionary of the United States Army*. 2 vols. Washington, D.C.: U.S. Government Printing Office, 1903.

Hodges, LeRoy. *Slavs on Southern Farms: An Account of the Bohemian, Slovak, and Polish Agricultural Settlements in the Southern States*. 63d Cong., 2d Sess., Sen. Doc. 595. Washington, D.C.: U.S. Government Printing Office, 1914.

U.S. Department of the Interior. *Register of Officers and Agents, Civil, Military, and Naval, in the Service of the United States on the Thirteenth of September, 1875*. Washington, D.C.: U.S. Government Printing Office, 1876.

———, Patent Office, Commissioner. *Report of the Commissioner of Patents for the Year 1854: Agriculture*. 33d Cong., 2d Sess., Sen. Exec. Doc. 42. Washington, D.C.: Beverley Tucker, 1855.

———. *Report of the Commissioner of Patents for the Year 1855: Agriculture*. 34th Cong., 1st Sess., Sen. Exec. Doc. 20. Washington, D.C.: A. O. P. Nicholson, 1856.

U.S. Department of State, Secretary. *Letter from the Secretary of State Transmitting the Annual Report of Passengers Arriving in the United States*. 33d Cong., 2d Sess., H. Exec. Doc. 77. Washington, D.C.: A. O. P. Nicholson, 1855.

———. *Letter of the Secretary of State Transmitting a Statement of the Commercial Relations of the United States with Foreign Nations*. 35th Cong., 2d Sess., H. Exec. Doc. 85. Washington, D.C.: James B. Steedman, 1859.

U.S. Department of War. *The War of Rebellion: A Compilation of the Official Records of the Union and Confederate Armies*. 130 vols. Washington, D.C.: U.S. Government Printing Office, 1880–1901.

———, Secretary. *Report of the Secretary of War, 1867*. 40th Cong., 2d Sess., H. Exec. Doc. 1, pt. 1. Washington, D.C.: U.S. Government Printing Office, 1867.

———. *Report of the Secretary of War, 1868*. 40th Cong., 3d Sess., H. Exec. Doc. 1, pt. 1. Washington, D.C.: U.S. Government Printing Office, 1868.

U.S. Immigration Commission. *Immigrants in Industries (in Twenty-five Parts); Part 24: Recent Immigrants in Agriculture (in Two Volumes)*. 61st Cong., 3d Sess., Sen. Doc. 663. 2 vols. Washington, D.C.: U.S. Government Printing Office, 1911.

Young, Edward. *Special Report on Immigration*. 42d Cong., 1st Sess., H. Exec. Doc. 1. Washington, D.C.: U.S. Government Printing Office, 1871.

Interviews

Where noted by (KB), Krystyna Baker assisted with the interviews.

Bensmiller, Mrs. Richard E. Panna Maria, Texas, 27 November 1971.

Kaczmarek, Clem. Panna Maria, Texas, 10 August 1973 (KB).

Karkosz, Franz, and Karkosz, Maria. Płużnica, Opole Voivodeship, Poland, 23 June 1972 (KB).

Karkosz, Rev. Jan. Piotrówka, Opole Voivodeship, Poland, 21 June 1972 (KB).

Kosub, Emil A. St. Hedwig, Texas, 27 November 1971.

Kuhnel, Fletcher B., Sr. Karnes City, Texas, 24 November 1971.

Lyssy, Mrs. Mary. Panna Maria, Texas, 10 August 1973.

Michałowski, Jacek, staff photographer, Museum of the Opole Countryside. Bierkowice, Opole Voivodeship, Poland, 8 July 1972 (KB).

Mika, Felix, Sr. Panna Maria, Texas, 27 November 1971 (KB).

Mika, Mrs. Mary. Panna Maria, Texas, 27 November 1971, 11 August 1973 (KB).

Moczygemba, Elias J. Panna Maria, Texas, 10 August 1973 (KB).

Moczygemba, Rev. Henry. Polish American Historical Association Convention, New Orleans, La., 27 December 1972.

Moczygemba, LeRoy. San Antonio, Texas, 6 December 1974.

Snoga, Mrs. Ella. Panna Maria, Texas, 11 August 1973 (KB).

Snoga, Felix V. Polish American Historical Association Convention, New Orleans, La., 27 December 1972.

Urbanczyk, Ben P. Panna Maria, Texas, 10 August 1973 (KB).

Urbanczyk, Rosie. Interview with John Pinkham, White Deer, Texas, 17 June 1974. Typescript. Panhandle-Plains Historical Museum, Canyon, Texas.

Yanta, Rev. John W. San Antonio, Texas, 9 August 1973.

Miscellaneous

Bedingungen der Ueberfahrt von Bremen nach den Vereiningten Staaten von Nord-Amerika, das Handelungshaus Carl Pokrantz & Comp. in Bremen Passagiere Annimmt und mit Vorzüglich Guten Schiffen Befördert [Conditions for Passage from Bremen to the United States of North America under Which the Trade House of Carl Pokrantz & Company Accepts Passengers and Transports Them on Exceptionally Good Ships]. Handbill. Bremen: Carl Pokrantz & Comp., 1855.

Bremen, Free Port of. *Bremens Schifffahrt von der Weser in Jahre 1855 von und nach Aussereuropäischen Plätzen und Gewässern* [Bremen Shipping on the Weser in the Year 1855 to and from Non-European Places and Waters]. N.p.: [1856]. Broadside. Bremen State Archives, Bremen, Federal Republic of Germany. Photocopy provided by Dr. Andrzej Brożek, Katowice, Poland.

"Ehrentafel für Unsere in Weltkrieg Gefallenen und Mitkämpfer Gross Pluschnitz" [Roll of Honor for Our Dead and Comrades of the World War from Płużnica]. Mounted photograph, ca. 1918, in possession of Mrs. Krystyna Popanda-Jaksik, Płużnica, Opole Voivodeship, Poland.

Everybody Invited to Historic and Significant Celebration Panna Maria, Texas Immaculate Conception Church Sunday, October 23, 1966 Celebrating the Millennium of Polish Christianity. N.p.: [1966]. Poster in possession of Felix Mika, Sr., Panna Maria, Texas.

"Hej Kolęda Polish Christmas Carols." Mimeographed. [Christmas carols sung by church choir at Panna Maria, Texas, 1970.] Booklet in possession of the author.

Nativity of the Blessed Virgin Mary Church, Częstochowa, Texas. Weekly parish news bulletins. Mimeographed. 10 January 1971, 21 November 1971, 7 July 1974. In possession of the author.

"P[olish] A[merican] P[riests] A[ssociation] Newsletter," 11 November 1976. Mimeographed. In possession of the author.

[Sacred Heart Church, White Deer, Texas]. "Polish Sausage Supper Work List—1973—White Deer, Texas." Mimeographed. In possession of the author.

St. Ann Church, Kościuszko, Texas. *Financial Report for the Year 1970 St. Ann's Church Kosciusko, Texas*. N.p.: [1971]. Broadside. In possession of the author.

———. Weekly parish news bulletin. Mimeographed. 10 January 1971. In possession of the author.

St. Francis Church, St. Francisville, Texas. Cemetery grave inscriptions.

St. Mary Church, Panna Maria, Texas. Weekly parish news bulletins. Mimeographed. 1 October 1972, 15 October 1972. In possession of the author.

Silas, R. M. "Plan of Property Belonging to the Galveston Wharf Co. 1859 as Contained, on Pages 10 & 11, in the Volume Known as 'The History of the Galveston Wharf Company,' in the Files of the Galveston Wharf Company's Main Office, R. M. Silas Chief Engineer January 12, 1926." Blueprint. Archives Division, Rosenberg Library, Galveston, Texas.

Index

Adamietz, Albert, 96, 194 n.27
Adamietz, Constantina (Pyka), 32–33, 35
Adamietz, John, 74–75, 96
Adamietz, M., 74
Adkins, Tex., 137
agriculture: cooperation in, 143–144; droughts and, 52–54, 67, 143; initial, 41; mechanization of, 141–144; in 1970's, 163; production in, by Silesians, 142, 164; significance of Silesian, 164–165; in Silesian colonies, 47–53, 135, 140–144, 151–155; in Upper Silesia, 3, 5, 9, 14
alcohol, 67–68, 84
Amandus, Rev. P., 68
Amarillo, Tex., 109
"America letters," 8–9, 17–18, 36, 168
Americanization, 124, 150, 161
American Revolution Bicentennial, 163
Americans: consider Silesians Poles, 168; employ immigrants, 41, 62; relations of, with Silesians, 61–63, 65–66, 84–98, 137, 151, 224 n.3
Anderwald, Anton, 75, 219 n.26
Anderwald, Gabe, 139
Anderwald, Valentine, 219 n.26
Anderwald, W., 194 n.27
Anderwald, Walek, 75
Anioł, James, 182 n.30
Anioł, Valentine, 182 n.30
anti-Catholic feeling, 62, 151–152
Antoinette (ship), 23, 25
Apostleship of Prayer Society, 132
architecture: of churches, 59–61, 100, 102–109, 124, 134; of initial shelter, 27, 42–43; of lean-to, 116; modified in Texas, 44; mortar preparation for, 213 n.43; of Post of Helena, 92; of schools, 103–104, 114–115, 120–123; Silesian peasant style of, in Texas, 42–44
Arkansas Post, Ark., 69–72, 155
Arkansas River, 70–71
Atascosa County: Confederate troops from, 74; Indian raids in, 45; Silesian colony in, 57–58
automobiles, 143, 148, 151, 158

Bakanowski, Rev. Adolf: blesses San Antonio church, 104; blesses Yorktown church, 106; conflicts of, with Kuhnel, 86–87, 93–96, 205 n.65, 206 n.71; and cowboys, 89; and defense of Panna Maria, 88–89, 90–91; early life of, 79–80; and education, 114–115, 120; and Panna Maria church, 100–102; on Polish spoken at Panna Maria, 169; on travel, 145–146; sent to Texas as mission head, 79–80
Balch, Emily Greene, 156–157
Bandera: arrival of 1855 immigrants in, 31; arrival of Resurrectionists in, 81; churches in, 61, 105; Civil War soldiers from, 69, 194 n.27; established by Americans, 25; first Poles employed by Americans in, 27, 41; Indian raids on, 25, 39, 45–46, 75, 139, 146–147; inheritance customs of, 130–131; misconceptions concerning history of, 181 n.21; Polish population of, 27, 59, 113; school of, 123; served by Rev. Julian Przysiecki, 56, 67; Silesian county officials in, 96; as site for Polish colony, 24–25, 39; travel to and from, 146–147
Bartole, Tex., 123
Barzyński, John, 58, 117

Barzyński, Joseph, Sr., 116, 145
Barzyński, Rev. Joseph, 122
Barzyński, Rev. Vincent: activities of, in San Antonio, 82, 103–104, 122, 138–140, 169; builds school at St. Hedwig, 121–122; and defense of Panna Maria, 91; life of, 80, 165; sent to Texas as missionary, 79–80
baseball, 154
Bavaria, 6–7, 16
Bednorz, Demas, 111
Bednorz, Sam, 111
Bee County, 91
beggars: in Upper Silesia, 10–11, 22
Benedictines, 68, 124
Berlin, Ger., 14, 15, 33
Bexar County: Silesian county officials in, 96, 137. *See also* Saint Hedwig; San Antonio
Białystok, Pol., 81
Biela, F., 187 n.49
Biela, Frank, 114
Biela, J., 187 n.49
Bier, Rev. C. J., 112
"Blue Sisters," 119–120, 122–123
Boguszyce, Upper Silesia, 6, 8
Bonk family, 57
Borysownia, Tex., 124
Boy Scouts, 159, 170
"Boże coś Polske" (song), 134
Bralewski, Rev. Teofil, 121
bread, 11, 35, 51
Bremen, Ger.: as port of departure, 20, 23, 30, 33, 34, 167, 182; Prussian consul at, 30, 167
Bremerhaven. *See* Bremen
Breslau. *See* Wrocław
Brotherhood of the Sacred Heart, 132
Brown, Capt. Wash: cavalry company of, 75
Brys, John, 73–74, 195 n.29
Butler, William, 62
Butler, William J., 73

Calaveras Creek, 47
Camp Butler, Ill., 71–72, 155
Camp Verde, Tex., 46
Carl Pokrantz Company, 28–29, 34–35
Carlsbad, N. Mex., 136
Carter's Brigade of Texas Mounted Volunteers, 70
Castroville, Tex., 8, 24, 25, 29, 46, 49, 54–56, 118–119
Catholic Church. *See* architecture, of churches; and church entries under individual colonies
Catholic Daughters (organization), 132
cattle: in Silesia, 5, 14; in Texas, 18, 30, 41, 48–50, 53, 63, 65, 67, 85, 88, 111, 128, 136–137, 143, 148, 155
celebrations: centenary of Panna Maria, 161; millennium of Polish Christianity, 161; reinterment of Moczygemba, 162; 75th anniversary of Panna Maria, 155
census. *See* United States census
Central Emigration Society for Silesia, 18, 21, 34, 167
Chicago, Ill., 117, 153, 165–166
Children of Mary Society, 132
cholera, 11, 12, 81
Christmas: carols, 102, 134; celebrations, 25, 102
churches. *See* architecture, of churches; and church entries under individual colonies
Cibolo, Tex., 8
Cibolo Creek, 24, 39, 62, 89, 106–108, 123, 141–142
Cieszyn, Upper Silesia, 10
Civil War, 64–77; veterans of, 155–156
clothing, 44–45, 66, 84, 101–102, 119, 158
Clover Bottom, Mo., 58
Coleto, Tex.: church built at, 105; Polish population of, 59; Silesian colony in, 57
Comal, Tex., 8
Confederate States of America: administration of, deteriorates, 82; army of, 64–66, 68–77, 165; lack of Silesian support for, 65–67; records of, 68
Congregation of the Resurrection: history of, 79; Texas missions of, 78–82, 86–89, 98–107, 114–122, 165, 169, 199 n.5
conscription: into Confederate army, 64–66; into Prussian army, 15–17; into U.S. Army, 150
corn, 47–48, 50–51, 53, 62, 66, 75, 111, 141, 144
Corpus Christi, Tex., 75

costume. *See* clothing
cotton, 47, 138, 141–142, 151–153, 157–158
Cotulla, Joseph, 32, 58, 76–77, 220 n.27
Cotulla, Tex., 76
Coy, Andreas, 51, 62, 138
Cracow, Tex., 24
Crimean War, 9, 10, 37
crop-lien system, 152
Curtis, —— (American at Bandera), 50–51
Cybis, Martin, 182 n.30
Czas (newspaper), 10, 15, 21, 32, 168
Czerner, Albert, 219 n.26
Czerner, Alexander, 28–29
Czerner, Cryspin, 111
Czerner, Henry, 110–111
Czerner, Mary (Mrs. Anton Urbanczyk), 109
Częstochowa, Tex.: agriculture of, 141–142, 152–153; as center of Polish population, 107–108; church of, 106–107, 134; founded, 106–107; inheritance customs of, 131; missed by railroad, 108; Polish spoken in, 158; Polish population of, 113; school of, 106, 123–124; settlers in, described as Poles, 168; visited by bishop, 163; wedding feast in, 127–128

Dallas, Tex., 159, 170
Davidson's Battalion of Louisiana Cavalry, 75
Davies, Navarro, 118
Davis, Edmund J., 82, 97
Davis, Sam, 97
Dembowski, Kazimierz, 116
Demner, John, 31
Democratic party, 82, 137
De Montel, Charles, 25, 46
De Witt County: in Helena district, 91; 1917 cotton harvest in, 151; Silesian colonies in, 56–57. *See also* Meyersville; Yorktown
diet: of Confederate troops at Arkansas Post, 70; during Civil War, 66–67; on emigrant ships, 35; during Great Depression, 154; of Silesian peasants in Europe, 9, 14; of Silesians in Texas, 50–51; during travel in Texas, 145; at wedding feasts, 128
Dlugosz, John, 41, 194 n.27
Dlugosz, Joseph, 195 n.29
Dobrodzień, Upper Silesia, 27
Dobrowolski, William, 142
dogs, 50, 145, 155
Dolna, Upper Silesia, 8
donkeys, 148
Dorstyn, Faustyna, 32
Dorstyn, John, 31–32
dress. *See* clothing
drewniaki (wooden shoes), 44–45
droughts: of 1856–1857, 53–54; of 1862–1865, 67; of 1870's, 143; of mid-1890's, 143
Dubuis, Bishop Claude-Marie, 78–81, 91, 106, 119, 121, 199 n.5
Dugi, A., 187 n.49
Dugi, Martin, 74, 76
Dupnik, Joseph, 75–76
dust storms, 154
Dziuk, Alexander, 62, 76, 96, 198 n.61
Dziuk, J., 187 n.49
Dziuk, John, 36

Ecleto Creek, 67, 148
Eighth Texas Cavalry, 75
Eighth Texas Infantry, 156
El Paso, Tex., 137
emigration: agents for, 18–19, 28–29; causes of, 5, 8–21, 37; decline of, 37; and departure from villages, 32–33; and disposal of property, 28, 33; encouraged by letters, 8–9; of poorer peasants, 30; prompted by landlords, 17; second year of (1855), 27–31; and "Texas fever," 21, 27–28; third year of (1856), 32; travel and, 33–37, 179–180 n.13. *See also* immigration
ethnicity, 167–170

Falls City, Tex.: church at, 109; founded, 108; Polish organizations in, 132; Polish population of, 113; schools in, 124; telephones at, 148; transportation in, 108, 147
federal army. *See* United States Army
Felician Sisters, 120, 122, 124
Felix, Cecylia (Sister Stanisław Kostka), 215 n.65

Fifty-fourth Missouri Militia, 76
First Texas Cavalry (U.S. Army), 77
fishing, 50, 131
floods, 12–14, 143, 146, 153
Florian, Erasmus Andrew, 27, 103
flour, 51, 53, 66, 151
Fly, Capt. B. F., 70
folk culture: opposed in Spper Silesia, 167; of Silesians in Texas, 126–134, 139–149, 163, 167–170
folk medicine, 127
food. *See* diet
Fort Chadbourne, Tex., 92
Fort Concho, Tex., 92
Fort Stockton, Tex., 96–97
Fort Worth, Tex., 111
Fourth U.S. Cavalry, 204 n.59
Franciscan Sisters, 124
Franco-Prussian War, 220 n.34
Franklin County, Mo.: Civil War soldiers from, 76; Barzyński moves to, 117; Silesian colonies in, 58, 191 n.88
Fredericksburg, Tex., 8, 54
Friars Minor Conventual: directs mission to Texas, 55–56; missions of, moved to northern states, 55; Moczygemba and, 6–7, 23, 52, 54–55; supported by Ludwig-Missionsverein, 60
Frydrychowicz, Rev. John, 93–94, 105–106

Gabrysch, Gervase A., 160–161
Galveston, Tex., diocese of, 6, 78; as port of entry, 7, 20, 23, 31, 32, 34, 36, 81, 82, 117, 179 n.13; Silesian soldiers in, 74–75
Gamble, William W., 89
Gasz, Christian, 191 n.88
Gawlik, John, 43, 60, 96, 114, 142, 187 n.49, 219 n.26
Gawlik, Joseph, 75
Gawlina, Bishop Joseph, 159–160
Germanization, 119, 167
Germans: as landlords in Upper Silesia, 3, 5, 15, 19; relations of, with Silesians in Texas, 56, 138–139; as settlers in Texas, 7–8, 37, 44, 46–47, 56, 68, 85–87, 93–96, 123, 167–169
Gessner (ship), 30–31
Gleiwitz. *See* Gliwice
Gliwice, Upper Silesia, 6, 13
Gochaczewski, Herman, 12
gold, 20, 36
Goliad, Tex., 74
Goliad County, 45, 91
Gola family, 57
Golla, Frank, 74
Golla, John, 195 n.29
Golla, T., 195 n.29
Gomula, Joseph, 191 n.88
Gonzales County, 91
Gordzelik, William, 111
Granger, Gen. Gordon, 82
grasshoppers, 47–48
Great Depression, 152–155, 159
Gregorczyk, John, 75
Groom, Tex., 110
Gross Strehlitz. *See* Strzelce
Gussett, N.: Company of Texas State Troops of, 74
Gwiazdka Cieszyńska (newspaper), 10, 15, 18, 167
gypsies, 11

Haiduk, Albert, 194 n.27, 219 n.26
Haiduk, Ben, 111
Haiduk, Charlie, 134
Haiduk, Rosie. *See* Urbanczyk, Rosie (Mrs. John Urbanczyk)
Haiduk, Vincent, 111; family of, 111–112, 142–143
Halamuda, Albert, 75
Halamuda, Jacob, 219 n.26
Hamburg, Ger.: as port of departure, 34, 182
Hardee, Col. W. J., 52
Hardin, John Wesley, 137
Hébert, Gen. Paul Octave, 65
Heinke, Rev. Anthony, 122
Helena, Tex.: Capt. Wash Brown's company organized at, 75; Confederate conscription at, 65; Silesians in, 66, 88–89; violence at, 83, 84, 85
"Helena duel," 201 n.28
Herndon, John H., 25
Hidalgo County, 154–155
highwaymen. *See* robbers
Historja polska w Ameryce (book), 157
Hobart, Timothy Dwight, 110

Hobson, Tex., 109
Holy Trinity School Club, 132
Hondo Creek, 94
horses: in Silesia, 14; in Texas, 48–50, 63, 66, 68, 70, 85, 87, 89, 109, 111, 133, 141–142, 145–148, 152, 155
Huffman, Jacob, 46–47
hunting, 50, 109, 131, 145–146
Hutch, Ignatz, 191 n.88
Hyères, Fr., 78

Iciek, Rev. Stanisław, 159
icons, 15, 100–101, 107
Illinois state legislature, 165
immigration: after Civil War, 113–114; of first peasants to Texas, 9, 21–25; of propertied peasants, 21–23; and travel from Texas coast, 36–37, 179 n.13. *See also* emigration
indentured servants, 30
Indianola: as port of entry, 23–24, 31–32, 34, 179 n.13
Indian raids: on Bandera, 25, 39, 75, 139, 146–147; on Silesians, 45–47; on South Texas, 70, 75
Inez, Tex.: Polish population of, 59; Silesians in, 57
inflation: during Civil War, 66; during drought, 53; in Upper Silesia, 9–11
Institute of Texan Cultures, 134, 140
"ironclad" oath, 85, 93, 96, 201 n.32
Italy, 6, 16, 39

jacales (huts), 43
James, John, 25
Jański, Bogdan, 79
Jarzombek, Anthony, 123
Jarzombek, Anton, 75
Jarzombek, Veronica (Mrs. John Kotara), 133
Jełowicki, Rev. Alexander, 78–80
Jemielnica, Upper Silesia, 8, 196 n.42
Jendrush, Edmund, 111
Jendrzej, Tom, 75
"Jeszcze Polska nie zginęła" (song), 134
Johnson, Lyndon B., 161, 168
Josko, Frank, 219 n.26
Josko, Joseph, 195 n.29
Josko, T., 195 n.29
Juarez, Mex., 136
Juleja, Jack, 111
Jurecki, P., 96

Kaczmarek, John, 195 n.29
Kaczmarek, Joseph, 195 n.29
Kaczmarek, Paul, 182 n.30
Kaczmarek, T., 195 n.29
Kahle (highwayman in Silesia), 11
Kajsiewicz, Rev. Jerome, 79
Kalka, Casper, 194 n.27
Kalka, Charles, 111
Kalka, Jos., 187 n.49
Kalka, Joseph, 194 n.27
Kamieniec Podolski, Pol., 80
Karnes City, Tex., 151, 160
Karnes County: Confederate sentiment in, after war, 84–85; lawlessness in, 67, 85–97; in Post of Helena district, 91; Silesian county officials in, 95–96; U.S. Army in, during Reconstruction, 92–95; value of land in, 52–53. *See also* Częstochowa; Helena; Karnes City; Panna Maria
Kasprzyk, Albert, 43, 96
Katowice, Upper Silesia, 11, 159, 170
Keller, Rev. Bonaventure, 7
Kindla, Theodore, 46
Kiołbassa, Adolph, 150
Kiołbassa, Bernard, 137
Kiołbassa, F., 195 n.29
Kiołbassa, Ignatz, 195 n.29, 196 n.42
Kiołbassa, Peter, 61, 69–72, 117, 165, 194 n.26, 195 nn.29–30, 196 n.42
Kiołbassa, Stanisław, 15–16, 28, 177 n.46
Kiołbassa, Thomas, 194 n.26
Klappenbach, August, 41
Kluczbork, Upper Silesia, 13
Knapick, Frank, 74–75
Kniejski, Albert, 114
Knox County, 109–110
Kolodziej, Simon, 76, 195 n.29
Kolodziejczyk, Joseph, 195 n.29
Kolodziejczyk, Thomas, 74
Korzekwa, Charles, 75
Kościuszko, Tadeusz, 108, 163
Kościuszko, Tex.: children of, described in 1930, 124; church of, 107; described by Szczepański, 158; estimated birthrate of,

127; founded, 108; land use at, 141; onions cultivated at, 152–153; school at, 107, 124; Polish population of, 113
Kosielsky, Anton, 195 n.29
Kossup,——(murdered Silesian), 84
Kossup, Thomas, 75
Kosub, Anton, 182 n.30
Kosub, Frank, 182 n.30
Kotara, Edward, 111
Kotara, John, 111, 127, 131, 133
Kotula, Edward, 135–136, 220 n.27
Kotzur, Urban, 154–155
Kowalik, Fabian, 154
Kowalik, John, 114
Kowalik, Mrs. John, 156
Koźle, Upper Silesia, 13, 33
Kozub, Thomas, 49
Krakow, Mo., 58
Kraków, Pol., 10, 25, 80, 162, 168
Krawiec, Ewa (Mrs. Leopold Moczygemba, Sr.), 6–7
Krawiec, Nicholas, 191 n.88
Krawiec, Thomas, 182 n.30
Krawietz, August, 96
Krawietz, Barbara (Sister Maria Kunegunda), 215 n.65
Krawietz, Kunegunda (Sister Maria Bronisława), 215 n.65
Krol, John, 110
Kuhnel, John, 86–87, 93–96, 169, 205 n.65, 206 n.69
Ku Klux Klan, 151
Kusar, John, 96
Kush, John, 74
Kyrish, Jacob, 83, 96, 114

Łabędy, Upper Silesia, 13
Labus, A., 187 n.49
Labus, Mat, 160
Labus, Paul, 191 n.88
land purchase, 51–53, 106, 110–111, 143–144
land reform: in Upper Silesia, 3, 5
land tenure: in Texas, 188 n.63
Las Gallinas, Tex.: Civil War soldiers from, 76–77; Polish population of, 58; Silesian colony in, 57–58
La Vernia, Tex.: Civil War soldiers from, 75; Poles attack freedman in, 96; Silesian injured in, 138
lawlessness: in Texas, 47, 67, 82–97; in Upper Silesia, 11, 22
Ledwig, Joseph, 75
Le Havre, Fr., 81
Leipzig, Ger., 33
Leon Creek, 97
Liberty Hill, Tex., 124
Ligota Toszecka, Upper Silesia, 6
Liskowacki, Florian, 27, 103
Littleton, Capt. John: Texas Cavalry company of, 75
Llano, Tex., 8
Longley, William Preston, 85
Lublin, Pol., 80
Lubliniec County, Upper Silesia, 5, 12–13, 22, 50
Lublinitz County. *See* Lubliniec County
Lubsza, Upper Silesia, 22
Ludwig-Missionsverein, 60
Lutosławski, Vincent, 156
Lyles, George B., 97
Lyssy, A., 195 n.29
Lyssy, Albert, 72–73, 195 n.29, 219 n.26
Lyssy, Frank, 219 n.26
Lyssy, Jacob, 74, 219 n.26
Lyssy, John, 219 n.26

McCook, Tex.: church at, 155; founding of, 154–155
McLean, Tex., 111
Martin, Paul, 194 n.27
Martinez, Tex., *See* Saint Hedwig
Martinez Creek, 31, 39–40, 45, 104
Mason, Gen. John S., 87, 89–90, 203 n.51
Maximilian (emperor of Mexico), 114
Mayfield, Albert, 66
Mazurek, Jacob Anthony, 136
Mazurek, Thomas, 111, 194 n.27
meat preservation, 50
Mexicans: assist in trading horses, 85; attack German immigrant, 47; and cost of labor, 142; cultural influence of, on Silesians, 138; and death of Kindla, 46; as renegades in South Texas, 67, 74; as teamsters, 37; killed by Indians, 147;

women of, in churches, 103; wood hauler killed, 97
Meyersville, Tex.: Civil War soldiers in, 75; language use in church in, 56, 138; Polish population of, 113; school in, 123; Silesian colony in, 56
Michalski, John, 75
Michalski, Joseph, 182 n.30
Mickiewicz, Adam, 123
midwives, 127
Mihalski, Alex, 137
Mika family, 158
Mikosz, Franz, 191 n.38
milk products, 50
Missouri. *See* Franklin County, Mo.
Mitchell, Capt. B.: company of, 69, 194 n.27
Moczygemba, Anton, 219 n.26
Moczygemba, Elias J., 150
Moczygemba, Frank, 195 n.29
Moczygemba, Frank T., 74, 130
Moczygemba, H., 223 n.1
Moczygemba, Hanka, 44
Moczygemba, Ignatz, 223 n.1
Moczygemba, J., 187 n.49
Moczygemba, Jacob, 149
Moczygemba, John, 30, 36, 49, 74, 96–97, 170, 187 n.49, 207 n.77, 219 n.26
Moczygemba, John T., 75
Moczygemba, Joseph, 74, 148–149
Moczygemba, Leopold, Sr., 6–7
Moczygemba, Rev. Leopold Bonaventura Maria: advises emigration, 36, 44–45; arranges land purchase at Panna Maria, 51–52; complains to Rome about Rossadowski, 56; early life of, 6–7; departs Silesian colonies, 54–55; describes agriculture, 47; effect of letters of, in Upper Silesia, 17–18; and immigrants, 23, 24–25, 29, 40–41; encourages immigration, 8–9, 17–18; later life of, 55, 166; and Panna Maria church, 52, 60, 102–103; plans Polish settlements in Texas, 8–9; on Polish ethnicity, 170; reinterred at Panna Maria, 162; on St. Hedwig, 40; seeks teacher for Panna Maria, 61
Moczygemba, Thomas, 36, 187 n.49
Moczygemba, Rev. Thomas J., 166
Moczygemba family, 158, 174 n.11
Morawietz, Joseph, 74, 194 n.27
Morawietz, Thomas, 74
Mozurów, Upper Silesia, 12
Mróz, Martin, 136–137
mules, 49–50, 141, 142, 148
Mushall, Florian, 219 n.26
music, 102, 119, 128, 134, 145
Musioł, Albina (Sister Maria Kazimierz), 215 n.65
Musioł, James, 195 n.29
Mutz, Franciszek, 123
Myslowice, Upper Silesia, 33

national consciousness, 167–170
nativism, 62, 151–152
naturalization, 86, 201 n.32
Negroes: agricultural production of, vs. Poles, 142; enfranchised after Civil War, 82–83, 85; attacked by Poles, 96; relations of, with Silesians, 138
Nesterowicz, Stefan, 157
New Braunfels, Tex., 8, 24, 54–55
New Orleans: as port of entry, 34
New York: as port of entry, 34, 82, 100–101
Niklewicz, Franciszek, 158, 169
North-Western Trust and Savings Bank, 166
Notatki z podróży (book), 157
Novack, John, 198–199 n.66
Nowiny Texaskie (newspaper), 140

Odin, Bishop Jean-Marie, 6–7
Odra River, 12–14
Oggersheim, Ger., 7
O'Keefe, J. Sid, 110
Olesno, Upper Silesia, 16, 27, 167
Olesno County, Upper Silesia, 5, 13, 17, 21–22, 28
onions: as a cash crop, 142, 152–153
Opiela, J., 195 n.29
Opiela, John, 195 n.29
Opiela, T., 195 n.29
Opole, Upper Silesia, 6, 8, 10–11, 18, 28–29, 33, 139, 162
Opole County, Upper Silesia, 5
Oppeln. *See* Opole, Upper Silesia

Oppenheimer, D. and A. (San Antonio merchants), 135
Olmsted, Frederick Law, 168
Order of the Immaculate Conception of the Virgin Mary, 119–120, 122–123
Orłowski, Leon, 153, 157–158, 169
Ostend (ship), 30–31
Our Lady of Częstochowa Grotto, 161
Our Slavic Fellow Citizens (book), 157
Owensville, Mo., 58
oxcarts, 24, 31–32, 34, 37, 135
oxen, 41, 48–50, 61, 135, 141. *See also* oxcarts

Panhandle (region of Texas): Silesians in, 109. *See also* White Deer
Panna Maria, Tex.: arrival of immigrants in, 24–25, 31; arrival of Resurrectionist missionaries in, 81–82; celebrations at, 155, 161; church of, 60, 94–95, 100–103, 168; Civil War difficulties of, 66; Civil War soldiers from, 69–76; described, 157, 159; drought and, 53; farming and, 41, 43; as first Polish colony in America, 25; founding of, 24–25; harassed by Ku Klux Klan, 151; mentioned by emigration agent, 29; missed by railroad, 108; named, 25; organizations at, 132; Polish population of, 59, 113; Reconstruction difficulties of, 84–96; school at, 61, 90, 114–121, 123; school children of, speak Polish, 158; served by Rev. Thomas Moczygemba, 166; site of, described, 39; transportation at, 144–147; visited by bishop, 163; WWI soldiers from, 150, 223 n.26
Panna Maria Grays, 69–70, 86, 194 n.26
Paris, Fr., 79–81
Paschall, Capt. J. M.: volunteer company of, 74
Pawełek, Albert, 134
peasant class: discussed, 21–22
Pedernales, Tex., 8
Pellicer, Bishop Dominic, 107, 119
Petrucha family, 57
Phillips' Cavalry Regiment of Green's Brigade, 75
Pierdoła, Adam, 182 n.30
Pierdoła, Martin, 182 n.30
Pierdolla, Joseph F., 75, 156
Pierdolla, Roma, 138
pigs, 48, 50, 152
Pilarczyk, Matthew, 114
Pleasantier, Peter, 97
Ploch, Anton, 75
Ploch, Lawrence, 182 n.30
Płużnica, Upper Silesia, 6–7, 9, 29, 42, 76, 148, 162, 223 n.1
Polack, Valentine, 194 n.26
Poland, Republic of: army of, 159; attempts to secure cotton from Texas, 157–158
"Polander Joe," 84
Polish American (newspaper), 221 n.41
Polish American Center (San Antonio), 161
Polish American Congress of Texas, 161–162
Polish American Priests Association, 161
Polish colonies: first in America, 3, 170–171; transportation between, 144–148; visitors to, 147–148, 153, 156–159
Polish culture. *See* folk culture
Polish Insurrection of 1830, 27, 31, 55, 79
Polish Insurrection of 1863, 68, 79, 80
Polish language: decline of use of, in Texas, 139–140; learned by non-Poles at Panna Maria, 169; Silesian dialect of, in Texas, 139; in Silesian colonies, 158, 168–169; spoken by Moczygemba, 7; spoken by Stanisław Kiołbassa, 15; in Upper Silesia, 3, 167
Polish National Alliance, 132–133, 161
Polish population: in Texas, 58–59, 112–113
Polish press: on emigration and its causes, 10–13, 15, 18–23, 30–32; in Missouri, 58, 117; in northern U.S., 165; on Silesians in Texas, 160, 167; in Texas, 140
Polish Roman Catholic Union, 132, 161, 165-166
Polish Village (St. Francisville), 57
Polish Young Men's Union, 132
Poniatowski, Darius, 78
Poniatowski, Denise, 78–79
Post of Helena, 91–95, 204 n.59
potato blight, 9–10
potatoes, 9–11, 14, 51
Poznan, Pol., 23

Praha, Tex., 81
prayer books, 78, 139
prisoners of war, 69, 71–73, 76
Prussian army, 16–17, 64
Przewlocki, Rev. Bronislaus, 137
Przybysz, Edward, 166
Przybysz, Philip, 43
Przybysz family, 158
Przysiecki, Rev. Julian: as only Polish priest in Texas, 67–68; serves Silesians in Texas, 56
Pułaski, Casimir, 163
Pulaski, Tex., 123
Pyka, Anton, 194 n.27
Pyka, Franciszka (Mrs. John Pyka), 130
Pyka, John, 49, 130

Quihi, Tex., 8

Rabstein, J., 187 n.49
Racibórz, Upper Silesia, 13, 33
Rafliczyn, Peter, 30
Ragsdale's Battalion of Texas Cavalry, 75
railways: in Upper Silesia, 9, 20, 23, 30, 32–34; in Texas, 108, 111, 147, 154–155
rattlesnakes, 40–41
Reconstruction: for Silesians in Texas, 82–98; in Texas history, 83
Reevey, Bill, 84
Regency of Opole, subdivisions of, 4–5
Republican party, 82, 86, 137
Resurrectionists. *See* Congregation of the Resurrection
Revolution of 1848, 15–16
Rhineland, Tex., 109–111
Rio Grande, 67, 74, 76, 114, 137, 142, 154
robbers: in Texas, 47, 67, 82–84; in Upper Silesia, 11
Rome, Ital., 55, 80–81
Rosary societies, 132
Rose, Oscar, 205 n.61
Rosenberg. *See* Olesno
Rosiński, Bolesław, 158, 169
Rossadowski, Rev. Anthony: departs Texas, 67; early life of, 55–56; erects church at St. Hedwig, 61; serves Silesians in Texas, 55–56
Rotterdam: as port of departure, 34
Rozmierz, Upper Silesia, 131
Ruckman, Thomas, 39, 120, 127, 141, 168
Russell, Charles A., 73
Russell, Lyman Brightman, 44, 194 n.26
Ryman family, 57
Rzeppa, Emanuel: activities of, at Panna Maria, 93–96, 118, 201 n.31; activities of, in San Antonio, 103, 201 n.31; as registrar of voters, 86–87; threatened by Kuhnel, 86–87
Rzeppa, John, 28–29, 43, 60, 195 n.29
Rzeppa, R. T., 194 n.26
Rzeppa, T., 195 n.29

Sacred Heart Society (St. Hedwig), 132
Saint Adalbert's Benevolent Society, 132
Saint-Andre, Mother, 119
Saint Francisville, Tex., 57
Saint Hedwig: agriculture at, 41, 49; arrival of priest in, 81; church at, 60–61, 104, 127, 210 n.11; Civil War soldiers from, 75; conscription evaded in, 65; death of Rev. Przysiecki at, 67–68; described by Moczygemba, 40; drought of 1856–1857 in, 53; founded, 31–32; German shop in, 138; isolation of farms at, 43; name chosen for, 104–105; Polish language spoken in, 169; Polish organizations at, 132; Polish population of, 59, 113; school at, 120–122; served by Przysiecki, 67; site of, described, 39–40; transportation at, 145–148
Saint Joe. *See* Częstochowa
Saint Stanislaus Kostka Church (Chicago), 165
Saint Stanislaus Kostka College (Chicago), 165
Saint Stephen's Singing Society, 132
Saint Vincent de Paul Society, 132
Saints Cyril and Methodius Seminary, 166
San Antonio: as agricultural market, 40; arrival of Polish immigrants in, 25, 31; arrival of Resurrectionist missionaries in, 82; church constructed in, 103–104, 209 n.9; Civil War soldiers from, 74–75; establishment of Polish colony, 27; immigrants employed by Americans, 41; immigrants use *jacales* in, 43; Poles invited to join German parish in, 138–139;

Polish language spoken in, 139–140, 169; Polish parish founded in, 27, 103–104; Polish population of, 27, 59, 113; Polish societies in, 132–133; press announces conscription in, 64–65; road from, to Helena terrorized, 83; school at, 120, 122; served by Rev. Thomas Moczygemba, 166; thieves in Polish Quarter of, 84; transportation from, 145–147; visited by bishop, 159
San Antonio and Aransas Pass Railroad, 108
San Antonio River, 24, 39, 54
San Antonio Weekly Herald (newspaper), 65
San Diego, Tex., 75, 155
San Fernando Church (San Antonio), 103
San Jacinto, Battle of, 159
Santa Clara, Tex., 8
Scapular Society (Panna Maria), 132
Schlesische Zeitung (newspaper), 10
Schönau, Bav., 7
schools: at Bandera, 123; at Częstochowa, 106, 123–124; at Falls City, 124; first Polish, in America, 3, 61, 114; at Kościuszko, 108; at Meyersville, 123; at Panna Maria, 61, 90, 108, 114–121, 123; at St. Hedwig, 120–122; at San Antonio, 120, 122; at Yorktown, 120, 122–123
Schüler, Julius Heinrich, 28–29, 32, 34
Seco, Tex., 8
Second Texas Infantry, 75
Seguin,Tex., 51
Semenenko, Rev. Peter, 79
Seminole War, 56
sharecropping, 152
shelter. *See* architecture
Silesians in Texas: birthrate of, 127; baptismal customs of, 126; contact of, with Poland, 140, 159–160, 163; case study of family of, 63; divorce among, 129; diet of, 50–51; ethnic leaders among, 165–166; family size of, 126–127; funerary rites of, 130; inheritance customs of, 130–131, 163; intermarriage of, 128–129, 138; isolation of, 43, 45, 126; national consciousness of, 167–170; political activity of, 64, 86–87, 91, 93–97, 137; poverty of, disputed, 41–42; sexual morality of, 129–130; significance of, 164–171; sleeping practices of, 133–134; social mobility of, 134–136; thieves attack, 47, 67, 82–84; wedding customs of, 88, 127–128. *See also* folk culture
Sisky family, 57
Sisters of Charity of the Incarnate Word, 120, 122–124
Sisters of Divine Providence, 118–119, 122, 215 n.65
Sisters of the Incarnate Word of the Blessed Sacrament, 124
Sixteenth Illinois Cavalry, 72–73
Sixth Texas Infantry, 72, 195 n.29
Sixth U.S. Colored Cavalry, 72
Skloss, Adam, 75, 156
Skull, Sally, 85
slaves, 64
Smith, Lt. George W., 205 n.61
Snigurski, Rev. Adolf, 117, 121, 139
social discrimination: in Texas, 62–63, 151–152, 224 n.3; in Upper Silesia, 14–16
societies. *See* organizations
Society of the Immaculate Conception, 132
Spanish language: learned by Silesians, 138; words borrowed by Silesians, 187 n.53
Staniszcze Małe, Upper Silesia, 30
Stanuś, Walter, 182 n.30
Star Land Company of Iowa, 110
stations of the cross, 101–102
steerage quarters (on emigrant ships), 21, 34–35
Stockdale, Tex., 108
Strzelce, Upper Silesia, 6, 11, 18, 23, 29, 33, 46
Strzelce County, 5, 8, 12, 32, 130–131, 182 n.28
Sucho Daniec, Upper Silesia, 32, 130
Sulisławice, Pol., 80
sweet potatoes, 51, 53
Świbie, Upper Silesia, 15–16, 28, 165
Szczecin, Pol.: as port of departure, 34
Szczepański, Alexander, 153, 158, 166, 169
Szeguda, Casimir, 191 n.88
Szymiszów Castle, Upper Silesia, 11

Tarnowskie Góry, Upper Silesia, 33
taxes: as cause for emigration, 10
Tenth U.S. Infantry, 204 n.59
Texas Centennial, 159, 170
Texas Polish News Publishing Company, 140
Thirteenth Battalion of Texas State Troops, 74
Thirty-first Texas Cavalry, 73–74
Thirty-second Texas Cavalry, 75
Thirty-fifth U.S. Infantry, 92
Thirty-sixth Texas Cavalry, 75, 156
Thompson, Ben, 83
Thompson, Bill, 83
Thompson, William Alexis, 93, 204 n.54
Times (London), 5
Tom, John F.: company of Texas State Troops of, 74
Tomaszów Lubelski, Pol., 80
Tost. *See* Toszek
Toszek, Upper Silesia, 6, 8, 9, 16, 23, 28–29, 33–34, 60, 86
Toszek-Gliwice County, Upper Silesia, 5, 11, 17, 28
Tudyk, F., 182 n.30
Tudyk, M., 182 n.30
Tudyk, Nicholas, 182 n.30
Tunnel Hill, Ga., 73
Twenty-fourth Texas Cavalry, 70–73, 195 n.29
Twohig, John, 24, 51–53, 60–62, 115
typhus, 11–12

Union Army. *See* United States Army
United States Army, 66, 68–73, 76–77, 82, 87, 90–97, 165; records of, 68–69
United States census, 48, 59, 112–113, 135
United States Immigration Commission, 157
Upper Silesia: described, 5; economic problems of, 5, 9–14, 20, 22–23, 37; emigration from (*see* emigration); history of, 3, 5; social discrimination in, 5, 14–16
Urbanczyk, Anton, 109–110
Urbanczyk, Ben, 110–111, 144
Urbanczyk, Felix, 111, 144
Urbanczyk, Jacob, 109
Urbanczyk, John, 74, 111–112, 143
Urbanczyk, Ladislaus, 111
Urbanczyk, M., 187 n.49
Urbanczyk, Mary (Mrs. Anton Urbanczyk), 109
Urbanczyk, Paulina (Sister Maria Jadwiga), 215 n.65
Urbanczyk, Rosie (Mrs. John Urbanczyk), 111–112
Urbanczyk, Thomas, 131
Urbanczyk, Tom, 74–75
Ursuline Sisters, 122

Van Buren, Ark., 73–74
Vandenburg, Tex., 8
Victoria, Tex.: mail carried to, 135; Polish population of, 59; Silesian colony in, 57
Victoria County, 91
Virchow, Rudolph, 12
Von Beaulieu (ship), 32
voting rights, 85–87

Waclawczyk, F., 194 n.27
Wade, Col. James F., 97
wagons, 31, 42, 84–85, 109, 145–147
Wardziński, Felix, 159
Warenski, Karol, 116–117
Warsaw, Pol., 117, 153, 156, 162
Waschka family, 57
Weser (ship), 23, 25, 30–31, 35, 109, 179 n.10
White Deer, Tex.: agriculture at, 142–143, 153–154; church at, 112; described, 112; Haiduk family experiences at, 111–112; inheritance customs at, 131; Polish colony in, 109–111; Polish population of, 113; school at, 148, 151–152; social discrimination in, 151–152; and transportation, 148
White Deer Land Company, 110–111
Wiatrek, J., 127
wild foods, 51, 54
Wilke, Capt. F. C., 70
Wilke's Twenty-fourth Texas Cavalry. *See* Twenty-fourth Texas Cavalry
Willke's Battalion of Light Artillery, 74
windmills, 148
Wiśnicze, Upper Silesia, 7, 16
Witte Memorial Museum, 134
Wnęk, Jacek, 170

Woitena, Stanisław, 75
Wojciechowski, Rev. Stanisław, 134
wood carving, 134
wooden shoes, 44–45
World War I, 150–151, 157, 167, 223 n.1
World War II, 159–161, 167
Wrocław, Silesia, 10–11, 12, 32, 33, 168
Wygladacz, Anton, 74

Yanta, Simon, 187 n.49, 201 n.32
Yanta, Valentine: family of, 148
Yorktown: church at, 105–106; Civil War soldiers from, 75–76; conscription officers at, 65; marriage patterns at, 129; Polish language spoken in, 139, 169; Polish population of, 59, 113; school at, 120, 122–123; served by Rev. Thomas Moczygemba, 166; Silesian colony in, 56
Yosko (surname). *See* Josko

Zahradniczek, Rev. Robert, 7
Zaiontz, Onufry, 150
Zaiontz, Wladyslaw, 150
Zając family, 158
Zając, Jacob, 182 n.30
Zając, James, 182 n.30
Zając, Ludwig, 61, 182 n.30
Zielinski, Rev. Anthony, 200 n.10
Ziemia (journal), 158
Zimmerman, Isabelle, 121
Zwiardowski, Rev. Felix: at Bandera, 105, 181 n.21; becomes Resurrectionist superior, 117; and Częstochowa church, 106–107; and defense of Panna Maria, 90–91; early life of, 81; founds order, 118–119; as missionary to Texas, 79–81; and Panna Maria church, 100–103, 107; on Polish spoken at Panna Maria , 169; returns to Panna Maria, 116; at St. Hedwig, 104–105, 116; as teacher, 115–116, 121; on travel, 146–147
Zwiastun Górnoszląazki (newspaper), 10, 15, 120